Reconsidering the Democratic Public

Reconsidering the Democratic Public

Edited by
George E. Marcus
and
Russell L. Hanson

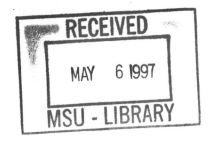

The Pennsylvania State University Press
University Park, Pennsylvania

Library of Congress Cataloging-in-Publication Data

Reconsidering the democratic public / edited by George E. Marcus and
Russell L. Hanson.

p. cm.
Includes bibliographical references and index.
ISBN 0-271-00917-9. — ISBN 0-271-00927-6 (pbk.)
1. Democracy. 2. United States—Politics and government.
3. Political participation. I. Marcus. George E.
II. Hanson. Russell L.
JC433.R317 1993
321.8—dc20 92-33653
CIP

Published by The Pennsylvania State University Press,
Suite C, Barbara Building, University Park, PA 16802-1003

It is the policy of The Pennsylvania State University Press to use acid-free paper for the first printing of all clothbound books. Publications on uncoated stock satisfy the minimum requirements of American National Standard for Information Sciences—Permanence of Paper for Printed Library Materials, ANSI Z39.48–1984.

To the memory of Richard Krouse,
valued colleague and good friend

Contents

Part III. Passion and Politics

Part IV. Democracy and Diversity

Acknowledgments

The editors would like to thank contributors for their cooperation in revising chapters for this volume. In turn, the contributors would like to thank George Marcus, first for organizing the symposium at Williams College, and then for his determination to publish its results. George's unflagging devotion sustained this project throughout its many phases, and we feel privileged to be part of his efforts to honor the memory of Richard Krouse. We would also like to thank Sandy Thatcher, who supported this project from beginning to end. Keith Monley edited the manuscript thoroughly and professionally, and Cherene Holland at Penn State University Press oversaw its production. We are grateful for their efforts to make this a better book.

Preface: Toward a More Democratic Political Science

George E. Marcus

The impetus for the Democratic Theory Symposium, held at Williams College from 30 July to 4 August 1989, was a conversation I had held some years earlier with Richard Krouse, a political theorist at Williams College. Dick and I had just completed a collaborative effort in which we discussed recent empirical findings of research on American political behavior in relation to American democratic theory (Krouse and Marcus 1984). We had so enjoyed the pleasure of the joint work—an attempt to better understand American democratic practices and the requirements of democratic theory—that we undertook to seek funding to host a symposium. The purpose of the symposium was to enable those political scientists who do empirical research and those who do philosophical research to come together in order to discuss and debate the study of democracy.

Dick's sudden and untimely death interrupted that project. However, the idea of the symposium proved to be a long-lasting one. With the help of an ever-widening group of enthusiastic scholars and the crucial and vital support of the National Endowment for the Humanities, the Ford Foundation, the Carnegie Corporation of New York, the Center for the Humanities and Social Sciences at Williams College, and the John M. Olin Foundation, the Democratic Theory Symposium was at last realized.

This preface is a remembrance of Richard Krouse, especially his intellectual appetite, personal humility, and commitment to rigorous argument. In appreciating these aspects of Dick's life, we can remind ourselves of the values that not only energized him but can energize all those interested in democratic life. These values bear on how the academy studies democratic politics, as well as on democratic experience itself.

The study of American politics has traditionally been carried out by scholars who have tended to compartmentalize themselves into relatively homogeneous fiefdoms. Dick was committed to a very different and noncompartmentalized understanding of academic life. He brought to his own work a deep commitment to the possibilities of achieving justice within a democratic polity. However much he became excited about the possibilities for gaining a firmer grasp on specific principles of justice, and however excited he became about a specific model of democracy, he never let these enthusiasms generate a certainty that his inquiry was completed. He never set aside his critical skills in the midst of intellectual inquiry. His curiosity was never limited by the artificial, internal boundaries imposed by our discipline.

Our discipline is, of course, frequently divided. Its divisions might best be understood in terms of the different orientations of different subfields, or more generally of political theorists and empiricists. Although all scholars have curiosity and imagination, these faculties are put to different tasks depending on the field of endeavor. The political theorist brings a wide range of analytical, conceptual, historical, and normative concerns and skills to the investigation of political life. He or she brings scrupulous attention to the formulation of political principles or to the narration of the changing histories of political ideas. The empirical political scientist directs his or her study to the observable events of experience and speculates about their causes and effects. Among the most useful skills of the empiricist is the systematic application of doubt to causal accounts and to the evidence upon which they ultimately rest.

The different orientations of skills would be wholly salutary, if it were not for another difference. Political scientists tend to distrust not only the prevailing wisdoms of their own subfields but often those of other subfields and even other subfields themselves. Thus, the political theorist mistrusts the conventional normative understandings that empiricists apply to the world and directs critical curiosity at the interpretive standards they frequently seem to endorse. The empirical political scientist, in turn, mistrusts the descriptive understanding theorists have of the world and directs critical curiosity at the ungrounded observations on which their interpretations rest. As a result, unfortunately, the empirical enterprise, as such, becomes the object of the theorist's mistrust, and the theoretical enterprise, in its various forms, becomes the object of the empiricist's mistrust. This pattern of competitive distrust, as it were, engenders antagonistic suspicions.

Such a division is not new. Alexis de Tocqueville—a frequent subject of Richard Krouse's scholarship—made a similar comparison between the *philosophes* and the Catholic church in the period before the French Revolution. The *philosophes* had no practical experience. But they did, nonetheless, offer diverse and simple rules of reconstruction to replace the existing state of affairs. Mindful as they were of the possibilities they envisioned, the *philosophes* were generally hostile to tradition and to the church, which they understood to be relics restricting progress. The church, for its part, was aggressive in its defense of the complexity of life and reliance on faith, dogma, and traditional mores. Were he alive today, Tocqueville might see a parallel in our warring camps: the political philosopher's yearning to identify the radical root on which the world can be modified, and the empiricist's reluctance to accept the conceptual idealization of the world as portrayed by his disciplinary companions.

The analogy to "clans" might be suggestive here. With clans, conversations among those who reside in one clan are more commonplace than between those of different clans. Intraclan conversations, while often competitive over position within the clan, are often premised on common agreements. Interclan conversations, if they are well mannered, will avoid by mutual understanding topics that inflame. So it was perhaps unusual that Dick and I came to have frequent conversations unconstrained by "clan" conventions. Maybe it had something to do with the Williamstown locale and tradition, the intimate scale of the rural college, and the removed location that offered freedom from clan oversight. It certainly had a lot to do with Dick's intellectual zeal and his deep concern for knowing more about democratic practices and possibilities. From whatever stimulus that gave it birth, the conversation turned to democracy.

Although it was not a formal point of departure or purpose—conversations frequently spring from less academic and strategic intentions—we discussed the talents and perspectives each could offer to the other. Dick hoped that empirical investigations could offer some guidance in the pursuit of the ideal. There being many different idealized versions of democracy competing for our attention and our support, he felt that the plausibility of their realization ought to be an important consideration in the choice of which to endorse and pursue. I hoped that a more precise portrait of the various ideals would offer some guidance in the study of the here and now. Careful attention to the construction of any particular ideal might be useful in identifying the crucial features of the sensible world. Furthermore, by attending to the different idealized versions of democracy, each of which rests on different assumptions, we would be able to investigate them comparatively, to evaluate one ideal against another, empirically as well as normatively. While that discussion led to a joint effort of modest scope, it also led to the idea for a symposium on democracy.

The symposium would bring together for conversation political theorists interested in democracy and empirical political scientists who study American politics. Because the discussions would focus on the particular projects that have long engaged the participants, we hoped that the discussions would be more productive, more sustained, and less restricted than conversations in more-traditional venues such as professional conferences. These hopes and expectations came to pass, and this volume contains the fruits of the NEH Democratic Theory Symposium.

Dick and I had hoped that the symposium would encourage many to see the benefits in the joint engagement of the philosophic and empirical enterprises. Some of those who participated in the symposium have become remarkably well versed in both sorts of undertakings. However, it was not Dick's hope that all those interested in democratic politics would become trained in both the philosophical and empirical faculties. Dick's dream was that the academy itself would become a democratic community fostering conversations among those who are diverse in beliefs, backgrounds, talents, and training. Such a community would be far more heterogeneous than each current clan within political science; it would have to learn how to engage, endure, and indeed flourish amid contention and dissonance. Dick's hope was not immodest. But then anyone as committed to democratic life as Dick was would have to be a great optimist. Dick was a person of great enthusiasm, gentleness, and optimism. If this symposium was able to encourage the kind of democratic academic life that he envisioned, then his legacy is all the more enriched.

Reference

Krouse, Richard, and George E. Marcus. 1984. "Electoral Studies and Democratic Theory Reconsidered." *Political Behavior* 6 (1): 23–39.

Introduction: The Practice of Democratic Theory

Russell L. Hanson
George E. Marcus

Our title, *Reconsidering the Democratic Public*, signals a deep dissatisfaction with previous descriptions of the general public's incapacity for democratic politics (Lippmann 1922; Converse 1964; and more recently, Neuman 1986; Smith 1989). These negative assessments have a long tradition: throughout history democracy has been condemned as a form

We are extremely grateful to Charles Anderson and an anonymous reviewer, who made valuable suggestions about the content of this introduction and the organization of the volume as a whole. James Farr also made helpful comments on an earlier version of this introduction. Lois B. Cooper gave us astute editorial advice. As always, it has been our distinct pleasure to work with Sandy Thatcher, who supported the project from start to finish. Naturally, we absolve these people of responsibility for whatever shortcomings remain.

of mob rule in which the least-qualified persons in society exercise dominion over their social betters. Few people any longer subscribe to the extreme versions of elitism, and we feel no special obligation to answer their objections here. But there are professed friends of self-determination who are unimpressed with the quality of citizenship in contemporary mass society, and they are the audience we want to reach.

Worries about citizens' democratic character surface quickly in discussions about how to invigorate the political experiences of ordinary people—and whether that is even a reasonable objective. Doubts on the latter score are most commonly expressed by self-styled realists who observe that citizens become active in politics under rare circumstances and then behave in ways that do not seem especially democratic. Consequently, realists fear that reformers who want to expand opportunities for participation in collective decision making are courting disaster; better to let sleeping dogs lie if citizens are likely to turn on one another upon waking to their newfound freedoms.

Some of these doubts about citizens' capacity for self-governance seem well founded; they rest on evidence gathered by social scientists during the post–World War II period. As several of our contributors note, social scientists have shown that American citizens' knowledge of politics is slim, their tolerance for others is low, and their preoccupation with self-interest leaves little room for contemplating the public good. This portrait is confirmed by other sources of information, including newspaper and television coverage of such deadly spectacles as the racial incidents that took place in Bensonhurst and Howard Beach. No wonder some observers suspect that Americans' contemporary "habits of the heart" are losing their power to sustain rich forms of democratic life (Bellah et al. 1985).

This reading of the accumulated evidence has led to massive revisions in democratic theory.[1] The role of citizens has been downgraded, in view of their undemocratic propensities. Conversely, many democratic theorists now place greater (but not unlimited) confidence in the wisdom of elected representatives, who seem more committed to the democratic creed. And institutions that insulate elites from mass sentiment are now

1. Schumpeter (1943) advanced this revision, which received strong support from Berelson, Lazarsfeld, and McPhee (1954) and other social scientists too numerous to mention here. The fullest and most provocative statement of the revisionists' position was given by Giovanni Sartori (1962). In 1987, Sartori forcefully restated his views in *The Theory of Democracy Revisited*.

highly valued by those who worry about the destructive and destabilizing consequences of democratic "overload" (Crozier et al. 1975). In short, the views of James Madison have been reaffirmed: realism has produced a highly restrictive interpretation of popular rule and its requirements, if not a qualified endorsement of the doctrine of popular sovereignty itself (Sartori 1987).

The movement toward theoretical realism has been resisted, most notably by advocates of participatory democracy (Bachrach 1967; Pateman 1970). Actually, several varieties of participatory democracy have been proposed; Robert Dahl's *Preface to Economic Democracy*, Benjamin Barber's *Strong Democracy*, and Carole Pateman's *The Sexual Contract* are only three of the better-known texts extending the principle of consent to new areas of social life.[2] What unites all participatory democrats is a vision of possibilities quite different from the realities of contemporary politics (broadly construed to include most, if not all, power relations). It is the way the world might be that interests participatory democrats, who stress the need for more, not less, involvement of citizens in collective decision making.

Participatory democrats are often impatient with arguments about the need for realism in theories of democracy. For them, no useful purpose is served by blaming the victims of insufficiently democratic institutions whose legitimacy is exempted from critical scrutiny. The point is made well by Benjamin Barber in his contribution to this volume. Barber insists that the language of democracy *assumes* that citizens are capable of ruling themselves; without this assumption, the idea of self-governance does not make sense. Therefore, the case for participatory democracy turns on arguments about the need to organize collective life in ways that respect and promote individual autonomy. Evidence concerning citizens' limitations is not immediately relevant to this kind of moral discourse and may even subvert democratic progress if it causes us to sacrifice democratic ideals in the name of misplaced realism.

2. Proponents of economic democracy are legion, but Dahl (1985), Green (1985), and especially Gould (1988) offer particularly good arguments on behalf of this version of expanded participation. The democratization of politics is also a popular theme, but two authors merit special consideration: Boyte (1981) analyzes the impact of the "new citizen movements" on local politics, and Barber (1984) discusses a variety of mechanisms for increasing political participation at all levels of government. Gutmann (1987) considers the importance of education in democracy and the role of democracy in education. Pateman's (1988) work is remarkable for applying democratic principles to the domain of private life, a project shared by Okin (1989). All of these authors provide numerous references to related works not catalogued here.

Ironically, a preoccupation with the normative dimension of democratic theory has probably caused participatory democrats to concede too much empirical ground to revisionists. Spurred by a desire to promote participatory democracy, many scholars have failed to challenge evidence of undemocratic proclivities among citizens. They have generally accepted an unflattering portrait of the masses and gone on to argue that undemocratic tendencies are to be expected from political systems that fail to provide citizens with meaningful opportunities for political participation. More-democratic institutions would produce more-democratic citizens, in their view.

Often, these proposals for increasing participation seem hopelessly utopian. In fact, that is the usual response to concrete suggestions for increasing the range and reach of democracy; critics are wont to ask how citizens could ever play the ambitious role assigned to them by participatory democrats and still lead lives of freedom and leisure. Would not their every waking moment be filled with deliberation and engagement of the sort that might exhaust the patience and wisdom of even the most dedicated philosopher-kings? As Walter Lippmann (1925, 20–21) observed, "Although public business is my main interest and I give most of my time to watching it, I cannot find time to do what is expected of me in the theory of democracy; that is, to know what is going on and to have an opinion worth expressing in every question which confronts a self-governing community. And I have not happened to meet anybody, from a President of the United States to a professor of political science, who came anywhere near to embodying the accepted ideal of the sovereign and omnicompetent citizen."

Participatory democrats are partly to blame for inviting this kind of response. In choosing not to challenge early studies of the public's performance, participatory democrats assumed responsibility for showing that citizens were nevertheless capable of fulfilling an expanded role in more-participatory settings. Such experiments are exceedingly hard to come by, and it has been almost impossible to provide compelling evidence of most citizens' propensity for democratic politics.[3] Consequently, the viability of reforms remains unproven or, worse, doubtful, given the preponderance of evidence on the undemocratic inclinations of mass publics.

3. Pateman 1970, Mansbridge 1980, and Greenberg 1986 are among the most interesting accounts of participatory democracy in action.

For participatory democrats, there is a way out of this impasse. The credibility of reforms would be enhanced by showing that suspicions about the incapacity of ordinary citizens are unfounded (or at least greatly exaggerated). As Thompson (1970) argues, calls for reforms that make unreasonable demands on citizens and require massive social reorganization are likely to fall on deaf ears. On the other hand, proposals that seem realizable within existing institutional and cultural settings are apt to be received more favorably. Hence, the cause of participatory democracy may be strengthened by evidence showing that citizens' political capabilities have been underestimated significantly.

Clearly, this involves a reconsideration of the evidence constituting the original indictment of the mass public—an exercise that is long overdue, in our opinion. If the evidence is found wanting, then the prospects for reform will certainly seem brighter, since the charge of utopianism will be removed, or at least reduced. And if the evidence withstands scrutiny, participatory democrats will be alerted to the need to bridge the "credibility gap" that now threatens their project.

Revisionists, too, have an interest in reviewing the standard description of mass sentiments and behavior. This is especially true of reluctant converts to the cause, those who regretfully placed their hopes for democracy in the hands of a guardian class. But all revisionists are committed to giving an accurate account of the citizens' commitment to democracy. The hard, cold facts about popular opinion and behavior are the basis of all revisions undertaken in the name of realism. So there can be no objection to reopening the investigation or, for that matter, to keeping it open on a continuing basis.

Thus, our aim in *Reconsidering the Democratic Public* is to advance the debate about democracy and its prospects by returning to the concerns about citizenship that spawned the discussion in the first place. We hope this move, and the new evidence that comes with it, will lead students of democracy to a better understanding of the opportunities for—and limits on—self-governance in modern times.

The Rational Public

Popular sovereignty is the essence of "democracy," a word that comes from the Greek *dēmokratia*, meaning rule by the people. Democrats believe that people ought to rule themselves, either directly or through the agencies of representative government. Government will then be the instrument of popular opinion; its policies will correspond to the wishes of the people—or at least a majority of those who participate in the selection of political leaders and policymakers. The congruence between public opinion and public policy will be greatest where plebiscitary instruments—for example, initiative, referendum, and recall—are in place and where parliamentary systems with responsible political parties exist. It will be weaker where representative government includes safeguards against the tyranny of the majority: the Madisonian separation of powers is a familiar American example. But even where minorities enjoy strong protection, the weight of public opinion must ultimately prevail in a properly functioning democracy, or so democrats hold.

Implicit in the idea of democracy is the belief that a sovereign people knows what it wants and is able to communicate its desires to political leaders, who then respond or are held accountable for their failure. If the public does not know what it wants, there is no popular will to reflect, and the whole idea of popular sovereignty is called into question. Similarly, if the public is incapable of expressing its views, political leaders can hardly be charged with making policies congruent with majority sentiment. How could they, given the absence of direction from the people? Thus, everything depends on public opinion, the greatest strength—and also the chief weakness—of democratic politics.

No one saw this more clearly than Walter Lippmann, one of the first democratic revisionists. For Lippmann, it was a mistake for democrats to invest so heavily in public opinion. According to Lippmann (1925), public opinion was no sovereign force; it was a "phantom." Most men, most of the time, simply were not interested in public affairs or, for that matter, in governing themselves. They became involved only when politics was made especially salient, usually by leaders seeking support for their policy proposals. Even then, the public's attention was shallow and fleeting; the public did not guide policy as devotees of popular sovereignty held. Public opinion merely decided who governed at any given moment, and nothing more.

That was as it should be, since the public had neither an interest in ruling nor any expertise in conducting the affairs of state, in Lippmann's view. Indeed, he believed that in the drama of modern politics, "the public will arrive in the middle of the third act and will leave before the last curtain, having stayed just long enough perhaps to decide who is the hero and who the villain of the piece" (Lippmann 1925, 65). To expect more from ordinary citizens was simply unreasonable, for "the individual man does not have opinions on all public affairs. He does not know how to direct public affairs. He does not know what is happening, why it is happening, what ought to happen. I cannot imagine how he could know, and there is not the slightest reason for thinking, as mystical democrats have thought, that the compounding of individual ignorances in masses of people can produce a continuous directing force in public affairs" (Lippmann 1925, 39).

At the heart of Lippmann's thoroughgoing revision of democratic theory was a "realistic" assessment of citizens' attitudes and behavior. He assumed that opinions were something people formed independent of politics. Some brought their opinions to politics; most did not. But in any case, opinions were not something to be discovered or refined in the course of political discussion. Lippmann further assumed that public opinion itself was nothing more than the aggregation of the opinions of individual citizens. Consequently, he thought that public opinion naturally exhibited the tendencies of individuals' opinions: like them, it was slow to crystallize, quick to dissipate, and never achieved much insight or depth. That was why Lippmann thought public opinion was incapable of being a "continuous directing force in public affairs," as earlier democratic theorists had wanted it to be.

Many subsequent investigators endorsed Lippmann's analysis of phantom public opinion—wrongly, in the view of Benjamin Page and Robert Shapiro, whose chapter begins Part I of this volume. Page and Shapiro acknowledge the well-documented cognitive deficiencies of individual citizens, so graphically described by Lippmann. Nevertheless, they insist that the electorate *as a whole* approaches political issues quite intelligently. Aggregate measures of opinion and policy preferences are not random and irrational, the evidence shows. They are generally stable, and when changes do occur, they reflect sensible reactions to events in the real world. In that sense, the public seems fully capable of participating in a dialogue with political elites, although leaders do not always allow this to happen.

Page and Shapiro explain how measurement errors and random fluctuations in individual persons' opinions are eliminated by the "miracle of statistical aggregation," producing a rational public, one whose collective opinion is reasonable and understandable, given the information available to it. From the otherwise unpromising raw material of individuals' opinions, a coherent—and collective—vision of the political world emerges. Lippmann was simply wrong to attribute characteristics of individuals' opinions to the public as a whole, and so the idea of a sovereign people does not seem so fantastic.

Page and Shapiro also discuss the social formation of preferences through collective deliberation. The opinions of people are not fixed, as many scholars seem to assume; they evolve over time, as new information becomes available and different interpretations of political events are circulated in the media and discussed by citizens. Opinion leaders play a crucial role in this process. They are in a position to educate opinion and also to deceive or mislead the people by suppressing vital information. That is why John Dewey (1927), Lippmann's contemporary and sometime adversary, insisted that the real problem of the public is not ignorance but inadequate opportunity for deliberation. It is imperfect methods of debate, discussion, and persuasion that compromise democracy.

For Dewey, the intelligence of democracy does not reside in the genius of individual leaders but in the public airing of issues and policy proposals.[4] Debate governs elites' behavior in a democracy, as John Kingdon argues in his chapter on the power of ideas in politics. Without denying the motivational importance of self-interest, Kingdon stresses leaders' need to explain themselves to the electorate in terms that justify their actions. The pressure to offer convincing explanations and, indeed, the very content of the explanations themselves act as constraints on elites' understanding and pursuit of self-interest. This does not rule out the possibility of strategic action; elites can, and do, explore different ways of framing political debate. But frame the debate they must, and that is why government by discussion still may be served by conditions that do not fully satisfy idealized visions of democratic discourse.

The full import of Kingdon's linguistic turn is brought out by Jane Mansbridge. She argues that democratic political communication requires much more than citizens conveying their preferences to policymakers, or representatives leading citizens to ratify their actions. Under the right conditions, communication is a form of deliberation in which

4. Dewey (1927, 211) makes a sharper criticism of those who scorn the ignorance of citizens: "The notion that intelligence is a personal endowment or personal attainment is the great conceit of the intellectual class, as that of the commercial class is that wealth is something which they personally have wrought and possess."

people discover and modify their preferences in light of other people's needs and interests. As such, democratic discourse has the capacity for resolving prisoners' dilemmas into cooperative enterprises where individuals benefit from what is good for the collectivity as a whole. When that happens, we move beyond adversarial models of democracy that do not comprehend anything other than the self-interested behavior of citizens and their leaders,[5] and we move toward the vision of democracy entertained by those who, like Dewey, believe that democracy forces a recognition of common interests and a discussion aimed at clarifying what those interests are.

That does not mean we can dispense with adversary democracy, where people with different interests oppose each other. Not all, or even most, of our interests are held in common, and so the choice is not between two all-encompassing and mutually exclusive forms of political discourse. Students of democracy face more-difficult, but also more-interesting, questions about the best way to balance adversarial and deliberative styles of communication.[6] Different areas of social life may require more of one and less of the other, and theories of democracy need to take this possibility into account. But, then, citizens already know that, for *Reconsidering the Democratic Public* leaves little doubt that their capacity for politics is far more complex than any theory has heretofore admitted.

The Reasonable Citizen

A stress on the formation of opinion leads away from characterizations of democracy as a system for registering citizens' opinions and converting them into policy. It leads toward conceptions of democracy that emphasize deliberation, for it is in debates and other political exchanges

5. Spragens (1990) and Anderson (1990) offer excellent, albeit quite different, accounts of deliberation in democracy. See also Ackerman 1980 on "neutral dialogue" and, of course, Habermas 1981 on communicative ethics more generally.

6. Warren (1992) suggests that transformative effects are most likely to emerge from discussions about social identity, since the value of the goods in question depends on social interaction and cannot be realized without common action. Goods with other characteristics may not lend themselves to democratic deliberation at all or may give rise to adversarial democracy instead of transformation.

that opinions are expressed, challenged, clarified, and sometimes altered. That is why recent treatments of democracy seek to identify the practices that sustain deliberation and the political, social, and economic conditions that determine the possibilities for democratic discourse.[7]

Ultimately, however, it is citizens and their leaders who deliberate. The institutions of "strong democracy" may facilitate deliberation, while others do not, as Benjamin Barber's chapter notes. But no political process can produce democratic results unless citizens themselves are willing and able to enter into deliberation. Advocates of participatory democracy believe that citizens will rise to the challenge, at least under the right circumstances. In this view of things, there are no inherently disabling traits that make it impossible or undesirable for ordinary citizens to play a significant role in governing themselves.

Other scholars are unwilling to accept this presumption at face value; for them, questions about individual citizens' political capacities are matters of fact. Like Lippmann, they seek a realistic account of democratic politics in mass industrial societies, not a utopian vision of democracy based on heroic assumptions about people's interest in public affairs. In their view, the new interest in deliberation only magnifies the problem because it fails to consider the possibility that an aroused and ill-tempered public might destroy democracy long before its opinions are refined and enlightened by participation in politics.

To realists, accumulating evidence about citizens' political attitudes and behavior is damning because it contrasts so sharply with the apparent requirements of democratic politics. Classical theories of democracy imply that citizens are knowledgeable about political issues, tolerant of opposing views on those issues, and capable of resolving differences of opinion (with the assistance of elected intermediaries). At least that is the image of the rational citizen abstracted from democratic theories by modern observers, including Joseph Schumpeter and a host of contemporary sociologists, political scientists, and economists.[8]

As is well known, this image of the democratic citizen is largely

7. In addition to Mansbridge's essay and the sources mentioned in footnote 5, see Fishkin 1991, Dryzek 1990, and Ackerman 1980. Popkin (1991) discusses voters' deliberations in the context of contemporary American elections.

8. More sophisticated readings of "classical" democracy are given by Cohen (1971), Pennock (1979), and Held (1987). All three of these authors place contemporary notions of democracy in historical perspective, while considering "problems of democracy" peculiar to the modern world.

mythical. Pateman (1970) and others had little difficulty showing that theorists such as Jean-Jacques Rousseau, John Stuart Mill, and Alexis de Tocqueville entertained few illusions about the character of ordinary individuals, especially as that was shaped by the institutions of representative democracy. Therefore, it was quite easy for critics of democratic revisionism to object that realists were applying an inappropriate standard of democratic attitudes and behavior and reaching unduly pessimistic conclusions about the capacity of ordinary citizens for democratic politics.

The objection is sound, but has an apologetic ring to it. It may indeed be unreasonable to hold citizens to an impossibly high standard of conduct, but how low must our standards sink before the average citizen passes the test? If most citizens show little interest in politics, have little knowledge about it, and express strong feelings of intolerance and impatience with democratic processes, why invest our hopes for democracy in deliberation or expanded participation more generally? The evidence seems to undermine the very possibility of transformative politics.

Fortunately, new evidence points to previously undetected capacities for deliberation and moderation. These capacities remained invisible to earlier researchers, whose investigations relied heavily on constructs derived from theories of social psychology. Such constructs informed survey questions put to respondents and shaped scholars' interpretation of answers given to pollsters. So, for example, people were asked if they respected the rights of extremist organizations like the Communist party. Qualified or negative responses were considered intolerant, with little or no regard for the reasons behind them. Subjective understandings of tolerance and its requirements were ignored in favor of researchers' a priori definitions of tolerant behavior.

The continued development of the behavioral sciences has brought home the extent to which findings of this sort are constrained by the conceptions and methods of researchers themselves. This has caused much soul-searching about the nature of objectivity, the authority of "facts," and the meaning of scientific revolutions precipitated by the discovery of new information (Kuhn 1970). It has also shifted attention from naive to sophisticated forms of falsification (Lakatos 1970) and even spawned a variety of epistemological anarchism (Feyerabend [1975] 1978).[9]

9. J. Donald Moon (1970) provides an excellent overview of these issues as they apply to

Ferment has reached the level of methods and measurements, too. A drive to eliminate "artifactual findings" and minimize problems of "response bias" has changed the conduct of opinion surveys and experiments. The subjects under investigation have moved to the foreground and have been allowed to speak more freely, while investigators have faded into the background and listened more attentively. Although this move toward what might be called subject-centered research is still in its infancy, its popularity has grown rapidly and seems likely to increase.

Subject-centered research is also certain to reveal a higher capacity for deliberation among citizens, as the chapters in Part II demonstrate. Thus, subjective understandings of freedom and its possibilities are the focus of James Gibson's contribution to this volume. He reports that people's perceptions of the range of personal freedom open to them vary tremendously; some feel quite free, while others perceive heavy constraints on their freedom. Indeed, a significant number of people say they would not express their opinion on controversial issues, because they do not believe government officials would permit it or because they fear social sanctions. Self-censorship is therefore a common form of behavior among American citizens.

Not surprisingly, the tendency toward self-censorship is particularly strong among African Americans, who have experienced discrimination and intolerance from whites. However, self-censorship is also common among older, more-dogmatic whites who place a high value on maintaining social order. They restrict their own freedom and also tend to be intolerant of others' exercise of liberty, especially when that proves disruptive. In turn, displays of intolerance may contribute to self-censorship on the part of those groups—for example, African Americans—vulnerable to the advocates of law and order.

The extent of self-censorship is both cause for alarm and grounds for hope. It is grounds for hope insofar as self-censorship offers a new interpretation of heretofore critical evidence on the political propensities of citizens. The extent of self-censorship suggests that many individuals' political apathy is not so much an indicator of their incapacity for democratic politics as it is the result of their perceptions of the possibilities for personal involvement in politics. Altering those perceptions, perhaps by altering the social, economic, and political circumstances

political science. Readers will also wish to consult Richard Bernstein 1976 and two books by Brian Fay (1975, 1987).

that give rise to them, may be extremely difficult. But advocates of democratic deliberation would certainly rather face that problem than struggle against the ostensibly limited capacity of citizens identified by an earlier generation of researchers.

Self-censorship is alarming insofar as it suggests that existing political institutions and practices do not seem very inviting to some groups, who therefore do not feel free to participate in democratic politics. However, as John Burke notes, there are many reasons for self-censorship, and not all of them point in the direction of democratic failure. Self-censorship arising from well-grounded perceptions of unfreedom *is* evidence of institutions or social conventions that do not adequately protect liberty. On the other hand, self-censorship may in some cases be the result of a deliberate balancing of democratic values: individuals may not feel free to exercise their liberty, because they respect the liberty of others or because other values, for example, a concern for equality or public safety, require personal restraint. Thus, we need to know more about the reasons behind self-censoring behavior before we are in a position to gauge the critical import of Gibson's finding.

The chapter by Pamela Conover, Stephen Leonard, and Donald Searing shows how to obtain additional information about the way in which citizens reason about their rights and balance their freedom against obligations to their fellows. Using focus groups, they recount how citizens in two North Carolina communities understand the complexities of citizenship in modern, pluralistic societies. Individual rights figure prominently in these subjects' understanding, but so do obligations to others; citizens draw simultaneously from liberal and communitarian traditions of political life. Moreover, people show a remarkable facility for differentiating between language appropriate for discourse among strangers and talk among friends or familiars—a point not always appreciated by theoreticians of democracy.

Thus, by attending to citizens' views of citizenship, Conover et al. uncover a level of public sophistication hidden from investigators employing more intrusive standards of democratic character. But Conover and her colleagues have only begun to tap the richness of the ordinary language of citizenship, if Mary Dietz is right, for their reading of the focus group protocols still owes too much to liberal and communitarian categories of thought. Or rather, the researchers' reconstruction of these categories distinguishes too sharply between rights and duties, and this causes them to misread citizens' recognition of duties as evidence of a communitarianism distinct from a liberal ethos. In Dietz's view, a more plausible interpretation is that citizens grasp the complementarity of rights and duties and are able to transcend one-dimensional conceptions of citizenship. Thus, she endorses an even deeper commitment to subject-centered research as a way of enriching theories of democratic citizenship.

North Carolinians' reconciliation of rights and duties under the rubric of citizenship is a specific example of a more general aspect of deliberation. When citizens deliberate, they aim to choose, not just between different ways of obtaining the same end but also among different ends. Moreover, the choice must be made against a backdrop of uncertainty, both about the effects of various actions and about their wisdom. Some participants may claim to know what is right, but in democratic politics such claims are contestable: there is always room for disagreement, since we lack perfect consensus on the way the world is or how it ought to be.

Hence, for citizens to engage in deliberation, they must tolerate ambiguity and appreciate contradiction without losing sight of the necessity for action. Doctrinaire thinking upsets democratic deliberation among people with different ideas about the proper course of collective action. As Marcus (1988) argues, accommodation is possible only when people are not rigidly committed to their opinions; a certain amount of ideological flexibility is necessary before compromise occurs. In her contribution to this volume, Jennifer Hochschild identifies two sources of ideological flexibility: disjunction, which arises when a person is uncertain about the applicability of a principle of justice to different areas of social life, and ambivalence, which occurs when an individual holds contradictory beliefs about a single issue.

Either disjunction or ambivalence can lead to political paralysis. People who are committed to equality in politics may not be egalitarian when it comes to economics; they are likely to feel conflict when confronted by questions at the boundary of the two spheres of life, for example, questions of redistributive policy. Similarly, people who are ambivalent may approach a political issue and see that it serves one of their cherished values, say liberty, but not another, say justice. They may be uncertain about where they stand, and so they may not act. This inaction is not a sign of some incapacity for politics; it is evidence of a capacity for deliberating about complex issues (just as self-censorship can sometimes be the result of deliberation).

Moreover, some of Hochschild's subjects reacted to their feelings of disjunction and ambivalence in ways that seem transformative. They tried to resolve their uncertainty by absorbing new information, seeking higher-order values capable of relaxing the tensions of disjunction and ambivalence, and even creating new identities out of their experiences. In so doing, these respondents proved their capacity for internal deliberation of a sort that both precedes and anticipates the "government by discussion" that is the essence of democratic communication. Consequently, the prevalence of disjunction and ambivalence among American citizens is a hopeful sign for democrats interested in the peaceful reconciliation of differences in the citizenry.

An openness to different points of view, and a willingness to submit those differences to the court of public opinion, helps explain the appeal of liberal democratic theory, which Donald Moon construes as an effort to show how people who disagree on important and enduring questions regarding the ends and purposes of life can nevertheless come to live together under rules that all accept. Put this way, the skills required of citizens are manifestly not those identified by researchers who stress the capacity for abstract thinking and ideological consistency. Rather, the requisite virtues include moderation, tolerance, a capacity for coping with disjunction and ambivalence, and a willingness to explore problematic issues with fellow citizens—all of which suggest that democratic citizens must be more like foxes than the hedgehogs of political philosophy and democratic revisionism.

Moon rightly observes that the virtues that define democratic character are not only or purely intellectual.[10] "The cognitive world of a fox cannot be divorced from its noncognitive elements—the capacity to tolerate ambiguity or ambivalence, the salience of different ideas and values, the affect with which certain ends and symbols are invested, and so on." Hence, the study of democratic citizenship must be concerned with emotional and affective traits as well, a point brought home forcefully in Part III of *Reconsidering the Democratic Public.*

Passion and Politics

When citizens deliberate, they weigh alternative courses of action. A jury decides whether an accused person is guilty or innocent and, hence,

10. Galston (1991) and Macedo (1990) provide extended discussions of liberal virtues and their inculcation via civic education.

whether that person will suffer criminal penalties or go free. A town council passes on the merits of developers' proposals, in light of environmental and social considerations. Voters choose between candidates with different ideas about the role of government in our lives. Sometimes voters directly decide questions of public policy in referenda. In each case, a deliberate choice is made, after presentation of the relevant information and discussion of alternatives. To that extent, at least, the process is rational, even if the outcomes are displeasing to some.

Democrats' emphasis on rationality is a child of the Enlightenment, which identified reason with deliberation and deliberation with democracy. Philosophers like Rousseau were not unaware of the emotional or affective bases of social life, and in fact they dwelt on the need for civic religions or other traditions capable of sustaining democratic politics. Yet they celebrated reason's role in taming the passions, especially those which undermined communal life. Modern democratic theorists implicitly endorse this view; they dwell on reason so strongly that emotions have been almost totally eclipsed in discussions of citizens' participation in politics. As a result, the "rational actors" of formal theory are only the most extreme representation of citizens qua cogitators in contemporary accounts of democratic life; less formal theories, however, are also preoccupied with reason.

Some of those concerned about democratic character object to this overwhelming stress on citizens' cognitive abilities (especially when these abilities are reduced to austere calculations of the most efficient means of achieving desired ends). Character is broader than cognition; it includes the emotional constitution of individuals, which both shapes and is shaped by cognition—and much else. The interplay of affect and cognition, or emotion and reason, is therefore a topic that has come into its own with the surge of interest in subject-centered research.

The connection with democratic theory is obvious, for the subjective understandings of citizens have special relevance for political toleration. Citizens' willingness to "live and let live" has long been considered an essential feature of democratic politics. How else could pluralism survive in the modern world, except for people's recognition of the rights of others, even—or especially—those with radically different ideas about life, work, and politics?

Perhaps this is why the discovery of high levels of intolerance by Samuel Stouffer (1955) was originally thought to be so incriminating; it strongly suggested that many people were uncommitted to basic political norms and were therefore a threat to democracy. Other researchers, for example, Prothro and Grigg (1960) and McClosky (1964), confirmed this impression, while adding additional information about elites' stronger dedication to the democratic cause. On the strength of these findings, it seemed as if elites, and not masses, were the carriers of the democratic creed, to use Robert Dahl's famous description of the ironic conclusion friends of democracy were driven to accept.

Researchers' understanding of tolerance and its implications played an obtrusive role in these early studies of tolerance, however. Citizens' interpretations of tolerance were not highlighted until much later, in connection with a debate over a contention that levels of tolerance increased during the 1960s and 1970s (Davis 1975; Nunn et al. 1978). New evidence suggested that masses were becoming more attached to basic democratic norms as the hysteria of the Cold War declined and as the ferment of the civil rights and antiwar movements increased citizens' exposure to dissenting opinions.

Sullivan et al. (1982) subsequently showed that the apparently significant increase in tolerance was overstated. A new conceptualization and measurement of political tolerance led them to this conclusion. Previous investigators presented respondents with a list of groups thought to be in greatest danger of being denied civil liberties, thereby imposing a particular construction of tolerance on respondents. Sullivan et al. were the first to ask respondents which groups they disliked, *before* asking if they were willing to respect the civil liberties of unpopular groups and individuals. This allowed citizens more room to express themselves on matters of tolerance or, more precisely, intolerance.

Use of a subject-centered measurement strategy showed that citizens were indeed more tolerant of Communists, socialists, and atheists, groups at the center of most measures of political tolerance. However, during the 1960s and 1970s people expressed dislike for other groups, for example, the Ku Klux Klan or the Symbionese Liberation Army. A pattern of "pluralistic intolerance" appeared, wherein citizens were intolerant of many different groups, depending on their personal predilections and dislikes. Although Sullivan et al. deplored this situation, they noted that democracy might survive the threat to civil liberties posed by pluralistic intolerance, unless intolerant attitudes were again mobilized and focused as they had been during the Red Scare of the 1950s.

James Kuklinski, Ellen Riggle, Victor Ottati, Norbert Schwarz, and

Robert Wyer agree that the dangers of intolerance are not receding, even though the public seems capable of greater deliberation than democratic revisionists claimed. In the first of three chapters in this volume that directly challenge the hegemony of reason among theorists of democracy, Kuklinski et al. dispute the assumption that a rational public is necessarily a tolerant one. Drawing on experimental data, Kuklinski et al. argue that deliberation on the part of citizens does not, by cooling their emotions, lead to a stronger sense of tolerance. Deliberation actually causes people to be *less* tolerant, as the negative consequences of tolerating such groups as the Ku Klux Klan come into view. This is true even when respondents are considering the consequences of tolerating actions undertaken by groups that enjoy high levels of public esteem. Hence, reason does not seem to be a force of enlightenment, at least where matters of tolerance are concerned.

Russell Hanson questions this conclusion, suggesting that Kuklinski et al. have underestimated the moderating role of reason in political deliberation, a point also made in John Burke's chapter. In Hanson's view, Elizabeth Theiss-Morse, George Marcus, and John Sullivan offer a more balanced account of the roles of reason and emotion in the psychology of most citizens. Theiss-Morse et al. show that emotions fulfill an important function in focusing people's attention on their political environment. Reason comes into play as citizens evaluate dangers posed by groups they dislike or fear. If the danger is thought to be slight, people are likely to tolerate the actions of the groups in question; but when the risks loom large, intolerance is the rule. Thus, Theiss-Morse et al. conclude that reason plays a larger role than Kuklinski and his colleagues admit, although both groups of scholars agree that emotional factors deserve much greater emphasis than they have received so far in democratic theory.

Neither of the studies presents any evidence that intolerant people act upon their feelings, and this widespread forbearance may be the key to democratic stability, as Hanson notes. Even if full-fledged expressions of intolerance were common, however, the place of emotions in theories of democratic politics would not be settled. Hadley Arkes readily concedes that the new studies show that emotions are an important, and often overlooked, determinant of political tolerance. However, from his point of view, the fact that emotions affect citizens' political orientations has no bearing on normative accounts of how democratic citizens *ought* to behave. If people's willingness to tolerate others is determined by emotions, that only highlights the need for civic education in moral reasoning as the foundation of democratic politics.

This raises questions long known to be central to democratic theory. Who is responsible for the moral instruction of citizens? Will leaders, as the acknowledged carriers of the democratic creed, perform this function? Or will they "demagogue the issues," appealing to citizens' emotions in order to advance their own careers and interests, as Kuklinski et al. suggest? If leaders abdicate their responsibility, have the people any indigenous capacity for refusing the low road in favor of democratic pluralism?[11]

Such questions are difficult to answer directly and definitively, but Denis Sullivan and Roger Masters provide relevant information from their experimental studies of political communication. They examine political leaders' use of nonverbal behavior to appeal to citizens' emotions, a very undeliberative style of communication. Citizens react to noncognitive messages sent by candidates' gestures and facial displays, which convey a sense of personal warmth or coldness as well as information about candidates' commitment to action. In this way emotional bonds form between citizens and candidates with similar feelings about politics and its possibilities.

The emotional reaction of citizens is independent of cognitively shaped attitudes. In fact, warm feelings toward candidates like Ronald Reagan cause people to be more supportive even when no new information about policy positions has been verbalized. Sullivan and Masters argue that the existence of powerful emotional ties between leaders and citizens requires a significant revision of democratic theories that fail to account for people's susceptibility to nonverbal appeals by prospective leaders. A full reckoning of the effects (positive as well as negative) of emotional bonds is needed to improve our understanding of democracy and its possibilities, they conclude.

Larry Preston's comments on the chapter by Masters and Sullivan echo Hadley Arkes's reply to Theiss-Morse et al., who emphasize the

11. Clearly, these are not simply theoretical questions, they are highly practical; and although the participants at the Williams Conference did not focus on citizenship training, others have. See, for example, Merelman 1984, Janowitz 1984, and Gutmann 1987, as well as efforts by Barber and others at Stanford University, Baylor University, Spellman College, Ohio University, and the University of Minnesota to promote civic education (Farr 1990). Still, Hanson (1979) is surely right about contemporary political scientists' general indifference to citizenship, one of the discipline's historic interests.

emotional foundations of tolerance. Preston wants students of democracy to consider what role emotions *should* play in political communication. Sullivan and Master's evidence about the importance of emotion is relevant, he acknowledges; it would be foolish to assume that emotions do not affect political communication between leaders or followers or that candidates will ignore strategically useful knowledge about the efficacy of emotional appeals. However, it would be equally mistaken to assume that emotions cannot be enlightened by reason and deliberation. Television campaigns for election may not lend themselves very well to this purpose, but other institutions might, and Preston urges students of democracy to imagine what sorts of practices would motivate leaders to act responsibly and citizens to think critically and self-consciously about their gut feelings on politics.

Democracy and Diversity

The structure of communication between leaders and followers is the principal concern of all considerations on representative government, a central and indispensable element of modern democratic theory. An unqualified commitment to direct democracy is impossible to maintain in large, diverse societies; for democracy to work on an extended scale, some decision-making powers must be delegated to representatives of the people.[12] Not everyone regrets this concession to reality, but all admit that a commitment to popular rule demands the closest scrutiny of how representation operates and how well various interests are politically incorporated.

The institution of representation is usually defended as a means of assuring some congruence between popular opinion and public policy; hence its utility in theories of popular rule or self-determination. Such theories stress the role of political parties, interest groups, and other organizations in conveying information between leaders and followers. Effective "linkage mechanisms" inform leaders of their constituents' policy preferences, assuring that representatives will either give the

12. Pitkin (1967) traces the historical development of representation in Anglo-American thought. Lindblom's (1977) brief, but telling, discussion of volition illuminates the operation of representation and its limitations in contemporary polyarchies. A classic study of representatives' relations to their constituents is Fenno 1978.

people what they want or suffer the political consequences of disregarding their will.[13] Of course, parties, interest groups, and the media also afford leaders a chance to persuade people of their wisdom and courage in managing the affairs of state, so that communication flows both ways (though not at the same volume or in the same channels, to be sure).

Thus, a healthy dialogue is essential to representative government. Sullivan and Masters' demonstration of the public's susceptibility to emotional appeals raises questions about the vitality of this dialogue in contemporary American politics. The success of "negative campaigning," especially during the presidential election of 1988, underscores citizens' apparent gullibility, while reinforcing doubts about elites' commitment to democratic discourse. There is a pressing need to reconsider the communicative links between leaders and followers, if we want to grasp the possibilities for democracy under representative government.

Donald Kinder and Don Herzog return to John Stuart Mill for suggestions about the proper role of people and their leaders under representative government. With Page and Shapiro, they insist that many citizens have the knowledge, interest, and cognitive skills necessary for "government by discussion," the findings of democratic revisionists to the contrary notwithstanding. Those findings assume that abstract, even ideological thinking is the hallmark of informed public opinion. But public opinion is not a rigid calculus; it is a fluid discourse, and in that respect public opinion provides substantial room for deliberation, as Kinder and Herzog read the evidence.

For Kinder and Herzog, communication among citizens, and especially between citizens and leaders, is mediated by interpretive "frames." These frames enable communication by supplying political vocabularies for exploring issues confronting the collectivity. Those who participate in political debate draw on these vocabularies in their struggle to understand problems, discover solutions, and mobilize support for

13. Many important works on representation are cited in Chapters 1, 3, and 17 of this volume, and so only a few references are needed here. Luttbeg 1981 is a standard overview of political linkages in American politics; Ginsberg (1986) offers a more critical evaluation of the connections between rulers and the ruled in the age of mass media. Lowi (1979) offers a provocative account of interest-group politics, and the role of political parties in democratic polities is considered in Schattschneider's (1942) classic essay, as well as in Ranney and Kendall 1956. Sartori (1976) explicitly treats parties as channels of communication and considers their role in fostering representation.

different kinds of action. Emotions figure prominently in frames, of course, but so do cognitions (in the form of explanations or justifications for actions). Thus, frames do not simply carry messages about the public's desires, they are the medium in which those desires are uncovered, shaped, and refined.

The discursive organization of frames makes them more congenial to democratic discourse than abstract, highly constrained belief systems of the sort admired by some democratic revisionists. Agreeing with Hochschild's chapter in this volume, Kinder and Herzog argue that rigid ideologies promote doctrinaire politics, whereas communicative frames facilitate the sort of exchange of ideas prized so highly by Mill and most other democrats. The prevalence of frames therefore implies that citizens are more sophisticated democrats than earlier researchers—for example, Converse (1964)—were willing to admit.

Although he welcomes the renewed interest in "government by discussion" that motives frame analysis, James Farr is not persuaded that John Stuart Mill offers the best guidance on these matters. Mill's interest in discussion stemmed from his concern over the political shortcomings of ordinary citizens. The public mind might be educated and improved by the exchange of ideas, but when all was said and done Mill refused to make a strong connection between discussion among citizens and the business of governance itself (as Rousseau had done when he refused to accept representation as a mode of democratic governance). As a result, the authority of the *vox populi* is only weakly recognized in Mill's account, which leaves ample room for elites to "frame" discussions with an eye toward legitimating their own policy preferences.

That is the sense in which frames, which allow for communication between leaders and followers, are open to manipulation and domination by elites. This is Farr's second point, which Kinder and Herzog acknowledge, while stopping short of saying what distinguishes "artful" frames from truly democratic ones. In Farr's view, this step must be taken, or else we may uncritically endorse frames that do not measure up to robust conceptions of government by discussion. As he puts it, we must "focus less on the ways in which the use of frames makes discussion cognitively possible and more on the ways in which discussion makes the use of frames practically democratic."

The analysis of public opinion and its formation is probably not the most promising site for uncovering the essential features of truly democratic frames. Farr suggests that jury discussions, town meetings, and even focus groups offer richer possibilities for frame analysis. Such naturally occurring deliberations allow participants to shape the agenda of discussion and to be involved in the actual resolution of issues. The risk of co-optation by elites is correspondingly reduced as the distinction between political leaders and citizen followers is reduced or eliminated in favor of the institutions that constitute "strong democracy."

Asymmetries of power are still present in these natural deliberations, of course. In juries and other small groups, task leaders emerge and exert disproportionate influence in collective decision making. By virtue of their individual talents and superior communication skills, these leaders will frame issues and alternative courses of action, reducing the impact of others. Yet the closeness of the exchanges and the need to persuade others to take action prevents leaders from gaining control of the process, particularly if they lack any formal powers of command. Thus, what Kingdon says about Congress applies even more to small-group dynamics.

Town meetings are larger affairs, and with increasing size the distribution of group powers becomes more important. Even (or perhaps especially) within open frameworks of discussion, strategic action is common where groups of citizens assert their interests and seek political support for them. To the extent that participating groups of citizens have unequal power, distortions of communication may emerge (Habermas 1981). As a result, minority points of view are especially likely to be ignored, unless protective coalitions with other influential groups can be forged or no clear majority forms—a possibility that Madison foresaw in large (and hence diverse) polities.

Strategies for protecting the interests of racial minorities are discussed by David Tabb in a chapter that deals not with town meetings but urban politics. Tabb outlines some of the conditions that favor the emergence of multiracial coalitions in urban politics. Some of these coalitions, Tabb notes, do little to redress the grievances of African Americans or Latinos, who may be co-opted by white factions. In a handful of cities, however, minority groups play a leading role in multiracial coalitions with white liberals. When these coalitions dominate city government, they not only protect the rights of individuals who are members of a minority, they also advance the group interests of the minority. For Tabb, this represents the only genuine accommodation of racial minorities in urban settings; the mere extension of formal rights to previously excluded individuals is not enough to meet the demands of democratic justice.

This attempt to privilege minority claims, or group rights, draws fire from Gary Jacobsohn. He sympathizes with minority complaints of unfair treatment and applauds the partial redress of these complaints by regimes that include minority representatives. However, Jacobsohn wonders whether *any* group's claims can be placed above others without undermining democratic principles of equality. As he suggests, an emphasis on group entitlements suggests that rights are a function of who one is, rather than an extension of one's commitment to the institutions and procedures that constitute a shared way of life. That is the sense in which a substantive recognition of differences among citizens can undermine the indeterminacy of outcome so often thought to be a strength of liberal democratic politics.

Jacobsohn worries that Tabb's version of minority incorporation is a step toward the idea of "differential citizenship" propounded by Iris Marion Young (1989), who roots the identities of individual citizens in the particular circumstances of their lives. The diversity of these circumstances ensures a heterogeneous polity composed of members with distinct claims and interests. Liberal democratic theory has long recognized this fact of political life, yet its image of "the people" suggests an assemblage of identical and interchangeable persons who stand equal before the law. Persons become citizens, acquiring a formal identity that is common to all and specific to none. Only then can the construction of neutral political processes take place, in theory or practice.

It would be convenient if citizens were not so different from one another, for that would make it easier to speak confidently of an overarching commitment to neutral procedures that treat everyone equally. But citizens *are* different from one another, and political arrangements that ignore those differences may produce undemocratic outcomes, as the final chapters in this volume note. Mary Shanley argues that conceptions of citizenship as a public affair necessarily discriminate against women and other groups whose access to political decision making is restricted by law and socioeconomic circumstance. The political incorporation of previously excluded groups may achieve formal equality, she argues, but it does not get at the root issue, the need for democratic theory to recognize gender, race, and class differences among citizens. This will entail a radical rethinking of rights and responsibilities in a democratic society composed not of abstract citizens but of variously embodied selves—each with concrete interests and needs—

the sort of people who participated in the focus groups organized by Conover et al.

Shanley's comments reinforce the conclusion of Virginia Sapiro's chapter, which is concerned with violence against women. The violence takes many forms, including sexual harassment, psychological abuse, battery, rape, and assault; and much of it occurs within families. The problem of violence against women is belittled by cultural beliefs that shift moral responsibility from the perpetrators of violence to their victims. "She asked for it" and "It's a private matter between husband and wife" are widely accepted excuses for violent behavior that, if it were directed against men, would not be tolerated.

Sapiro contends that democrats have generally failed to meet the challenge of domestic violence, because they accept too readily the distinction between public and private affairs. Public affairs, and especially political decision making, receive a great deal of attention from democrats who insist on the importance of obtaining the consent of the governed and who are critical of institutions that evidently rely on tacit or implied consent for their authority. Yet in the realm of private matters, critical scrutiny seems to dissipate: power relations frequently remain unanalyzed, and imputations of consent are accepted without much examination. As a result, women's interests are routinely neglected or are even subordinated to those of men as private life is excluded from political consideration.

Sapiro challenges democratic theorists to reconsider their allegiance to a distinction between public and private life that blunts examination of violence against women. Hers is a call for more subject-centered research, not only because it provides a more accurate account of what citizens do and think but also because attention to the identity of our subjects reveals lacunae in our conceptions of democracy as a form of life. Like Dietz and Farr, Sapiro feels that our abstract analyses of democracy would be substantially enriched if our research came into much closer contact with the experiences of ordinary citizens; after all, they are "the people" of whom democratic theorists speak and in whom our hopes for a more democratic life reside.

The Conduct of Research

We do not want to leave readers with the impression that all of the contributions to *Reconsidering the Democratic Public* are utterly consistent with one another. There are indeed many points of intellectual contact, and this lends coherence to the volume. However, "contact" allows for conflict and the expression of differences of opinion, of which there are many in *Reconsidering the Democratic Public.* Some of the differences arise in unexpected quarters: witness the contrasting findings of Theiss-Morse et al. and Kuklinski et al., teams of researchers most closely identified with the "empirical" camp at the Williams symposium. For their part, "theorists" seem divided over the wisdom of Barber's and Arkes's characterization of the role of facts in moral theory and their unyielding insistence on the primacy of the normative project of democratic theory.

Nevertheless, it is undoubtedly true that the sharpest differences are between "empiricists" and "theorists." This is hardly surprising, given the division of labor that now characterizes the discipline of political science in general and democratic theory in particular. Yet the differences of opinion expressed herein do not support the conclusion that neither side has much to learn from the other, or that each should go its separate way. To the contrary, *Reconsidering the Democratic Public* suggests that the two camps cannot do without each other, or at least they cannot do very well alone.

That is because a deeper understanding of democracy requires knowledge of the real world of politics, as well as critical perspective on it. It is not enough to say "this is the way democracy really is," nor is it sufficient to insist that "we must search in this direction for democracy." Both types of investigation are needed to grasp whatever potential for democracy exists in contemporary society. Therefore, the existing division of labor must be rejected as being counterproductive.

It is easy to claim that normative and empirical inquiry must join in democratic theory, but it is much harder to say how this can be managed. It would certainly help if "empiricists" and "theorists" stopped ignoring each other. The estrangement of the two has deepened over the past three decades as each pursued its own concerns about democracy more or less independent of the other. As a result, the harsh and generally sterile debates of the late sixties and early seventies have disappeared, but potentially more constructive exchanges have been a casualty, too.[14]

14. The current situation is captured quite literally in Almond's (1988) discussion of "separate tables" in the lunchrooms of political science. Gibbons (1990) takes issue with Almond's description of the conversation that goes on at some of these tables, but he endorses

David Ricci blames both "empiricists" and "theorists" for the tragic decline of scholarship on the problems of democracy. By his telling, the former's pursuit of a scientific understanding of politics has taken political science ever farther from moral issues and concerns vital to the health of democratic politics. Theorists, too, have made themselves irrelevant to politics by ignoring the findings of "mainstream political scholars who strive to uncover the salient facts of political life, fleeting though they may be" (Ricci 1984, 321). Thus, neither camp has much to offer in the way of advice to practicing democrats.

The Democratic Theory Symposium at Williams College was explicitly designed to overcome the alienation of "empiricists" and "theorists," as the Preface to this volume explains. The format of the conference is reflected in the following chapters: empirically minded researchers presented the results of their investigations and received comments from a political theorist. Both were then given a chance to revise their work in light of the other's remarks and the reaction of the other participants in the conference. The final chapters therefore represent an advanced stage in an ongoing conversation.

The arrangement works surprisingly well, at least insofar as it produces stimulating discussions about problems of democracy. We hope that *Reconsidering the Democratic Public* will have a similar effect on the discipline as a whole, rekindling a debate gone prematurely cold. But we also believe that it is possible to move beyond an adversarial relationship between "empiricists" and "theorists" and toward collaborative explorations of current prospects for democratic politics. The Conover, Leonard, and Searing team, as well as the partnership between Kinder and Herzog, demonstrates the special value of such joint undertakings: normative and empiricist concerns are fused from the start, affecting all phases of research, from problem formulation to interpretation of the findings and their implications for democracy. The results speak for themselves, proving the potential of joining forces (and the folly of choosing sides).

Of course, there must be grounds for collaboration between "empiricists" and "theorists." Such grounds do not exist where the former confine their attention to the "real" world of democracy, while the latter

the call for more communication between them. Since Gibbons's complaint involves Almond's telling of the history of the discipline, readers may profit from Dryzek and Leonard (1988) and their exchange with Farr et al. (1990).

contemplate the "ideal" of democracy. However, between the real and the ideal lies the realm of democratic possibilities. This realm encompasses institutions and practices that do not exist now and may never come to be unless someone does something to "realize" them. The realm of possibilities, we suggest, represents the common ground where empirical and theoretical interests meet.[15]

A number of questions are likely to be debated when democratic possibilities are considered. The probable starting point is a sense that things are not as they should be in a democracy, since discontent with the status quo is the usual source of reform suggestions. The discontent may stem from the moral judgments of political theorists, or it could be discovered by researchers attentive to the complaints of ordinary citizens; there is no reason to assume that representatives from either camp will fill this role completely. But wherever it originates, some critical perspective is the foundation of any study of democratic possibilities, as the contributors to this volume all insist.

Of course, discontent has no creative outlet if things are as they must be. Hence, the delineation of alternative institutional arrangements is fundamental to the exercise, although it, too, involves collaboration. The theorist has a role to play insofar as some alternative arrangements may not be at all democratic (and the democratic ones may not be equally praiseworthy). But the empiricist contributes information about the processes that govern the realization of different alternatives. Such information is useful in separating "realistic" proposals from utopian projects insofar as it contributes to an assessment of their relative odds of success and plays a role in mobilizing opinion in support of one proposal over others.

Empirical research may also help us understand the costs of implementing reforms in the name of democracy, just as normative theories gauge the effects of failing to make democratic progress. An intelligent assessment of democratic possibilities must weigh the gains of reforms against the costs of bringing them about, not only because the costs might exceed the gains in democracy but also because the value of democracy itself may be limited by other values. To take an obvious,

15. Bobbio (1987) and Dahl (1989) offer considerable insight into the feasible futures of democracy. Essays in the fourth section of Duncan 1983 also consider democratic possibilities, although they pay less attention to constraints that make some possibilities less likely than others.

albeit hypothetical, example, if participation in the workplace leads to dramatic losses in productivity and declining standards of living, that is a relevant consideration—for citizens who must live with the consequences, if not for some students of democracy.

Prudence demands that risks associated with change be considered, too. Reforms undertaken with the best intentions can have disastrous, but unforeseen, consequences. No theory provides a certain guide to the future, and any theory with such pretensions is almost certainly undemocratic. For it is a peculiarity of democratic change that it emanates from political decisions that are not predetermined; the possibility of changing directions while sailing toward the future makes truly democratic reform an inherently uncertain prospect. It is therefore necessary to consider what new possibilities—not all of them democratic—might be opened if we act to realize democratic alternatives.

Thus, students of democracy find themselves in much the same position as their subjects, citizens who are engaged in political discussions about the best course of action to pursue in an uncertain world of possibilities. Given the similarity of predicament, it would be perverse of "empiricists" and "theorists" to remain intellectual adversaries while extolling the virtues of reasonable accommodation to citizens. Surely we have learned more than that from considering the democratic public—and if we have not, it really is time for *Reconsidering the Democratic Public.*

References

Ackerman, Bruce. 1980. *Social Justice and the Liberal State.* New Haven: Yale University Press.

Almond, Gabriel. 1988. "Separate Tables: Schools and Sects in Political Science." *PS: Political Science and Politics* 21 (4): 828–42.

Anderson, Charles. 1990. *Pragmatic Liberalism.* Chicago: University of Chicago Press.

Bachrach, Peter. 1967. *The Theory of Democratic Elitism: A Critique.* Boston: Little, Brown.

Barber, Benjamin R. 1984. *Strong Democracy: Participatory Politics for a New Age.* Berkeley and Los Angeles: University of California Press.

Bellah, Robert, Richard Madsen, William M. Sullivan, Ann Swidler, and Steven M. Tipton. 1985. *Habits of the Heart: Individualism and Commitment in American Life.* Berkeley and Los Angeles: University of California Press.

Berelson, Bernard R., Paul F. Lazarsfeld, and William N. McPhee. 1954. *Voting: A Study of Opinion Formation in a Presidential Campaign*. Chicago: University of Chicago Press.

Bernstein, Richard. 1976. *The Restructuring of Social and Political Theory*. New York: Harcourt Brace Jovanovich.

Bobbio, Norberto. 1987. *The Future of Democracy*. Minneapolis: University of Minnesota Press.

Boyte, Harry C. 1981. *The Backyard Revolution: Understanding the New Citizen Movement*. Philadelphia: Temple University Press.

Cohen, Carl. 1971. *Democracy*. New York: Free Press.

Converse, Philip E. 1964. "The Nature of Belief Systems in Mass Publics." In *Ideology and Discontent*, ed. David Apter, 206–61. New York: Free Press.

Crozier, Michel J., Samuel P. Huntington, and Joji Watanuki. 1975. *The Crisis of Democracy: Report on the Governability of Democracies to the Trilateral Commission*. New York: New York University Press.

Dahl, Robert A. 1956. *A Preface to Democratic Theory*. Chicago: University of Chicago Press.

———. 1985. *A Preface to Economic Democracy*. Berkeley and Los Angeles: University of California Press.

———. 1989. *Democracy and Its Critics*. New Haven: Yale University Press.

Davis, James A. 1975. "Communism, Conformity, Cohorts, and Categories: American Tolerance in 1954 and 1972–73." *American Journal of Sociology* 81:491–513.

Dewey, John. 1927. *The Public and Its Problems*. New York: H. Holt and Company.

Duncan, Graeme, ed. 1983. *Democratic Theory and Practice*. Cambridge: Cambridge University Press.

Dryzek, John S. 1990. *Discursive Democracy: Politics, Policy, and Political Science*. New York: Cambridge University Press.

Dryzek, John S., and Stephen T. Leonard. 1988. "History and Discipline in Political Science." *American Political Science Review* 82:1245–60.

Farr, James. 1990. "To Do Political Science Democratically." Remarks at a roundtable discussion on the Williams Conference, presented at the annual meeting of the American Political Science Association.

Farr, James, John Gunnell, Raymond Seidelman, John Dryzek, and Stephen T. Leonard. 1990. "Controversy: Can Political Science History Be Neutral?" *American Political Science Review* 84:587–607.

Fay, Brian. 1975. *Social Theory and Political Practice*. London: George Allen & Unwin.

———. 1987. *Critical Social Science: Liberation and Its Limits*. Ithaca, N.Y.: Cornell University Press.

Fenno, Richard F. 1978. *Home Style: House Members in Their Districts*. Boston: Little, Brown.

Feyerabend, Paul. [1975] 1978. *Against Method*. London: Verso.

Fishkin, James. 1991. *Deliberation and Democracy: New Directions for Democratic Reform*. New Haven: Yale University Press.

Galston, William A. 1991. *Liberal Purposes: Goods, Virtues, and Diversity*. New York: Cambridge University Press.

Gibbons, Michael T. 1990. "Political Science, Disciplinary History, and Theoretical Pluralism: A Response to Almond and Eckstein." *PS: Political Science and Politics* 23 (1): 44–46.
Ginsberg, Benjamin. 1986. *The Captive Public: How Mass Opinion Promotes State Power*. New York: Basic Books.
Gould, Carol C. 1988. *Rethinking Democracy: Freedom and Social Cooperation in Politics, Economy, and Society*. Cambridge: Cambridge University Press.
Green, Philip. 1985. *Retrieving Democracy: In Search of Civic Equality*. Totowa, N.J.: Rowman & Allanheld.
Greenberg, Edward S. 1986. *Workplace Democracy: The Political Effects of Participation*. Ithaca, N.Y.: Cornell University Press.
Gutmann, Amy. 1987. *Democratic Education*. Princeton: Princeton University Press.
Habermas, Jürgen. 1981. *Theories des Kommunikativen Handelns*. 2 vols. Frankfurt: Suhrkamp.
Hanson, Donald W. 1979. "The Education of Citizens: Reflections on the State of Political Science." *Polity* 11:457–77.
Hanson, Russell L. 1985. *The Democratic Imagination in America: Conversations with Our Past*. Princeton: Princeton University Press.
Held, David. 1987. *Models of Democracy*. Stanford: Stanford University Press.
Janowitz, Moriss. 1984. *The Reconstruction of Patriotism: Education for a Civil Consciousness*. Chicago: University of Chicago Press.
Kuhn, Thomas. 1970. *The Structure of Scientific Revolutions*. 2d ed. Chicago: University of Chicago Press.
Lakatos, Imre. 1970. "Falsification and the Methodology of Scientific Research Programmes." In *Criticism and the Growth of Knowledge*, ed. Imre Lakatos and Alan Musgrave, 91–196. Cambridge: Cambridge University Press.
Lindblom, Charles E. 1977. *Politics and Markets: The World's Political-Economic Systems*. New York: Basic Books.
Lippmann, Walter. 1922. *Public Opinion*. New York: Macmillan.
———. 1925. *The Phantom Public*. New York: Harcourt, Brace.
Lowi, Theodore J. 1979. *The End of Liberalism: Ideology, Policy, and the Crisis of Public Authority*. 2d ed. New York: W. W. Norton.
Luttbeg, Norman. 1981. *Public Opinion and Public Policy: Models of Political Linkage*. Itasca, Ill.: F. E. Peacock.
McClosky, Herbert. 1964. "Consensus and Ideology in American Politics." *American Political Science Review* 58:361–82.
Macedo, Stephen. 1990. *Liberal Virtues*. Oxford: Clarendon Press.
Mansbridge, Jane J. 1980. *Beyond Adversary Democracy*. New York: Basic Books.
Marcus, George E. 1988. "Democratic Theories and the Study of Public Opinion." *Polity* 21:25–44.
Merelman, Richard M. 1984. *Making Something of Ourselves: On Culture and Politics in the United States*. Berkeley and Los Angeles: University of California Press.
Moon, J. Donald. 1975. "The Logic of Political Inquiry: A Synthesis of Opposed Perspectives. In *The Handbook of Political Science*, ed. Fred I. Greenstein and Nelson W. Polsby, 1:131–228. Reading, Mass.: Addison-Wesley.

Neuman, W. Russell. 1986. *The Paradox of Mass Politics: Knowledge and Opinion in the American Electorate*. Cambridge, Mass.: Harvard University Press.

Nunn, Clyde A., Harry J. Crockett, and J. Allen Williams. 1978. *Tolerance for Nonconformity*. San Francisco: Jossey-Bass.

Okin, Susan M. 1989. *Gender, Justice, and the Family*. New York: Basic Books.

Pateman, Carole. 1970. *Participation and Democratic Theory*. London: Cambridge University Press.

———. 1988. *The Sexual Contract*. Stanford: Stanford University Press.

Pennock, J. Roland. 1979. *Democratic Political Theory*. Princeton: Princeton University Press.

Pitkin, Hanna Fenichel. 1967. *The Concept of Representation*. Berkeley and Los Angeles: University of California Press.

Popkin, Samuel L. 1991. *The Reasoning Voter: Communication and Persuasion in Presidential Campaigns*. Chicago: University of Chicago Press.

Prothro, James W., and Charles W. Grigg. 1960. "Fundamental Principles of Democracy: Bases of Agreement and Disagreement." *Journal of Politics* 22:276–94.

Ranney, Austin, and Willmoore Kendall. 1956. *Democracy and the American Party System*. New York: Harcourt, Brace.

Ricci, David. 1984. *The Tragedy of Political Science: Politics, Scholarship, and Democracy*. New Haven: Yale University Press.

Sartori, Giovanni. 1962. *Democratic Theory*. Detroit: Wayne State University Press.

———. 1976. *Parties and Party Systems*. Cambridge: Cambridge University Press.

———. 1987. *The Theory of Democracy Revisited*. 2 vols. Chatham, N.J.: Chatham House Publishers.

Schattschneider, E. E. 1942. *Party Government*. New York: Rinehart.

Schumpeter, Joseph A. 1943. *Capitalism, Socialism, and Democracy*. London: George Allen & Unwin.

Seidelman, Raymond, with the assistance of Edward J. Harpham. 1988. *Disenchanted Realists: Political Science and the American Crisis, 1884–1984*. Albany: State University of New York Press.

Smith, Eric R.A.N. 1989. *The Unchanging American Voter*. Berkeley and Los Angeles: University of California Press.

Spragens, Thomas A., Jr. 1990. *Reason and Democracy*. Durham, N.C.: Duke University Press.

Stouffer, Samuel. 1955. *Communism, Conformity, and Civil Liberties*. New York: Doubleday.

Sullivan, John L., James Piereson, and George E. Marcus. 1982. *Political Tolerance and American Democracy*. Chicago: University of Chicago Press.

Thompson, Dennis. 1970. *The Democratic Citizen: Social Science and Democratic Theory in the Twentieth Century*. New York: Cambridge University Press.

Warren, Mark. 1992. "Democratic Theory and Self-Transformation." *American Political Science Review* 86(1): 8–23.

Young, Iris Marion. 1989. "Polity and Group Difference: A Critique of the Ideal of Universal Citizenship." *Ethics* 99 (January): 250–74.

I

The Rational Public

1

The Rational Public and Democracy

Benjamin I. Page
Robert Y. Shapiro

Democratic theories of various sorts ask various things of the citizenry. Many emphasize the need for public support of democratic processes and political liberty. Some demand a high level of participation in politics (Pateman 1970; Barber 1984). Others are satisfied with a pluralistic clash among interest groups that may or may not represent everyone (Truman [1950] 1971) or with a public that simply forms retrospective judgments of government performance and holds officials accountable through contested

We are grateful to Ben Barber, Jane Mansbridge, Virginia Sapiro, Roger Masters, James Gibson, and other participants in the Democratic Theory Symposium for comments and suggestions on this paper. Our intellectual debts for the research project as a whole are vast and are partially enumerated in Page and Shapiro 1992.

elections (Schumpeter [1942] 1975; Key 1961, 263–87, 472–80; Fiorina 1981).

In a large, diverse nation like the contemporary United States, where face-to-face interaction and participation by all citizens is generally impossible and where interests tend to clash in an "adversary" fashion (Mansbridge 1980), we believe that direct participatory democracy is bound to play a limited part. Representative institutions are necessary. Yet representation need not entail an attenuated, Schumpeterian form of democracy; it is not necessarily incompatible with a vigorous, majoritarian, populistic democracy in which governments respond to the policy preferences of the public.

James Mill long ago sketched out a utilitarian rationale for majoritarian representative democracy: the business of government is to "increase to the utmost the pleasures, and diminish to the utmost the pains, which men derive from one another"; if powers are put into the hands of one or a few, they will take from the rest of the community wealth and the objects of desire and use terror to impose their will; the community itself, or a portion of the community with interests identical to those of the whole, must choose the representatives and check their actions periodically ([1820] 1978, 56, 72–77). In short, only citizens themselves can be trusted to control government in their own interests. Democratic politician-theorists like Thomas Jefferson, Andrew Jackson, Abraham Lincoln, and Woodrow Wilson articulated increasingly broad conceptions of who should choose representatives and how closely those representatives should adhere to the public's wishes. Faith in majoritarian democracy has become deeply embedded in the American consciousness. James Mill's utilitarian heirs among contemporary economists have argued that governments should respond faithfully to citizens' policy preferences, so long as that is feasible (Arrow [1951] 1963); they have demonstrated that majority rule is the only way to respond decisively, anonymously (that is, in egalitarian fashion), and neutrally to individuals' preferences (May 1952); and they have shown how officials in a competitive two-party electoral system may be led, through their own self-interest, to respond to majority will (Hotelling 1929; Downs 1957; Davis and Hinich 1966; McKelvey and Ordeshook 1986).

A nagging difficulty, however, is that majoritarian democracy seems to require a great deal of the public: well-formed, deliberative policy preferences that accurately reflect citizens' values and interests, preferences that are sufficiently firm and well reasoned to constitute the bedrock of government decision making. It is commonplace to deny that the public is capable of forming such preferences, to disdain public opinion as ignorant, capricious, and dangerous, and to argue that majoritarian democracy is neither feasible nor desirable. When we use the phrase "rational public," some think it is an Irish bull—a contradiction in terms, involving a ludicrous inconsistency. Surely we must mean the "irrational" public. Is not public opinion notoriously ill informed, evanescent, fickle, and unreasonable?

We are serious about public rationality. We maintain that critics of the public have either misunderstood what is required for majoritarian democracy or have misinterpreted the available evidence as showing the public to fall short. Our own new evidence supports a picture of rational collective public opinion that is quite consonant with majoritarian democratic theory.

Critics of the Public

Disdain for public opinion and fear of it have an impressive pedigree. Many of the earliest users of the concept—such as eighteenth-century French theorists, even Rousseau—referred to "public opinion" mainly to urge writers and statesmen to resist it, rise above it, or manage it (Gunn 1989). The founders of the U.S. federal government often spoke of the "errors" and "delusions" of the public and of "fluctuations" in opinion and designed political institutions to check the will of the majority. James Madison, defending the constitutional provision for the U.S. Senate, declared that such a "select and stable" body would serve as "an anchor against popular fluctuations and delusions" (Hamilton et al. [1787–88] 1961, 384). Alexander Hamilton, arguing for an energetic and independent executive, insisted that the republican principle does not require an unqualified complaisance to every "sudden breeze of passion" or to every "transient impulse" of the public (Hamilton et al. [1787–88] 1961, 432).

Similarly, Alexis de Tocqueville ([1835, 1840] 1954) was concerned about the "tyranny of the majority," which he feared would squelch dissent. Walter Lippmann, in his important book *Public Opinion*, argued that objective reality differs sharply from the "pictures in our heads," which often mislead men in their dealings with the world outside. He spoke of "stereotypes" that guide most people's thinking and quoted Sir Robert Peel on "that great compound of folly, weakness, prejudice, wrong feeling, right feeling, obstinacy, and newspaper paragraphs which is called public opinion" (1922, 18, 127).

And in the early Cold War years Gabriel Almond ([1950] 1960) set forth a "mood theory" of public opinion. He said that "foreign policy attitudes among most Americans lack intellectual structure and factual content. Such superficial psychic states are bound to be unstable." He argued that only immediate threats break into the focus of attention and that the moment the pressure is reduced, there is a "swift withdrawal, like the snapping back of a strained elastic" (69, 76).

Now of course some of the observers we have quoted wrote a long time ago and had access to no systematic evidence about public opinion. No opinion polls or surveys were available to Madison or Tocqueville. They had to rely upon their own impressions and judgments. But when survey research got under way in the 1930s, putting political questions to representative samples of Americans, many of the results seemed to confirm these skeptical views of public opinion. Right up to the present day the skeptical views have been widely shared.

Paul Lazarsfeld and his fellow sociologists at Columbia University, for example, found in their 1940 and 1948 election studies that few citizens paid much attention to politics, that most made up their minds long before election day, apparently on the basis of group identifications rather than issues, and that many people were confused about what the candidates stood for (Lazarsfeld et al. [1944] 1968; Berelson et al. 1954).

Then, in the 1950s, Angus Campbell and other survey researchers at the University of Michigan found that most Americans knew little about the stands of political parties or about what their government was doing in specific policy areas; most voted on the basis of long-term party loyalties or the personal characteristics of candidates, rather than on issues (Campbell et al. 1960).

Since that time, surveys have repeatedly demonstrated that many or most Americans do not have a great deal of political information. Many people do not know such things as the name of their congressperson, which party controls Congress, where foreign countries are located, or the meaning of various political terms and concepts (see, for example, Erikson et al. 1988). The fact of low levels of information is well established and not controversial. Certainly we do not dispute it.

Perhaps the most important evidence that has contributed to an unflattering picture of public opinion involves the instability of individuals' stated opinions about government policies. Philip Converse (1964) at the University of Michigan found that when ordinary citizens were repeatedly asked the same questions about their policy preferences, they tended to give different answers at different times. And the changes in responses did not seem to fit any reasonable pattern; they looked altogether random. Converse (1970) coined the term "nonattitudes" to refer to these responses. He claimed that many or even most people do not have any real opinions at all about what the government should do in various policy areas; when survey interviewers come to the door, these people just give "doorstep opinions" or meaningless responses.

Subsequently, several scholars (e.g., Achen 1975) have argued that the instability of individual citizens' responses to surveys may partly result from measurement errors: from questions that are ambiguous or that force people to choose answers they do not like, and from errors in recording and keypunching and storing the data. But on the face of it, this still controversial claim seems to provide only limited consolation; it suggests that even if people have real opinions, we may never be able to learn what they are, because survey research is imperfect and there is no feasible alternative to it. And the evidence has kept piling up that in fact many people do give unstable, fluctuating responses to survey questions about their policy preferences.

A Theory of Collective Rationality

Despite all this evidence, and despite the skepticism about public opinion that goes back to Lippmann and Tocqueville and the Founding Fathers, we want to offer a series of propositions that say something very different about public opinion in the United States. These propositions add up to the general claim that collective public opinion is real, measurable, and rational—by which we mean not necessarily right or correctly calculated, but reasonable and understandable, given the information the public has at hand.[1]

1. The word "rational," of course, means many things to many people. We mean that citizens' policy preferences are instrumentally rational, intended to seek desired political consequences. But this does not at all imply a narrowly self-interested calculation of material benefits. The desired consequences may concern loved ones or particular social groups or the

Here we will present some evidence and illustrations supporting our propositions. Much more evidence appears elsewhere (Page and Shapiro 1992).

Our propositions are as follows:

1. Collective public opinion is real. The U.S. public as a collectivity has genuine preferences about most of the policy issues of the day, not just random, meaningless "nonattitudes" or "doorstep opinions."
2. Public opinion is measurable through survey research. We can rather accurately learn what these collective policy preferences are, through interviews with representative samples of citizens.
3. Collective opinion forms coherent patterns that differentiate among alternative policies in reasonable ways that reflect Americans' values and beliefs.
4. Collective public opinion is generally quite stable. It does not often change by very large amounts, and it only very rarely fluctuates back and forth.
5. When public opinion changes, it does so in regular, understandable ways. Changes are not capricious or whimsical or inexplicable but follow clear principles and patterns.
6. Furthermore, public opinion nearly always changes in reasonable, sensible ways. That is, it changes in response to objective events, to changes in reality that affect the costs and benefits of policy alternatives, and in response to new information conveyed through the mass media. The public reacts in sensible ways to the information that is made available to it.

For all these reasons, we believe that public opinion need not be feared but can and should be relied upon as the chief engine of democratic government. The American public is capable of the task that majoritarian democratic theory sets.

How is this possible? How could these propositions be true in the face of the evidence about low information levels and unstable survey

---

nation as a whole or all of humankind, not just the self; and they may involve nonmaterial (for example, aesthetic or emotional) matters. Moreover, we do not insist that behavior be calculated or even conscious in order to possess the characteristics of instrumental rationality. Thus, we use the term more in the sense espoused by V. O. Key, Jr. (1966), than in that of economics-style rational-choice models.

responses by individual citizens? The answer involves the distinction between individuals' opinions and *collective* public opinion. Many observers have mistakenly assumed that collective public opinion and collective survey responses have the same characteristics as the opinions and responses of each individual making up the public. But individual and collective opinion are actually quite different, for two reasons. The first has to do with the *statistical aggregation* of individuals' opinions, and the second has to do with what might be called *the social formation of preferences* through *collective deliberation* involving division of labor and elaborate systems of communication.[2]

Statistical aggregation bears upon the reality, the measurability, and the stability of collective public opinion. Even if individuals' responses to opinion surveys are partly random, full of measurement error, and unstable, when aggregated into a collective response—for example, the percentage of people who say they favor a particular policy—the collective response may be quite meaningful and stable. This is just an example of the law of large numbers. Under the right conditions, individual measurement errors will be independently random and will tend to cancel each other out. Errors in one direction will tend to offset errors in the opposite direction. The result will be accurate measurement of collective public opinion. (These collective properties would follow, for example, from the kind of errors in measurement of individuals' preferences postulated by Achen [1975].)

Moreover, the same reasoning applies not only to measurement errors but also to real fluctuations in individuals' opinions, provided that those fluctuations are independent of each other. Even if many individuals change their opinions back and forth in a haphazard fashion, so long as they each have an underlying tendency of opinion, those temporary changes may offset each other and produce a highly stable collective public opinion.

There is nothing magical about this contrast between individual and collective opinion. It follows from simple statistics.

2. In referring to the "social formation" of preferences we do not mean to embrace the term "socialization," which suggests that citizens are entirely passive and that their minds are blank slates written upon by forces beyond their control. We see citizens as both more active and more resistant than that. Most people hold basic values and beliefs, grounded in experience, that are hard to budge; most do some thinking and talking about politics, question what they hear, and exercise judgment. We believe that the phrase "collective deliberation" better describes the processes by which collective policy preferences develop and change, but we also want to emphasize that deliberation occurs in a social context.

Perhaps even more important is the social formation of preferences through collective deliberation. Because of these social processes, even if most individuals are poorly informed about the details of politics, collective public opinion can act in highly informed, reasonable, sensible ways that we call "rational." In an uncertain and changing world, individuals' preferences are not fixed but develop and change in response to new information and new interpretations. Information and interpretations are not necessarily derived by atomistic individuals working on their own but are often produced and disseminated through an elaborate social structure involving specialized division of labor and extensive communications networks. Experts and researchers and government officials learn new things about the political world. They make discoveries and analyze and interpret new events. These analysts pass along their ideas and interpretations to commentators and other opinion leaders, who in turn communicate with the general public directly through newspapers, magazines, and television and indirectly through social networks of families, friends, and coworkers. Members of the public think and talk among themselves and often talk back to elites, questioning, criticizing, and selecting ideas that are useful. Most citizens never acquire much detailed information about politics, but they do pay attention to and think about media reports and friends' accounts of what commentators, officials, and trusted experts are saying the government should do. And they tend to form and change their policy preferences accordingly.

As a result, new information and ideas can affect collective public opinion even when most members of the public have no detailed knowledge of them. Even when most individuals are ill informed, collective public opinion can react fully and sensibly to events, ideas, or discoveries. (What this system of collective deliberation may not guarantee, however, is that the information conveyed to the public is always truthful, helpful, and unbiased, a point to which we will return in our brief discussion of opinion manipulation.)[3]

3. The reader should keep in mind that our propositions about rationality refer to collective policy preferences being reasonable or sensible given the information made available to the public. The heart of our concern is with the capacities of the public; our argument is entirely consistent with the possibility that misinformation or misleading interpretations may be provided and the rational public deceived.

Data and Methods

Thus, there are theoretical reasons for supposing that collective public opinion might be rational despite discouraging evidence about individuals' attitudes and behavior. Let us turn to some concrete empirical evidence.

For more than a decade, we have engaged in a study of Americans' collective policy preferences. In the course of this work, we gathered a large collection of data from many hundreds of opinion surveys conducted over a period of more than fifty years, starting with the first Gallup surveys of the 1930s and continuing into 1991. In fact, we tried to find all available national surveys that asked policy preference questions: surveys by Gallup, Harris, Roper, and the like; surveys by academic organizations like the Center for Political Studies at the University of Michigan and NORC at the University of Chicago; surveys by television networks and newspapers; and surveys by market research and political consultant firms. We gathered a total of more than ten thousand policy preference questions that were asked of national samples.

In order to study opinion stability and change, we looked for questions that were asked more than once, with identical wording, so that we could see whether the collective responses altered. Among the ten thousand questions, we found over one thousand (actually 1128) that were repeated at least once in identical form. These 1128 questions are very diverse. They cover a broad range of policies, somewhat more than half, domestic, and somewhat less than half, foreign. They deal with government spending, taxes, laws, regulations, court decisions, and officials' actions. They concern executive, legislative, and judicial policies at all levels of government—mostly national policies but also many state and local issues.

For each of the 1128 questions, we recorded the "marginal frequencies" of responses—that is, the percentages of the public saying they favored or opposed particular policies each time the question was asked. We also calculated the percentage points of opinion change, if any, from one survey to another. We checked how many of those apparent changes were statistically significant, since small observed changes could result from sampling errors in the surveys rather than real alterations of opinions. We also calculated the rate (in percentage points per year) at which opinion change occurred. We categorized the significant changes as abrupt (if they occurred at a rate of 10 percentage points or more per year) or as gradual. And for the questions that were repeated frequently enough, we checked whether opinion fluctuated, that is, whether it moved back and forth by significant amounts in opposite directions: two or more changes within two years, or three or more within four years.

Next we studied the historical context of each of the significant opinion changes to see what was happening in the United States and in the world when collective public opinion changed. And for a special set of eighty survey questions that were repeated at very short intervals, we studied the impact of the mass media on public opinion, measuring what kinds of stories appeared on network television news between surveys and using them to account for the extent and direction of change in public opinion.

Findings

Some highlights and some illustrations of our findings follow.

First, we found a remarkable amount of *stability* in collective public opinion. For example, out of our total of 1128 repeated survey questions, more than half—58 percent—showed no significant opinion changes at all. That is, on *more than half* of these issues there was no observed change of 6 percentage points or more, which is what it takes to be fairly sure there was a real change. Domestic-policy opinions were somewhat more stable than those in foreign policy, with 63 percent (vs. 51 percent) showing no change. But even in the realm of foreign policy, where the "mood theory" was invented, half our repeated questions showed no significant opinion change. That is true even though many of these questions were repeated a number of months or years apart, and many were repeated a number of times, so there was plenty of opportunity for change. Still, on most issues, public opinion stayed about the same. These findings are summarized in table 1.1.

Moreover, as table 1.2 indicates, when collective public opinion did change, the changes were usually not very large. The 473 survey questions with one or more significant opinion changes revealed a total of 556 instances of change. Nearly half of the 556 changes, 44 percent of

Table 1.1 Significant Changes in Repeated Policy Questions

	No Change		Change		Total Questions	
	%	N	%	N	%	N
Foreign and defense policy	51	215	49	210	38	425
Domestic policy	63	440	37	263	62	703
Total items	58	655	42	473	100	1128

NOTE: Gamma = Yule's Q = −.24; p < .05.

Table 1.2 Magnitudes of Significant Changes in Policy Preferences

	6–7%		8–9%		10–14%		15–19%		20–29%		30% +		Total	
	%	N	%	N	%	N	%	N	%	N	%	N	%	N
Foreign and defense policy	21	54	22	55	28	71	15	38	12	30	3	7	46	255
Domestic policy	24	71	21	62	30	91	14	41	8	23	4	13	54	301
Total	22	125	21	117	29	162	14	79	10	53	4	20	100	556

NOTE: Gamma = −.05 (n.s.).

them, were less than 10 percentage points. Most of those involved changes of just 6 or 7 percentage points, which is statistically significant but not very substantial. Very large opinion changes, of 20 percentage points or more, were quite uncommon. They constituted only 14 percent of our 556 instances of significant change. Or, to put it another way, out of our total of 1128 repeated survey questions, we found only 73 cases in which public opinion changed by 20 percentage points or more. And there were only 20 cases in which opinion changed by 30 percentage points or more. Some of those cases are interesting and important, and we present some graphs of them below, but they are very unusual. There was no significant difference between foreign and domestic policy in the magnitude of changes (see table 1.2 and Shapiro and Page 1988).

Furthermore, we found that collective public opinion very rarely fluctuates. When we looked at 173 survey questions that were repeated often enough to reveal fluctuations in opinion, we found actual fluctuations, back-and-forth movements, in only 18 percent of the cases (21 percent of the foreign-policy questions and only 14 percent of the domestic). And when we looked more closely at those cases, we found that most of them involved what we call shifting referents, in which the meaning of the survey question, rather than the opinions of the public, shifted from one survey to the next. Questions that ask whether "too much" is being spent on foreign aid or whether "too many" sacrifices are being made for defense refer to the policy that is current at the moment the question is asked; if that policy changes (e.g., if the government is now spending much more or much less than when the question was previously asked), naturally people's reactions may change, even if their policy preferences stay constant. So our 18 percent figure, small as it is, probably overstates the extent to which collective policy preferences fluctuate.

It seems to us that these findings establish clearly that collective policy preferences in the United States are not changeable, fluctuating, or capricious. For the most part they are very stable. Most changes are gradual. This conclusion is also supported by regression analyses that reveal that the level of public opinion on a given issue at time 1 is a very strong predictor of the level of opinion on that issue at time 2. (In a multivariate model using a cross-section of observations from pairs of surveys, the estimated coefficient is a remarkably high 0.97.)

Our findings may seem to conflict with impressions of fluctuating public opinion that are sometimes conveyed by newspaper and television stories about poll results, but those stories may give a misleading impression: (1) The public's policy preferences are much less volatile than its attitudes about political candidates and presidents, which get a lot of publicity. (2) Many reports of "changes" in collective policy preferences are erroneously based on responses to questions with different wordings. It should be no surprise when different questions yield different answers. (3) The magnitude of actual opinion changes is often exaggerated by "chopped top" graphs that make small shifts of 5 or 6 percentage points fill up a whole graphic. (4) Cases of change get more attention than cases of stability because change is more interesting; journalists and pollsters would much rather write about it. In fact, that is even true of the data available for us to analyze, since pollsters are most likely to repeat questions when they expect change; and within those data, it is true of the graphs we will present here, because we do not want to bore readers with many pictures of flat lines.

The evidence of collective-opinion stability is overwhelming. But that fact, in itself, does not conclusively demonstrate the rationality of public opinion. For one thing, opinion stability might not be particularly sensible in a changing world. Some critics like Tocqueville and Lippmann have argued that public opinion is actually too stable and does not react sufficiently to changed circumstances. For another thing, the fact of stable collective survey responses does not even prove that public opinion is real or meaningful, because totally random responses could produce collective stability. If every citizen flipped a mental coin and gave survey responses randomly, with equal probability, each time a question was asked, then about the same proportion of citizens would respond the same way each time. We would observe great stability in collective responses without any real public opinion existing at all.

Fortunately, we can easily reject this idea of random stability because the patterns we observe in public opinion are not consistent with it. It is simply not the case that when the public is asked about two alternatives, half the people generally favor one and half the other, or that the public generally divides equally among multiple policy options. The distributions of responses vary widely. Some policy alternatives are rejected overwhelmingly, while others are endorsed almost unanimously by the public. This is not just an artifact of question format or "response sets," either; it often occurs with a constant question format when the substantive content is altered. Moreover, collective responses to different questions form coherent patterns that distinguish in reasonable ways among policies.

Furthermore, we have found that changes in public opinion follow predictable, regular, and sensible patterns. When we examined all 556 instances of significant opinion change in our data, investigating what was happening in the political world at the time of each change, we found that the vast bulk of changes, particularly the larger ones, came in response to changing circumstances and changing events. Wars and international crises were especially important. World War II, for example, and the events leading up to it, brought many changes in public opinion concerning preparedness, defense spending, alliances, foreign aid, and the like, as well as price controls, taxes, desired peace terms, international organizations, and many other matters. The Korean and Vietnam wars had similar effects.

On domestic issues, changes in the economy often affect public opinion. Recessions, for example, generally lead to less support for discretionary government spending and more support for tax cuts. Also, gradual social and economic trends have affected public opinion. Economic growth has led to the desire for shorter workweeks and higher minimum wages, as well as to increased willingness to spend money on workplace safety, protection of the natural environment, and other things once viewed as luxuries. Urbanization and rising crime rates have increased the desire for strict courts and harsh punishments. Rising levels of formal education have contributed to increased tolerance and support for civil liberties. Migration of blacks to the North and black people's economic and cultural successes (together with the civil rights movement) contributed to the great shift of opinion in favor of civil rights.

Each of these events and historical changes involves a complicated story that is better told in a book than in a brief chapter (see Page and Shapiro 1992). But the point is that virtually every significant opinion change we have found makes sense in terms of changing realities or changing ideas and information that affect citizens' assessments of the costs and benefits of public policies. Opinion changes are not capricious or whimsical; nearly all of them follow sensibly from changes in political reality, as reported to the public.

In order to pin down more precisely the mechanisms of opinion change and to study the role of network television news, we used eighty policy preference questions that were repeated at short intervals. We found it remarkably easy to account for short-term changes in the level of collective support for a given policy, in terms of the television news stories relevant to that policy that appeared between two opinion surveys. In particular, we found that stories featuring commentators, experts, and popular presidents had a strong impact on collective public opinion. When commentators and experts were reported as saying something supportive of a particular policy, public opinion moved markedly in a direction more favorable to that policy (Page et al. 1987; similar results based on newspaper data are reported in Page and Shapiro 1984).

This helps explain the mechanism by which public opinion changes in response to events and historical changes. It also helps show how public opinion is able to react to new information even when most citizens do not know the details. Experts, commentators, and political leaders process the information and convey their policy conclusions to the public, which thinks and talks and reacts. We see it as quite reasonable for citizens to change their policy preferences in accord with the views of opinion leaders they trust, particularly when that trust is contingent upon citizens' own experience and judgment.

From our historical research and our media impact studies, we have concluded that public opinion—when it changes at all—almost always changes in ways that are predictable and in ways that are generally reasonable or sensible, given the information that the public is provided. Of course, that information is not always accurate or unbiased; at times it may be misleading or downright deceptive, and it is important to learn about the quality of the information and interpretations that affect public opinion. But given the available information and ideas, the public as a collectivity generally reacts in a sensible fashion.

Some Trends in Collective Public Opinion

A few concrete illustrations, using graphs, can highlight trends in collective public opinion. We should mention that in these graphs "don't know" and "no opinion" responses are excluded, so that in most cases one can tell what proportion of the public took the opposite side on an issue simply by subtracting the displayed percentages from one hundred.[4] Trend lines are displayed within the full 0–100 percent range of possible variation in collective opinion so that the extent of change is not exaggerated.

The first example shows an abrupt change in foreign-policy opinion: people's characterizations of themselves as "hawks" or "doves" before and after the 1968 Tet Offensive in Vietnam. As figure 1.1 indicates, in December 1967 Gallup found that about 60 percent of those with opinions called themselves "hawks," meaning that they wanted to step up the U.S. military effort in Vietnam. When the Tet Offensive occurred

4. Since the proportion of "don't know" and "no opinion" responses is not usually large—seldom exceeding 10 or 15 percent—we are not disregarding a large fraction of the population. Nor are we necessarily excluding an ignorant portion; a number of well-informed respondents say "don't know" in order to indicate ambivalence or uncertainty. It is desirable to exclude "don't know" and "no opinion" responses not only because so doing facilitates the description of collective-opinion changes—so that a single percentage at each time point can be used to chart trends—but also because "don't know" responses are relatively sensitive to variations in interviewing techniques and organizational practices, so that they are not always comparable over time or across survey organizations.

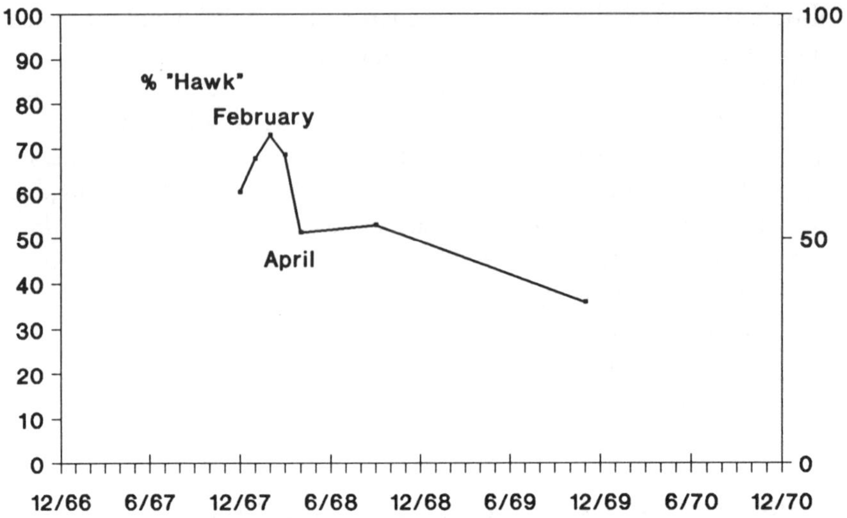

Fig. 1.1. Abrupt opinion changes: the Vietnam War

in January and February 1968, with National Liberation Front, or Vietcong, uprisings throughout South Vietnam, including an attack on the American embassy in Saigon, the initial reaction was belligerent. Toward the end of February, 73 percent of those with opinions called themselves hawks. But a chorus of criticism and disillusionment came from antiwar politicians like Eugene McCarthy and Robert Kennedy and from commentators like Walter Cronkite and even the *Wall Street Journal*, arguing that the war was probably unwinnable and not worth the cost. In March, President Johnson turned down the military's request for more troops and announced a partial bombing halt. The proportion of hawks dropped to 51 percent in early April, a remarkable drop of 22 percentage points in two months.

The size of that sudden change is quite unusual. It resulted from an exceptionally dramatic event and a sharp switch of signals by many different experts and commentators and politicians of both parties. But the Tet case is typical in the sense that many opinion changes in foreign policy are abrupt (58 percent of them, compared with only 27 percent on domestic policy). And most of those changes are sensible, in light of the information the public receives through the mass media.

The next graph illustrates the public response to the broad foreign-policy issue of interventionism or isolationism, namely, whether it would be best for the United States to "take an active part" in world affairs or to "stay out" of world affairs. Figure 1.2 shows the percentage of Americans, at various times from 1945 through 1990, who said the United States should take an "active part," in response to a number of surveys by Gallup and NORC that asked identical questions.

This case is unusually informative in having so many repetitions of the question, but it is fairly typical in its combination of stability and change. As figure 1.2 makes clear, there was a drop in foreign-policy activism between late 1946 and middle 1947 (a drop from 81 percent to 72 percent favoring an "active part"); World War II had ended, and people wanted to turn their attention to domestic concerns. But with the Truman Doctrine and the beginning of disputes with the Soviet Union, the "active part" responses edged back up to about 75 percent, where they stayed rather steady for nearly a decade, despite the turmoil of the Cold War and the Korean War. (This was the same time that Almond [(1950) 1960] was writing about "moods" in foreign-policy opinions. See Caspary 1970.)

Because of gaps in the data, we cannot be sure exactly what was happening to the public's attitudes during much of the 1960s, but clearly

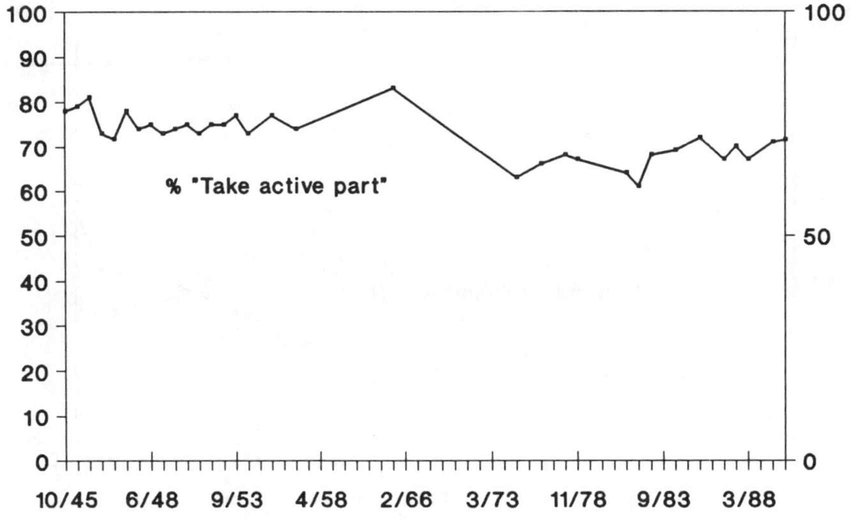

Fig. 1.2. U.S. involvement in world affairs, 1945–90

there was a rise in "active part" responses to an all time high of 83 percent in 1965, presumably in reaction to Kennedy's foreign-policy activism and initial support for the Vietnam War. This fell substantially to the 66 percent range after the failure of the war and then eventually rose a bit to hover around the 70 percent level in the Reagan and Bush years—not very different from what it had been in the 1950s. So here we see both general stability and some changes in reaction to events.

An example of a fairly gradual long-term trend in foreign-policy opinion is the rise in support for admitting mainland China to the United Nations. Figure 1.3 shows that trend. In July 1954, not long after American soldiers had been fighting Chinese soldiers in Korea, only 8 percent of those with opinions said Communist China "should" be admitted as a member of the United Nations. Over the next two decades this proportion rose fairly steadily until it reached 55 percent in May 1971, during the early publicity about Nixon and Kissinger's opening to China. That is, by 1971 a clear majority of Americans who had opinions favored admission of China to the United Nations.

There were some ups and downs when events like the Quemoy-Matsu crisis and the Cultural Revolution made some people skeptical of the desirability of dealing with China and when the Chinese testing of a

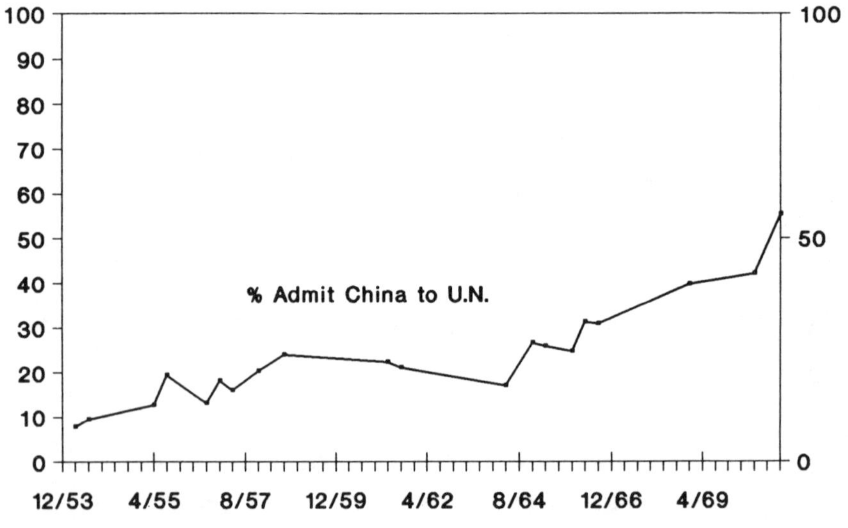

Fig. 1.3. Admission of China to the United Nations, 1953–71

thermonuclear device in 1964 apparently led more Americans to think that China would have to be taken into account in world affairs. But the most striking thing is the trend, most of which occurred long before Nixon's conciliatory moves and in spite of considerable hostile publicity from the Committee of One Million and other anti-Communist groups.

A final example from foreign and defense policy is the trend between 1971 and 1991 in collective responses to Gallup, Trendex, Roper, and NORC questions about the level of defense spending. People were asked whether they thought the government was spending "too much" money, "too little," or "about the right amount" on defense. Figure 1.4 shows the percentages of people who said "too little," that is, who wanted the government to spend more.

As the Roper and NORC series in figure 1.4 indicate, in the early 1970s, when the Vietnam War was ending, only 15 or 20 percent said we were spending "too little" on defense; many more said "too much." But beginning in the middle and late 1970s, publicity about a Soviet arms buildup and Soviet activism in Africa and elsewhere led to a substantial rise: in December 1976, 25 percent said "too little" was being spent on defense; in December 1978, 35 percent; and in December 1979, 45 percent, even before the full impact of the Iranian hostage crisis and the

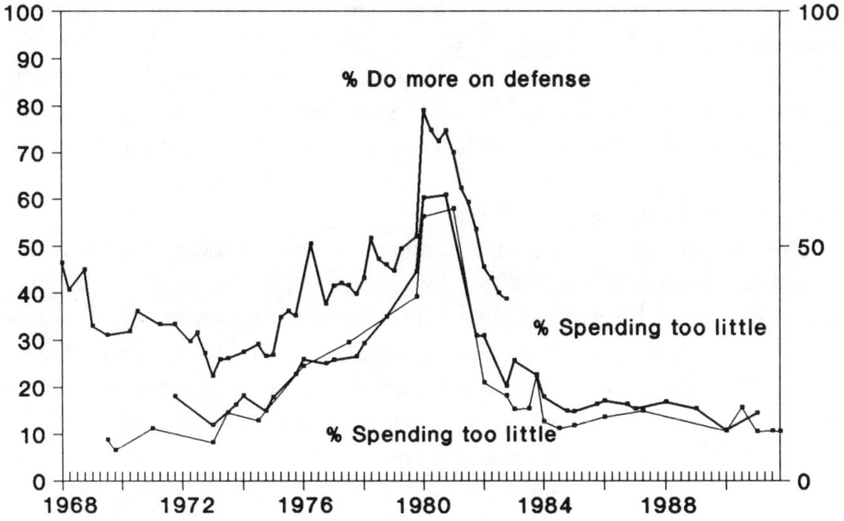

Fig. 1.4. Defense, 1968–91

Soviet intervention in Afghanistan had been felt. Then in 1980, as those events continued and Ronald Reagan talked about U.S. weakness and a strategic "window of vulnerability" in his presidential campaign, the "too little" responses reached a peak of 61 percent. As soon as Reagan took office, however, they fell sharply, and eventually settled down to the same 15–20 percent range as in the early 1970s. (The Gulf War produced only a very small and temporary rise in "too little" responses.) The Gallup and Trendex series track very similar trends.

A warning: one has to be careful about interpreting these trends, because the questions involve what we have called shifting referents; they implicitly refer to the contemporary level of spending, so that those in 1982 who no longer said "too little" was being spent on defense were reacting to the new, higher level of spending. The actual level of spending they favored may not have changed at all. Thus, this graph probably exaggerates the extent of changes in collective policy preferences. Still, the unusually big changes in survey responses are dramatic and interesting.

On domestic policy, public opinion seldom changes abruptly in the way it does on foreign policy. There are not so many sudden, policy-relevant events of the sort that occur in international affairs. Instead, opinion usually remains stable over a long period or follows gradual trends.

Figures 1.5 and 1.6 show the high and fairly stable proportions of Americans who have said we were spending "too little" on health, education, and fighting crime. Those are very popular government programs. Substantial majorities of Americans have wanted to spend more, rather than the same or less, on crime, health, and education in nearly every year since the NORC General Social Survey began asking these questions in the early 1970s.

One interesting aspect of the graphs is that the supposed "right turn" in public opinion in the 1980s is barely visible, if visible at all. In fact, looking across a large number of domestic policy issues, it is difficult to find much substantial evidence of a right turn, outside certain scattered issues. When the Reagan administration moved in a conservative direction on domestic policies, it was not following any marked shift in public opinion (see Ferguson and Rogers 1986).

Another interesting aspect of these graphs is that they help illustrate how the public has regularly drawn sharp distinctions among different government programs. At exactly the same time (in March 1988) that 68

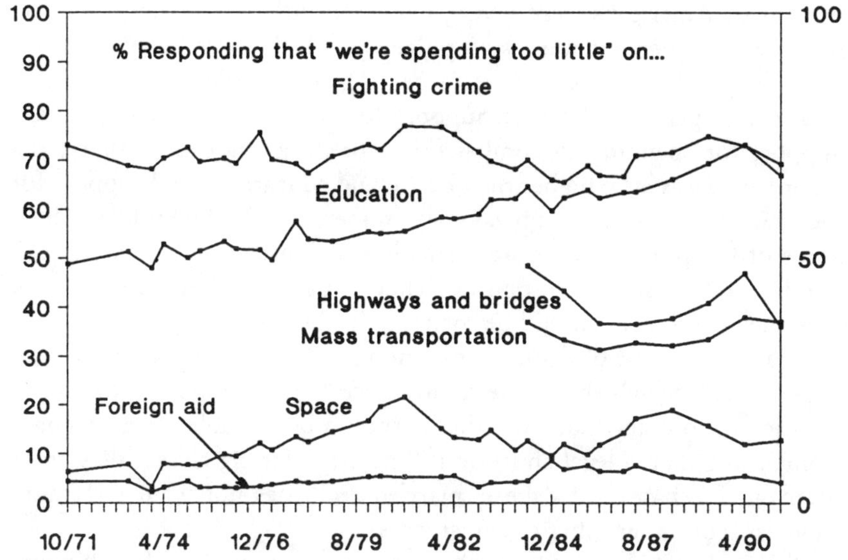

Fig. 1.5. Stable spending preferences, 1971–91

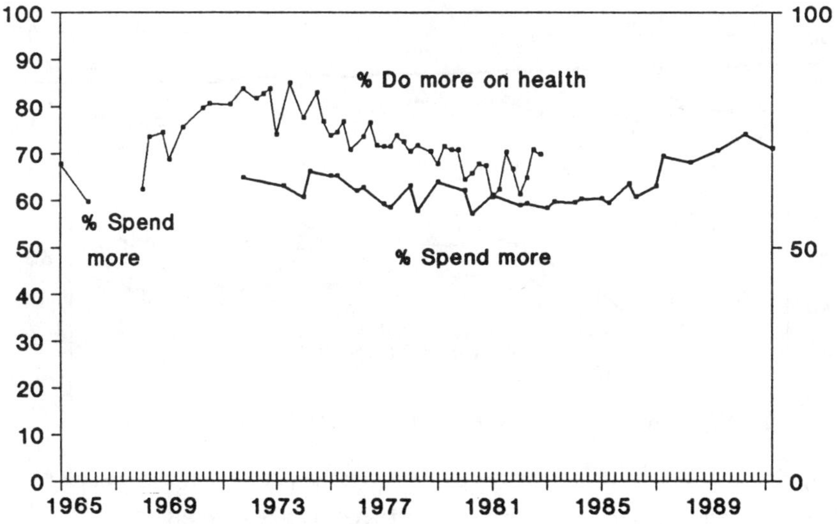

Fig. 1.6. Health measures, 1965–91

percent of Americans were saying that "too little" was being spent on health and 66 percent were saying that "too little" was being spent on education, only 17 percent (see figure 1.4) were saying that "too little" was being spent on defense. Support for foreign aid was still lower. Support for spending to combat crime or drugs (not shown), on the other hand, was even higher than health and education. And support for the space program and highways was somewhere in the middle. These kinds of sharp distinctions are certainly not consistent with the idea of purely random survey responses. They suggest a differential view of how the government should be spending its money.

Another example of distinctions among different policies can be seen in figure 1.7, which shows the trends since 1962 in responses to several questions about abortion: whether it should be possible for a pregnant woman to obtain a legal abortion if "there is a strong chance of serious defect in the baby," if "she is married and does not want any more children," or under other circumstances.

Obviously there is a strong trend of increasing approval for abortion under any of the mentioned circumstances between 1965 and the spring of 1973 or 1974. Nearly all the change occurred before *Roe* v. *Wade*, which was decided in January 1973. The change seems to have resulted

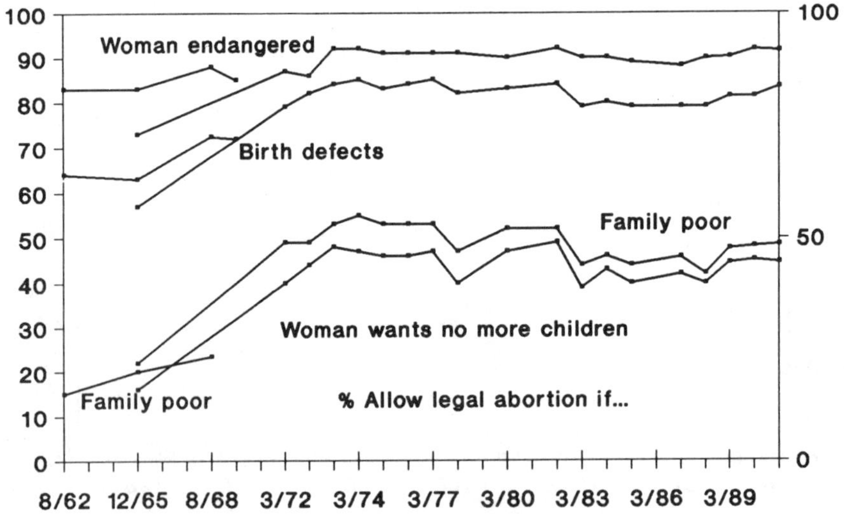

Fig. 1.7. Large, gradual opinion change: legal abortion, 1962–91

largely from such factors as increases in the number of women working outside the home and the rise of the women's movement. Approval of legalized abortion in case of birth defects was already high in 1965, at 57 percent; it rose to 79 percent in spring 1972 and 84 percent in spring 1973. Approval in the case of wanting no more children started very low, at only 16 percent in 1965, but rose to 40 percent in 1972 and 48 percent in 1973. After that, all four lines form fairly flat plateaus through the 1970s and 1980s, with some back-and-forth movement on the "want no more children" and "family poor" questions, and a bit of a dip on all questions around 1983 and then a gradual rise through 1991.

But what we want to emphasize here are the sharp distinctions among the items. The public does not simply react to some general stimulus like the word "abortion." NORC General Social Survey data show the highest level of support for legal abortion, usually around 90 percent or even higher, when the health of the mother is seriously threatened. Cases of rape get the next highest support (not shown), generally over 80 percent—a bit higher than the birth defect line in figure 1.7. All of these could be considered involuntary and health-related reasons for abortions. But under more discretionary circumstances, support for abortion is considerably lower. Approval of abortion when a woman is single and does not want to get married (not shown) is generally even lower than the "want no more" question: around 39 or 40 percent. And for the case of people who are poor and cannot afford more children, it is only a bit higher, around 45 to 50 percent. So there are clear distinctions among circumstances. Furthermore, some of the trend lines move differently. The poverty and single-parent numbers dropped the most in the 1980s, for example, as many people's ideas about poverty and the family changed, focusing more on individual responsibility.

Again, this kind of differentiation seems consistent with the idea of what we call rational collective public opinion. It certainly does not fit with the notion that people are simply flipping mental coins when they respond to surveys.[5]

Some readers may already be familiar with these General Social Survey trends, which James Davis and Tom Smith and others at NORC have

5. One might reply that people respond as if flipping biased coins—their responses have both a random component and a central tendency. Aside from the negative connotations of the word "bias," that is precisely our point: the central tendencies of responses represent the cores of individuals' opinions, which surveys aggregate into accurate measures of real collective opinion.

reported. So we would like to include some less well known issues, one of them concerning whether members of the Communist party in this country should be allowed to speak on the radio. The proportions of people who would not allow Communists to speak, at various times between 1946 and 1963, are plotted in figure 1.8, together with related items through 1991.

This graph casts rather a different light on one of the most famous findings of the General Social Survey, which is that—since Samuel Stouffer's study in 1954—Americans have become much more favorable to the civil liberties of Communists, socialists, and atheists to speak at meetings, to have books in public libraries, and to teach in schools (Stouffer 1955; Davis 1975). Tolerance, at least for these groups, seems to have gone way up.[6] Since people with more formal education tend to be more tolerant, this trend is often attributed to rising levels of education.

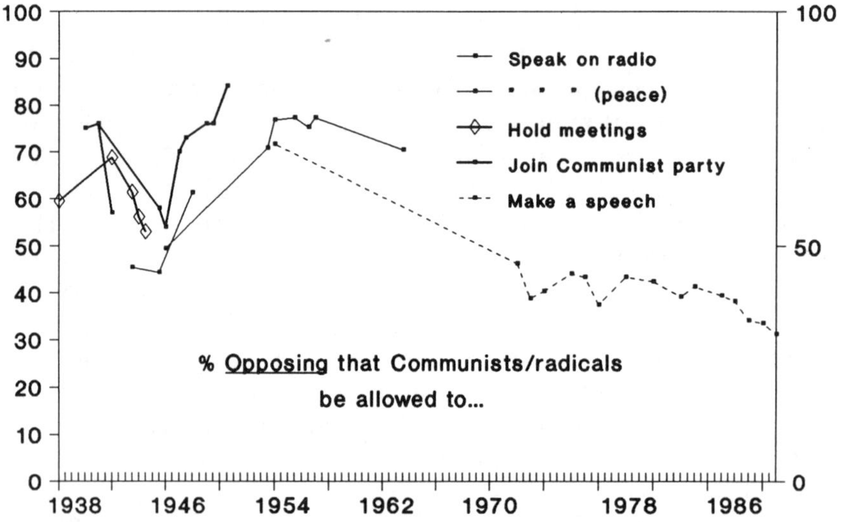

Fig. 1.8. Free speech for radicals and Communists, 1938–91

6. The increased tolerance of Communists, socialists, and atheists may (in whole or part) reflect, not a rise in generalized tolerance, but rather a reduced level of distaste for these particular groups. As Sullivan et al. (1982) show, Americans remain quite intolerant of their least-liked groups, which at the end of the 1970s included the KKK, the PLO, and elements of the New Left.

In figure 1.8 one can see the beginnings of a trend toward more tolerance between 1957, when 77 percent of those with opinions said Communists should not be allowed to speak on the radio, and 1963, when the figure fell to 70 percent. But bigger and more interesting is the earlier movement in the opposite direction: the sharp rise between 1946, when only 49 percent were opposed, and January 1954, when the proportion went up to 77 percent. This suggests that there was no simple tendency for rising education to bring more tolerance for Communists. Americans were certainly getting more education between 1946 and 1954. But the end of wartime cooperation with the Soviet Union and the rise of the Cold War and McCarthyism led to strong public desire to crack down on domestic Communists. That anti-Communist trend in opinion apparently peaked at just about the time Stouffer did his study. Then the gradual easing of the Cold War and the increasingly obvious irrelevance of the U.S. Communist party contributed to much greater tolerance. (For further discussion, see Page and Shapiro 1992, 85–90.)

A final graph depicts the classic, and quite remarkable, case of large increases in the proportions of Americans saying that white students and Negro (or black) students should go to the same schools rather than separate schools. In 1942, only 30 percent said "the same schools"; in 1985, 92 percent did so—a complete turnaround, an amazing increase of 62 percentage points. Table 1.1 indicates just how rare such big changes are. Out of our 1128 repeated survey questions, only 20 cases involved 30 percentage points or more of opinion change. By now, in fact, we have mentioned a good many of those 20, concerning abortion, civil liberties, various aspects of civil rights, and relations with China. There exist only a few other really large changes—shifting opinions about the impeachment of President Nixon, for example. Again, the reader should remember that our graphs overemphasize change.

We cannot tell from figure 1.9 how much of the change in opinions about school desegregation was caused by the 1954 Supreme Court decision, *Brown* v. *Board of Education*, since the decision came during a gap in the survey data. But other race relations questions give reason to doubt that the Court had much effect, if any at all. All the available questions about civil rights for black people, whether dealing with racial intermarriage or integration of public accommodations, jobs, or housing, show strong prointegration trends beginning in the 1940s (or whenever the questions were first asked) and continuing through the 1970s and 1980s. (Even busing for school desegregation, which is

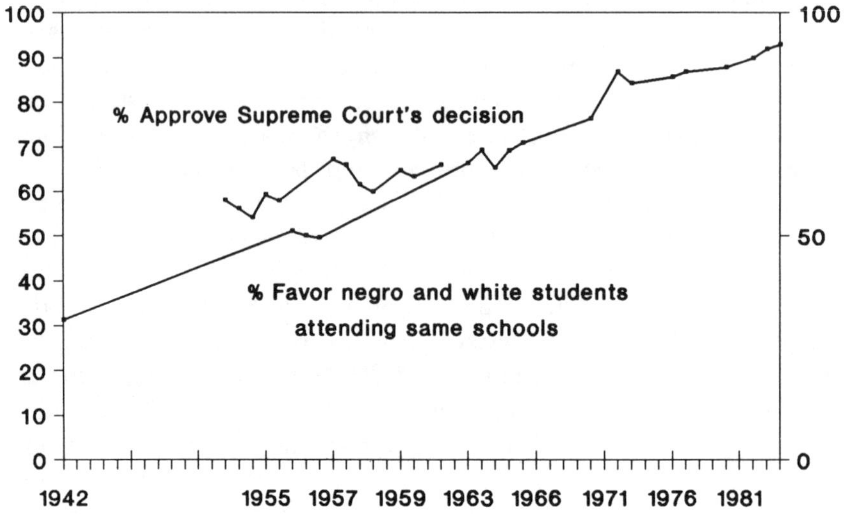

Fig. 1.9. Large, gradual opinion change: school desegregation, 1942–85

generally unpopular, won substantially increased support in the 1980s, increasing from 16 percent in favor in 1976 to 34 percent in favor in 1988.) The fairly steady upward trend on desegregation questions suggests that fundamental and long-lasting social changes were at work. Among the basic causes seems to be a steady decline in whites' beliefs that black people are somehow inferior, which probably has to do with blacks' migration to the North, their service in the armed forces, their economic and cultural successes, and of course the civil rights movement.

Obviously none of this means that racism has disappeared from America, but something very important and hopeful has happened.

In conclusion, let us recall the propositions we listed earlier: that collective public opinion about policy is *real*; that it is *measurable* through survey research; that it forms *coherent patterns*; that it is generally *stable*; that when public opinion changes, it generally does so in *regular and understandable* ways; and that it nearly always changes in *reasonable and sensible* ways in response to objective events and to the new ideas and interpretations provided to it. We believe that public opinion nearly always reacts reasonably—that is, in a politically instrumental fashion, in harmony with citizens' basic values and beliefs—to the information that is made available.

If this picture of a rational public is correct, it has several implications. One is that there is less reason to fear majoritarian democracy than many elite scholars and leaders suggest. The point is not that the public is never wrong or that it is necessarily the highest fountain of wisdom in society. But the American public, as a collective body, does seem to have a coherent set of policy preferences that fit with people's basic values and that respond to changing realities and changing information. Lacking a supply of philosopher kings or a reliable means of identifying them, it is not easy to find a better source of guidance on what a government should do than the preferences of its citizenry.

Populistic democracy can work, at least in the sense that the general public is capable of forming reasonable policy preferences to which its representatives can respond. (Some evidence indicates that they do in fact tend to respond, though not perfectly; see Page and Shapiro 1983.) We do not mean to counsel complacency about the state of democracy in America; much can and should be improved. We favor more responsiveness to the citizenry—less influence by money and organized interests, for example—and better collective deliberation, with citizens given more helpful information and more opportunities to participate actively and to discuss and consider the public good. But our evidence indicates that any defects of American democracy lie primarily at the elite level and in the structure of society, not in a lack of capacity among the citizens.

In particular, our work suggests that proponents of democracy should look very closely at how information and interpretations are produced and communicated to the public and at the quality of information and interpretations. In most of the examples we have given here, the public probably got a reasonably accurate picture of what was going on in the country and the world. But in some cases, it seems to us, the public has been told misleading tales or falsehoods, and public opinion has been manipulated. This may happen fairly often in foreign affairs, especially during real or manufactured crises, when government officials tend to have monopoly control over information and can conceal or misrepresent the facts. (Needless to say, this is no reason to take political power from the deceived and give it to the deceivers.) In other, more frequent cases, information and interpretations provided by the media may, without necessarily reflecting any conspiracy or conscious intent, be misleading or biased; the range of options may be restricted in public discourse; certain ideas may gain hegemony (Page and Shapiro 1989; Page and Shapiro 1992, chap. 9).

The rational public can be fooled. When the public is deceived, democratic responsiveness is not worth much. It is important to discover when and how this happens and to figure out what to do about it. The ideas of Dewey (1916, [1927] 1954) and Habermas ([1964] 1974) about public education and the nature of the public sphere point toward what would be required for a perfectly functioning democracy.

What we are suggesting is that the cure for most of the ills of democracy is not less democracy but, rather, more democracy: more responsiveness to the general public, together with improvements in the system of collective deliberation. As Thomas Jefferson put it in a famous passage of his 28 September 1820 letter to William C. Jarvis, "I know of no safe depository of the ultimate powers of the society but the people themselves, and if we think them not enlightened enough to exercise their control with a wholesome discretion, the remedy is not to take it from them but to inform their discretion by education" (Jefferson 1955, 93).

References

Achen, Christopher H. 1975. "Mass Political Attitudes and the Survey Response." *American Political Science Review* 69:1218–31.

Almond, Gabriel A. [1950] 1960. *The American People and Foreign Policy.* New York: Praeger.

Arrow, Kenneth J. [1951] 1963. *Social Choice and Individual Values.* 2d ed. New York: Wiley.

Barber, Benjamin R. 1984. *Strong Democracy: Participatory Politics for a New Age.* Berkeley and Los Angeles: University of California Press.

Berelson, Bernard R., Paul F. Lazarsfeld, and William N. McPhee. 1954. *Voting: A Study of Opinion Formation in a Presidential Campaign.* Chicago: University of Chicago Press.

Campbell, Angus, Philip E. Converse, Warren E. Miller, and Donald E. Stokes. 1960. *The American Voter.* New York: Wiley.

Caspary, William R. 1970. "The 'Mood Theory': A Study of Public Opinion and Foreign Policy." *American Political Science Review* 64:536–47.

Converse, Philip E. 1964. "The Nature of Belief Systems in Mass Publics." In *Ideology and Discontent,* ed. David E. Apter, 206–61. New York: Free Press.

———. 1970. "Attitudes and Non-attitudes: Continuation of a Dialogue." In *The*

Quantitative Analysis of Social Problems, ed. Edward R. Tufte, 168–89. Reading, Mass.: Addison-Wesley.

Dahl, Robert A. 1956. *A Preface to Democratic Theory*. Chicago: University of Chicago Press.

Davis, James A. 1975. "Communism, Conformity, Cohorts, and Categories: American Tolerance in 1954 and 1972–73." *American Journal of Sociology* 81:491–513.

Davis, Otto A., and Melvin Hinich. 1966. "A Mathematical Model of Policy Formation in a Democratic Society." In *Mathematical Applications in Political Science*, vol. 2, ed. Joseph L. Bernd, 175–205. Dallas: Southern Methodist University Press.

Dewey, John. 1916. *Democracy and Education: An Introduction to the Philosophy of Education*. New York: Macmillan.

———. [1927] 1954. *The Public and Its Problems*. Athens, Ohio: Swallow Press.

Downs, Anthony. 1957. *An Economic Theory of Democracy*. New York: Harper & Row.

Erikson, Robert S., Norman R. Luttbeg, and Kent L. Tedin. 1988. *American Public Opinion: Its Origins, Content, and Impact*. 3d ed. New York: Macmillan.

Ferguson, Thomas, and Joel Rogers. 1986. *Right Turn: The Decline of the Democrats and the Future of American Politics*. New York: Farrar, Straus & Giroux.

Fiorina, Morris P. 1981. *Retrospective Voting in American National Elections*. New Haven: Yale University Press.

Gunn, J.A.W. 1989. "Public Opinion." In *Political Innovation and Conceptual Change*, ed. Terence Ball, James Farr, and Russell L. Hanson, 247–65. Cambridge: Cambridge University Press.

Habermas, Jürgen. [1964] 1974. "The Public Sphere: An Encyclopedia Article (1964)." Trans. Sara Lennox and Frank Lennox. *New German Critique* 3:49–55.

Hamilton, Alexander, James Madison, and John Jay. [1787–88] 1961. *The Federalist Papers*. Ed. Clinton Rossiter. New York: New American Library.

Hotelling, Harold. 1929. "Stability in Competition." *Economic Journal* 39:41–57.

Jefferson, Thomas. 1955. *The Political Writings of Thomas Jefferson: Representative Selections*. Ed. Edward Dumbauld. New York: Liberal Arts Press.

Key, V. O., Jr. 1961. *Public Opinion and American Democracy*. New York: Knopf.

Key, V. O., Jr., with the assistance of Milton C. Cummings, Jr. 1966. *The Responsible Electorate: Rationality in Presidential Voting, 1936–1960*. Cambridge, Mass.: Harvard University Press.

Lazarsfeld, Paul F., Bernard Berelson, and Hazel Gaudet. [1944] 1968. *The People's Choice: How the Voter Makes Up His Mind in a Presidential Campaign*. 3d ed. New York: Columbia University Press.

Lippmann, Walter. 1922. *Public Opinion*. New York: Macmillan.

McKelvey, Richard D., and Peter C. Ordeshook. 1986. "Information, Electoral Equilibria, and the Democratic Ideal." *Journal of Politics* 48:909–37.

Mansbridge, Jane J. 1980. *Beyond Adversary Democracy*. New York: Basic Books.

May, Kenneth O. 1952. "A Set of Independent, Necessary, and Sufficient Conditions for Simple Majority Decision." *Econometrica* 20:680–84. (Reprinted in

Rational Man and Irrational Society? ed. Brian Barry and Russell Hardin, 299–303. Beverly Hills, Calif.: Sage Publications, 1982.)

Mill, James. [1820] 1978. "Essay on Government." In *Utilitarian Logic and Politics: James Mill's Essay on Government, Macauley's Critique, and the Ensuing Debate*, ed. Jack Lively and John Rees, 53–95. Oxford: Oxford University Press.

Page, Benjamin I., and Robert Y. Shapiro. 1983. "Effects of Public Opinion on Policy." *American Political Science Review* 77:175–90.

———. 1984. "Presidents as Opinion Leaders: Some New Evidence." *Policy Studies Journal* 12:649–61.

———. 1989. "Educating and Manipulating the Public." In *Manipulating Public Opinion: Essays on Public Opinion as a Dependent Variable*, ed. Michael Margolis and Gary A. Mauser, 294–320. Pacific Grove: Brooks/Cole.

———. 1992. *The Rational Public: Fifty Years of Trends in Americans' Policy Preferences*. Chicago: University of Chicago Press.

Page, Benjamin I., Robert Y. Shapiro, and Glenn R. Dempsey. 1987. "What Moves Public Opinion?" *American Political Science Review* 81:23–43.

Pateman, Carole. 1970. *Participation and Democratic Theory*. New York: Cambridge University Press.

Schumpeter, Joseph A. [1942] 1975. *Capitalism, Socialism, and Democracy*. 3d ed. New York: Harper & Row.

Shapiro, Robert Y., and Benjamin I. Page. 1988. "Foreign Policy and the Rational Public." *Journal of Conflict Resolution* 32:211–47.

Stouffer, Samuel A. 1955. *Communism, Conformity, and Civil Liberties*. New York: Doubleday.

Sullivan, John L., James Piereson, and George E. Marcus. 1982. *Political Tolerance and American Democracy*. Chicago: University of Chicago Press.

Tocqueville, Alexis de. [1835, 1840] 1954. *Democracy in America*. 2 vols. Ed. Phillips Bradley. New York: Random House.

Truman, David B. [1950] 1971. *The Governmental Process*. 2d ed. New York: Knopf.

2

Reductionist Political Science and Democracy

Benjamin R. Barber

Benjamin Page and Robert Shapiro have martyred their time and energy to a battle that ought not to have needed waging at all. But the persistence of an obstinately reductionist social science in certain parts of the discipline apparently requires that it be fought and refought. With care and diligence, they have once again shown what it is that theory requires of any regime that claims to be democratic. They have proven the obvious: that voters act in a relatively rational manner; that they are relatively autonomous and relatively thoughtful beings whose political participation is premised on deliberation and judgment rather than merely on opinion and prejudice; and that collective political opinions are stable over time and that when they change, they change in a rational fashion. And, finally, they have proven that this holds true not only for ideal democracies but for compromised versions, like our own.

Now, any social scientist conversant with the literature of political philosophy (although this leaves out those for whom dead philosophers can mean only dead philosophies) knows that democracy can be distinguished from the many forms of despotic and heteronomous rule only by the measure of rational autonomy and that to treat voters as anything other than rational freemen and freewomen is therefore to undermine the very language of democracy. To be governed by the passions of a thousand men is little different than to be ruled by the passions of one. Traditional democratic theory (say in Machiavelli, Montesquieu, Harrington, Rousseau, and J. S. Mill) thus incorporates ideas of disinterestedness, civic virtue, education, and competent citizenship into the generic notion of popular rule. For citizens to rule themselves (as Rousseau and Kant teach), they must rule themselves *literally*, must control heteronomous forces operating within them as well as without. In short, the very idea of self-rule entails both the idea of autonomy and the idea of rationality. Without them, democratic rule is (as its elitist critics, denying both popular reason and popular liberty, have insisted it always was) only a rationalization for the rule of prejudice—force legitimized by numbers.

Page and Shapiro know, however, that they cannot count on a sound background in theory among all of their empiricist colleagues, and they work painstakingly to remind them that actual survey instruments demonstrate vividly that there is such a thing as public judgment (even when we call it public opinion); that it can be measured; and that when it is measured, it turns out to be stable and reasonable, so that when it changes, it changes in rational and regular ways that reveal a relatively competent and rational electorate.

It will seem to many theorists that Page and Shapiro are traversing ancient, if not hallowed, ground, trying to avoid determinist sinkholes. Much of their argument is devoted to the reiteration of familiar rationalist themes. Voters, they recall, may sometimes seem to be mere creatures of an overdetermined world in which their decisions and actions are so many reflex responses to fixed environmental stimuli, but they nevertheless do think when they vote and reflect when they act; they impinge on the environment impinging on them.

However, there is reason to think that the model social scientist to whom Page and Shapiro endeavor to prove the obvious is not so much avoiding sound theory as avoiding sound science. Indeed, this latter-day positivist sometimes seems to resemble not a cautious student of human behavior but a rash metaphysician hoping to instantiate esoteric theories of environmentalism and stimulus-response behaviorism in unruly human actions that do not necessarily lend themselves to such theories. Page and Shapiro, on the other hand, are acute observational scientists simply making sense out of what citizens do.

Yet Page and Shapiro do have a methodological problem. The issue between them and their behavioral voter-studies opponents is not really scientific at all; that is to say, it does not turn on empirical matters. By assuming that it does, they not only circumvent the real disagreement, they inadvertently cede ground to their adversaries, primarily by allowing themselves to be drawn onto rhetorical (thus theoretical) turf better suited to the determinist than to the rationalist.

The underlying quarrel is between two orientations toward human conduct. One, variously called environmentalism or determinism or stimulus-response mechanism, attempts to reduce conduct to determined behaviors that can be predicted and thus can be both generalized as science and manipulated as politics; the other, rooted in models of autonomy and reason, assumes the independence and willfulness of voluntary beings whose actions are by definition resistant to reductive strategies. The difference between the two has little to do with "facts." Each theory gives its own account of the same elementary data. As the case of B. F. Skinner suggests, reductionists are unlikely to be disabused of their biases against human rationality and liberty by a rationalist reconstruction of behavior they already "understand" as emotive. For reductionists reject the very language of liberty and reason, recasting its referents in their own language of prior causality.

This is where Page and Shapiro through rhetorical indirection give up the victory they have tried to secure for rationalism through direct empirical demonstration. For they utilize a language—the conventional language of voter studies and opinion research—that is in many ways better suited to antirationalist reductionism than to civic liberty. They risk snatching defeat from the jaws of victory. It is as if Socrates had tried to persuade Thrasymachus to embrace a more noble conception of justice by arguing with him in the language of interest: "No Thrasymachus, justice is not the interest of the stronger, it is the interest of the wiser." So, while they hope to construe political women and men as interdependent social beings defined by social communities, beings whose interdependence with others is ineluctable and thus must be legitimized by liberty and good reasons, they nonetheless deploy a language of opinion, feeling, private interest, and radical individualism. And this language, unfortunately for them, is far more conducive to a conception of women and men as solitary beings defined by their boundaries, beings whose interaction with others is produced by desires and productive of conflict. The aim is a voluntarist conception of democratic life rooted in rich understandings of judgment, deliberation, public good, and citizenship; but the medium of discourse is interest politics, and it is very difficult to liberate democratic theory from determinism while wedded to such heavily freighted rhetoric.

To argue against the conception of voters as self-interested individuals for whom political participation means the expression and aggregation of private opinions, and against the conception of politics as a vector product of reactive interests reflecting nothing more than forces of class, race, and gender, it is necessary first of all to put aside such a conception's facilitating vocabulary. The vocabulary of democracy speaks in terms of deliberate and competent citizens who render public judgments in a civic context where they are compelled to consider public interests—their own interests reconceived in terms of their civic interests. It points with carefully chosen words to the distinction between interested individuals and deliberative citizens, elucidating the Rousseauist distinction between the will of the individual and the general will. The term "opinion" is patently loaded, suggesting a view of human thought processes as reflexively linked to interests without the intervention of rationality (other than as instrumental reckoning of the kind Hobbes depicted) or collective judgment (other than as an aggregating mechanism for interests). The Greeks spoke of opinion pejoratively (as *doxa*, the root of our term for unreflected dogma or "orthodoxy") and took it to denote firmly held but weakly grounded preferences—such preferences being expressions of undeliberated interests spawned by individuals engaged in self-preservation and its concomitants (acquisition, appropriation, labor, and—in Locke's sense—liberty, as the condition for the pursuit of interests). To the extent "reasons" were involved in opinion, they took the form of rationalization, the sort of pseudothinking that is slave to base interests.

When, today, pollsters inquire after public opinion, what they really tap is the status of private prejudices. To take the public pulse means only to take the measure of aggregated impulse, to elicit undeliberated biases unmediated by reason or common deliberation. For example, in talking about the changes that occur in popular attitudes toward tolerance for Communists speaking on the radio or for school integration, the authors suggest that "opinion" has been affected by information, education, and other outside stimuli. But this language makes terms like rationality and liberty suspect from the outset. Perhaps a better way to depict the sort of change the authors discern would be to say that over time, private and unreflected prejudices are transformed by education, exposure to other views, and political experience into civic judgments; that wholly privatized views give way to views reflecting membership in a community that evokes an obligation to consider the needs and interests of others.

Democratic politics is transformative, and it is its capacity for civic self-transformation (among other things) that distinguishes it from despotism. Democratic participation turns self-interested private beings into citizens with a concern for the community. This is not a matter of egoists becoming altruists but of bridging the gap between the two. In the absence of a language of civic transformation, we cannot escape the prison of heteronomy that is invariably established by the language of opinion, interest, and radical individualism. Moreover, the difference between opinion and judgment is also the difference between what is private and what is public. Political judgment is necessarily rooted in common deliberation and occurs only when citizens are joined together. As I have argued at length in *The Conquest of Politics*, it is a social and political faculty depending on political interaction, rather than—as it has often been depicted from Kant to Arendt—an exclusively cognitive faculty.

In sum, what the authors are lacking is not empirical evidence, for there is a great deal of evidence that can be construed as supporting the hypothesis of the rational voter (V. O. Key was developing that data thirty-five years ago, well before *The American Voter* was first conceived). Yet that same evidence, in another interpretive construction, may be seen as consistent with a purely behavioral explanation as well. A clever Thrasymachean reductionist can take this proposition, "As a free and autonomous individual who has engaged in common deliberation with a community of her fellow citizens, X holds rationally grounded and carefully deliberated aims Alpha and Omega to be public goods," and restate it in this form, "As a bundle of desires and drives in whom 'will' is but the final cause of a deterministic train in which rationality plays no role, X wants to gratify private desires A and Z, which, however, she cynically labels Alpha and Omega, so that she can pretend to the community she wishes to deceive that A and Z are actually public goods." There is no argument here about facts—X "chooses" A/Alpha and Z/Omega—only a dispute about their significance and meaning, which is all wrapped up (so to speak) in the labeling.

Page and Shapiro are faced with a theoretical debate rather than an empirical test. Their interpretive framework is what is at stake. This makes their job easier and harder. Easier, because they need not conduct endless surveys or haggle over who did what to whom—when, where, and how. Harder, because there is no datum that will make their case conclusively or definitively. It is helpful to try to adduce some relation between beliefs and citizenship, but their real task is to defend a certain understanding of what it means to hold beliefs (the differences among prejudice, opinion, conviction, and truth, for example), and to explicate how citizenship might differ from mere voting or the articulation and aggregation of interests. As understood by classical democratic theory, rationality is an aspect of citizenship, in an analytic referent; so to set about trying to establish a synthetic linkage between the two is not of much use.

The appropriate way to address the theory of the overdetermined voter is to argue its theoretical incoherence, its internal inconsistency with the liberty it necessarily entails, in other words, to argue its implausibility. It should be the job of the language of autonomy and judgment to demonstrate that the very idea of democracy becomes incoherent—or wholly pejorative, as in "the rule of the passions"—in the absence of such a language. This will hardly convince the diehards, but neither will the "facts," which belong to whatever theory can minimally account for them—that is to say, to more than just one. Thoughtful political scientists already know, as Sir Karl Popper has spent a lifetime saying, that the entire edifice of empiricism is built on sand, and they will require better theory rather than just more data. Ordinary citizens are even more likely to respond to an argument for liberty and rationality as concomitants of genuine democracy, for they will see in the language of choice and freedom a reflection of what they take themselves to be doing, however incompletely, when they try to live up to their vision of what it means to be a citizen. And, of course, for both observers and practitioners of democracy, the real question then becomes, What are the conditions under which opinion can be transformed into judgment, and private individuals can see themselves as public citizens with wider interests that incorporate civic obligations into the community as a whole? Voters may not always behave rationally, but that only proves that many regimes so called are not actually or always democratic. The step from passivity to voting is a large one, but the step from voting to full citizenship is still larger, and until it is taken, it may be inappropriate to employ fully the language of democracy.

Once we acknowledge this, the task of the political scientist becomes to hold up to critical examination, in the light of the actual practices of a regime, the theorist's democratic interpretation of what citizens are doing, how power is distributed, what constitutes civic judgment, and so forth. Systems that are nominally democratic are often captive to forces of irrationality and heteronomy (hidden perhaps, but the more insidious for that) that belie the democratic claim and make hypocrites of their defenders. Pareto, Mosca, Schumpeter, and their counterparts on the Left are not necessarily disbelievers in the moral power or the liberating prospect of democracy; they simply do not believe that political systems that carry the name generally work democratically, even when they possess what pass as democratic political institutions or constitutions. What they are seeking is the kind of guarantees afforded by an unconditioned democracy—what Habermas calls undominated communication and what French social theorists from Montesquieu and Rousseau to Tocqueville and Durkheim and Raymond Aron have agreed is indispensable to the successful working of a democratic constitution.

The authors take a step down this road when, toward the end of their chapter, they talk about the need to "look very closely at how information and interpretations are produced and communicated to the public and at the quality of information and interpretations." Do the media make us more or less autonomous in our judgment? Does education liberate us from or reinforce our prejudices? And what do we mean by "education"? What kind of political institutions force us to face our social or communal being—our dependency and our social embeddedness, whether we recognize them or not? What kinds of intercourse allow us not only to "change opinions" but to change private opinions into public judgments? To transform prejudice into deliberation? To make *doxa*, or orthodoxy, over into *epistēmē* or at least right opinion? Indeed, what *is* political judgment, that crucial notion that entails a distinction between private opinion and public deliberation?

As Page and Shapiro say, the cure for the ills of democracy is more, rather than less, democracy. But until we know more of what, we cannot really confront the elitist critics of democracy, who may believe men *can* be free but who are persuaded that they rarely (or never) *are* so. And we will certainly not be able to rebut determinist critics of democracy, who deny that women and men are liberty-capable, so to speak, at all.

Whatever force this response to Page and Shapiro may have applies equally to other essays in this volume and much of the work being done by social scientists interested in democracy. The message theorists bring to empirical political scientists wishing to make a case for (or against) democracy is that the empiricist's ultimate task is theoretical, that the persuasiveness of an argument about democratic politics will turn on the persuasiveness of the theory in which it is grounded (whether consciously or not). And that the first thing that needs to be done on the way to addressing the theoretical argument is to examine not simply the facts and the data but the vocabulary in which they are expressed. For in that vocabulary will be found the beginnings (and often the essence) of theories that, acknowledged or not, are the common ground of political philosophy and political science. And if political theorists need constantly to be reminded that the political theories they adduce are pointless other than as vehicles for the understanding and practice of politics (and it is the special character of *political* theory that it regards understanding and practice as inextricably bound together), political scientists need constantly to be reminded that the political data they adduce are utterly devoid of meaning except as they are explained and given significance by words and the ideas words make possible. The point then is not to emphasize the differences between political science and political theory; nor is it to make the thin case that they are complementary or mutually reinforcing. It is to insist they are two aspects of a single, integral task: political understanding.

3

Politicians, Self-Interest, and Ideas

John W. Kingdon

Americans tend to think of politicians as self-interested. The Founders (e.g., Madison, in *The Federalist* No. 10) found it prudent to assume that politics would bring out self-interest, and they built the constitutional system on their assumption that human nature included a healthy dose of self-interest motivation. Mark Twain often "confused" politicians with crooks and got a good laugh every time. Journalists, in their

This essay is a shortened, updated, and revised version of a paper I gave at the annual meeting of the American Political Science Association in 1988. I wrote that paper at the Center for Advanced Study in the Behavioral Sciences at Stanford, a marvellous place to write and to recharge the intellectual batteries. For parts of my work there, I am grateful for the support of the National Science Foundation (#BNS-8700864). I am deeply indebted to many colleagues among the Fellows at the Center and to many at Stanford University and the University of Michigan for endless hours of conversation, seminars, and mutual paper-reading that have contributed in so many ways.

attempt to look beneath the surface and describe what is "really" going on in politics, routinely portray politicians as ambitious for higher office, interested in maximizing votes or campaign contributions, or self-interested in other ways.

This assumption of self-interest has its scholarly counterpart. Scholars portray parties as seeking power in government and acting to maximize their chance of election (Downs 1957) and incumbent politicians as single-minded seekers of reelection (e.g., Mayhew 1974). Government action is interpreted as the outcome of a struggle among interest groups vying with one another for benefits (e.g., Truman 1962). Bureaucrats are seen as occupied with protecting their turf and building the support of clients (e.g., Rourke 1984) or acting to maximize their budgets (Niskanen 1971). Rational-choice modeling, though not necessarily bound to an assumption that actors are self-interested, still often does make such an assumption in practice.

Clearly, individuals and groups do look after their own interests, and politicians do pay close attention to interest-group pressure and to the consequences of their actions for their parties and for their own elections. But scholars are increasingly expressing their uneasy feeling that something is missing in a self-interested account of the world. Many actions seem driven by more than self-interest, and many governmental outcomes cannot be fully explained by the pursuit of self-interest. So Kelman (1987a, 1987b) argues that "public spirit" is important in the formation of public policies both descriptively and prescriptively. Reich and his colleagues (1988) argue for "the power of public ideas." Stone (1988) explores policy principles and political reasoning. Herson (1984) links themes in American political theory with patterns of public policy. And Mansbridge (1990) edits a volume entitled *Beyond Self-Interest*.

The "something" that is missing in accounts of self-interested motivation is often taken to be "ideas" (e.g., see Reich 1988; Herson 1984). Although precise definitions of the word are not often offered, ideas in general refer either to goals or motivations other than self-interested pursuits or to theories about how the world works that could be put to use in the pursuit of self-interest as well as other goals (see Kingdon 1988). Thus, self-interest is thought to be not a wrong but an incomplete account of motivation, in the sense either that goals other than self-promotion affect behaviors and outcomes or that even self-interest needs notions of cause and effect, or knowledge of processes, to be pursued.

This chapter reviews some of the literature in political science related to self-interest and ideas, concentrating particularly on politicians and legislatures.[1] It highlights some empirical findings and presents some reasons for greater scholarly attention to the world of ideas at this point in the discipline's development, not in place of models based on self-interest but in addition to them. Among other things, I argue, contrary to an assumption common in many recent writings, that ideas are not opposed to self-interest. Instead, self-interest and ideas, though different, are also inextricably intertwined.

Before beginning, let me clarify one preliminary point. This chapter is not "against self-interest," either descriptively or prescriptively. Descriptively, self-interest is in fact important; the social sciences have made many advances based on assumptions of self-interest, and ideas and interest are difficult to disentangle, in any event. Prescriptively, pursuit of "the good" is not necessarily superior to the pursuit of self-interest. Indeed, a lot of harm has been done throughout history in the name of some "good." But I do notice that the balance in the social sciences between self-interest and ideas has been decidedly in favor of the former, particularly recently, and that it probably needs redressing.

Limitations of Self-Interest

This section notices that self-interest is an incomplete explanation for elite behaviors and policy outcomes. The next section then presents several reasons for greater attention to ideas and politics. Two aspects of the limitations of self-interested explanations for behaviors or outcomes are discussed here. First, there is a good bit of empirical evidence that self-interest does not explain actual behavior very well. Second, there may not be a good theoretical basis in the first place for expecting self-interest to be a very complete explanation.

Empirical Considerations

As an example, consider the Congress. Legislators are of course concerned about reelection, and they do respond to interest groups, presi-

1. Findings in public opinion research are discussed in other papers in this symposium. Although I consider some of their findings and arguments in this chapter, I concentrate on elite and governmental levels. I have reviewed a larger range of literatures and issues elsewhere (Kingdon 1988).

dential persuasion, and other pressures. They are constrained by constituents. But saying that they are constrained by constituents is quite different from saying that they are single-mindedly serving constituency preferences. There are many indications that a lot more than reelection drives their behavior.[2] As they decide how to vote on the floor, for instance, they take cues from fellow legislators, and a major criterion for choosing to follow one colleague rather than another is philosophical agreement (Kingdon 1989, 75). It is also hard to account for observed voting structures without invoking some version of legislators' ideology or conception of good public policy as a major part of the explanation (see Clausen 1973; Poole and Rosenthal 1988; Schneider 1979; Smith 1981). In committee, pursuit of good public policy also contributes to an explanation of outputs, along with reelection and seeking intra-House power (Fenno 1973).

A similar point could be made about other elites. Presidents seem driven by their desire to make a mark, affect the course of history, and change public policy. Bureaucrats are as devoted to the missions of their agencies, the subject matter with which they deal, and the values of their professions as they are to their paychecks, job stability, agency turf, and budget maximization. Courts are affected by the political system, to be sure, but also decide in the world of ideas. Precedents, legal reasoning, and policy principles all play a part in judicial outcomes (e.g., see Howard 1968). None of this argues that ideas supplant self-interest, only that full understandings of behavior must include motivations beyond the promotion of self-interest.

As to collective outcomes, sometimes public policy changes because of the appearance of a new interest group, the activities of existing groups, or the appearance of some new force in constituencies that alters reelection incentives. But at least as often, particularly with major changes, an idea sweeps across the land, bowling over powerful interests in its path and resulting in many changes, including changes in public policy. Such an idea might well be accompanied and buttressed by self-interest, but it also has a life of its own. This power of ideas has been found in consumer protection (Nadel 1971), nuclear deterrence and environmental policy (Schulman and Cook 1987), the move to deregu-

2. Mayhew (1974) and Fiorina (1977) are both quite clear that their assumptions about politicians as seekers of reelection are devices for building theory and are not intended to represent the actual range of politicians' motivations.

late (Derthick and Quirk 1985), and many other cases. It is difficult to understand the origins, attraction, and tremendous power of such movements as abolition, civil rights, environmental protection, feminism, and consumerism without resort to the power of ideas.

In agenda setting, Kingdon (1984) portrays policy change as the result of changes in separate streams of problem recognition, policy-proposal formation, and politics, and the joining of those streams at critical junctures. In that way of thinking, ideas do not drive changes by themselves, since they must be coupled with more conventional political forces, but ideas do have considerable impact on the outcomes independent of such self-interested factors as interest-group pressure and reelection incentives that political scientists often study.

Theoretical Considerations

Aside from the empirical work that suggests that self-interest is not a very complete explanation for behaviors or outcomes, there may not be a very good theoretical basis for thinking of self-interest as an explanation. We are accustomed to thinking of self-interest as quite a sure guide to action. In an economic sphere, for instance, we think we know what it means for individuals to maximize their wealth. In politics, interest groups ought to know what they want to achieve; politicians want to win elections and can devise ways to maximize their chance of doing so; political parties want to gain and hold power. In a hard-nosed, "realistic" mode of calculating, promoting one's self-interest should be pretty straightforward.

Actually, self-interest is not nearly as sure a guide to action as we customarily think. The case of interest groups illustrates. When Bauer et al. (1964, 127) began their study of reciprocal trade, they were told that groups' interests would be easy to discern; once they knew what a group's members produced, they could tell what their interest was in the field of trade. Actually, they found the definition of a group's interest to be highly problematic; in fact, the group itself spent a lot of time and energy trying to define it. Furthermore, if the group could define its interest, it was unclear how that interest should be applied in a given situation. If this surprising finding was true of narrow interests like those of the National Association of Widget Manufacturers, it was even harder for larger, more heterogeneous groups with vaguer purposes to define their interests.

This conclusion about interest groups raises a fundamental point. People often have a difficult time deciding what is in their own interest. One reason might be that even if they are motivated to behave in their self-interest, they are implicitly choosing among conceptions of the self. A president interested in the judgment of history, for instance, is implicitly choosing between long-run stature and short-run approval. Both might be versions of self-interest, but we need to sort out which version controls the president's behavior. Even more broadly, self-interest is not self-evident but is culturally constructed. At some times and in some cultures, for example, the idea that a politician might vote with constituents and against his or her own principles might not be acceptable; but at other times and in other cultures, it might be commendable. Self-interest cannot be expressed or defined except in ideas; people have ideas about their self-interest.

To turn to the example of representatives as single-minded seekers of reelection, much of the modeling assumes that a constituency preference should be readily discernible. Actually, much of the time, it is not. On many issues, most constituents have no opinion. The preferences of those that do not have an opinion may be incompatible. There may be varieties of constituents in the geographical district: some attentive and others not, with varying intensities and stakes in the issue, with varying involvement and proclivity to hold opinions at all, and with varying positions when they do hold opinions. Even if there is a clear constituency preference, it is not clear whether that preference will have future electoral effects. It is therefore difficult to know how a given action (e.g., a roll call vote) would affect one's prospects for reelection. Constituency preferences also might change in ways that cannot be anticipated very well. Constituents might have vague opinions, but how they would translate those opinions in application to the concrete issues before the Congress is not at all clear. Even a highly homogeneous district may not give a politician much guidance a lot of the time. There is a substantial literature (e.g., Dexter 1957; Fenno 1978; Kingdon 1989; Miller and Stokes 1963) that reinforces this picture of the constituency. Seeking reelection, in short, is not a very clear guide to action.

This characterization of the constituency leads to thinking of constituency as a constraint on action, rather than as a guide to action (Kingdon 1989, 68, 288): not as directing a legislator *to* act in a certain way, but as telling him how *not* to act. The mass public in a district sets rather broad boundaries beyond which the legislator may not go; they are there, but are vague. Attentive people and elites in districts narrow those boundaries; they will allow a narrower range of options than the mass public. The politician's supporting coalition narrows the range of the possible even further. But much of the time there is still considerable discretion available to the legislator.

A final theoretical reason for caution about the pursuit of self-interest involves a distinction between means and ends. It is quite possible that politicians' interests in reelection and pursuit of power are not ends in themselves but means to other ends. Politicians could conceivably be primarily interested in the pursuit of good public policy and could reason that the best way to pursue that goal is to remain in office (see Fiorina 1977, 39). Thus, reelection has instrumental value but is not a motivational primitive. What we often take as the pursuit of self-interest or the maximization of one's own utility might often be a means to another end. And theorizing that assumes the pursuit of these self-interested goals (e.g., reelection, power) does not necessarily deny the importance of other goals.

Curiously, self-interest may not be as sure a guide to action as ideas. Let us portray decision makers as rational, but boundedly so. They are purposive, but they operate in an uncertain world with incomplete information; they do not search for alternatives very systematically; and they do a lot of satisficing rather than maximizing (e.g., March and Simon 1958; Cyert and March 1963). In such a world, people look for shorthand ways to make decisions. In politics, ideology and party are pretty good rules of thumb.

For a legislator, for example, if the world sorts itself roughly into liberal versus conservative and Democrat versus Republican, then it is not too difficult to decide most things, and certainly a lot easier than divining the preferences of constituents. Thus, cues for floor voting tend to be taken from colleagues on the committee who share the deciding member's party and ideology (Kingdon 1989, 75). And for more complicated or specialized issues, such as one might find in technical committee work, ideas about good public policy and the most efficacious means of achieving policy goals would seem to be even more important than on the floor.

Of course, ideology is a less precise guide than one might like, needing a good bit of specification before being applied to particular decisions. Also, different principles might conflict with one another, necessitating research into ideology as a guide to action in the case of such conflict

(Schumaker 1988). Still, ideology provides decision makers with considerable guidance.

The Importance of Ideas

There are several reasons to pay greater attention to ideas at this stage in the development of political science as a discipline. I have just discussed several empirical and theoretical reasons that self-interest is not a very complete explanation for political behaviors and policy outcomes. If something is missing, scholars naturally turn their attention to that "something." I have concentrated particularly on considerations at the elite or governmental levels.

In fact, there have also been excellent studies of non-self-interested motivations in mass public opinion. For instance, Sears and his colleagues (1979, 1980) have pointed out that compelling symbols do better than private self-interest in explaining various political behaviors. To the extent that economics affects voters, furthermore, people make judgments about the overall performance of the economy and the incumbent administration as much as, and probably more than, their own economic circumstances (Kinder and Kiewiet 1981). Constituents' preferences for public goods, rather than their own private interests, also seem to affect legislation (Jackson and King 1989). Even to vote at all cannot be explained in terms of self-interest (Downs 1957); instead, senses of citizen duty and efficacy seem to account for the act of voting.

Several of the essays in this volume grapple with the ways in which rank-and-file citizens think about political issues. At least individually, people do not normally seem to be highly informed about or involved in politics and government, and their opinions apparently do not fall into highly constrained ideological dimensions (Converse 1964). But as Kinder and Herzog argue in Chapter 17, there is good evidence that people do hold real opinions, and those opinions have reasonable, understandable roots in their interests, social attachments, and values. They also argue that people are capable of more sophistication than is generally thought, if media and politicians give them more information than they usually provide. Page and Shapiro, furthermore, argue in Chapter 1 that collectively, as opposed to individually, public opinion makes a good deal of sense. It is relatively stable across time, and when it does change, it changes in response to salient events or interpretations offered by trusted public figures.

As Kinder and Herzog as well as Page and Shapiro argue, these observations provide some reason for thinking that there are, within the world of ideas, important connections between the public and government. At this point in the development of the literature, scholars have not developed as complete an understanding of those connections as we might like. But it could turn out that common frames, themes, and orientations that are developed in a process of relatively free democratic discussion tie citizens and government together. As Kinder and Herzog point out, these frames and common understandings may not always be healthy, but they may nonetheless exist and be quite important.

Beyond these indications of the importance of ideas at the level of mass public opinion, there are a number of reasons to concentrate on the importance of ideas at the elite level and in government. These reasons augment my previous argument about empirical and theoretical reasons for questioning the dominance of self-interest.

First, consider the time, money, and energy that people in and around government spend on ideas. They hire analysts; they marshal arguments and collect evidence in support of those arguments; they reason and persuade (see Majone 1989; Sabatier 1988). Even the most hard-bitten, self-interested lobbies have policy analysts and do not rely simply on appeal to their self-interest or on their political muscle. On the assumption that these practitioners know what is a productive use of their resources and that this behavior reveals something of their motivations, one must conclude that ideas are important. If they were not important, then savvy people would not invest so much in them.[3]

Second, study of the world of talk gives us clues about the world around the talker. Assume for a moment that politicians never reveal what is "truly" driving their behavior (an assumption that is probably wrong, but useful for current purposes). They must couch what they want, not in terms of their own crass advantage, but in terms of some larger theme that others will find attractive. Why do they choose certain words rather than others? The answer is that they find certain words

3. Alt (1987) discusses the importance of investment in ideas. People spend resources on ideas, build institutions around them, and have costs sunk in them. Ideas are not just free-floating. Once investments have been made in ideas, one can observe the importance of those ideas and can predict that the ideas will be used. I return to this point below.

have some appeal to larger publics, to undecided fellow legislators, to constituents, or to whoever is important to them in that situation. Certainly in a strategic sense, one needs ideas to build coalitions in politics. Often, two opposing sides are both motivated by self-interest but find that they must appeal to a set of decisive actors in the middle. Those uncommitted actors, for whom the persuaders' or their own self-interest may not be controlling, may be persuaded by argument and evidence rather than by appeal to their self-interest.

In short, politicians use words to make sense of their behavior for others, to persuade others of the rightness of their actions, or to persuade others to join their cause. If that is true, and if these politicians are astute, then a study of their words indicates something about the context within which the politicians work—the culture surrounding them, the nature of the times, the coalitions they try to build, the kinds of justifications that would appeal to constituents or other important people—even though that study cannot tap their motivations or the causes of their behavior (see Tidmarch 1987). By studying politicians' ideas as expressed, we may learn as much about the people to whom the remarks are expressed and the context within which politicians operate as we learn about the politicians themselves.

Third, once politicians are committed to this world of talk, they end up being constrained by it. They make a tremendous investment in developing arguments, in marshaling supporting information, and in persuading those around them. It is highly unlikely that they expend all of this effort without being at least somewhat convinced of the rightness of their arguments. Furthermore, once they take public positions, buttressed as elaborately as they often are, it is extremely difficult to back away from them. Once advocated, ideas take on a life of their own, and politicians become committed to them. They also become committed to the very process of argumentation and persuasion, having invested so much in it.

Fourth, ideas are important whether or not they affect decisions (Schneider and Ingram 1988). Once an authoritative decision is made (e.g., a statute is passed and signed into law), the law embodies ideas that have consequences, even if the law was entirely the result of the push and pull of interest groups, electoral considerations, or other self-interested forces. That being true, it makes sense to study the content of ideas in authoritative decisions, whether or not they drive the policy-making process, because those ideas have consequences.

Distinguishing Ideas from Self-Interest

Much of the current writing on ideas and politics takes the posture that ideas are quite different from self-interest and that the two also work at counterpurposes. Running through much of the writing of Kelman (1987a, 1987b) and Reich (1988), for instance, is an implicit assumption that self-interest can be distinguished from ideas and, furthermore, that self-interested motivations are less lofty and less desirable.

In empirical research, therefore, perhaps scholars could devise ways of distinguishing the effects of ideas from those of self-interest and of comparing the weights of the two in accounting for behaviors and outcomes. If one could specify a set of cases of policy-making, for instance, or a set of individual behaviors, in which one could clearly predict (or postdict) one outcome on the basis of self-interest and a contrary outcome on the basis of ideas, then one could test which explanation seems to hold over those cases, how frequently, and under what conditions. One recent, but flawed, attempt is the effort to isolate the effect of ideology in congressional roll call voting.[4]

In my view, by contrast, a major problem with attempts to distinguish between explanations based on self-interest and on ideas may be that the two cannot be disentangled, and therefore the whole enterprise may be doomed. To illustrate, let us return to the case of the reelection-maximizing legislator. In the selection process that brings victory to one candidate rather than another, candidates whose policy views are wholly unlike those of the majority of constituents tend to be weeded out. Thus, the recruitment process brings incumbents to office whose views are similar to constituency views (see Kingdon 1989, 45; Miller and Stokes 1963). Of course, incumbents' views do not always match con-

4. These studies (e.g., Kalt and Zupan 1984; Nelson and Silberberg 1987) usually take as a dependent variable a set of roll call votes on some issue (e.g., strip mining or defense spending), specify a model with various independent variables that include several constituency or economic variables and something like ADA scores (the measure of ideology), enter these into a logit analysis, and find that ideology has a measurable effect independent of the "political" or "economic" variables. I think they are right in the result, but flawed in the methodology. Because both the measure of ideology and the dependent variable are constructed from roll call votes, they are probably both tapping the same dimension in the roll calls, and the result is tautological. Researchers need some measure of ideology that is independent of the roll call votes themselves. See Carson and Oppenheimer 1984 and Jackson and Kingdon 1992 for critiques.

stituency views perfectly, and there are many issues on which the constituency does not have a clear preference; still, incumbents are like constituents in rough terms. If that is true, then it is usually impossible to distinguish the cases in which the legislators are voting according to their own policy preferences from the cases in which they are voting to maximize their chances of reelection. Most of the time, constituency views and the representative's personal preferences point in the same direction. Most of the time, legislators take *both* the expedient course *and* the principled course at once.

To stipulate that the constituency is the dominant coalition of elites in the district rather than a majority of the rank and file does not fundamentally alter the argument. There may be some room for politicians to select among coalitions in the district. A constituency is often sufficiently complex that different winning coalitions can be built within it (Dexter 1957; Fenno 1978; Kingdon 1989). With this freedom to construct a coalition, the effective constituency (the winner's supporting coalition) and the politician's own ideology reinforce each other and make the task of disentangling the motive of reelection from that of ideology very difficult (Poole 1988). If the district is quite homogeneous, as many House districts are, then it is all the more likely to select an incumbent whose views are within the dominant coalition of the district. Mansbridge (1988) makes a similar argument.

If ideas and self-interest reinforce each other with legislators, the same is likely true of other actors. When bureaucrats take a position, for instance, both their dedication to agency mission and their desire to maximize their budgets often point them in the same direction. If that is true, then it is difficult to identify a case that clearly distinguishes self-interest from ideas. Also, when interest-group leaders push for something, they could be motivated both by ideology and by a drive for power and self-promotion at the same time. The likelihood is really quite general.

The problem of disentangling self-interest from ideas carries over into interpretation of policy-making cases. For instance, the 1986 tax reform act might be portrayed as the triumph of the idea of tax reform over the phalanxes of entrenched interests bent on preserving their tax preferences (Birnbaum and Murray 1987). But it probably also involves politicians sensing a popular thing at that time and running with it as a way to promote their careers and enhance their reelection chances. Or, for another example (see Derthick and Quirk 1985; Kingdon 1984), early in the consideration of airline deregulation, the careerists at the Civil Aeronautics Board (not just the in-and-out political appointees) took the position that their agency should be abolished, which should be clear evidence for the power of ideas. They bought the argument for deregulation, even though it meant the loss of their agency and their jobs. But even in such a clear-cut case of the power of ideas, these civil servants may also have seen themselves as did the professional economists, seen that economists generally favored deregulation, and so figured that they were actually enhancing their future career prospects inside or outside of government by taking that position. Again, the outcomes involve some mix of ideas and self-interest, and the effects of the two are extremely difficult to disentangle empirically.

Beyond that practical research problem, ideas and self-interest are also inseparable in principle—different, but inseparable. People need to attach meaning to their behavior, even if that behavior is motivated by self-interest (Geertz 1973, 40, 218; Wood 1979). That need for meaning does not simply involve rationalization, although there certainly is plenty of ex post rationalization to go around. Nor is it merely cloaking self-interested motives in symbolic politics, although again there is plenty of manipulation of symbols to go around (Edelman 1964; Elder and Cobb 1983). Meaning is always present in action.

One implication is that the meanings people find in their actions affect those actions. For instance, legislators may vote against constituency wishes if they can gracefully explain their votes, but without such an explanation, they will not take the unpopular position (Kingdon 1989, 47). The explanation is neither superfluous nor a mere political cover; it is part and parcel of the decision. By persuading others, politicians also persuade themselves. Kertzer (1988, 3) makes a similar point about ritual: "Ritual [is not] mere embellishment for more important, 'real' political activities. In fact, ritual is an integral part of politics in modern industrial societies." March and Olson (1983, 1984) point out that both periodic attempts to adopt comprehensive administrative reform and the literature on the "new institutionalism" suggest the central importance of cherished meanings, interpretations, and symbols. The world of talk is as important as the world of action. Indeed, words cannot be separated from acts (Rodgers 1987, 5). Similarly, argument, persuasion, and reasoning are central to the process of public policy formation, not mere rationalizations after the fact (Kingdon 1984, 131). People often find it impossible to pursue only their "raw" self-interest. They cannot arrive at positions without both self-interest and principle.

Conclusion

I do not recommend abandoning self-interest as an object of theory or empirical research; nor do I want to replace self-interest with altruism as an assumed guiding force in politics, descriptive or prescriptive; nor do I claim that behaviors or policy outcomes result solely from ideas. But a new balance probably needs to be found in theory building and in empirical research, and more attention should be paid to the world of ideas. We should study the place of ideas in politics for its own sake, not because ideas form some kind of alternative to self-interest, but because ideas are important in their own right.

Assumptions make a major difference in what scholars choose to study and in what other observers choose to concentrate on. To take the legislative example again, if we see legislators as driven only by the pursuit of power or career advantage (self-interest), we will study strategies that marshal votes and campaign contributions. But if we also see legislators as driven by the desire to achieve policy goals and promote a public interest, then we will also study strategies that marshal arguments and evidence. If we see the construction of legislative coalitions only as a process of giving side payments in return for support, we will study which goodies are handed out to which legislators to buy votes. But if we also see coalitions as constructed by processes of persuasion, as well as the process of exchanging favors, we will study how arguments are built and why some are more successful than others and in which contexts.

In some respects, the study of ideas and politics has not been encouraged by the discipline's usual assumptions concerning self-interested motivations for political action. In other respects, of course, an interest in ideas and politics represents a return to other honored traditions in political inquiry that have always considered ideas as central to political behaviors and outcomes. In Chapter 4, Mansbridge discusses that historical context very nicely.

Mansbridge also raises a set of normative concerns. It is tempting to find great solace in the observation that ideas matter (e.g., Kelman

1987a). But it is not at all clear to me that political behaviors or policy outcomes driven by ideas are necessarily preferable to those driven by self-interest. As I said at the beginning of this chapter, a lot of damage has been done throughout history in the name of some good idea. I might also add that processes driven by bargaining, exchange, and vote mobilization sometimes produce excellent results. A slippery politician may sometimes be preferable to a rigid ideologue.

Despite quite a volume of existing work on ideas and politics, there remains a whole world of research yet to be done. Eventually, we will want to construct understandings that take account of the wide variety of ideas and that model the range of interactions between ideas and self-interest. Another whole world of thinking needs to be done about the normative consequences. Under what conditions would we prefer ideas to drive behaviors and outcomes? Which sorts of ideas? In what contexts? With what results? We have quite a bit of empirical and normative work to do.

References

Alt, James E. 1987. "Crude Politics: Oil and the Political Economy of Unemployment in Britain and Norway, 1970–85." *British Journal of Political Science* 17:149–99.

Bauer, Raymond, Ithiel Pool, and Lewis Dexter. 1964. *American Business and Public Policy*. New York: Atherton.

Birnbaum, Jeffrey H., and Alan S. Murray. 1987. *Showdown at Gucci Gulch*. New York: Random House.

Carson, Richard A., and Joe A. Oppenheimer. 1984. "A Method of Estimating the Personal Ideology of Political Representatives." *American Political Science Review* 78:163–78.

Clausen, Aage R. 1973. *How Congressmen Decide*. New York: St. Martin's Press.

Converse, Philip E. 1964. "The Nature of Belief Systems in Mass Publics." In *Ideology and Discontent*, ed. David Apter, 206–61. New York: Free Press.

Cyert, Richard M., and James G. March. 1963. *A Behavioral Theory of the Firm*. Englewood Cliffs, N.J.: Prentice-Hall.

Derthick, Martha, and Paul J. Quirk. 1985. *The Politics of Deregulation*. Washington, D.C.: Brookings Institution.

Dexter, Lewis Anthony. 1957. "The Representative and His District." *Human Organization* 16:2–13.

Downs, Anthony. 1957. *An Economic Theory of Democracy*. New York: Harper & Row.

Edelman, Murray. 1964. *The Symbolic Uses of Politics*. Urbana: University of Illinois Press.
Elder, Charles D., and Roger W. Cobb. 1983. *The Political Uses of Symbols*. White Plains, N.Y.: Longman.
Fenno, Richard F. 1973. *Congressmen in Committees*. Boston: Little, Brown.
———. 1978. *Home Style: House Members in Their Districts*. Boston: Little, Brown.
Fiorina, Morris P. 1977. *Congress: The Keystone of the Washington Establishment*. New Haven: Yale University Press.
Geertz, Clifford. 1973. *The Interpretation of Cultures*. New York: Basic Books.
Herson, Lawrence J. R. 1984. *The Politics of Ideas*. Prospect Heights, Ill.: Waveland Press.
Howard, J. Woodford. 1968. "On the Fluidity of Judicial Choice." *American Political Science Review* 62:43–56.
Jackson, John E., and David King. 1989. "Public Goods, Private Interests, and Representation." *American Political Science Review* 83:1143–64.
Jackson, John E., and John W. Kingdon. 1992. "Ideology, Interest Group Scores, and Legislative Votes." *American Journal of Political Science* 36:805–23.
Kalt, Joseph P., and Mark A. Zupan. 1984. "Capture and Ideology in the Economic Theory of Politics." *American Economic Review* 74 (June): 279–300.
Kelman, Steven. 1987a. *Making Public Policy: A Hopeful View of American Government*. New York: Basic Books.
———. 1987b. " 'Public Choice' and Public Spirit." *The Public Interest* 87(Spring):80–94.
Kertzer, David I. 1988. *Ritual, Politics, and Power*. New Haven: Yale University Press.
Kinder, Donald R., and D. Roderick Kiewiet. 1981. "Economic Discontent and Political Behavior." *American Journal of Political Science* 23:495–527.
Kingdon, John W. 1984. *Agendas, Alternatives, and Public Policies*. Boston: Little, Brown.
———. 1988. "Ideas, Politics, and Public Policies." Paper delivered at the annual meeting of the American Political Science Association.
———. 1989. *Congressmen's Voting Decisions*. 3d ed. Ann Arbor: University of Michigan Press.
Majone, Giandomenico. 1989. *Evidence, Argument, and Persuasion in the Policy Process*. New Haven: Yale University Press.
Mansbridge, Jane. 1988. "Motivating Deliberation in Congress." In *Constitutionalism in America*, ed. Sarah Baumgartner Thurow, 2:59–86. Landham, Md.: University Press of America.
———, ed. 1990. *Beyond Self-Interest*. Chicago: University of Chicago Press.
March, James G., and Johan P. Olsen. 1983. "Organizing Political Life: What Administrative Reorganization Tells Us About Government." *American Political Science Review* 77:281–96.
———. 1984. "The New Institutionalism: Organizational Factors in Political Life." *American Political Science Review* 78:734–49.
March, James G., and Herbert A. Simon. 1958. *Organizations*. New York: Wiley.
Mayhew, David R. 1974. *Congress: The Electoral Connection*. New Haven: Yale University Press.

Miller, Warren E., and Donald E. Stokes. 1963. "Constituency Influence in Congress." *American Political Science Review* 57:45–56.

Nadel, Mark. 1971. *The Politics of Consumer Protection*. New York: Macmillan.

Nelson, Douglas, and Eugene Silberberg. 1987. "Ideology and Legislator Shirking." *Economic Inquiry* 25(January):15–26.

Niskanen, William A. 1971. *Bureaucracy and Representative Government*. Chicago: Rand McNally.

Poole, Keith T. 1988. "Recent Developments in Analytical Models of Voting in the U.S. Congress." *Legislative Studies Quarterly* 13(February):117–33.

Poole, Keith T., and Howard Rosenthal. 1988. "The Spatial Stability of Congressional Voting, 1789–1985." Paper delivered at the Conference on Legislative Institutions, Practices, and Behavior, Hoover Institution, Stanford.

Reich, Robert B., ed. 1988. *The Power of Public Ideas*. Cambridge, Mass.: Ballinger.

Rodgers, Daniel T. 1987. *Contested Truths: Keywords in American Politics Since Independence*. New York: Basic Books.

Rourke, Francis E. 1984. *Bureaucracy, Politics, and Public Policy*. 3d ed. Boston: Little, Brown.

Sabatier, Paul A. 1988. "An Advocacy Coalition Framework of Policy Change and the Role of Policy-Oriented Learning Therein." *Policy Sciences* 21:129–68.

Schneider, Anne, and Helen Ingram. 1988. "Filling Empty Boxes: A Framework for the Comparative Analysis of Policy Designs." Paper delivered at the annual meeting of the Western Political Science Association.

Schneider, Jerrold. 1979. *Ideological Coalitions in Congress*. Westport, Conn.: Greenwood Press.

Schulman, Paul R., and Brian J. Cook. 1987. "Political Science and the Analysis of Policy Ideas." Paper delivered at the annual meeting of the American Political Science Association.

Schumaker, Paul. 1988. "Urban Ideologies, Political Principles, Policy Preferences, and Issue Outcomes." Paper delivered at the annual meeting of the Midwest Political Science Association.

Sears, David O., Carl Hensler, and Leslie Speer. 1979. "Whites' Opposition to Busing: Self-Interest or Symbolic Racism?" *American Political Science Review* 73:369–84.

Sears, David O., Richard Lau, Tom Tyler, and Harris Allen. 1980. "Self-Interest Versus Symbolic Politics in Policy Attitudes and Presidential Voting." *American Political Science Review* 74:670–84.

Smith, Steven. 1981. "Consistency and Ideological Structure." *American Journal of Political Science* 25(November): 780–95.

Stone, Deborah A. 1988. *Policy Paradox and Political Reason*. Boston: Little, Brown.

Tidmarch, Charles M. 1987. "The Language of Legislative Life: Discursive Practices in Congressional Politics." Paper delivered at the annual meeting of the American Political Science Association.

Truman, David B. 1962. *The Governmental Process*. New York: Knopf.

Wood, Gordon S. 1979. "Intellectual History and the Social Sciences." In *New Directions in American Intellectual History*, ed. John Higham and Paul Conkin, 27–41. Baltimore: Johns Hopkins University Press.

4

Self-Interest and Political Transformation

Jane Mansbridge

The Revolt Against Economism

John Kingdon's chapter in this volume contradicts a major thrust of empirical work on Congress since World War II by adding the power of *ideas* to self-interest in explaining the motivations of elected representatives. Until very recently in this postwar period, the assumption of self-interest in human motivation dominated not only the study of Congress but also the profession of political science and indeed most of the social sciences in the United States.

The trend toward explaining behavior as based in self-interest began in the seventeenth century. In economics, the assumption of self-interest

Portions of this chapter have been adapted from Mansbridge 1990b and 1990c. I am also indebted to the lively discussion of this paper at the Democratic Theory Symposium at Williams College, 1989.

began to dominate scholarly work in the eighteenth century; in psychology, the trend began in the late nineteenth century; in political science, interpretations of behavior based exclusively on self-interest did not emerge until the early twentieth century. The drive to make political science into a genuine "science"—a drive that culminated after World War II—involved, in large part, trying to reduce human motivation to self-interest. Only in the last decade have researchers throughout the social sciences been undermining this assumption.[1]

In postwar pluralism, the reigning paradigm in political science was what I have called elsewhere "adversary democracy" (Mansbridge [1980] 1983). This model of democracy assumes fundamentally conflicting interests, which have to be resolved by fair procedures, since there is no hope of agreement on substance. Systems that in theory guarantee each person an equal vote, or an equal effect on the outcome, are fair when no individual can claim that his or her wants have a higher standing than those of any other individual. In this theory the vote serves as a weapon with which each individual can protect his or her interests. As Colonel Rainborough argued, in the first intimation of this theory of democracy that I have seen in print, if the poor did not have the vote, the rich would "crush" them ([1647] 1957, 59).

Although this understanding of democracy began to evolve in the mid-seventeenth century and in embryonic form had some influence (often exaggerated) on the framers of the U.S. Constitution, it did not reach its most developed formulation until 1942, in the works of the economist Joseph Schumpeter. In democracy as Schumpeter understood it, there is no common good or public interest. Voters pursue their individual interests by making demands on the political system in proportion to the intensity of their feelings. Politicians, also pursuing their own interests, adopt policies that buy them votes, thus ensuring accountability. In order to stay in office, politicians act like entrepreneurs and brokers, looking for formulas that satisfy as many and alienate as few interests as possible. From the interchange between self-interested voters and self-interested brokers emerge decisions that come as close as possible to a balanced aggregation of individual interests (Mansbridge [1980] 1983, 17).

At the time I wrote *Beyond Adversary Democracy*, in 1980, this was

1. For a history of the self-interest assumption and advances beyond that assumption since 1980, see Mansbridge 1990c.

the commonly accepted understanding of democratic practice in American political science. Particularly among empirical political scientists it was also a major normative contender for a workable and just democratic theory. The study of pluralism, interest groups, and who gets what, where, when, and how, typically assumed both that citizens (and their representatives) were self-interested and that their interests would conflict. Even those who criticized the American polity, either from the mainstream or from the Left, agreed with these underlying assumptions but correctly pointed to major inequalities that left most citizens, and particularly the working class and poor, unable to defend their interests as well as a minority of the more powerful. Marxist critics pointed to structural imbalances involving massive inequalities of power; mainstream critics pointed out that "those who may need governmental assistance the least participate the most" (Verba and Nie 1972, 12).

Building on Schumpeter, Anthony Downs's 1957 *Economic Theory of Democracy* began the process of rendering in more-formal terms the assumptions of the theory of adversary democracy. This book, which launched the "rational-choice" school of analysis in political science, was part of a more general trend of "economic imperialism," by which scholars in the discipline of economics began increasingly to turn the tools of their trade to analyzing phenomena in arenas other than the market—arenas traditionally analyzed by scholars in other disciplines. The tools of analysis these economists brought to bear included, first, the two critical features of "economic man"—that he pursue his self-interest and that he maximize, choosing consistently more, rather than less, of whatever served his self-interest—and, second, the techniques of formal modeling, with their frequently accompanying equations. Because modeling through reduction to a single motive can generate important and useful insights,[2] most elite academic departments soon came to want at least some "rational-choice" analysts on their faculty. In some universities this perspective came to dominate whole departments.

In the field of congressional studies, works in the 1970s by David Mayhew (1974) and Morris Fiorina (1977), in which the analysis required

2. For example, insights derived from the following ideas: that in a two-party system both parties will move toward the center to capture the middle votes, that unanimity can be achieved through side payments to those who do not agree with the proposed policy, or that a rationally self-interested person will not usually contribute to providing a good that, once provided, would be available to all.

seeing members of Congress as single-minded seekers of reelection, typified the temporary triumph of the kind of "economism" that required a focus on self-interest and thought of democratic politics as only the aggregation of interests.

But beginning around 1980, empirical political scientists began to rediscover another world, closer both to reality and to the earlier understanding of the political process that animated the framers of the Constitution. In this understanding, motives are manifold, and certain conflicts are not irreconcilable. In some contexts citizens and their representatives can both discover and create a common good through deliberation.

In 1979 a prescient paper by Joseph Bessette, presented at the American Political Science Association annual meeting but never published, gave evidence that in Congress deliberation on matters of the common good plays a much greater role than either the pluralist or the rational-choice schools had realized. In 1982 William Muir wrote *Legislature: California's School for Politics*, arguing both that legislators often want to make good public policy for its own sake and that specific governmental institutions could encourage this public-spirited motivation. In the next year, 1983, Arthur Maass's *Congress and the Common Good* contended that members of the U.S. Congress deliberate to reach agreement on what Maass called "the standards of the common life" at least as much as they aggregate particular self-interests. In 1985, David Vogler and Sidney Waldman's *Congress and Democracy* applied to Congress my distinction between "adversary" democracy and one aimed at the common good, producing as evidence instances in which members of Congress appeared to be influenced primarily by considerations of good public policy. In the same year, Martha Derthick and Paul Quirk's *Politics of Deregulation* (1985) reported hundreds of legislators and other political actors acting orthogonally to or against their own self-interest because they had been convinced that deregulation was in the interest of the public as a whole. As John Kingdon points out, a host of more-recent authors, both economists (Kau and Rubin 1982; Kalt and Zupan 1984; Nelson and Silberberg 1987) and political scientists (Kelman 1987; Reich 1988), have amassed evidence against the view that congressional action can be understood by positing that its members seek only their own reelection. Kingdon also points out that the behavior of bureaucracies, presidents, and courts cannot be explained solely in terms of self-interest.

In almost all the empirical branches of the profession of political science, a mini-revolt has now begun against the self-interested model of the way a democratic polity actually works.[3] Although the revolt is taking place in the descriptive, empirical wing of the discipline, it has prescriptive implications. The surprise is how tangentially this revolt is related to the strands in normative democratic theory that since World War II have come to focus on this issue.

Deliberation—traditionally defined as reasoned public discussion on questions of the common good[4]—was the essence of democracy in the normative prescriptions as well as the empirical descriptions of major nineteenth- and early twentieth-century writers like John Stuart Mill ([1861] 1958), Walter Bagehot ([1867] n.d.), and Ernest Barker ([1942] 1967). After World War II, when empirical description began to focus more and more on self-interest, the normative concern for a politics that transcended self-interest was preserved by philosophers in several almost independent traditions—the antimodernist tradition associated with Leo Strauss (1973), the republican virtue tradition associated with the historical work of J.G.A. Pocock (1975), the communal tradition associated with Sheldon Wolin (1960), and the Frankfurt tradition associated with Jürgen Habermas ([1968] 1971). Many contemporary democratic theorists, like Benjamin Barber (1984) or Hanna Pitkin (1981, 1984, and, with Sara Shumer, 1982) stress transformation of self and policy through communal deliberation. Recent "communitarian" theorists like Michael Sandel (1982) and Charles Taylor (1989) put collective attributes at the core of individual identity, pointing out that the self must always be "situated" and "encumbered," and that many goods, like language, are "irreducibly social." Feminist theorists have turned political thinking away from individual rights and toward mutual relationships, suggesting, for example, that mothering is a model of human behavior as applicable to political life as contract (Held 1990; see Mansbridge 1993 for a review). Yet while the insights of rational choice have informed political philosophy (e.g., Rawls 1971; Taylor 1976), the concerns of philosophers for deliberation and the transformation of interests through polit-

3. See citations in Kingdon (in this volume) and in Mansbridge 1990a. Studies of social movements, for example, have documented the political effects of non-self-interested motivation among activists (Mansbridge 1986; Conover and Gray 1983), and studies of citizens have shown how little, in some cases, narrow self-interest explains citizen attitudes and voting behavior (Sears and Funk 1990; Kinder and Keiwiet 1979, 1981).

4. See below for a critique of this definition of deliberation.

ical discourse have had relatively little effect on either rational choice or empirical political science.

Bridging the Gap

John Kingdon's chapter in this volume begins to bridge this gap. Along with documenting the fact that ideas affect—often in dramatic ways—the behavior of elected representatives, bureaucrats, and courts, Kingdon goes on to explore the theoretical problems behind the very notion of self-interest. Several of his points are critical for linking the empirical description of democracy and the philosophical analysis of democratic ideals.

Changing Preferences, Changing Selves

First, Kingdon points out that people, and groups, often do not have a clear idea what their interest is in a given situation. They need to consider what their interests are, usually through a process that combines collective deliberation, action, and personal reflection. By deliberation I mean, as I will explain below, a process that creates new selves and new interests as well as revealing underlying interests. Deliberation uncovers both conflict and commonality, and requires both reason and emotion. Beyond deliberation, probing one's interests adequately also requires taking action and experiencing the results of that action. Even narrow trade groups must sometimes, as Kingdon says, spend "a lot of time and energy trying to define" their interests.

Kingdon's important empirical observation returns deliberation, broadly defined, to a central place in the study of practicing democracies. It suggests that political scientists would do well to study not only how constituent preferences are transmitted through the policy-making machine but also how various institutions, in and outside formal government, help citizens decide what they want and then influence the content of those wants. A research agenda focused on the deliberative process broadly defined would investigate any act of communication that helped individuals "probe their volitions" (Lindblom 1990).

Through deliberation, action, and reflection, members of a group or potential group not only can discover that their underlying interests differ from their previous preferences but also, by creating themselves anew, can create new interests.[5] Empirical political science cannot easily observe and measure the processes in which people evolve new identities, adopting new political preferences and interests, but these processes are not impossible to document (see Kingdon on Bauer et al. 1964 [citation in Chapter 3]). Kinder and Herzog as well as Page and Shapiro (in this volume) indicate how those who are not politically active form and express preferences and how the larger deliberative process aggregates those individual conclusions, nonconclusions, decisions, and decisions not to decide. In-depth interviews would illuminate the internal dynamics of political transformation, including the role of ideas, among both activists and the general public.

More easily than documenting internal psychological processes, political scientists can observe and analyze how political institutions help people change their preferences and their identities. Researchers in the field of political communication could move beyond one-way theories of top-down media manipulation to theories of mutual influence, mediated by ideas, between media producers and consumers. Scholars who specialize in the professions could look at the effects of professional socialization, including socialization to specific ideas, on identity, values, and political interests—particularly in fields that channel many of their members into professional policy-making. Specialists in interest groups could look at the deliberative functions of these groups, since, as Kingdon indicates, a strong case can be made that "trying to define" their interests is a major part of what these groups do (Mansbridge 1992). Kingdon's point that an important part of politics consists in trying to clarify one's interests should set an agenda focused on deliberation and political transformation for the next generation of empirical political scientists.

Political philosophers, also, are turning their attention these days to political transformation through deliberation, action, and reflection (e.g., Warren 1992). In promoting deliberation, however, they often forget that deliberation should uncover not just commonality but conflict (e.g., Bessette 1979; Barber 1984; Habermas [1981] 1984; Sunstein

5. I define "interest" here as an enlightened preference, the preference one would have if one had perfect information, including inner knowledge of the person one would become with each choice and the experience of discussing the choices with others in a nonoppressive setting. See Mansbridge [1980] 1983, 24–28, esp. nn. 1–9, and Habermas [1981] 1984.

1988; Cohen 1989a, 1989b). Claus Offe and Helmut Wiesenthal (1980), for example, following Jürgen Habermas, focus on the discovery and creation of collective interests. They ask what kinds of institutions foster the transformation of interests, conclude that such institutions must be deliberative (or, in their word, "dialogic"), and suggest, correctly, that the procedures of what I call "adversary" democracy do not promote the dialogic interaction that facilitates interest transformation. Unions (and, I would add, towns, cities, states, and nations) need deliberative arenas that allow their members and citizens to discuss, come to understand, and possibly transform their interests. Yet Offe and Wiesenthal, like many others, seem to assume that dialogic political transformation should and will move the participants in a communal direction. Deliberation, like all political participation, should instead ideally allow participants to investigate where their considered interests lie and to create new interests that will be good for them. When warranted, a good discussion should let some participants see that what they previously thought was a common good actually disguised underlying conflict.

Institutions that lead people to transform their preferences and themselves tend to have several features. At least in Western culture, such transformative institutions give individuals a chance to ask questions that are on their minds, speak their puzzlements, and declare aloud their conclusions.[6] Transformative institutions also promote the human emotions of hatred and empathy, either through face-to-face contact or through dramatic evocations of the difference or commonality of others and the evil inflicted by or upon others. Institutions that transform in a communal direction will, in addition, tend to promote acting according to principle, or duty, sometimes by establishing as a spoken or unspoken rule that one speak only of what would benefit the collective and not oneself (see Barber 1984), and sometimes through charismatic or otherwise compelling role models.[7]

Each practice that facilitates transformation—whether in a communal or self-interested direction—has the potential both for good and for bad. A Khomeini, an Inquisition, or a Hitler can use for political transformation any technique, including decisions announced in public, height-

6. Kurt Lewin (1947) has shown that in the United States, middle-class women who discuss and announce their conclusions and their commitment to a new course of action in a small group are more likely than others to change their behavior and stick by that change.

7. At least in the United States, exposure to someone performing an altruistic action increases one's chances of performing such an action oneself (Krebs 1970).

ened affect, suppression of self-interest, and charisma. Empirical political scientists studying political transformations thus need philosophical help, for it is harder in transformative politics than in aggregative politics to devise a simple noncontroversial measure for judging the process. In a purely aggregative, or "transmission belt," model of democracy, where preferences are taken as given, one might argue that the larger democratic process should approximate what would happen in a reasonably well-informed, well-conducted referendum. A system would be democratic to the degree that political outcomes were congruent with the majority's political preferences (as expressed, say, in surveys), each counting for one, and none for more than one. An empirical researcher could simply approve, implicitly or explicitly, of high representative-constituency congruence and disapprove of its opposite. To judge a more transformative model of democracy, however, the researcher needs a theory of what is good for specific people (or, as Kinder and Herzog say in Chapter 17, what is "healthy" for them) or at least what is bad for them. Absent such a strong theory, the researcher needs a theory of what kinds of processes might generate good transformations. One might follow Habermas ([1981] 1984), for example, in concluding that true interests are likely to emerge through consensual discussion in a nonoppressive setting, where speakers' statements are subject to a variety of challenges. Or one might improve on Habermas's rationalistic analysis by adding a consideration of the role of the emotions in deliberation.

The processes of deliberation, action, and reflection require a mixture of emotion and reason. Although in ordinary speech the words "deliberation" and "reflection" have strong rational overtones, actual deliberation and reflection require emotional investment, even if only in the minimal sense that one's emotions must be engaged in order to address a problem. More substantively, productive deliberation requires that the individuals involved have some understanding of their own needs and the needs of others in the decision. Understanding one's own needs requires gaining insight into why one fears, hates, loves, feels sorry for, and feels proud of aspects of oneself and other individuals and groups. That gain in insight cannot be a purely rational process. It must involve experiencing the emotions and testing them against expected future emotions, testing, for example, feeling toward the different aspects of the person one is and wants to be. Understanding others' needs requires the same process of emotional sympathy, identification, and judgment, directed outward. Beyond understanding, the emotional aspects of deliberation should help participants, when warranted, to make the interests of others and of the whole their own. The use of emotion (as against reason) in public deliberation is not bad in itself; what is good or bad is the use to which the emotion is put. Sullivan and Masters's work, along with that of Kuklinski et al. and Theiss-Morse et al.—all in this volume—points out that emotions can play a positive role in deliberation, while Kinder and Herzog also suggest that political emotions, like political symbols, can have both good and bad uses.

Living Ideas

Kingdon argues that while politicians use ideas to persuade others, in the process they are often persuaded themselves. We persuade ourselves through our own ideas not only because we do not like being liars or think that the most efficient way to persuade others we are sincere is to be sincere. Ideas are not inert objects that we can appropriate or not as suits our interest. Ideas often become part of our identity, even when the practical consequences of an idea work against our material self-interest.

Ideas have a life of their own. Prescriptive ideas, ideals, have implications for practice that are not always congruent with the self-interest or other ideals of those who hold them. When one's prescriptive ideas come in conflict with other ideals, they create a tension that demands resolution or repression. In combination with other ideals or in combination with practice, ideals generate new ideals that take the individuals that hold them in unexpected directions. Descriptive ideas, too, can get out of any individual's control. Descriptive theories and descriptive analogies are either upheld or undermined by facts. The political influence of the idea of deregulation, for instance, rested in part on classic economic theory, which predicted greater efficiency if the market took its course. The influence of that theory in turn rested in part on facts. The idea of deregulation would not have had the political influence it did without a host of empirical studies seeming to demonstrate that in states trying deregulation, the enterprises affected became more efficient, and potential negative consequences, like airline abandonment of small routes, did not follow (Derthick and Quirk 1985). People find it hard to maintain their descriptive ideas when empirical studies provide evidence that the description is factually wrong.

Because ideas have a life of their own, not fully under the control of those who may want to use them to serve their self-interest, the course of an idea may take a turn that works against the material self-interest of those who espouse it. But by then those who espouse the idea may have been persuaded by the congruence of a prescriptive idea with their other values or by the factual accuracy of a descriptive idea. They cannot then easily let the idea go. If they have argued that a policy generated by the idea will foster the public good, their interest may come to include both the promotion of this idea and concern for the public good.

People create and adopt ideas, and are transformed by them, when the ideas flow logically or emotionally from previously held premises. Once we have invested our labor in an idea, we have made it ours. It becomes, for a shorter or longer time, part of our identities. As a consequence, few human beings can pick up and drop ideas the way we can pick up and drop a material object. Ideas can have a profound impact, not only on the legislators, bureaucrats, and judges who are the principal subjects of Kingdon's analysis, but also on the policy-oriented public and, through the processes that Kinder and Herzog, and Page and Shapiro analyze, on the larger public as well.

Ideas and Self-Interest Entangled

Because we are "intellectually constituted" as well as "socially constituted," Kingdon argues convincingly that ideas and self-interest are not easily disentangled. I would add that even altruistic motivation and self-interest are not easily disentangled.

We normally see self-interest and altruism as at opposite poles. Conceptually we know what we mean by altruism only by contrasting it with self-interest. We *know* that love (empathy with others in and outside one's group) or duty (commitment to a principle or to a course of action because of arguments that it is right) is at work only when an action could not possibly have been taken for reasons of self-interest. Empirically we demonstrate that people are acting for unselfish reasons by devising situations in which they act *against* their self-interest.

In practice, however, altruism must coincide with self-interest sufficiently to prevent the extinction of either the altruistic motive or the altruist. Duty and love, though valuable in themselves, must be sustained by an environment that provides enough self-interested return to both motivations to prevent actions based on them from being excessively costly.

In practice we often try hard to arrange our lives so that duty (or love) and interest coincide. Eighteenth-century writers often exaggerated the degree of coincidence. (When Thomas Jefferson directed his overseer to ease the work of pregnant slaves in order to prevent miscarriages, he chillingly commented, "In this, as in all other cases, providence has made our interests and our duties coincide perfectly" [(1819) 1953].) Today, in the interests of misplaced "realism," we often exaggerate in the other direction, claiming that if we can detect any self-interested reason to act in a particular way, this reason provides the only explanation we need. Yet self-interest does not automatically drive out duty, in spite of the conceptual opposition between the two. In my own case, I have a duty to care for my child, and I am made happy by his happiness, and I get simple sensual pleasure from snuggling close to him as I read him a book. I have a principled commitment to work for women's liberation, and I empathize with other women, and I find a way to use some of my work for women as background to a book that advances my academic career. Duty, love (or empathy), and self-interest intermingle in my actions in a way I can rarely sort out (Mansbridge 1990b). Because we have worked to entangle them, both the way ideas entangle with self-interest and the way altruism entangles with self-interest persistently evade the empirical researcher's quest for explicit categorization.

A Philosophical Agenda

Kingdon makes a distinct contribution to the description of American national government when he insists on the importance of ideas in addition to narrow self-interest. He opens the door to philosophical inquiry when he points out that preferences and selves are changed through deliberation, that ideas have a life of their own, and that ideas cannot easily be disentangled from self-interest. For philosophers, the task remaining is to analyze the normative and philosophical implications of this revised description.

A recent stream of philosophical writing has concluded that selves are neither atomistic and unencumbered by communal identities and obligations nor unchangeably situated, but are complexly created and self-creating (Sandel 1982; MacIntyre [1981] 1984; Okin 1989; Benhabib [1987] 1988; Flanagan 1991; McLaren 1991). Public and private deliberation, public and private action, and personal reflection all help form the political aspects of the self. Such deliberation, action, and reflection will almost inevitably include, and should include, self-interest as well as love and duty, emotion as well as reason, conflict as well as commonality with others, and the independent power of ideas, which become entangled with the self.

Philosophers have investigated the potential role of self-interest in morality (Gauthier 1986; Rawls 1982) and the relation of self-interest to love and duty (Sen [1978] 1990; Elster 1990; Jencks 1990; Mansbridge 1990b; Okin 1989). The next step would be to look more closely at self-interest, love, and duty in the construction of self, particularly the construction of selves through political deliberation. Feminist theorists have led the way in reintegrating the emotions into moral and political philosophy (see review in Mansbridge 1993). Here, too, the next step would be to investigate the interpenetrating roles of "reason" and "emotion" in the public and private construction of political selves.

Thought about the role of deliberation in the construction of political selves needs to avoid, like thought about democracy in general, settled adherence to either an adversary view of democracy that assumes self-interest and conflicting interests, and requires fair mechanisms (such as "one person, one vote") for aggregating preferences, or a communal view of democracy that assumes citizens can and should make the good of the whole their own. Communal processes, which induce some to make the good of others their own through duty or love, can transform collective decisions from "prisoners' dilemmas," in which each individual potentially benefits from harming the others, into cooperative enterprises, in which the individual benefits from what is good for the group.[8]

8. For a description of the prisoners' dilemma, see Axelrod (1984) or Mansbridge (1990b). This two-person dilemma is one of many "social dilemmas" in which actions that are to the self-interest of each individual separately produce, in interaction with other self-interested individual decisions, worse outcomes than more-cooperative behavior. The prisoners' dilemma makes an analytic advance over Hume's ([1739–40] 1978) stress on "remote," as against "proximate," self-interest and Tocqueville's ([1835, 1840] 1954) stress on "self-interest rightly understood," by revealing that it is often in the individual's self-interest—both in the short and the long run, and correctly understood—to act in a narrowly self-interested manner, provided that others act cooperatively. In the absence of love, duty, or communal sanctions, each individual has an interest in "free riding" on others' efforts (Olson 1965). Human societies have therefore traditionally remedied this destructive logic of collective action by creating informal punishments for the noncooperative in small groups (Taylor 1976) and formal punishments in nation-states (Hobbes [1651] 1950; Hardin 1982), by instilling conscience or a sense of duty toward others in members of the group (Campbell 1975), and by promoting love

But if political institutions assume only common interests, elites who dominate the agenda and language of discourse can obscure what is in others' interests and possibly induce those others to participate in their own oppression. Political deliberation should also produce transformations of self that recognize underlying conflict and incorporate engagement in that conflict as a part of one's identity.

As for the role of ideas in the political process, political philosophers can draw on the philosophy of the self, on Marxist materialist versus antimaterialist debates, and on the philosophy of the emotions to pursue the question of how in a political context an idea might be said to have a life independent of the material interests of those who espouse it. In some ways, for example, the formal demonstration that two plus two equals four "commands" our assent. Decision theorists speak in a similar way of "Eureka" problems, whose solutions depend on factual premises: once any member of a group points out the relevant fact, the solution commands the group's assent.[9] Because problems like these are essentially uncontested, many political philosophers consider them not "political." But problems of this nature are frequently embedded in more-contested issues as segments of more-complex ideas. Part of political deliberation consists in separating out and "solving" the uncontested aspects of a problem, thus both clarifying the remaining conflict and creating an experience of mutual gain that promotes future collaboration. It obscures the political process to rule out of the realm of the political those parts of an idea that upon deliberation turn out to be uncontested or that even before deliberation all participants acknowledge to be uncontested. For more-contested problems, Jürgen Habermas ([1981] 1984) suggests criteria that explain when we might rationally give assent to an idea or (to move both from Habermas's language and his thought) how an idea might legitimately command our assent.

The emotional components of ideas, including the sympathies and hatreds introduced through collective deliberation, also take hold or fail to take hold in a way not fully in the control of those who introduce

---

or a sense of "we-feeling" with others in the group (Dawes et al. 1990). Mansbridge (1990b) discusses these options.

9. In the "NASA" problem used in some group research, for example, the group must rank several pieces of equipment in order of their usefulness on a trip to the moon. The nature of the pieces is such that once anyone in the group points out certain facts about them, everyone agrees on their appropriate ordering. The emergency flare, for example, is always ranked last because it requires oxygen to work.

them. We do not have, however, a set of Habermasian criteria that might help us normatively judge the emotional components of deliberation and self-transformation, other than a crude functionalism suggesting that whatever emotional components survive across time as positively loaded aspects of human normative systems may have something good about them.[10]

As empirical political scientists begin to make the processes of political deliberation and self-transformation a more central part of their inquiry, philosophers can help clarify the normative questions involved. Neither self-interest nor altruism, neither emotion nor reason, neither conflict nor commonality is good or bad in itself. When democratic processes, intimately entangled with ideas, transform participants by helping them understand their interests and create new interests and new selves, the normative judgment of that transformation and its direction must depend on its content, context, and place in a larger theory of human interests and justice. Such a philosophical focus on political transformation is long overdue.

References

Axelrod, Robert. 1984. *The Evolution of Cooperation*. New York: Basic Books.

Bagehot, Walter. [1867] n.d. *The English Constitution*. Garden City, N.Y.: Doubleday.

Barber, Benjamin R. 1984. *Strong Democracy: Participatory Politics for a New Age*. Berkeley and Los Angeles: University of California Press.

Barker, Ernest. [1942] 1967. *Reflections on Government*. London: Oxford University Press.

Benhabib, Seyla. [1987] 1988. "The Generalized and Concrete Other." In *Feminism as Critique*, ed. Seyla Benhabib and Ducilla Cornell, 77–95. Minneapolis: University of Minnesota Press.

Bessette, Joseph M. 1979. "Deliberation in Congress." Paper delivered at the annual meeting of the American Political Science Association, Washington, D.C.

Campbell, D. T. 1975. "On the Conflicts Between Biological and Social Evolution and Between Psychology and the Moral Tradition." *American Psychologist* 30:1103–26.

Cohen, Joshua. 1989a. "Deliberation and Democratic Legitimacy." In *The Good Polity*, ed. Alan Hamlin and Phillip Pettit, 17–34. Oxford: Blackwell.

10. One could interpret in this way Aristotle's starting with Greek proverbs, Hume's reliance on habit, and MacIntyre's criterion of historical survival.

———. 1989b. "The Economic Basis of Deliberative Democracy," *Social Philosophy and Policy* 6:25–50.
Conover, Pamela Johnston, and Virginia Gray. 1983. *Feminism and the New Right: Conflict over the American Family.* New York: Praeger.
Dawes, Robyn, Alphons J. C. van de Kragt, and John M. Orbell. 1990. "Cooperation for the Benefit of Us—Not Me, or My Conscience." In *Beyond Self-Interest*, ed. Jane J. Mansbridge, 97–110. Chicago: University of Chicago Press.
Deci, Edward L. 1971. "Effects of Externally Mediated Rewards on Intrinsic Motivation." *Journal of Personality and Social Psychology* 18:105–15.
Derthick, Martha, and Paul J. Quirk. 1985. *The Politics of Deregulation.* Washington, D.C.: Brookings Institution.
Downs, Anthony. 1957. *An Economic Theory of Democracy.* New York: Harper & Row.
Elster, Jon. 1990. "Selfishness and Altruism." In *Beyond Self-Interest*, ed. Jane J. Mansbridge, 44–52. Chicago: University of Chicago Press.
Fiorina, Morris. 1974. *Representatives, Roll Calls, and Constituencies.* Lexington, Mass.: Lexington Books/D. C. Heath.
Flanagan, Owen. 1991. *Varieties of Moral Personality.* Cambridge, Mass.: Harvard University Press.
Gauthier, David. 1986. *Morals by Agreement.* Oxford: Oxford University Press.
Gilligan, Carol. 1982. *In a Different Voice.* Cambridge, Mass.: Harvard University Press.
Habermas, Jürgen. [1968] 1971. *Knowledge and Human Interests.* Trans. Jeremy Shapiro. Boston: Beacon Press.
———. [1973] 1975. *Legitimation Crisis.* Trans. Thomas McCarthy. Boston: Beacon Press.
———. [1974] 1979. *Communication and the Evolution of Society.* Trans. Thomas McCarthy. Boston: Beacon Press.
———. [1981] 1984. *The Theory of Communicative Action.* Vol. 1. Trans. Thomas McCarthy. Boston: Beacon Press.
Hardin, Garrett. 1968. "The Tragedy of the Commons." *Science* 162:1243–48.
Hardin, Russell. 1982. *Collective Action.* Baltimore: Johns Hopkins University Press.
Held, Virginia. 1990. "Mothering Versus Contract." In *Beyond Self-Interest*, ed. Jane J. Mansbridge, 287–304. Chicago: University of Chicago Press.
Hobbes, Thomas. [1651] 1950. *Leviathan.* London: J. M. Dent & Sons, 1947; New York: E. P. Dutton.
Hume, David. [1739–40] 1900. *A Treatise of Human Nature.* Ed. L. A. Selby-Bigge. Oxford: Oxford University Press.
———. [1739–40] 1978. *A Treatise of Human Nature.* Ed. L. A. Selby-Bigge. 2d ed., ed. P. H. Nidditch. Oxford: Oxford University Press.
Jefferson, Thomas. 1953. *Farm Book.* Ed. Edwin Marry Betts. Princeton: Princeton University Press.
Jencks, Christopher. 1990. "Varieties of Altruism." In *Beyond Self-Interest*, ed. Jane J. Mansbridge, 53–67. Chicago: University of Chicago Press.

Kalt, Joseph, and Mark A. Zupan. 1984. "Capture and Ideology in the Economic Theory of Politics." *American Economic Review* 74:279–300.

Kau, James, and Paul Rubin. 1982. *Congressmen, Constituents, and Contributors.* Boston: Martinus Nijhoff Publishing.

Kelman, Steven. 1987. *Making Public Policy: A Hopeful View of American Government.* New York: Basic Books.

Kinder, Donald R., and D. Roderick Kiewiet. 1979. "Economic Discontent and Political Behavior: The Role of Personal Grievances and Collective Economic Judgments in Congressional Voting." *American Journal of Political Science* 23:495–527.

———. 1981. "Sociotropic Politics." *British Journal of Political Science* 11:129–61.

Krebs, Dennis L. 1970. "Altruism: An Examination of the Concept." *Psychological Bulletin* 73:258–302.

Lindblom, Charles E. 1990. *Inquiry and Change: The Troubled Attempt to Understand and Shape Society.* New Haven: Yale University Press.

Maass, Arthur. 1983. *Congress and the Common Good.* New York: Basic Books.

MacIntyre, Alasdair. [1981] 1984. *After Virtue.* Notre Dame, Ind.: University of Notre Dame Press.

McLaren, Margaret. 1991. "Complex Identity." Ph.D. diss., Department of Philosophy, Northwestern University.

Mansbridge, Jane J. [1980] 1983. *Beyond Adversary Democracy.* Chicago: University of Chicago Press.

———. 1986. *Why We Lost the ERA.* Chicago: University of Chicago Press.

———. 1988. "Motivating Deliberation in Congress." In *Constitutionalism in America*, ed. Sarah Baumgartener Thurow, 2:59–86. New York: University Press of America.

———, ed. 1990a. *Beyond Self-Interest.* Chicago: University of Chicago Press.

———. 1990b. "On the Relationship of Altruism and Self-Interest." In *Beyond Self-Interest*, ed. Jane J. Mansbridge, 133–43. Chicago: University of Chicago Press.

———. 1990c. "The Rise and Fall of Self-Interest in the Explanation of Political Life." In *Beyond Self-Interest*, ed. Jane J. Mansbridge, 3–22. Chicago: University of Chicago Press.

———. 1992. "A Deliberative Theory of Interest Representation." In *The Politics of Interests: Interest Groups Transformed*, ed. Mark P. Petracca, 32–57. Boulder, Colo.: Westview Press.

———. 1993. "Feminism and Democratic Community." In *Democratic Community: NOMOS XXXV*, ed. John W. Chapman and Ian Shapiro. New York: New York University Press.

Mayhew, David R. 1974. *Congress: The Electoral Connection.* New Haven: Yale University Press.

Mill, John Stuart. [1861] 1958. *Considerations on Representative Government.* New York: Bobbs-Merrill.

Muir, William K., Jr. 1982. *Legislature: California's School for Politics.* Chicago: University of Chicago Press.

Nelson, Douglas, and Eugene Silberberg. 1987. "Ideology and Legislator Shirking." *Economic Inquiry* 25 (January): 15–28.

Offe, Claus, and Helmut Wiesenthal. 1980. "Two Logics of Collective Action: Theoretical Notes on Social Class and Organizational Form." In *Political Power and Social Theory*, ed. Maurice Zeitlin, 1:67–115. Greenwich, Conn.: JAI Press.
Okin, Susan. 1989. "Reason and Feeling in Thinking About Justice." *Ethics* 99 (January): 229–49.
Olson, Mancur. 1965. *The Logic of Collective Action*. Cambridge, Mass.: Harvard University Press.
Pitkin, Hanna Fenichel. 1981. "Justice: On Relating Public and Private." *Political Theory* 9:327–52.
———. 1984. *Fortune Is a Woman*. Berkeley and Los Angeles: University of California Press.
Pitkin, Hanna Fenichel, and Sara M. Shumer. 1982. "On Participation." *Democracy* 2:43–54.
Pocock, J.G.A. 1975. *The Machiavellian Moment*. Princeton: Princeton University Press.
Quirk, Paul J. 1988. "In Defense of the Politics of Ideas." *Journal of Politics* 50:31–41.
Rainborough, Colonel Thomas. [1647] 1957. In *Puritanism and Liberty*, ed. A.S.P. Woodhouse, 53–74. Chicago: University of Chicago Press.
Rawls, John. 1971. *A Theory of Justice*. Cambridge, Mass.: Harvard University Press.
Reich, Robert B., ed. 1988. *The Power of Public Ideas*. Cambridge, Mass.: Ballinger.
Sandel, Michael J. 1982. *Liberalism and the Limits of Justice*. Cambridge: Cambridge University Press.
Schumpeter, Joseph A. [1942] 1962. *Capitalism, Socialism, and Democracy*. New York: Harper & Row.
Sears, David O., and Carolyn L. Funk. 1990. "Self-Interest in Americans' Political Opinions." In *Beyond Self-Interest*, ed. Jane J. Mansbridge, 147–70. Chicago: University of Chicago Press.
Sen, Amartya K. [1978] 1990. "Rational Fools." In *Beyond Self-Interest*, ed. Jane J. Mansbridge, 25–43. Chicago: University of Chicago Press.
Strauss, Leo. 1973. *The Political Philosophy of Hobbes*. Chicago: University of Chicago Press.
Sunstein, Cass R. 1988. "Beyond the Republican Revival." *Yale Law Journal* 97:1539–90.
Taylor, Charles. 1989. "Irreducibly Social Goods." In *Proceedings of the Conference on Rationality, Individuality, and Public Policy*. Canberra: Australian National University.
Taylor, Michael. 1976. *Anarchy and Cooperation*. London: John Wiley & Sons.
Titmuss, Richard M. 1970. *The Gift Relationship*. London: George Allen & Unwin; New York: Pantheon, 1971.
Tocqueville, Alexis de. [1835, 1840] 1954. *Democracy in America*. New York: Vintage Books.
Verba, Sidney, and Norman H. Nie. 1972. *Political Participation in America: Political Democracy and Social Equality*. New York: Harper & Row.

Vogler, David J., and Sidney R. Waldman. 1985. *Congress and Democracy*. Washington, D.C.: Congressional Quarterly Press.

Warren, Mark. 1992. "Democratic Theory and Self-Transformation." *American Political Science Review* 6:8–23.

Wolin, Sheldon S. 1960. *Politics and Vision*. Boston: Little, Brown.

II

The Reasonable Citizen

5

Political Freedom: A Sociopsychological Analysis

James L. Gibson

Few political concepts have been as thoroughly investigated as that of political freedom. From the ancient Greeks to modern political philosophers, scholars have attempted to identify the essence of political free-

This chapter is based on research funded by the National Science Foundation (SES 86-06642). I am deeply indebted to Felice Levine at NSF for support for the project. A number of colleagues have contributed significantly to the development of the research, including Jonathan Casper, James Davis, Jennifer Hochschild, Stanley Presser, Lee Sigelman, Paul M. Sniderman, John L. Sullivan, and Thomas Tyler. I am also indebted to the National Opinion Research Corporation—and especially Dick Rubin—for their excellent execution of the survey. Bernadette McKinney, Steven Shamberger, and Marilyn Yale provided quite helpful research assistance. This is a revised version of a paper delivered at the Democratic Theory Symposium, Williams College, August 1989. I am especially grateful for the comments of Betin Bilir, John Burke, James F. Farr, George Marcus, and Laura J. Scalia on an earlier version of this chapter.

dom and to design political systems that are compatible with desired levels of freedom. For democratic theorists, political freedom is an integral part of the function of government itself.

It is not surprising that such an important concept has been analyzed from a variety of theoretical perspectives and normative and empirical objectives. Freedom has long been a staple of the intellectual diet of philosophers, both analytical philosophers, who are concerned more with the logic of the concept, and normative philosophers, who would structure the political world around certain desiderata. Yet for all that is known about freedom as a concept and as an attribute of institutions and systems, we understand very little about *freedom as an attribute of individuals.* What does freedom mean in the context of the individual within the polity? To what extent do individuals have and perceive political freedom? Are perceptions of freedom measurable, quantifiable? If so, do some people perceive more freedom than others, and if they do, why do they? What implications flow from political freedom? Are citizens who feel more freedom more politically active? Are political systems composed of citizens with more freedom more democratic? Freedom is a concept that has been thoroughly analyzed as a macro-level concept, yet the analysis of freedom as individuals perceive it has been neglected.

In this chapter I address the problem of perceived political freedom at the micro level. My objectives are (1) to develop a conceptualization of political freedom that is appropriate for micro-level analysis; (2) to construct operational indicators of perceived personal political freedom; (3) to determine how widespread perceptions of political freedom are in the United States; (4) to test various hypotheses about the social, political, and psychological origins of perceived political freedom; and (5) to identify some of the political implications—both at the micro and macro levels—of personal freedom. Ultimately, the goal of this analysis is to contribute rigorous social scientific evidence on the meaning, causes, and consequences of personal political freedom.

The political freedom with which I am concerned is not the freedom that is found in law books or even in actual constitutional practice; it is the freedom that individuals perceive, that they believe is available to them. There may be some connection between the "law in the books" and the "freedom as perceived," but it is not necessary to *assume* that the connection exists or that it is of any strength. For the moment, it is only necessary to devise a strategy for allowing people to report on their own experiences with freedom. Such a strategy first requires that "freedom" be given some conceptual meaning. Fortunately, there are those who have considered this problem before.

Conceptualizing Personal Political Freedom

A common understanding of "freedom" within modern Anglo-American liberalism is "the ability of individuals to pursue personal goals without burdensome restraints or coercion" (Preston 1982, 73).[1] For Preston, the essence of the problem of freedom is "that of distinguishing consciously determined, free activity from behavior which is controlled or manipulated by other causes" (82). Thus, "conscious deliberation" is an important distinguishing characteristic of free choice. But since it is so difficult to observe the interior workings of the deliberative mechanism—the human brain—Preston takes one step back. He argues that "freedom can only be examined by determining whether individuals possess, when they act, the essential *capacities and conditions* for deliberative choice" (74, emphasis added). By capacities he means "skills, abilities, or understanding essential for deliberate choice with respect to a given problem." Conditions "refer to the presence of genuine opportunities in a given decision-making environment which either (1) support the development of needed capacities or (2) permit action in pursuit of freely selected goals" (84). Threats and physical coercion are of course incompatible with these conditions. Thus, Preston melds various views of freedom by proposing external but to some degree subjective standards for judging the capacities and conditions for freedom.[2]

1. Similarly, Perry (1944, 521) has defined liberty (the same thing as freedom) as "the absence of external obstacles which prevent, and the presence of resources and capacities which promote, the power of any individual to realize his desires or execute his will." For Pennock (1979, 28) liberty is "the opportunity for spontaneous and deliberate self-direction in the formation and the accomplishment of one's purposes."

2. I recognize that a distinction is typically made between "negative" and "positive" conceptions of freedom (see Berlin 1958). The negative view of freedom argues that to free people is to remove restraints on their actions. Rights perform this function by guaranteeing broad areas of autonomous activity within which the individual can make free choices. The positive view of freedom emphasizes rational self-determination. Freedom is thus assessed, not in terms of whether conditions for free choice prevail, but rather by the objective rationality of the choice. Decisions that are irrational, but seemingly unrestrained, are not free choices.

The distinction between negative and positive freedoms has been subjected to a variety of

This view of freedom is useful because it implies that a key element of the capacities and conditions for deliberative choice is the *perception of the ability to make such choices freely*. People cannot be free unless they perceive opportunities for self expression.[3] To the extent that some perceive constraints on their freedom, liberty is diminished.

This conceptualization of freedom is also salutary because it renders the concept susceptible to empirical investigation. Although Preston is correct when he says that we cannot get easy access to the interior workings of the brain, we can certainly assess people's perceptions of the conditions for deliberative choice. Most basically, do people perceive such conditions as available to them? Certainly those who perceive the likelihood of sanctions for political activity have neither the capacity nor the conditions for free action. Although freedom is more than merely perceptual, the beliefs of individuals are important for understanding their own levels of freedom.

Democratic Freedom

Just what sort of activities are of concern when we speak of "freedom to act"? Though there are many domains of activity that may be of interest, my concern in this chapter is limited to *political* freedom, and mainly within the context of liberal democratic theory. Consequently, it is useful to provide a brief outline of the meaning of freedom within this body of theory.[4]

---

attacks and has been much debated (e.g., MacCallum 1967). For my purposes, it is more important to distinguish between subjective (perceived) and objective freedoms than positive and negative freedoms. Preston's conceptualization allows me to do just that.

3. There is a certain asymmetry to my argument. Perceived restraints on choices—perceptions that certain political activities will generate adverse repercussions—certainly are evidence of lack of freedom, even if I am on less certain ground when I claim that the *absence* of perceived restraints is equivalent to freedom. Nonetheless, if the absence of perceived constraints is grounded in reality, then this is an important component of positive freedom. Clearly, those who expect to be penalized for their political activity are not free. In this sense, my conceptualization of freedom is closer to the negative view than to the positive view.

4. The most useful conceptualizations of freedom are embedded in larger theories of politics. The theory I employ is most generally liberal democratic, with specific reference to Dahl's (1971) theory of polyarchy. This perspective emphasizes obstacles that individual citizens might perceive to frank political expression. This is not a freedom of unconstrained licentiousness; instead, it is freedom to engage in political activity that is essential to the effective functioning of polyarchies. It is quite possible for others to conceive of freedom differently, emphasizing, for instance, the potential of individuals—whether perceived or not—to develop nascent capacities for expression.

Relying on Dahl's (1971) theory of polyarchy, I postulate that in a democracy, citizens must have the opportunity to communicate with their fellows and to join together in political parties and pressure groups to press their political demands. Within this framework, a liberal democracy is a political system that requires unimpaired opportunities for all full citizens

> 1. To formulate their preferences
> 2. To signify their preferences to their fellow citizens and the government by individual and collective action
> 3. To have their preferences weighed equally in the conduct of the government, that is, weighed with no discrimination because of the content or source of the preference. (Dahl 1971, 2)

Liberal democracies need not allow all political interests equal *influence* over public policies, but they must allow all political interests *equal opportunity to compete* for the control of public policies.

If polities circumscribe this right, then political freedom is limited. As McClosky and Brill put it:

> Freedom of expression is obviously essential for registering popular consent and holding rulers accountable. To be genuine, consent must be freely given; and to be freely given, it must be the product of unhindered communication. At a minimum, all citizens must have the opportunity to obtain the information they need to evaluate their rulers fairly. They must be free to exchange opinions, to persuade others by facts and argument, and to be persuaded in turn. Effective consent and accountability presuppose the unhampered opportunity for citizens to test the truth or falsity of government claims; to evaluate the government, its policies, and its officeholders; and to participate (via speech, press, assembly, and association) in efforts to achieve peaceful and orderly change. (1983, 39)

Such an approach to the definition of democracy places great emphasis on political competition. Because democracy is a style of government that must maximize the opportunities and avenues of the entire citizenry to compete for control of political power and influence over public policy, the ability to compete, to dissent, to challenge the actions of government is crucial. Thus, from the perspective of democratic political systems, political freedom includes institutional guarantees of the right to engage in oppositionist political activity: to speak, to assemble, to organize, to proselytize, to compete for political power.[5] From the perspective of the freedom of individual citizens, my concern is whether individuals perceive the opportunity to express themselves on political matters.

Caveats

I must acknowledge that this view of personal political freedom is focused on the individual citizen—it looks directly toward the attributes and beliefs of individuals, as well as their interactions with their immediate environments, to try to understand freedom.[6] In adopting this approach, I do not deny or discount the utility of alternatives—for instance, studies that focus on the attributes of cultures or polities. But my basic premise is that what people believe about their own freedom is important, that what they perceive about the opportunities for political expression and the costs associated with such expression has much to do with their exercise of freedom, and that it is useful to think about the degree of freedom available and the patterns of allocation of freedom within a polity as ultimately reducible to a study of the beliefs of individual citizens. I do not gainsay the utility of thinking about other sorts of freedom, and at a later point in this analysis, I try to identify some linkages between the individuals and the larger social and political environment within which they function. But the approach here must be recognized from the beginning as a particular and not necessarily inclusive approach to the problem of perceived personal political freedom.

As much as I might wish to avoid the issue, it is necessary as well to

5. There are of course alternative conceptualizations of democracy and of democratic freedom, and I certainly do not claim this as the only legitimate approach. The emphasis I place on democracy as procedure, without much regard for substantive public policy, must be borne in mind throughout the analysis that follows.

6. Bay (1970) also recognizes this distinction and provides a quite useful review of the views of several political philosophers on this issue (see esp. chap. 2). Those who look inside individuals to understand freedom he refers to as "idealists," as distinguished from "empiricists," who focus on freedom in terms of relations between people. My own approach is a blend of these two ideal types.

acknowledge the distinction between objective and subjective freedom. My approach is to study subjective freedom—the freedom that is perceived by individuals. A different sort of freedom—for instance, the degree of freedom acknowledged by law—might be measured more objectively (and as an attribute of polities, not of individuals). Within my conceptualization of the problem, there is no necessary relation between objective and subjective freedom. People may perceive themselves as free even in the most repressive conditions (and that sort of "false consciousness" is not addressed in this research). Alternatively, people may not perceive the freedom that is truly available to them. When I refer to freedom, I refer to the freedom that exists in the minds and hearts of citizens, not to the freedom that exists in the law books or even in the broader political culture.

Do individuals perceive the availability of such political freedom? Until now, the answer would be largely that we do not know. Empirical inquiries into perceived levels of personal political freedom have not previously been conducted. At this point, let us consider how such perceptions might be measured.

Operationalizing Personal Political Freedom

Within this conceptualization of perceived freedom, I recognize two primary sources of constraints on liberty: the larger political system and the immediate interpersonal context. Citizens may perceive that public expressions of their political views are circumscribed by the laws and actions of the state. This external censorship is the most consonant with traditional notions of political repression. In addition, however, both public and private expressions may be constrained by interpersonal norms, by pressures toward conformity, and sanctions for deviance. Local networks of friends, family, and associates may impose substantial restrictions on a citizen's freedom. To the extent that the political culture to which the individual is exposed does not reinforce political diversity and respect nonconformity, individuals with unpopular views may perceive significant repercussions for expressing their opinions. Personal political freedom is minimal when perceptions of repercussions from expressing one's views are maximal. Thus, in measuring personal political freedom, we must be sensitive to constraints emanating from the larger political system, as well as from the personal network of the individual.[7]

This approach to personal political freedom makes it amenable to consideration through survey research. In order to assess the levels of freedom in the United States, I conducted a national survey in the summer of 1987. In addition to a typical national sample of white Americans, a special "oversample" of African Americans was selected. Thus, the survey allows an unusual opportunity to explore racial differences in perceptions of freedom and liberty. The data and analysis that follow are drawn from that survey.

Personal Political Freedom in the United States

Perhaps the easiest of these dimensions to measure is perceptions of what sort of political activity the government will permit. Table 5.1 reports responses to a question asking whether the government would allow the respondent to engage in certain types of political activities. The responses were collected through a four-point response set, although table 5.1 reports percentages based on collapsing the categories "probably not allow" and "definitely not allow."[8]

Table 5.1 reveals that significant numbers of Americans perceive that the government would *not* allow them to express their opposition to government policy through conventional and unconventional political activity. Racial differences on these items are dramatic: blacks are much

7. I recognize that irrespective of the freedom allowed by the larger political system or local networks, individuals may by unwilling to express themselves politically for completely psychological reasons. For instance, lack of self-confidence may lead people to be unwilling to risk the opprobrium of others (Bay [1970] terms this psychological freedom). Although the effect of psychological attributes may be interactive (in the sense that personality attributes structure perceptions of and reactions to external environmental stimuli), the effect may exist completely apart from the objective attributes of the environment.

This sort of psychological freedom is not addressed in this research. Instead, the psychological attributes of individuals are treated as independent variables, as predictors of social and political freedom. Thus, rather than assert that psychologically based risk aversion is a sign of unfreedom, I prefer to test the hypothesis that those who perceive less freedom are more risk-averse and psychologically insecure.

8. Those who "don't know" whether the government would allow them to engage in the activity might legitimately be included with those believing that they would not be allowed to do these actions. Since the numbers of subjects who "don't know" are quite small—ranging from twelve to twenty-six respondents—I have simply excluded them from the calculations of the percentages.

Table 5.1 Views of Governmental Constraints on Political Opposition, Black and White Mass Publics, 1987

	Blacks %	Whites %
Those believing that the government would *not* allow them to		
Organize a nationwide strike of all workers	85.9	79.0
Organize public meetings	63.7	39.5[a]
Organize protest marches and demonstrations	54.5	35.3[a]
Make a speech criticizing the actions of the government	55.6	29.6[a]
Publish pamphlets	53.0	28.1[a]

NOTE: The question stem read, "Suppose you felt very strongly that something the government was doing was very wrong and you wanted to do something about it. Do you think the government would definitely allow, probably allow, probably not allow, or definitely not allow you to . . ." The weighted number of black respondents ranges from 181 to 184; for whites, the range is from 962 to 974.

[a]Racial difference is significant at .01 or less.

more likely to perceive constraints on their freedom than are whites. Perhaps most surprising are the substantial numbers of both blacks and whites who feel that the government would not allow them quite conventional means of political participation. From roughly one-quarter to two-fifths of white Americans believe that the government would prohibit them from expressing their opposition through conventional speech-and-assembly activities. For blacks, the percentages range from 53 to 64. And although it is perhaps a bit fanciful for ordinary people to imagine organizing a nationwide strike, four in five black and white Americans believe that the government would prohibit such efforts. The level of perceived *governmental* constraints on political opposition is remarkably high.

Perceptions of governmental limitations on political freedom represent an external form of censorship. Internal censorship, or self-censorship, can be measured by asking whether individuals are willing to express themselves politically when their views are unpopular with the majority. Consequently, I attempted to measure the beliefs Americans hold that might justify self-censorship. The respondents were given the opportunity to accept or reject a variety of statements that might explain reluctance to talk about politics with their families and friends. Each of these statements represents the belief that there are significant personal costs to be paid for expressing one's views. Table 5.2 reports their responses to these statements.

Many of these responses reflect strong reservations about political expression. Politics is perceived as sometimes leading to arguments (58 percent of blacks, 47 percent of whites) and as creating enemies (42 percent of blacks, 37 percent of whites). There is also a substantial minority of respondents that is worried about nonconformity. Generally, many seem to believe that political discussions can be associated with unwelcomed repercussions from their friends and family.

The racial differences observed in perceptions of the governmental constraints on political action are not as stark here, but nor are they trivial. Blacks are significantly more likely to fear expressing their views, because people would think them strange, are more fearful of repercussions from the government, and are more self-censored by a distaste for political argument. Special note should be taken of the nearly 13 percent of the black sample that is reluctant to talk about politics due to a worry "that the government might find out about me." This is an astounding level of concern among African Americans and represents a very serious perceived threat to personal political freedom.

I also asked the respondents whether they would be willing to engage in certain sorts of activities to express views that they knew would be unpopular with others. These items represent a form of behavioral self-censorship. Table 5.3 reports the results from these questions.

A substantial number of Americans are reluctant to express unpopular political views. The figures range from roughly three-fourths who are unwilling to place a sign in front of their home or apartment to announce

Table 5.2 Reluctance to Talk About Politics, Black and White Mass Publics, 1987

	Percentage Agreeing	
	Blacks	Whites
I don't like arguments	58.3	46.5[a]
It creates enemies	42.3	37.3
People would think my political views were strange	28.7	18.7[a]
I worry about what people would think of me	18.2	12.5
I worry that the government might find out about me	12.5	2.4[a]

NOTE: The stem of each of the items is "I am sometimes reluctant to talk about politics because . . ." Responses were recorded as "true" or "false." The weighted number of black respondents ranges from 183 to 186; for whites, the range is from 974 to 983.

[a]Racial difference is significant at .01 or less.

Table 5.3 Self-Censorship: Political Behavior, Black and White Mass Publics, 1987

	Blacks %	Whites %
Those unwilling to		
Write a letter to one of your elected representatives	37.1	30.3
Sign a petition that would be published in the local newspaper with your name on it	51.4	39.1[a]
Wear a button to work or in public	51.4	55.8
Participate in a demonstration	55.7	61.8
Put a bumper sticker on your car	59.5	68.8
Put a sign in front of your home or apartment	71.0	77.2

NOTE: The question read, "Let's say you did have a political view that you knew would be very unpopular with others. Would you be willing to . . ." The percentages reported exclude those who would not do the activity under any circumstances, regardless of the popularity or unpopularity of the view. The weighted number of black respondents ranges from 175 to 183; for whites, the range is from 930 to 962.

[a]Racial difference is significant at .01 or less.

an unpopular view, to one-third who would not write a letter to one of their elected representatives.[9] It is not particularly surprising that large majorities would be unwilling to announce an unpopular view with a bumper sticker or a yard sign—to advocate such a view in this way makes one's property vulnerable to those who find the position offensive. But a majority of Americans are also unwilling to express an unpopular opinion through less risky activities such as wearing a button or participating in a demonstration. Only one-sixth of the respondents would engage in all six of the activities; fully 28 percent claim that they would do *none* of the activities. In general, the greater the direct personal accountability for the view, the less likely the respondents are to want to engage in the activity (although it should be reemphasized that nearly one-third of the respondents would be unwilling to write a letter to one of their elected representatives to express an unpopular view).

Racial differences in behavioral self-censorship are less pronounced than on the other sets of items. Blacks are significantly less likely than whites to be willing to sign a petition that would be published in the

9. Note that these figures exclude those who would not engage in the activity under any circumstances, regardless of the popularity or unpopularity of the view. For most of the actions this number is inconsequential; however, forty-four subjects claim they would not put a bumper sticker on their car under any circumstances, and twenty-nine would not wear a political button under any circumstances.

local newspapers, but none of the other differences is statistically significant. For some activities, whites are substantially (but not significantly) *less* likely to be willing to express themselves. For instance, nearly 10 percent more whites claim to be unwilling to put a bumper sticker on their cars. The differences in these frequencies suggest that the sources of self-censorship may be different for whites and for blacks.

Indexes of Political Freedom

In order to examine the causes and consequences of perceived political freedom it is useful to construct some indexes of political freedom. The advantage of using indexes is that the findings are not dependent upon responses to particular questions that may be idiosyncratic. I employ factor analysis to construct the measures. The advantage of using factor scores is that the items are weighted unequally, according to their correlation with the factor. This is preferable to assuming equal weights, as would be the case in forming a simple summated scale. Since all of the factor analysis results support the assumption of the unidimensionality of the measures, scores from the first unrotated factors serve as the specific indexes.

The first component of freedom is the perception that the government would allow political activity. An index was constructed by taking the mean of the responses shown in table 5.1, above. This index is quite reliable (alpha = .88) and can serve as a measure of perceived external governmental censorship of political behavior.[10] As expected, racial differences on this index were extremely significant, with blacks perceiving substantially more political repression.

A second major component of perceived political freedom concerns the beliefs held about the opportunities to express oneself politically. The items in table 5.2, above, represent such beliefs. An index of perceived social censorship of political expression was derived from the items shown in the table. This index is quite reliable, with an alpha of .70.[11] On this index, blacks are significantly more fearful of political expression than are whites.

10. The first unrotated factor from the common-factor analysis had an eigenvalue of 3.4 and accounts for 68 percent of the variance in the items. The second factor that emerged from the analysis had an eigenvalue of .72 (explaining just 14 percent of the variance) and was therefore ignored.

11. The first unrotated factor had an eigenvalue of 2.3 and explained 46 percent of the

An index of behavioral self-censorship can be constructed from the items shown in table 5.3, above. The reliability of this index is also quite high (alpha = .86), and all of the items contribute roughly equally to the scale.[12] Racial differences on this index are *not* significant.

Since I am interested in whether the subjects would be willing to engage in open expressions—verbal or behavioral—of unpopular political views, a summary measure of self-censorship was constructed from these last two factor scores. Thus, the two measures of perceived political freedom that are used in this chapter are perceptions of governmental censorship and self-censorship (verbal and behavioral). These two variables are moderately correlated (among blacks, r = .31; among whites, r = .38)—those who perceive greater governmental censorship are more likely to report an unwillingness to express themselves politically.

Validity

It is instructive to compare these indexes to the measure of perceived political freedom developed by Samuel Stouffer as part of his trailblazing study of political intolerance. After probing respondents on their perceptions of the political freedom of others, Stouffer asked, "What about you personally? Do you or don't you feel as free to speak your mind as you used to?" He discovered that 13 percent of ordinary Americans felt less free to speak their minds in 1954 (Stouffer 1955, 80).[13] This question was repeated on the 1987 survey. In 1987, 21 percent claimed to feel less free to speak their minds than they used to. Perhaps more important than the simple frequencies are the intercorrelations of this item with the indexes of perceived political freedom that I have developed from the 1987 survey. Are they measuring the same thing that Stouffer was?

There are highly significant differences in perceptions of government censorship between those who claim to feel free to express themselves and those who do not, just as there are highly significant differences in self-censorship. Those who claim to be free generally perceive less repression and are less likely to engage in self-censorship. This is true

variance in the items. The second factor, which was not used, had an eigenvalue of .93 (accounting for 18.5 percent of the variance).

12. The first unrotated factor had an eigenvalue of 3.6 and explained 59.4 percent of the variance in the items. The second factor, which was not used, had an eigenvalue of .84 (accounting for 14.0 percent of the variance).

13. By 1973, this figure had climbed to 20 percent (Nunn et al. 1978, 33).

for both blacks and whites. Although the correlations are not overly strong, these findings do serve at least to some degree as a testament to the validity of the measures. Consequently, the two summary indexes of perceived personal political freedom will be used in the remainder of this analysis.

Test-Retest Reliability

One of the means by which the reliability of measures can be assessed is through test-retest correlations. That is, subjects are asked to respond to identical measures at two points in time. To the extent that the responses are similar, the measures are said to be reliable (on reliability and validity generally, see Carmines and Zeller 1979).[14]

The white respondents who completed the summer reinterview were asked to complete a short questionnaire during the winter of 1987. Only the white respondents were selected due to resource constraints. This third-wave of the panel was conducted wholly by mail, with a response rate of approximately 70 percent. Several measures of perceptions of freedom were included on the third-wave instrument, so some indication of the degree of test-retest reliability of the freedom measures can be gleaned.

The measures of perceived governmental constraints on freedom are reasonably reliable. The reliability coefficients for the individual items range from .50 to .57. The correlation between the mean responses to the items at both times is .62. Thus, I am entitled to conclude that the measures are fairly reliable.

Some of the measures of perceived social censorship of political expression were also included on the winter questionnaire. The reliability coefficients for these items range from .28 to .46. The correlation of the mean responses to the items is .56, which also indicates reasonable

14. There are several limitations to thinking of reliability in this fashion. Most important, all change between administrations of the test is assumed to be due to the unreliability of the measures. That is, it is assumed that there is no *true* change. Thus, the reliability coefficient *underestimates* reliability to the extent that there is actual opinion change within the sample. Of course, to the extent that respondents remember their initial answers and try to duplicate them at the second interview, reliability is overestimated. Since roughly five months separated the interview and the questionnaire, I assume that the bias due to remembering the earlier response is negligible.

reliability. Thus, these measures of perceived political freedom appear to be both valid and reliable.

Summary

According to the results presented above, political freedom is not widely perceived in the United States. Levels of perceived governmental constraints on freedom and of self-censorship are surprisingly high. Moreover, perceived freedom seems to be allocated unevenly across racial groups. African Americans perceive themselves as having less liberty, like nearly everything of value in American society. It remains to consider whether variation *within races* can be accounted for.

The Origins of Personal Political Freedom

Among the many possible causes of perceptions of personal political freedom, four sorts of variables stand out. Perceived freedom may be a function of social class, levels of political involvement, basic political values, and individual personality attributes. In addition, it is necessary to control for relevant demographic attributes. Because racial differences in perceptions of freedom are so strong, it is essential to conduct the analysis separately on blacks and whites. I will consider each of these factors in turn.

Social class. I hypothesize that political freedom is distributed by social class in the United States and, thus, that there is a relation between perceptions and socioeconomic status. To the extent that one has economic resources, one can be less restricted by the sorts of constraints under consideration here. Those of lower socioeconomic status are more dependent upon the polity and lack the autonomy that is a condition of political freedom. Several measures of socioeconomic status are employed, including level of education, occupational prestige, income, and class self-identification.

Political interest. I also expect that those who are more knowledgeable about politics are more likely to perceive political freedom. This may be due to social learning that occurs as citizens are socialized to norms that favor political freedom. Thus, I hypothesize that those who are more interested in politics, more knowledgeable, who serve as opinion leaders, and who have a greater sense of political efficacy will perceive greater political freedom.

Basic political values. The political beliefs individuals hold may be of some consequence for their perceptions of freedom. In particular, individuals who tend to value liberty more than they value order are more likely to perceive freedom. To the extent that order is valued over liberty, individuals may be unwilling to risk the disruptions caused by political conflict. They may also perceive government efforts to limit dissent as more justified—that is, for some of these people, the question whether the government "would" allow political dissent may be understood as "should" the government allow such activity.

Similarly, those who are politically intolerant are expected to perceive less political freedom. To the extent that individuals are unwilling to allow others to express their political views, they may find it more acceptable to be denied liberty themselves. Similarly, those who are more supportive of the norms of democracy (cf. Sullivan et al. 1982) are expected to perceive more freedom.

Finally, there may be a relation between ideology and perceptions of freedom, with liberals perceiving less political freedom.

Personality attributes. It is possible that perceptions of freedom reflect the internal psychological makeup of the individual as much as external political reality. To test this general hypothesis, two personality attributes were measured. The first attribute is "closed-mindedness," or dogmatism. Those who are more closed-minded are more likely to perceive greater political repression and exercise self-censorship, due to the tendency to perceive the world in the dichotomous terms of "good versus evil." The tendency to characterize one's political opponents as evil makes them more dangerous and hence more threatening to a sense of personal political freedom.

Similarly, I hypothesize a relation between perceptions of freedom and self-esteem: those with a lower sense of personal unworthiness are more likely to perceive political repression and exercise self-censorship, due to their psychological aversion to risky behavior. Expressions of political views create the possibility of disagreement with and rejection by others that is more disruptive to those low in self-esteem.

Background attributes. The two most relevant additional background attributes are gender and age. I hypothesize that women and older citizens perceive less political freedom, due to their more marginal position within American politics.

Results

Table 5.4 reports the bivariate correlations necessary to assess these various hypotheses for the whites in the sample, as well as correlations between perceptions of freedom and the demographic attributes. Gen-

Table 5.4 The Origins of Perceptions of Personal Political Freedom, White Mass Public, 1987

	Government Constraints on Political Opposition		Self-Censorship	
	r	Beta	*r*	Beta
Social class				
Level of education	−.45	−.15[a]	−.25	.05
Occupational prestige	−.34	−.07	−.19	−.04
Income	−.26	.02	−.20	−.02
Class self-identification	−.12	.05	−.04	.05
Political involvement				
Interest in politics	−.25	−.06	−.22	−.14[a]
Political knowledge	−.13	−.03	−.05	.01
Opinion leadership	−.21	−.02	−.21	−.06
Political efficacy	−.27	−.03	−.20	−.02
Ideology				
Commitment to social order	.56	.29[a]	.36	.17[a]
Support for the norms of democracy	−.40	.02	−.25	.01
Political tolerance	−.49	−.12[a]	−.28	−.02
Self-identification	.07	−.02	.07	−.00
Personality				
Dogmatism	.48	.12[a]	.36	.13[a]
Self-esteem	−.29	−.09[a]	−.29	−.14[a]
Gender	.17	.10[a]	.06	.00
Age	.16	−.02	.24	.15[a]
R^2	.41		.23	

[a]Standardized regression coefficient is significant at .01 or lower.

erally speaking, nearly all of the hypotheses are supported by the bivariate results, although the correlations are stronger for perceptions of government censorship than for self-censorship. Those perceiving greater governmental and cultural repression are more strongly committed to liberty, are more tolerant, and more supportive of the norms of democracy. They are also more politically involved and are of higher socioeconomic status. In terms of personality attributes, greater dogmatism and lower self-esteem are associated with perceptions of more censorship. Finally, women perceive greater governmental constraints but do not necessarily censor themselves more than men, while older white Americans perceive less freedom to be available.

Using the variables reported in table 5.4, over 40 percent of the variance in perceptions of repression and nearly 25 percent of the variance in self-censorship can be explained. In both instances, the best predictor (as indicated by the multivariate betas) is the "commitment to social order" index. Those who more strongly value liberty are less likely to perceive repression and are less likely to engage in self-censorship. Turning the correlation around, those who value liberty less strongly than order are less likely to perceive personal political freedom. This may reflect a projection of the individual's values onto society more generally, or a selective perception process. Those who value liberty less perceive greater limits on their own freedom.

This finding raises an intriguing possibility: *perhaps those who do not perceive freedom for themselves accept their situation because they view social liberty as too disruptive.* Indeed, perhaps they are not even bothered by their lack of freedom. Just as they are willing to deny liberty to their political opponents (e.g., the correlation with political tolerance), they do not find it unreasonable that the government would deny them liberty or that they would have to engage in self-censorship. The original, implicit premise of the survey was that respondents who believe that the government would not let them express themselves would find that objectionable. Maybe that assumption was incorrect. It seems that some segment of the white mass public not only does not perceive freedom but would prefer it that way!

Several other conclusions can be drawn from the multivariate analysis. First, perceptions of political repression are largely concentrated among those who have less formal education, who are more intolerant and more dogmatic, who have lower self-esteem, and among women. Levels of political involvement are unrelated to perceptions of freedom in the multivariate case. This suggests that freedom is most widely perceived among those who interact with the world in a more informed, pragmatic fashion. To the extent that citizens confidently assert freedom, it seems to be available to them.

Those whites likely to engage in self-censorship tend to be older, are less interested in politics, have lower self-esteem, and are more dogmatic (in addition to being more strongly committed to social order). These are most likely people who have almost completely withdrawn from politics. It should also be noted that there is little relation to socioeconomic status: self-censorship seems to be as common among high-status whites as among low-status whites.

The findings for African Americans are weaker than the findings for whites but are generally similar (see table 5.5). Blacks more strongly committed to liberty tend to perceive fewer governmental constraints on politics and tend to engage in less self-censorship. Levels of political involvement are unrelated to perceptions of governmental censorship and only weakly related to self-censorship. Tolerance has little impact on perceived freedom, although black liberals tend to perceive more governmental constraints on politics. The influence of personality attributes is similar, and, as with whites, little relation between perceived freedom and social class exists. Perhaps the most important differences observed across races are the considerably stronger effect of age on self-censorship among blacks (older blacks tending to engage in considerably more self-censorship), and the greater effect of levels of education on perceptions of governmental constraints among whites.

Generally, this analysis reveals that basic political values structure views of political freedom among both blacks and whites (cf. Hurwitz and Peffley 1987). Perhaps the most important implication of these findings is that many Americans seem to be quite willing to accept significant constraints on their own political freedom. Social scientists have long known that substantial numbers of Americans would limit the freedom of dissident groups—these findings suggest that they would also limit *their own* freedom. In a sense, they are applying their intolerance in a uniform and consistent way—they would not even tolerate themselves![15]

15. These findings also have implications for the study of political tolerance. Sullivan et al. (1982) have argued that political tolerance becomes relevant *only* in the context of disapproval and have focused on disapproved groups. Perhaps that is reasonable. But these data suggest that there is an unwillingness to support some civil liberties that extends across all groups that

Table 5.5 The Origins of Perceptions of Personal Political Freedom, Black Mass Public, 1987

	Government Constraints on Political Opposition		Self-Censorship	
	r	Beta	*r*	Beta
Social class				
Level of education	−.13	.02	−.28	.03
Occupational prestige	−.14	−.03	−.22	−.07
Income	−.19	−.06	−.20	−.00
Class self-identification	−.01	.00	.01	−.01
Political involvement				
Interest in politics	−.11	−.03	−.22	−.14
Political knowledge	−.10	−.04	−.19	−.12
Opinion leadership	−.05	.08	−.14	−.05
Political efficacy	−.25	−.06	−.17	.01
Ideology				
Commitment to social order	.47	.35[a]	.30	.23[a]
Support for the norms of democracy	−.27	.01	−.15	.03
Political tolerance	−.26	−.00	−.18	.01
Self-identification	.16	.14	.08	.03
Personality				
Dogmatism	.36	.15	.26	.05
Self-esteem	−.22	−.05	−.29	−.16
Gender	.11	.05	−.02	−.10
Age	.08	−.00	.28	.27
R^2	.29		.27	

[a]Standardized regression coefficient is significant at .05 or lower.

Implications for Political Behavior

The above analysis may say something about the origins of perceptions of personal political freedom, but it does not address the more basic question of whether the perceptions predict anything. Does perceived political freedom have any implications for ordinary political participa-

would make a claim on liberty, even groups that are not disliked and threatening. That this has been largely unnoticed in the literature (but see Lawrence 1976 and Gibson and Bingham 1985) is due to the tendency to focus on groups rather than on activities. I suspect that many Americans do not support the right to assemble in the streets no matter who is assembling.

tion? I hypothesize that those who perceive greater political freedom are more likely to engage in political activity. Perhaps a portion of the explanation of the relatively low levels of political participation in the United States is that many Americans perceive significant costs associated with political participation.

A variety of indicators of political activity have been assembled in order to construct an index of political activism. These include (1) the frequency of political discussions, (2) the frequency of voting, (3) the frequency of other sorts of participation in electoral politics, (4) the frequency of interest-group participation, and (5) involvement in local politics. When factor-analyzed, a single strong dimension emerges that explains nearly one-half of the variance in the items (eigenvalue = 2.89).[16] The index of political activism is thus simply the factor scores from the first unrotated factor. The relations between perceived political freedom and political activism are shown in table 5.6.

Among whites, there is a reasonably strong relation between political activism and perceptions of freedom. Those who perceive more constraints on their freedom are significantly less likely to participate actively in politics. The greater effect is from perceptions of governmental constraints on political opposition. To the extent that the government is perceived as not allowing oppositionist activity, the respondents are themselves less likely to participate.

The relations among blacks are quite weak. Just as with whites, there is some tendency for those who engage in more self-censorship to

Table 5.6 The Impact of Perceived Personal Political Freedom on Political Activism, Black and White Mass Publics, 1987

	Perceptions of Government Constraints		Self-Censorship		
	r	Beta	*r*	Beta	R^2
General political activism					
Blacks	−.05	−.01	−.14	−.14	.02
Whites	−.33	−.28[a]	−.22	−.12	.12[a]

[a]Standardized regression coefficient is significant at .05 or lower for blacks; .01 or lower for whites.

16. Because no additional significant factor emerged (the eigenvalue of the second factor is .90), no rotation was necessary.

participate less, but the tendency is not at all strong. Surprisingly, there is no relation at all between perceptions of governmental constraints and activism. Perhaps this is because levels of participation among blacks are low in the first place. Consequently, perceptions of freedom, which are also low, do not allow blacks to overcome the hurdles to participation. Such perceptions are not as important among blacks because blacks lack the other resources necessary for effective participation in the first place. Because whites are more likely to have the initial resources, their perceptions matter more.

This conclusion, however, may be based on spurious relations. As we have seen above, some portion of those who perceive constraints on their political activity are politically unknowledgeable and *unlikely to participate in the first place*. Thus, it is essential that a control for other known antecedents of political participation be included in the analysis.

To simplify the analysis, only two variables are included as controls: level of political efficacy and level of interest in politics. In earlier research each of these has been found to have a substantial impact on political participation. The use of these variables allows for statistical controls that do not so completely determine the dependent variable that perceptions of personal political freedom could not have a statistical impact.

As expected, perceptions of personal political freedom do not add a great deal to the variance explained by efficacy and political interest—the increment in R^2 is relatively small, with interest in politics being by far the strongest predictor of political activism among both blacks and whites. Nonetheless, within the white sample, perceptions of governmental constraints on freedom have a statistically significant impact on activism: those who perceive greater governmental constraints are less likely to participate, even controlling for levels of efficacy and political interest (beta = −.17). There is little effect of the self-censorship measure. Thus, there is some evidence among whites that perceptions of freedom influence levels of political participation.

Among blacks, no such relation exists. Only interest in politics is significantly related to levels of participation. Those who perceive more freedom available do not participate at any higher levels than those who perceive less freedom. This is most likely due to other structural impediments to black political participation.

From this chapter's preliminary inquiry into the perceptions of personal political freedom held by Americans, several significant findings emerge. First, Americans perceive significant and substantial constraints on their political expression. These constraints emanate from the political system and from the political culture. The intolerance that is so widespread in American political culture seems not to have gone unnoticed. Whatever the reality of objective political freedom, subjective political freedom in the United States knows real limits.

Second, substantial racial differences exist in perceptions of freedom. Just as in so many areas of American life, African Americans share much less in the freedom enjoyed by the white majority. Some of these differences are very substantial indeed.

At the same time, the views of blacks are less predictable than the views of whites. For instance, while level of education is a good predictor of white perceptions, blacks with different levels of education do not differ in their views of freedom. Perhaps there is a certain degree of commonalty in the experiences of African Americans that reduces the ability of these other variables to discriminate between those who feel more free and those who feel less free.

Third, these perceptions are rooted in part in the values and personality attributes of Americans. Tolerance for sociopolitical disorder as a price of liberty is strongly related to perceptions of freedom. Those valuing liberty more are more likely to perceive freedom. Perhaps one of the most surprising findings is that those who are intolerant of others also perceive greater political repression and exercise more self-censorship. It is a mistake, apparently, to assume that everyone values freedom highly, that everyone seeks broad opportunities for political expression. Many seem not to want such opportunities, either for themselves or for others.

Finally, though the independent impact is not great, the amount of freedom available has some impact on levels of political participation among whites. Those who perceive greater freedom are more likely to exercise it. Those who rarely participate have neither the resources (e.g., information) nor the perceptions of opportunities to do so. Perhaps the perceptions are to some degree a rationalization of a general lack of interest in politics.

This research cannot address the question whether perceptions of lack of freedom are grounded in the reality of American politics and culture. There are snippets of evidence that suggest a connection to reality—

blacks feel less free than whites, and older black Americans perceive much less freedom than younger black Americans—but it is impossible to know whether subjective freedom is closely connected to objective freedom.

This is particularly troublesome when we consider the implications of freedom perceptions for political activity. Have some Americans sought political expression and been rebuffed, or have perceptions that freedom is too costly preempted efforts to participate in politics? Have people learned from their environment not to risk political expression, or have they simply never tested their families, friends, coworkers, and their government and thus never learned the true extent to which freedom is actually available? These are important questions that, unfortunately, cannot be addressed with the data at hand.

What implications do these findings have for our understanding of American democracy? First, this analysis suggests the utility of distinguishing between cultural democracy and institutional democracy. What people think about their liberty may diverge substantially from formal structures and institutions. Second, the United States ought to be seen as a country in need of further cultural democratization. Not only are black Americans less fully enfranchised by the culture than white Americans, but many whites as well do not perceive liberty. Finally, we have seen just how important basic values are to the development and maintenance of democracy. Without citizens who are predisposed to risk a bit of social disorder for the sake of liberty, democracy cannot flourish.

References

Acock, Alan, Harold D. Clarke, and Marianne C. Stewart. 1985. "A New Model for Old Measures: A Covariance Structure Analysis of Political Efficacy." *Journal of Politics* 47:1062–84.

Bay, Christian. 1970. *The Structure of Freedom*. Stanford: Stanford University Press.

Berlin, Isaiah. 1958. *Two Concepts of Liberty*. London: Oxford University Press.

Carmines, Edward G., and Richard A. Zeller. 1979. *Reliability and Validity Assessment*. Beverly Hills, Calif.: Sage Publications.

Dahl, Robert A. 1971. *Polyarchy: Participation and Opposition*. New Haven: Yale University Press.

Gibson, James L., and Richard D. Bingham. 1985. *Civil Liberties and Nazis: The Skokie Free-Speech Controversy*. New York: Praeger.

Hurwitz, Jon, and Mark Peffley. 1987. "How Are Foreign Policy Attitudes Structured? A Hierarchical Model." *American Political Science Review* 81:1099–1120.

MacCallum, Gerald C., Jr. 1967. "Negative and Positive Freedom." *The Philosophical Review* 76:312–34.

McClosky, Herbert, and Alida Brill. 1983. *Dimensions of Tolerance: What Americans Believe About Civil Liberties*. New York: Russell Sage Foundation.

Nunn, Clyde Z., Harry J. Crockett, Jr., and J. Allen Williams, Jr. 1978. *Tolerance for Nonconformity*. San Francisco: Jossey-Bass.

Pennock, J. Roland. 1979. *Democratic Political Theory*. Princeton: Princeton University Press.

Perry, Ralph Barton. 1944. *Puritanism and Democracy*. New York: Vanguard Press.

Preston, Larry M. 1982. "Individual and Political Freedom." *Polity* 15:72–89.

Rokeach, Milton. 1960. *The Open and Closed Mind*. New York: Basic Books.

Sniderman, Paul M. 1975. *Personality and Democratic Politics*. Berkeley and Los Angeles: University of California Press.

Southwell, Priscilla L. 1985. "Alienation and Nonvoting in the United States: A Refined Operationalization." *Western Political Quarterly* 38:663–75.

Stouffer, Samuel C. 1955. *Communism, Conformity, and Civil Liberties*. New York: Doubleday.

Sullivan, John L., James Piereson, and George E. Marcus. 1982. *Political Tolerance and American Democracy*. Chicago: University of Chicago Press.

6

Freedom in American Democracy: A Commentary on Gibson's "Political Freedom"

John P. Burke

Where there is no law, there is no freedom.
—John Locke

Political freedom is central to the project of liberal democratic politics. Although democracies serve a number of different individual and collective purposes—providing for the common welfare, establishing fair processes of political participation and deliberation, and regulating social and economic institutions and relations, to name but a few—it is the protection and enhancement of individual liberty that stands at democracy's core. Democratic government, as even its most vocal adherents must admit, surely sometimes fails to achieve its goals. But the gap between ideals and reality notwithstanding, these ends are central to the concept and logic of democracy, liberty most particularly.

James Gibson invites us to consider the place of political freedom as an "attribute of individuals," that is, to consider the beliefs individuals have about their political freedom and the relation of these beliefs to forms of political behavior that are generally characteristic of democratic politics. He thus raises an important—and neglected—empirical question, as he notes, about "the meaning, causes, and consequences of personal political freedom" in ostensibly democratic systems.

Taken at face value, Gibson's findings should be unsettling to defenders of American democracy: substantial numbers of black and white Americans perceive various kinds of constraint on the exercise of their liberty, and black citizens are more likely to feel such constraints than are white citizens. And, as Gibson notes in his conclusion, the implications of his study suggest a need for "further cultural democratization" and the need to risk a "bit of social disorder" so that democracy can flourish.

In the interests of argument, let me suggest a rather different interpretation: although not matching the ideals of political freedom that some democratic theorists might embrace, the kinds and degrees of perceptions about political freedom in Gibson's findings may be both less descriptively apparent than he sets out and less normatively problematic than he concludes.[1]

A Lack of Political Freedom?

Consider the question whether Gibson's findings do in fact suggest significant perceptions of constraint on political freedom. First, we do not know whether, *generally speaking*, individuals feel that they are politically free or unfree. Although it is *likely* that individuals who feel that government might restrain certain activities or who feel pressure from family, friends, or self against engaging in certain political activities believe they are not free in some significant way, it is also plausible that individuals may still perceive a significant degree of political freedom even though they are *sometimes* reluctant to talk about politics—for a variety of reasons—or though they feel that government might repress certain forms of political behavior, especially if those are rather unlikely,

1. Gibson's study also raises a number of important methodological issues that space considerations will not permit me to consider fully.

if not extreme, forms of behavior, such as organizing nationwide strikes or protest marches and demonstrations.

Second, are the numbers all that bad? All of the activities that Gibson lists in table 5.1 fall within the range of activities that are currently permitted in American politics. Gibson is correct to assert that the perception of governmental restraint seems considerable for both white and, especially, black respondents. But is the degree of political repression really all that high? Among white respondents, over 60 percent on two measures and over 70 percent on two other measures believe that government *would* allow them to engage in the activity, which could be taken to suggest a considerable degree of perceived freedom among white citizens.[2] (Similar conclusions can be drawn from the items in tables 5.2 and 5.3).[3]

On the fifth activity, organizing a nationwide strike of all workers, almost 80 percent of white respondents feel that the government would not allow them to undertake such activity. But a *nationwide* strike of *all* workers is a rather extreme expression of individual liberty. Furthermore, a strike is a more indirect measure of *political* liberty: an exercise of economic power, albeit one that is usually politically protected.

Third, can we be sure that Gibson's respondents are really telling us something about their perceptions of political freedom in the way the study would like them to? This is a problem inherent in survey research, but especially tricky in this instance, since important distinctions among the three types of repression rest, in part, on the stems used in the wording of the questions—motivational antecedents ("Suppose you felt very strongly. . . . Do you think the government . . ."; "Let's say you had unpopular views, would you . . .") that link certain forms of behavior to certain hypothetical situations involving repression of freedom. Thus, the items in table 5.3, for example, may not necessarily be tapping some sense of social constraint—based on information provided in the stem—but negative feelings about the activity: one might be unwilling to write a letter to an elected representative because one felt it

2. It should also be noted that Gibson's data on the negative responses to the question collapse the responses "probably not allow" and "definitely not allow" into one number. Depending upon what respondents mean by "probably" and the size of this group (which Gibson does not report), the negative response may, arguably, overstate the number of people who perceive a lack of political freedom.

3. The lower positive response on the part of the black respondents remains more problematic.

was an activity that had no political effect, save for added work for legislative staffers. One might not wear a political button to work, not because one was somehow afraid (for fear of repression) to do so, but because one deemed it inappropriate in such a setting. One might not put a sign in front of one's home or a bumper sticker on a new car for purely aesthetic reasons. Each of these rationales for failing to participate, to the extent they are present, may not necessarily involve a sense of repression and, therefore, may not be meaningful reflections about perceptions of freedom or its absence.[4] It all depends on which parts of the stem the respondent is focusing on.

Perceiving Political Freedom

Let us move beyond the largely empirical parameters of Gibson's project and consider its normative implications. The *perception* of freedom as a test of democracy raises some interesting issues in this regard. It seems entirely plausible, for example, that individuals who perceive some constraints on their freedom may in fact enjoy more actual freedom than those who perceive less constraint. To use an analogy, the connoisseur of expensive wines is able subjectively to differentiate two expensive *grands crus* and to perceive, let us suppose, one wine as less in quality compared to the other. But is the less favored wine a bad bottle? It would all depend, I suppose, on one's own standards and pocketbook. To push the example further, let us suppose that one's dissolute colleague is perfectly satisfied with a cheap bottle of sweet muscatel. Would one

4. Similar difficulties are present in table 5.2, which apparently is designed to measure the social constraint coming from friends, neighbors, and associates. Reluctance to talk about politics because others around one hold the same views or because they do not care about politics, for example, might be rational calculations of the utility of such activities rather than examples of repression. Later on in his analysis, Gibson combines tables 5.2 and 5.3 for a summary measure of self-censorship. The problem here is that the two tables do not seem to represent two measures of the same conceptual distinction, which might be profitably combined into a summary measure. Table 5.3 seems to measure—if it does even measure—reluctance to engage in certain forms of political behavior, while table 5.2 offers a range of reasons—political, social, and personal—for not engaging in a particular form of political behavior: talking about politics. The combination thus joins in an odd way what may be, in table 5.3, a measure of behaviors with a single motivational antecedent with, in table 5.2, a single behavior (reluctance to talk about politics) and a range of motivational antecedents.

conclude that the "bad" bottle of *grand cru* is still to be disvalued, compared to the other two? Would one even say that the good bottle is equal to the cheap muscatel? I know which two I would pick, but reliance on perception of quality seems to suggest a different answer. So too, perhaps, with freedom.

The Place of Liberty in Democracy

Underlying any normative assessment of Gibson's findings must be a question whether constraint on liberty is symptomatic of problems in a democracy or whether, in fact, constraint may be necessary to democratic politics, reflecting a necessary balancing of liberty with other political values, such as political order or equality. The sheer presence of the perception of constraint is not necessarily a meaningful test of freedom's place in democratic practice. All democratic theorists are willing to consider some compromises of individual liberty, in varying degrees and types, to further other political goals and values. Kant argues that individuals do not have valid claims for disobeying political authorities even when the latter violate the ideals of moral and political right. Rousseau unambiguously expects conformity to the general will at the explicit expense of the individual will. Mill's tolerance of the liberty of those he disapproves still can justify severe restrictions upon their exercise of it. Tocqueville is sensitive to Americans' passion for equality as well as their love of liberty, and he celebrates self-interest, but "properly understood." For Rawls, the equality called for by the difference principle generally leads to some substantial compromises of individual liberty. Indeed in any democratic state governed by some constitutional structure, it is likely—indeed rightfully expected—that liberty at times will be compromised by the power vested in the state or the rights granted to others (hence the notion of *civil* liberties). Even in our own political tradition, the Rehnquist Court notwithstanding, the equalitarian principles of the Fourteenth Amendment have led to substantial restrictions on the exercise of liberty.

In analyzing the place of liberty in democratic theory and practice, care must be taken in how far we are willing, to trade on Dworkin's phrase, to take liberty seriously. Clearly *some* liberty must matter, but the exercise of liberty is by no means the only principle that a democratic (as opposed, say, to a libertarian) polity embraces. A concern for equality, respect for the rights and privileges of others, civility in the expression of one's opinions, fairness in the consideration of the views of others, deference to the rightful exercise of political authority, and a recognition of the need for some measure of political order also have a place in the hierarchy of democratic values. And they ought to have a place in the minds of democratic citizens. Legitimate limits on the exercise of individual liberty, which citizens might feel, may be a vital necessity in democratic politics, rather than a cause for alarm. The question remains, of course, whether Gibson's respondents are in fact balancing liberty against other values that limit liberty and, if so, whether those liberty-limiting values fall within or outside constraints on liberty that are legitimate for liberal democratic polities.

Explaining Perceptions of Freedom

The final step of Gibson's empirical study is an analysis of the "origins" of citizens' perception of political freedom. In table 5.4 Gibson considers sixteen factors in all: four measures of social class (educational level, occupational prestige, income, and class identification), four measures of political involvement (interest in politics, political knowledge, opinion leadership, and political efficacy), four measures of ideology (commitment to social order, support for democratic norms, political tolerance, and self-identification), two measures of personality (dogmatism and self-esteem), and two demographic measures (gender and age).

I will not repeat Gibson's conclusions, but several of his findings deserve particular emphasis. First, the data indicate that his "commitment to social order" variable has strong effect upon the perception of liberty. This suggests that individuals perceive liberty in trade-off with other values. This is an important empirical finding. From a normative perspective, it may indicate that the perception of some constraint on freedom may not necessarily be unhealthy for democracy; as noted above, most democratic theorists of varying stripe are willing to compromise liberty with other political goals. Moreover, democratic citizens are not only willing to compromise the liberty of others, they are also willing to limit their own liberty in furtherance of other political ideals they value—another limit on liberty, now self-imposed, that may be vital for a viable democracy.[5]

If individuals see liberty in tension with other political values, an interesting question is raised about what precisely those other values are. What, for example, are the particular aspects of the broader concept of social order that individuals value? Are there any other political values, besides social order, that individuals balance against liberty? Answers to these questions will enhance our empirical understanding of citizens' conceptions of liberty, and they are critical in determining the normative import of these findings. Gibson is to be credited for setting an important research agenda for the future.

Gibson also considers the important issue whether perceptions of political freedom affect political participation, in effect asking the critical question about the relation between subjective freedom and the objective exercise of that freedom as political participation. Gibson indicates that, controlling for political efficacy and interest in politics, self-censorship does not have a statistically significant impact on participation and that the perception of governmental repression has only some (beta = −.17) impact. These links between perceptions of political freedom and the exercise of that political freedom are surprisingly weak. They suggest that other factors, such as political efficacy and interest in politics (and those factors that in turn affect them) may have more to do with the practice of freedom in democratic politics than perceptions of freedom. Even if Americans, both black and white, perceive significant governmental constraints on freedom and are willing to censor themselves in response to their social and cultural environment, these perceptions about the limits of freedom do not *strongly* affect political participation. This raises an interesting puzzle: perception of the lack of freedom is only weakly related to the most central exercise of freedom in democratic politics, political participation.

Finally, the differences between black and white respondents are an especially important part of Gibson's study. Gibson explores these differences in his chapter, but it is striking to note that (1) the self-identification measure in tables 5.4 and 5.5 differs among the two groups

5. I thus interpret this finding a bit differently from Gibson: it is not that citizens are "intolerant" not only of others but also of themselves; rather, it could be that citizens are willing to limit the liberty of others, for good reason, and their own liberty, again for good reason.

(−.02 for whites; +.14 for blacks); (2) the overall R^2 statistics are somewhat higher for blacks on self-censorship (.27 versus .23 for whites) but lower for blacks on governmental constraint (.29 versus .41 for whites); and, especially, (3) correlations between political activism and repression (in table 5.6) are negligible (R^2 = .02) for blacks.

Some Final Points

Analysis of the sort Gibson has undertaken undoubtedly enhances our understanding of freedom in the minds of democratic citizens. But there are other questions about the place of freedom in a democracy that also deserve attention.

The static versus dynamic character of our perceptions about freedom calls for analysis. Perceptions of freedom can change in response to changes in the broader political environment. For example, I suspect that responses to the burning of an American flag were quite different in January 1989, before the Supreme Court's controversial decision, than they were in the aftermath of the Court's ruling. What does this shift tell us about the perception of freedom?

How individuals come to perceive their own deprivation of freedom and then aspire to exercise freedom seems especially critical in understanding how free governments and societies are created and sustained. Events in Eastern Europe provide dramatic testimony about how both the subjective perception of freedom and its objective realization can rapidly develop. The 1989 student demonstrations in China are revealing both about the rapid and widespread development of democratic sentiment and about what happens to such sentiment in the face of real governmental repression. The demand for freedom can arise in spontaneous and often unlikely circumstances; analysis of these historically momentous developments may be especially telling about what freedom actually means in a democracy and among people who aspire to such.

Although Locke is right to suggest that we must usually understand freedom within the constraint of law, the project of creating a free and democratic society often involves the quest for freedom against political systems that do not embody democratic forms of politics and even sometimes against democratic systems and their laws when they fail to live up to their own principles. Analysis of freedom in these circumstances may be the most revealing of all.

7

Duty Is a Four-Letter Word: Democratic Citizenship in the Liberal Polity

Pamela Johnston Conover
Stephen T. Leonard
Donald D. Searing

People make the city and not walls or ships without people in them.
—Nicias, addressing the defeated Athenians at Syracuse

As Nicias realized, the polis is its citizens. It stands or falls on the character of its constituent members; it exists in their shared identity, the privilege they believe citizenship bestows, and the responsibilities they think citizenship entails. Of course this construction begs more

We gratefully acknowledge the generous support of the Spencer Foundation for this research and for the larger project of which it is a part. Matthew Burbank and Jenifer MacGillvary provided much-appreciated assistance in gathering the data, and Mary Dietz provided much-appreciated comments and criticisms on an earlier draft.

questions than it answers, for the substantive content of citizenship—how citizens understand themselves, what privileges they claim for themselves, what common commitments they must engage—has been a topic of dispute ever since the Greeks began to reflect on the distinction between membership in the polis and membership in other types of human associations.

In the modern democratic polity, these questions have been no less central to discussions of citizenship. And among contemporary political theorists, the dispute over an adequate conception of democratic citizenship has been dominated by the terms set in the debate between defenders of "liberalism" and liberalism's "communitarian" critics.[1] Interestingly enough, this debate has moved steadily in the direction of attempts to assess the practical implications of assumptions found in liberalism and communitarianism regarding the identity, commitments, privileges, and responsibilities of citizens in modern democracies.

This "historical," or "contextualist," emphasis reflects a broader movement found in much contemporary political theory, one that challenges many alternative understandings of theoretical justification and adjudication (see Kloppenberg 1989). But, for our purposes, its most interesting feature is that it implicitly involves a recognition of the necessary link between normative and empirical claims. This is brought out clearly by John Wallach (1987, 585), who notes that "one of the curiosities of the liberals/communitarians debate is how each side claims that the other fails to understand 'our' shared understandings, which are 'latent' or 'hidden' within us." In this respect, the arguments of liberals and communitarians may be understood as turning on claims about both the desirability of their respective positions and the extent to which these positions are part and parcel of the self-understandings of "ordinary agents" in modern democracies. One question, then, opened by the liberal-communitarian debate is whether liberals and communitarians have adequately interpreted the actual self-understandings of agents in modern democratic polities. And as for the desirability of liberal or communitarian conceptions of citizenship, this question too can now be

1. The "liberal-communitarian debate" was initiated by communitarian critics of liberalism. Among the most influential of these works are Barber 1984, Bellah et al. 1985, MacIntyre 1984, 1988, Sandel 1982, 1984, Sullivan 1986, and Walzer 1976, 1983. Among contemporary defenses of liberalism, some notable arguments are those of Berlin (1969), Dworkin (1977), and Rawls (1971). Work defending liberalism against communitarian critiques may be found in Galston 1989, Gutmann 1985, Herzog 1986, Hirsch 1986, Downing and Thigpen 1986, and Thigpen and Downing 1987. Much of the character of this contemporary dispute was anticipated in the work of Talmon (1952) and Salkever (1974).

understood as turning in part on the ways in which liberal and communitarian self-understandings actually reflect how "ordinary agents" understand themselves.

In this chapter we probe some of the implications of this opening provided by the liberal-communitarian debate with an eye toward rethinking what a coherent and defensible theory of democratic citizenship should look like. For the most part, our organizing theoretical frameworks are drawn from liberal and communitarian arguments. But our respondents also offer conceptualizations that suggest interesting insights into the strengths and weaknesses, the applicability and limitations, of these theoretical frameworks. These results suggest the need for greater sensitivity to the ways in which understandings of "ordinary agents" may provide useful correctives to—and in this instance, more complex and promising (even if only implicit) versions of—conceptions of citizenship adequate to the demands of life in highly complex, pluralist societies such as those found in the United States.

As we see it, our effort does not so much represent a fusing of empirical and normative inquiry (a dichotomy we take to be suspect) as much as it demonstrates the way in which empirical and normative inquiry are mutually constitutive and informing.[2] In this respect, we hope our work embodies the spirit and aim of the conference at which it was presented, a conference we think itself embodies the spirit and aim of an important and long-overdue movement on the part of many scholars in the discipline to bridge the gap between "political theory" and "political science." Most important, however, we also hope that our work represents a contribution to the development of a "democratic political science"—a form of inquiry that is empirically and normatively defensible, taken up with the expressed intent of better enabling us to understand the prospects for and obstacles to the kind of democracy worthy of our collective assent.

Citizenship in the Liberal Democratic Polity: Theoretical Considerations

The "contextualist" turn in recent political theory has radically transformed the disagreements between defenders and critics of liberalism,

2. The issues here are obviously wide-ranging and complex, and certainly beyond the scope of this essay. One of the best treatments of these questions in the vast literature on the philosophy of social inquiry remains Bernstein 1976.

including the terms of the liberal-communitarian debate. Although it has been fashionable for both sides in the debate to criticize apparent "foundationalist" tendencies in the other, increasingly this sort of criticism appears anachronistic because, as many liberals and communitarians themselves seem to suggest, the grounding and defensibility of normative principles derives from those traditions of discourse and practice of which they are the expression. This metatheoretical agreement does not, however, mean that there are no differences between liberals and communitarians. And the conceptions of citizenship that emerge from liberal and communitarian arguments indicate just how fundamental these differences may be.

A composite of liberal conceptions of citizenship might run as follows.[3] Liberalism portrays individuals as autonomous rational agents who seek to pursue their own life plans, their own interests, without interference from other agents. Any society capable of preserving this autonomy must therefore ensure the freedom of its constituent members to follow their chosen life plans—which is, in fact, the central point of Virginia Sapiro's chapter in this volume. Of course, this does not necessarily entail the claim that agents may do whatever they wish, for the exercise of autonomy must also be constrained by respect for the intrinsic worth and autonomy of others. It is in specifying the conditions under which individuals may act to preserve their autonomy and the autonomy of others that a liberal conception of citizenship takes shape.

First, from the assumption of autonomy, liberalism posits the "body politic" as an association in which there "is no meaningful or necessary element of 'common good,' of common or public purpose or public

3. We do not assume that liberalism (and liberal democratic theory) is a monolithic theoretical entity (see John Gray's [1986] useful little book on liberalism). Although we do not wish to minimize the fact that there are important substantive differences between the ways that various liberals might flesh out the implications of citizenship, family resemblances warrant the suggestion that there is a more or less shared set of assumptions undergirding liberal conceptions of citizenship. We would also note that, like liberalism, communitarianism is quite diverse. Communitarian criticisms of liberalism and communitarian conceptions of citizenship reflect this diversity. As with our characterization of liberalism, we do not want to suggest that substantive differences in this literature do not exist, but we also think that a relatively coherent communitarian conception of citizenship may be reconstructed from these arguments without doing excessive violence to the differences involved. Finally, we recognize that liberalism and communitarianism do not exhaust the discourse on citizenship. We focus on these two understandings as a basis for our discussions because, again, they represent the dominant forms in which much of the contemporary discourse on citizenship in political theory is conducted.

interest" (Tussman 1960, 4)—or at least none that extends beyond the preservation of individual autonomy. Liberalism is therefore said to embody a "negative" conception of political freedom. To the extent that liberal citizens share any sense of "common good," it is one defined in negative terms: "not being interfered with by others" (Berlin 1969, 122, 123). This means, second, that as citizens we may claim for ourselves particular privileges—in the idiom of liberalism, "rights"—against interference in our choices from other individuals, society, or government. This does not mean, however, that citizens are therefore freed of responsibilities toward other citizens, for the exercise and maintenance of individual rights requires reciprocity; we must recognize that our own autonomy is contingent on the duty to respect, and preserve as far as possible, the autonomy of others. Thus—and this is a third central precept of a liberal conception of citizenship—the rights of citizens imply a responsibility, or duty, to maintain the rights of others, although this duty demands no action beyond those minimally required for the preservation of individual autonomy.

As for the place of democracy in this understanding of citizenship, many contemporary liberals have argued that democracy must be "liberal" in character. Thomas Spragens, for example, makes this connection clear when he argues that "the ultimate value of liberal democracy lies in its contribution to the flourishing of individual lives" (1986, 42), and John Rawls insists that democracy should be preferred by liberals because it "treats everyone equally as a moral person, . . . [and] does not weight men's share in the benefits and burdens of social cooperation according to their social fortune or luck in the natural lottery" (Rawls 1971, 75).

This is a rather terse, perhaps overly simplified, account of different liberal versions of the substantive content of rights, duties, and the relation between liberalism and democracy. But if the arguments of contemporary communitarian critics of liberalism are taken to heart, there is also something fundamentally askew in liberal conceptions of citizenship. Communitarians see the liberal commitment to the preservation of individual autonomy as a disabling, perhaps even pernicious, foundation for an adequate conception of citizenship.[4] Michael Sandel, for instance, makes the strong claim that we need to move beyond

4. For claims to this effect, see, for example, Barber 1984, Daggar 1981, Portis 1985, Sullivan 1986, and Walzer 1970.

individualism and recognize that "we can know a good in common that we cannot know alone" and that "we cannot justify political arrangements without reference to common purposes and ends, and that we cannot conceive our personhood without reference to our role as citizens, and as participants in a common life" (Sandel 1984, 183, 5).

Implied in this criticism is an alternative understanding of citizenship, one apparently at odds with liberal accounts. Communitarians often seem to argue that it is a mistake—a mistake having highly undesirable practical consequences—to overlook the fact that we are "encumbered"; we must recognize that it is "as members of this family or community or nation or people, as bearers of this history, as sons and daughters of that revolution, as citizens of this republic," that we are "the particular persons we are" (Sandel 1982, 179).

From this it follows that the kinds of commitments we, as citizens, should embrace are those which involve " 'reappropriating tradition'—that is, finding sustenance in tradition and applying it actively and creatively to our present realities" (Bellah et al. 1985, 292). The privileges and responsibilities of citizens follow the logic of this commitment. Rather than see ourselves as individual bearers of "abstract rights," we ought to recognize that "the civic bond is in fact the one bond that orders and governs all others" (Barber 1984, 217). As for our responsibilities or duties as citizens, communitarians call for us to see ourselves as a collective body aiming at a collective good, a call clearly expressed in Benjamin Barber's conception of "a citizenry capable of genuinely public thinking and political judgement and thus able to envision a common future in terms of genuinely common goods" (Barber 1984, 197).

Liberals have been skeptical about communitarianism, which they accuse of advocating a "conservative," even reactionary, defense of standing traditions and practices, the consequences of which can be the repression of the pursuit of individual life plans (Gutmann 1985, 309; Thigpen and Downing 1987, 642). On this view, communitarians are tendering a vision of active citizenship that is a "dangerous and anachronistic ideal" (Hirsch 1986, 441). Amy Gutmann (1985, 319) expresses this objection vividly when she argues that "the common good of the Puritans of seventeenth-century Salem commanded them to hunt witches; the common good of the Moral Majority of the twentieth century commands them not to tolerate homosexuals. The enforcement of liberal rights, not the absence of settled community, stands between the Moral Majority and the contemporary equivalent of witch hunting."

Gutmann's comments bring us directly to the issues central to our essay. For both liberals and communitarians claim that their accounts are not just abstract utopian ideals but reconstructions of the self-understandings of real citizens. This is the source of John Wallach's (1987, 585) observation, cited in our introduction, that "one of the curiosities of the liberals/communitarians debate is how each side claims that the other fails to understand 'our' shared understandings, which are 'latent' or 'hidden' within us." However, as Gutmann's comments seem to suggest, the self-understandings of citizens may not fit easily into either conceptual framework; in short, "liberal" and "communitarian" conceptions of citizenship may be common among the citizenry of modern democratic polities like the United States. To be sure, there is nearly universal agreement that liberalism is the dominant discourse of citizenship in liberal democracies, but it does not follow from its being dominant that it is the only one. Of course, communitarians see the practical implications of their arguments as demanding that communitarian elements be strengthened and liberal beliefs beaten back, whereas liberals draw exactly the opposite conclusions. But neither liberals nor their communitarian critics have offered much in the way of empirical accounts specifying how liberal or communitarian concepts and categories are actually embodied in the self-understandings of ordinary citizens. To the extent that liberals and communitarians seek to transform or strengthen citizens' self-understandings, it would make good sense to move from the level of broad generalizations to a more concrete specification of what these citizens actually think about the privileges and responsibilities of citizenship. It is here that empirical research proves itself an essential feature of any coherent and defensible theory of democratic citizenship.

Framework and Method of Analysis

To understand how citizens think about citizenship, we shall focus on how they think about their privileges and responsibilities in both concrete and abstract terms. To get at this, we have adopted a method that is seldom used in political science: focus groups. Focus-group discussions are carefully planned group conversations that are tape-recorded and, in some cases, videotaped as well (Krueger 1988). Focus groups offer several advantages. Although (like all forms of dialogue) the responses are constrained by the moderator's questions, the discussion format of the focus group encourages people to respond in the language and categories that they typically employ in their own thinking. This tendency is promoted by the exchanges between participants in the focus group: they address one another, rather than simply react to the questions and language of an interviewer in a one-on-one situation. Finally, the focus groups provide an opportunity for group influence (Krueger 1988) and thereby mirror the group or social context within which many people experience citizenship.

We think that the use of focus groups is particularly appropriate to the study of citizenship. They not only offer researchers unusual opportunities for understanding the conceptual schemes of their subjects, including the disjunction and ambivalence that Jennifer Hochschild discusses in Chapter 9, but, perhaps more important, they provide a forum for a discursive exploration of the meaning of citizenship in which citizens can listen, respond to others, and reflect on their own self-understandings. This is not to suggest that focus groups are the only appropriate method for research on citizenship, nor should we overlook the drawbacks to this approach. Since participants are not representative of any particular population, the results are not generalizable in a statistical sense. There are social-desirability effects. And the open-ended, discursive nature of the discussions makes interpretation particularly difficult. Nonetheless, if we are really to understand how people in liberal polities think about citizenship, it makes good sense to begin by listening to how they themselves talk about it. Only after we have allowed them to articulate their own ideas in their own words does it become meaningful to contemplate more quantitative methods of study.

Here, we draw on our discussions with four focus groups: two composed of citizens of Chapel Hill, North Carolina, and two of citizens of Pittsboro, North Carolina, a small rural community south of Chapel Hill. The four groups were stratified according to urban-rural residence and familiarity of the participants with one another.[5] Previous research suggests that urban-rural residence as well as two of its corre-

5. By stratifying according to urban-rural residence, we have also indirectly stratified according to socioeconomic status.

lates, community size and level of social integration, are likely to shape the nature of citizenship (see Barber 1984; Daggar 1981; Kasarda and Janowitz 1974). By stratifying according to residence, we sought to increase the variety in responses to our questions. By stratifying according to whether the subjects were strangers or acquaintances, we sought to vary the impact of group influences over individual responses. These focus groups contained both men and women and ranged in size from seven to nine participants, including the moderator, who led the discussions.

Each group was asked thirteen basic questions accompanied by specific probes. Seven of these questions presented hypothetical dilemmas to be solved; the remainder were more abstract inquiries about citizenship. The discussions lasted two hours, with a short break in the middle, and each discussion produced, on average, forty-five pages of transcribed text. These transcripts were analyzed in three stages. First, they were read to identify descriptive and inferential codes for classifying the respondents' statements. Thus, although our initial questions were organized around the concepts of the liberal-communitarian debate, in our coding we were primarily guided by the respondents' discussions rather than our own preconceptions. Next, the transcripts were reread in order to classify statements according to the scheme developed on the basis of the first reading. Finally, these coded statements were subjected to a pattern analysis to identify common themes in the understanding of particular concepts and relations among concepts (see Miles and Huberman 1984 for a discussion of the development of coding schemes for qualitative data analysis).

Citizenship in the Liberal Democratic Polity: Empirical Considerations

The focus group transcripts were analyzed with the key categories of citizens' privileges and responsibilities in mind. As we have seen, liberal and communitarian theorists provide different perspectives on the nature of these concepts and the relations between them. And, as we shall see, our focus-group participants also differ in this regard, though not always in ways so easily categorized as "liberal" or "communitarian."

The Privileges of Citizens

To explore how our respondents conceptualize the privileges of citizens, we initially cast our questions in terms of "rights." In particular, we asked, What rights do citizens have? Political theorists such as T. H. Marshall (1977) suggest a threefold classification: civil rights, political rights, and social rights. These types of rights are very unevenly represented in our respondents' comments. In strikingly similar discussions of this question, all four groups focused overwhelmingly on civil rights: freedom of speech, freedom of religion, freedom of movement, freedom to become whatever one wants to become. The Bill of Rights is much more than a constitutional symbol for Americans. Its emphasis on civil rights actually defines the very substance of how we think about rights. Thus, when Americans are asked explicitly to think about their rights, they think about the rights that are essential for the preservation of their private lives, the rights that are necessary for the maintenance of independence and individualism in liberal society, the rights that are central to a liberal account of citizenship.

This is not to suggest, however, that people do not recognize the existence of political rights and "positive" social rights. They do mention them, but with less frequency and, in the case of social rights, with more ambivalence. In response to the direct question "What rights do citizens have?" our discussants mentioned civil rights ten times more frequently than political rights. The right to vote, a key political right, was also mentioned spontaneously in response to other questions, but typically, people tended to see voting as a duty as much as a right. Social rights were mentioned even less often than political rights. When asked about the rights of citizens, only one citizen suggested that people have a right to "the basic necessities . . . a place to live, food to eat, . . . health care." Others went out of their way, in response to the hypothetical situations, to reject or at least express ambivalence toward the idea that people have a right to expect that their basic needs will be met by the community. Thus, although many political theorists (King and Waldron 1988, 417) now assume that "welfare rights are integral to the contemporary sense of citizenship," American citizens may regard such rights with some skepticism.

People's lists of rights, as well as the language they use to discuss them, reveal the meanings associated with this term. Underlying the dominant focus on civil rights is an understanding of rights as legal guarantees: "Rights is a strong word . . . it gets legal"; "Rights are things guaranteed legally by a document." Specifically, there is the sense that rights are guarantees that ensure people's choices against interference by other individuals, society, or government. Rights are seen as necessary to prevent people from doing things that "may impact negatively on someone else." Thus, people tend to have a negative view of the nature of rights, a view most congruent with liberal politics.

That these Americans think of rights as legal protections makes their ambivalence over social rights understandable. Many found it difficult even to talk about whether their fellow citizens have a right to expect help in a disaster or a right to the basic necessities of life. For them, it is inappropriate to stretch the language of liberalism to encompass such rights. As one woman protested, "It's not kosher to talk about people having a right to help"; or, as another noted with frustration, "You don't say, 'Do people have a right to love?' or 'Do people have a right to be nurtured?' . . . There's certain innate things that I don't even associate as being a right." Most of our discussants expressed genuine compassion for the homeless and for victims of disasters, but they nonetheless bristled at the idea that such people have a "right" to be assisted by others.

Their objections to the idea of positive social rights stem from two related sources. First—and as stated most forcefully by members of the rural focus groups—the idea of social rights rubs up against the values of individualism and self-sufficiency, both crucial to liberal beliefs. To say someone has a right to food, shelter, or help is "like saying you owe me"; and, as one citizen angrily added, "I'm sorry but there are no free lunches. Nobody owes you anything anymore." Second, and perhaps more surprising, some people feel very strongly that talking about helping other citizens and meeting their basic needs as a matter of rights strips the emotional content and moral worth of these acts as voluntary acts. The notion of rights, they say, "leaves out the moral issue of citizenship." If someone has a right to help, then they themselves may have a duty to help. And, as we shall see later, it is this duty to help, as much as the right to help, that they find objectionable. Most of our discussants felt that it was far preferable for individuals to provide food or shelter to a needy person out of a "sense of friendship or love or community involvement," to provide because one is virtuous, rather than because one is compelled to do so by some legally sanctioned social right. This ambivalence about the existence of social rights reflects the influence of liberalism on our understanding of legally established rights as claims of forbearance against interference, rather than as morally grounded guarantees to provide assistance.

Finally, our discussants put forward relatively sophisticated accounts of the origins of rights, accounts that have a strikingly "contextualist" flavor to them. To begin with, nearly everybody expressed skepticism over the existence of natural rights. "You're definitely not born with rights just by virtue of the fact that you are a human being," they argued. In keeping with their legalistic interpretations of the nature of rights, our citizens understand these rights as something guaranteed by law and "given" by government. This is a point well worth emphasizing, for in the liberal tradition it has often been assumed that individual rights should be legally enforced natural rights. But while our respondents were ready to refer to their "inalienable rights," their discussions of these rights clearly suggest that they view them as "inalienable" *only for citizens.* Just as the government can "give us a right," so the government "can take it away."

In effect, they believe that rights are not universal, that they depend instead on the country and the historical period within which one lives. If they have certain "inalienable" rights as Americans, this is only because they have been born in a country founded, in part, to guarantee them these rights: "Our Founding Fathers thought . . . that we should have certain rights when you're born, and they couldn't find them in other countries . . . that's why they established this country, because they felt like some of these rights you should have been born with." Moreover, they recognize that the rights that Americans enjoy as seemingly inalienable may not exist in other countries, because rights "don't really exist unless the whole country agrees that they exist." In short, rights "are relative to where you happen to be born."

In summary, our focus-group discussions reveal that many citizens share common understandings of the content, nature, and origins of rights. When these people think about rights, they most naturally think about civil rights. Underlying this shared focus is a legalistic, basically negative understanding of the nature of rights, an understanding that fits easily with the existence of civil rights but that in their minds is incongruent with the existence of positive social rights. Thus, it would appear that liberalism is the dominant discourse underpinning citizens' conceptions of their privileges qua citizens. Their list of rights is a liberal list; their understanding of the character of rights is a liberal understanding; their language of rights is a liberal language—the preservation of individual autonomy is the operative principle involved. Yet their understanding of the origins of rights is surprisingly illiberal. Because rights are often seen as "alienable" and historically constituted, they are neither natural nor secure. This suggests that it would be unwarranted to conclude that citizens in the liberal democratic polity are liberals through and through—which becomes even more evident when we consider how they understand the responsibilities and duties of citizenship.

The Responsibilities of Citizens

"What are the duties or responsibilities of citizens?" As with rights, our discussants in all four groups clearly shared a common understanding, which they articulated in response to this question. In particular, *political* responsibilities came immediately to mind. The "duty to pay taxes," the "duty to defend the country," and the "duty to vote" were mentioned repeatedly, though discussants differed over the status of the duty to vote. Some believe that people who fail to vote "are not carrying out their primary responsibilities as citizens," whereas others say that not voting "does not make someone a bad citizen." More of this shared understanding was revealed when people were asked: "If you were a bad citizen, what duties would you neglect?" They simply assumed that virtually all citizens would automatically fulfill duties essential to the preservation of *civility* and *individual autonomy.* Thus, a "bad citizen" is someone who "fails to abide by the law," "violates the rights of others," or "does something to detract from the country or hurt other citizens." Once again, the core of the common understanding that our discussants share here is basically liberal in character (see Galston 1988).

But once we move beyond this core, we find considerable disagreement about what further responsibilities, if any, citizens must fulfill. Most of this disagreement concerns public involvement and social needs: political participation beyond voting, community service, participation in community organizations, educating children (both one's own and those of strangers), helping those in need, protecting the vulnerable, and preserving the environment. Evidence regarding the status of these activities as citizen duties comes from two sets of questions.

The first question explicitly asked whether people who engage in volunteer work and participate in the community are "extra good citizens or simply behaving as all citizens should." There was much discussion and much disagreement here. Less than a quarter of our citizens answered using a language of duty that appeared communitarian in character, but those who did so expressed their feelings strongly: "We all have a moral obligation to help in any disaster," they argued. "People have an obligation to help out and do things in the community." By contrast, the majority struggled for a while with the same question and then answered it using a language of choice rather than obligation (e.g., should or ought, as opposed to must). That is, they had a sense that such activities are clearly desirable—and that those who perform them are likely virtuous[6]—but that such activities also go beyond the normal responsibilities of citizens in a liberal polity (see Galston 1988). As one noted, "I think that you should make some kind of contribution, but I don't think everybody can necessarily get involved in working for a political movement." Or, "I think all citizens ought to do things like that, but . . . those of us who do go out and contribute . . . are extra good because . . . to get out and do it is . . . a little bit more." Finally, a small group of citizens immediately rejected the idea that such activities are either obligatory or meritorious as voluntary acts.

For some, the distinction between obligatory and voluntary "duties" blurred when they were presented with a series of hypothetical dilemmas about helping disaster victims, protecting the vulnerable, educating children, and engaging in community service. Responding to the dilemma of a young mother being hassled by teenage boys as she waits in an airport line, they assure us that they would certainly intervene, and even add, emphatically, "we *really* have a *responsibility* to protect the vulnerable and to help people in distress." Similarly, when asked what to do about a small boy who is destroying public property, they say, "People have a responsibility to try and educate the young about what is appropriate behavior. . . . Somebody's got to teach this child. Apparently the parents haven't instilled in him to care for things . . . so I would try to make a difference." Thus, some citizens who abhor the notion of duty in the abstract nevertheless adopt a communitarian-like

6. Some discussants wondered how virtuous were people who did volunteer work and became involved in the community. Several people expressed the sentiment that "it's not all giving, they're receiving some things back, or they wouldn't be doing it." And one of the Pittsboro groups engaged in a lengthy discussion of whether one can judge an act virtuous without considering the underlying motives. One woman said, "In order to classify someone as good—good citizen, good person—you've got to look at their motives"; in response, another said, "But, if the end result is good, then what difference does it make?"

language of duty when confronted with specific situations that force them to consider the practice of citizenship in context.

These different languages suggest two basic understandings of duty, or responsibility. Those discussants who limit themselves to the core responsibilities have a typically liberal understanding of duties, an understanding that limits duty to those requirements necessary for the preservation of primarily negative rights. From this perspective, duties are things "you sort of have to do," things that reflect a "formal relationship with your government." In short, duties are "what legally we are held accountable for . . . everything else is extra." Thus, not only are duties understood negatively, but they are seen as carrying legal consequences. Duties are the "things they can get you on"; or, as one discussant wryly observed, "Duty is a four-letter word." Given this perspective, it should not be surprising that such discussants view the performance of duties as activities bereft of real concern for communal integrity and moral responsibility to the collective, and even as cynical expressions of self-interest. People who understand citizen duties in this legalistic, negative fashion prefer a world with relatively few duties, a polity where people engage in virtuous behavior because they "want to do it," because of a "mothering instinct" or a "sense of humanity," because "it benefits my family," because of "care for another human being," even because of "selfish motives"—but definitely not because they are compelled to do so by a (legalistic) commitment. That is, they prefer a polity where, rather than obey dutifully as citizens, they can choose freely as autonomous individuals to engage in desirable civic behaviors or to shun them.

A second view of the nature of citizen duties stands in stark contrast to this first understanding. Here people see duties as obligations that go beyond legal requirements. They have difficulty finding language to express this understanding of obligation. They try with phrases such as "they [duties] aren't written; they're just there," or by characterizing them as "moral obligations." But in any case, these discussants see duties not as negative but rather as positive obligations that provide opportunities for demonstrating commitment and pride in the community. For them, more extensive responsibilities of citizenship seem a necessary, unquestioned part of life: "If you have pride in your country and your community . . . you feel you want to share in these duties. You want to contribute in that way." Moreover, the performance of duties is often infused with positive emotions. One feels "sympathy and passion for others" when fulfilling one's commitments toward the community. In effect, these people are comfortable with a rich and complex language of duty. They prefer a world where people engage in virtuous behaviors out of a sense of duty, because "they must," because they are "obligated to do so," because they "have a responsibility," or because it is the "natural thing to do." Clearly, a purely liberal account of duties cannot fit these conceptualizations without grossly distorting the practice of citizenship and the vision of the polity they express.

This point can be further explicated by considering the origins of duties. Not surprisingly, those who possess a negative understanding explain such origins in legalistic, utilitarian terms. Citizens have legal responsibilities "in order to keep society and government running." By virtue of being a "legal resident you have certain responsibilities." In contrast, those who see citizen duties in a more positive light understand them as necessary elements of communal life. "If you're part of a community, and you've been a member of that community," they say, then "you have certain obligations that you have to fulfill." If you enjoy the benefits of the community, then you "are obligated to give something in return." Duties grow naturally out of the attachments that people feel for one another and out of the sense of community and tradition that develops over time; they are taught from generation to generation as an almost unconscious part of the socialization process. Thus, when asked where her duties as a citizen came from, this respondent replied, "It's our families; it's our upbringing. It's what our grandparents, our great grandparents, and on and on have taught us. They always worked together just like, you know, when they came and started building the colonies. Everybody worked together. . . . If one family couldn't afford it then the other family provided, and it's always been that way . . . it's almost like being brainwashed." For some citizens, duties are a legal by-product of their formal status as citizens. For others, they emerge from the fabric of everyday life.

What is most interesting about the positions revealed in these answers is that once we move beyond the commonly agreed core duties of citizenship, there are several possible patterns of thinking. First, a small minority of our discussants see no merit whatsoever in looking for citizens' duties beyond this core. Second, the majority have a different and fundamentally liberal understanding of responsibilities. This leads them to restrict their listing to the core activities but at the same time to conceive virtuous behaviors that the "extra good" citizen engages in as a matter of choice. Moreover, for at least some people, the boundaries between these two ways of thinking are fluid; when confronted with specific situations, what they previously regarded as merely virtuous behaviors exercised by choice sometimes become morally and politically necessary responsibilities. Third, a significant minority clearly extend their conceptions of citizenship duties to encompass a very wide range of additional behaviors that suggest necessary orientations. They use the language of duty to discuss their active engagement in community and political activities. For them, community service is as much a responsibility of citizens as is, say, voting.

In summary, our focus groups share a common "liberal" understanding of the core responsibilities of citizenship. Central to this understanding are fundamental duties necessary for the preservation of civil life (e.g., obedience to the law, respect for the rights of others) and the political system (e.g., paying taxes, serving on juries, and, occasionally, voting). But people differ sharply over other forms of citizen behavior. Most argue that other types of citizen behavior (e.g., public service, aid to the needy, political participation beyond voting) are not so much responsibilities of citizenship as they are virtuous behaviors that individuals might or might not choose to do. Underlying this assessment is a liberal perspective: a basically negative view that characterizes duties as legal requirements stripped of emotional attachment to other members of the polity, as unavoidable by-products of legal citizenship. In contrast, a sizable minority of the discussants incorporate such citizen behaviors into their conceptions of the duties of a citizen. Underlying their interpretation is a communitarian perspective: a basically positive view that characterizes duties as moral obligations infused with a sense of care and concern, as necessary for the collective pursuit of a shared good. But whether "liberal" or "communitarian" or some mixture of the two, our discussants' responses nonetheless indicate that most, if not all, place a high value on those sorts of activities that go beyond the minimal requirements of core duties. They may attribute different status to the demand that one take up these activities, but we should note that there appears to be more complexity in many citizens' self-conceptions than the arguments of liberals and communitarians would suggest.

Discussion

The general dominance of the discourse of liberalism can best be seen in the common understanding that nearly all our respondents share with respect to rights. More diverse segments of the public may hold conceptions of rights different from those we have seen. But we are impressed by the extent to which a single understanding of rights, a liberal understanding, has dominated the discussions in all four focus groups. Thus, our discussants nearly all conceive of rights as legal guarantees for negative freedom. They conceive of them as legalistic protections against interference with their individual choices, protections against interference from government, society, or other individuals. In their discussions, they concentrate on the rights that are necessary for maintaining their independence and individualism in a liberal society: civil rights such as freedom of speech, freedom of religion, freedom of movement, freedom to become whatever one wants to become. They talk about political rights, such as the right to vote, but much less than they talk about these civil rights. And they are very skeptical about the status of social rights, like the right to health care, which they occasionally hear articulated in the media.

The discussants we have come to think of as our liberal citizens (who are the dominant group) and those whose inclinations appear more communitarian—all share a commitment to the belief in "political" duties such as paying taxes, voting, and defending the country. These duties are cast in terms that imply a reciprocity with negative rights; the responsibilities of citizens are defined as duties required to maintain these rights. Beyond agreement on such "core" duties, however, we find considerable disagreement, in particular about the nature of responsibilities toward public involvement and community service.

Those who seem to be more "liberal" citizens see such activities as virtuous but not as obligatory. Their view of citizen duties is legalistic and utilitarian; they would rather not call community involvement part of their responsibilities as "citizens." Thus, they understand their participation in community and political activities as acts of choice rather than as obligations. To participate may be virtuous, but avoiding participation does not reflect badly on one's character: "I can choose whether to volunteer. . . . I don't have to work for the community to maintain my respect." And to choose to participate is definitely, in their minds, to act "as a human being, not a citizen."

Like the citizens liberal theory would have them be, they also seem relatively uninterested in discussions of the land, its traditions, its history. When they do talk about such topics, their contributions sound more cognitive and abstract than emotional and concrete, for it is not terribly important to them to feel rooted in the community. Likewise, they display fewer signs of "civic wisdom," the capacity to envision and discuss a common good. And when they do act to benefit the community, they give these acts a distinctly liberal interpretation that is devoid of notions of a common good. Thus, they would intervene to prevent a child from destroying public playground property, but they would intervene because "my taxes are paying for the playground," "if it's a public park it's my property too." They would act to support community service programs, but they would do so because "it benefits the *individual*; they learn something for life," or "it's for what you get out of it."

The more "communitarian" citizens place much more emphasis than do the liberals on an expanded sense of citizen responsibilities, particularly on duties that concern public involvement and community service. They may share with their liberal neighbors a commitment to strictly "political" duties, but they see their responsibilities to other citizens as extending beyond their ties to each other via government. "Helping is what it means just to be," they say. "Helping is part of our consciousness." When it comes to involvement in the local community, it is not for them a matter of choice, since not to be involved is unthinkable. This point was made clearly when our focus group of rural neighbors was asked how they would react if Ronnie, who was seated at the table, chose not to help out during a community crisis. Everyone groped unsuccessfully for an answer until one of them eventually said, "It is inconceivable . . . that's not even a possibility." On this they all agreed, including Ronnie, who explained that he would simply "have to" help out because the members of a community "have obligations to one another." Ronnie and his neighbors lead "encumbered" lives and, for the most part, would not have it any other way.

Finally, our communitarian citizens express signs of some of the "civic wisdom" that their liberal counterparts seem to lack. They not only willingly engage in activities that benefit the community, but in explaining why they do so, they are also more likely than the liberals to suggest a vision of a common good. Thus, they too would stop the destructive child in the playground, but they would do so because "it's our property, community property." They too would support community service programs, but they would do so because community service "can build awareness of community need," because community service "motivates" people in a way that "benefits the country and the community."

Not surprisingly, most of the discussants who express these communitarian dispositions come from the small rural community of Pittsboro. This is consistent with the notion that communitarian forms of citizenship flourish among people who have face-to-face relations and regard themselves as friends and neighbors. It is also not surprising that most of those who express liberal sentiments come from Chapel Hill, a university town whose population is dominated by people who have little in the way of a "local identity."

Of course it is not news that citizenship in America seems to be predominantly liberal in character. Nor is it news that within this liberal context some communitarian orientations can be plainly seen. What is perhaps news, however, is the way that these different approaches to citizenship are manifested empirically. Our "liberal" citizens show a marked disdain for the language of community; nonetheless, they are willing to consider the merits of community involvement, even if they do not cast this involvement in terms of "citizenship." And our "communitarians" show a marked concern for community integrity and moral virtue, which they readily articulate in terms of "citizenship," yet they also recognize that abstract, legalistically defined, even "negative," rights are an important feature of citizenship in the United States.

Despite these significant differences in our respondents' conceptions of citizenship, we should take care not to lose sight of very real similarities among them. Whether they have a more restricted or more extended concept of citizenship, it is still the case that they share similar attitudes regarding appropriate action in particular situations. Given this, the differences they express when conceptualizing their different accounts of citizens' responsibilities seem less important than the fact that they would still act in similar ways. Meals on wheels are delivered and school bonds passed by both "liberals" and "communitarians." Individuals' rights to exercise autonomy in their life plans are respected by both "liberals" and "communitarians." The point here is that the reasons may be different, but the effect is the same.[7]

7. We should note that in a more representative population our "liberal" citizens might not prove to be so participatory. Our discussants were paid volunteers, but the fact that they were volunteers may have produced a participatory bias. Moreover, we recognize that different understandings of duties and responsibilities may incline citizens to extend or withhold support for public projects, depending on whether they see these projects as "protecting" their own

Neither liberal nor communitarian theorists offer conceptual frameworks adequate to account for this constellation of issues and, in particular, for the ways in which citizens readily reconcile (even if not always in the language of "citizenship") what are in "theory" mutually exclusive ideals. The difficulty lies with the language of liberalism and communitarianism itself, which is precisely why we think that an adequate conception of citizenship must move beyond the liberal-communitarian debate.

Rethinking Democratic Citizenship

Communitarian critics of liberalism (e.g., Barber 1984; Sandel 1984) see liberal citizens as passive, detached from others and disengaged from community activities. But what we have discovered is what has long been suspected by some of liberalism's defenders (Yack 1988): that liberal citizens do not always "live down" to liberal theory. In particular, our apparently "liberal" discussants report that they participate in local community activities nearly as much as do their more "communitarian" counterparts.

Liberal critics of communitarianism (e.g., Thigpen and Downing 1987; Gutmann 1985) see communitarian citizens as too active, too ready to trample the rights of individuals in the pursuit of some "higher" collective good. But we have also discovered that communitarians do not always "live down" to communitarian theory. Our apparently "communitarian" discussants do subscribe to a conception of a shared life and the pursuit of a common good, but the visions on which they draw are more or less "liberal" in character. When they talk about the responsibilities they have as citizens, more often than not these are responsibilities that enable the preservation of individual autonomy and a way of life that benefits not just a few but also (as one discussant put it) "the country and the community."

Now, none of this is meant to suggest that communitarians are wrong

---

interests or as serving a more general common interest. Our only point here, and as we argue later, is that support for public projects cannot be exclusively conceptualized in either liberal or communitarian terms. Whether on "obligatory" or "voluntary" grounds, there is a remarkable willingness on the part of citizens to consider the merits of public (private and governmental) provision of goods and services.

about the excesses to which liberal ideals are subject, nor is it meant to disparage liberal fears of communitarian tyranny. It is, however, to suggest that communitarians who think that liberalism constitutes an obstacle to an active democratic citizenry have simply failed to see that the traditions of liberalism itself may be a source of citizen activity. And it is also to suggest that liberals who think that appeals to tradition, a shared way of life, and conceptions of a common good are dangerous ideals threatening individual autonomy have simply failed to see that such appeals may actually serve to ground the commitments of those who would seek the preservation of autonomy. Thus, we would argue that an adequate conception of democratic citizenry entails neither abandoning liberalism for communitarianism nor vice versa. Rather, it entails a recognition, as James Kloppenberg (1989, 18) puts it, that "the intermingling of these styles of discourse has been as clear as their competition has been. A liberalism without any responsibilities accompanying rights, and communitarianism without any concern for individual liberties, are projected fantasies."

If nothing else, our research indicates that such an intermingling best captures the sensibilities of our discussants. But perhaps the strongest argument we would make is that there is a sense in which, despite their differences, our discussants are appealing not to two distinct conceptions of citizenship but to a single, albeit (as Hochschild would put it) "disjunctive," viewpoint. The citizens in our study seem most "liberal" with regard to their citizenship in the nation. When they focus on the local community context, by contrast, they begin to behave and speak like "communitarians" and articulate an expanded sense of responsibility, although not all of them articulate the language of obligation, let alone the duties of citizenship. Those who do are for the most part speaking as "friends and neighbors," as members of a community in which there is a strong sense of local identity, whereas those who do not are speaking as "strangers," as members of a community in which local ties and rootedness tend to be weaker.

There are, we think, important lessons in this. In a society of strangers, the language of liberal citizenship seems most appropriate, whereas in a society of friends, the language of community makes perfect sense. Modern liberal democratic polities are neither societies of friends nor societies of strangers. Instead, they are both—and our citizens seem to have recognized this fact by developing conceptions of citizenship appropriate to both. What this suggests to us is that an adequate theory of democratic citizenship suitable to a pluralistic culture ought to be able to account for contexts in which it is appropriate to think of citizenship among "friends" and also for contexts where it is appropriate to think of citizenship among "strangers." These may be, but need not be, mutually exclusive. One can certainly question whether a society in which citizens are strangers can sustain its collective identity and whether a society of friends can sustain the individuality and autonomy of its members. But if our discussants' responses suggest anything, it is that "strangers" are willing to act to sustain their communities and that "friends" are willing to respect those rights that preserve autonomy and individuality.

Our conclusion, however, is not that all is as it should be in the liberal democratic polity. We are concerned that, for many, the language of citizenship does not comport at all well with their own understanding of their responsibilities to other citizens. But by showing that it is possible to reconcile commitments to liberal rights and commitments of responsibility to others, we hope to have shown that the language of citizenship need not entail the choice between leaving others to fend for themselves or enforcing a mindless conformity.

Moreover, all of this begs the question whether our citizens actually translate their commitments into practice. It is one thing to articulate the privileges and responsibilities of citizenship, quite another to enact those understandings. Whether, and how, citizens articulate in their actions the relation between autonomy and community, between preserving a sphere in which their own choices are taken as inviolable and defining a sphere of action in which they must act in concert, remains to be more fully explored. And there are good reasons—as both liberals and communitarians have argued—for doubting the possibility of balancing liberal and communitarian ideals. Yet there are, as we hope to have shown, also good reasons for believing that citizens' own self-understandings already embody the conceptual resources from which this possibility might be realized. Democratic theory and democratic political science would do well to take heed of them, for they are the resources from which the future of democracy will be forged.

References

Barber, Benjamin. 1984. *Strong Democracy: Participatory Politics for a New Age.* Berkeley and Los Angeles: University of California Press.

Bellah, Robert N., Richard Madsen, William M. Sullivan, Ann Swidler, and Steven M. Tipton. 1985. *Habits of the Heart: Individualism and Commitment in American Life*. Berkeley and Los Angeles: University of California Press.

Berlin, Isaiah. 1969. *Four Essays on Liberty.* Oxford: Oxford University Press.

Bernstein, Richard J. 1976. *The Restructuring of Social and Political Theory.* Philadelphia: University of Pennsylvania Press.

Daggar, Richard. 1981. "Metropolis, Memory, and Citizenship." *American Journal of Political Science* 25:715–37.

Downing, Lyle, and Robert Thigpen. 1986. "Beyond Shared Understandings." *Political Theory* 14:451–72.

Dworkin, Ronald. 1977. *Taking Rights Seriously.* Cambridge, Mass.: Harvard University Press.

Galston, William A. 1988. "Liberal Virtues." *American Political Science Review* 82:1277–90.

———. 1989. "Community, Democracy, Philosophy: The Political Thought of Michael Walzer." *Political Theory* 17:119–30.

Gray, John. 1986. *Liberalism.* Minneapolis: University of Minnesota Press.

Gutmann, Amy. 1985. "Communitarian Critics of Liberalism." *Philosophy and Public Affairs* 14:308–22.

Herzog, Don. 1986. "Some Questions for Republicans." *Political Theory* 14:473–93.

Hirsch, H. N. 1986. "The Threnody of Liberalism: Constitutional Liberty and the Renewal of Community." *Political Theory* 14:423–49.

Huntington, Samuel P. 1981. *American Politics: The Promise of Disharmony.* Cambridge, Mass.: Harvard University Press.

Kasarda, J. D., and Morris Janowitz. 1974. "Community Attachments in Mass Society." *American Sociological Review* 39:328–39.

King, Desmond S., and Jeremy Waldron. 1988. "Citizens, Social Citizenship, and the Defence of the Welfare State." *British Journal of Political Science* 18:415–43.

Kloppenberg, James. 1989. "Why Does History Matter to Political Theory?" Paper presented at the annual meeting of the American History Association.

Krueger, Richard A. 1988. *Focus Groups: A Practical Guide for Applied Research.* Newbury Park, Calif.: Sage Publications.

MacIntyre, Alasdair. 1984. *After Virtue.* 2d ed. Notre Dame, Ind.: University of Notre Dame Press.

———. 1988. *Whose Justice, Which Rationality*? Notre Dame, Ind.: University of Notre Dame Press.

Marshall, T. H. 1977. *Class, Citizenship, and Social Development.* Garden City, N.Y.: Doubleday.

Miles, Matthew B., and A. Michael Huberman. 1984. *Qualitative Data Analysis: A Sourcebook of Methods.* Beverly Hills, Calif.: Sage Publications.

Portis, Edward B. 1985. "Citizenship and Personal Identity." *Polity* 18:457–72.

Rawls, John. 1971. *A Theory of Justice.* Cambridge, Mass.: Harvard University Press.

Salkever, Stephen G. 1974. "Virtue, Obligation, and Politics." *American Political Science Review* 68:78–92.

Sandel, Michael J. 1982. *Liberalism and the Limits of Justice*. Cambridge: Cambridge University Press.

———. 1984. "The Procedural Republic and the Unencumbered Self." *Political Theory* 12:81–96.

Spragens, Thomas A. 1986. "Reconstructing Liberal Theory: Reason and Liberal Culture." In *Liberals on Liberalism*, ed. A. J. Damico, 34–53. Totowa, N.J.: Rowman & Littlefield.

Sullivan, William M. 1986. *Reconstructing Public Philosophy*. Berkeley and Los Angeles: University of California Press.

Talmon, J. L. 1952. *The Origins of Totalitarian Democracy*. Boulder, Colo.: Westview Press.

Thigpen, Robert B., and Lyle A. Downing. 1987. "Liberalism and the Communitarian Critique." *American Journal of Political Science* 31:637–55.

Tocqueville, Alexis de. [1835, 1840] 1969. *Democracy in America*. Trans. George Lawrence. Ed. J. P. Mayer. Garden City, N.Y.: Doubleday, Anchor Books.

Tussman, Joseph. 1960. *Obligation and the Body Politic*. Oxford: Oxford University Press.

Wallach, John R., 1987. "Liberals, Communitarians, and the Tasks of Political Theory." *Political Theory* 15:581–611.

Walzer, Michael. 1970. *Obligations: Essays on Disobedience, War, and Citizenship*. Cambridge, Mass.: Harvard University Press.

———. 1976. "Civility and Civic Virtue in Contemporary America." *Social Research* 41:593–611.

———. 1983. *Spheres of Justice: A Defense of Pluralism and Equality*. New York: Basic Books.

———. 1989. "Citizenship." In *Political Innovation and Conceptual Change*, ed. Terence Ball, James Farr, and Russell Hanson, 211–19. Cambridge: Cambridge University Press.

Yack, Bernard. 1988. "Liberalism and Its Communitarian Critics: Does Liberal Practice 'Live Down' to Liberal Theory?" In *Community in America: The Challenge of Habits of the Heart*, ed. Charles H. Reynolds and Ralph V. Norman, 147–72. Berkeley and Los Angeles: University of California Press.

8

In Search of a Citizen Ethic

Mary G. Dietz

Long before it degenerated into the "L-word" and became the stuff of electoral campaign sloganeering in the United States, liberalism was of scholarly interest to students of American political life. Almost since the inception of the discipline (see Ricci 1984), and certainly since *The American Voter* (Campbell et al. 1960), empirical political scientists have been concerned to trace the impact of liberal values on public opinion and electoral politics. Following the publication of John Rawls's *A Theory of Justice* (1971), political theorists grew increasingly absorbed with the premises and principles of liberalism and various challenges to them. As a rule, however, these "empirical" and "theoretical" enterprises have unfolded in separate, though proximate, spheres. Hence, scholarship on liberalism (or theories of citizenship in general) is only infrequently informed by the beliefs and opinions of real citizens, and empirical studies of American public opinion or voter preferences are rarely attentive to the conceptual complexities that inhere in liberalism as a theoretical tradition.

"Duty Is a Four-Letter Word" is a refreshing exception to the separate-spheres rule. By uniting the conceptual sensibilities and research expertise of political science and political theory, Pamela Conover, Stephen Leonard, and Donald Searing confirm that political theory and empirical political science can be compatible partners. Their work employs a promising method and reaches some intriguing conclusions concerning the nature of political discourse and the meaning of citizenship in a liberal democratic polity. Even if they continue to position themselves in different domains, political scientists and political theorists might learn much from the example of this fruitful joint enterprise.

Studying Democracy Democratically

A decisively normative and theoretical question underlies the project of Conover et al.: What constitutes a "coherent and defensible theory" of citizenship? The authors intend to approach this question in a very specific way. Hence, they turn to the communitarian critique of liberal theories of citizenship—to date, largely confined to the windy reaches of academic political theory—and make the liberal-communitarian debate a matter of empirical research. Their attempt to sort out two competing political theoretical accounts of citizenship begins on the fruitful plain of citizen discourse itself, where the "self-understandings of 'ordinary agents' in modern democracies" can be uncovered and assessed. What Conover et al. want to see is whether real citizens actually express themselves in the "rights-bearing" terms liberal theorists promulgate (and communitarians challenge) or in ways that capture the language of liberalism's communitarian critics. Which, if either, "citizen ethic"—to borrow a characterization of Michael Sandel's (1984a)—distinguishes ordinary Americans?

The first merit of this project, then, lies in its attempt to bring liberal and communitarian political theories into the polity and see whether they adequately frame actual citizens' discussions of citizenship. Conover et al. rightly anticipate that however unsystematic the political views of citizens, they may themselves provide useful evaluative insights into the more systematic and formalized theories of citizenship that liberal and communitarian political theorists develop. Thus, one of the authors' aims is to hold political theories accountable to the beliefs, ideas, and political values expressed within the very "publics" political theorists presume, if not to represent, at least to understand.

In setting out the approach that guides their study, the authors observe that if we want to know how citizens think about citizenship, "it makes good sense to begin by listening to how they themselves talk about it" and by encouraging citizens "to articulate their own ideas in their own words." Although the specific methodologies best suited to this sort of enterprise are numerous, implicit in the authors' formulation is the sense that some methods are perhaps more democratic than others and therefore more appropriate to the study of citizens and citizenship. Put otherwise, if we understand the concepts "citizen" and "democracy" as normative and not just neutral, or "descriptive," terms, then some methodological approaches might recommend themselves over others. Particularly appropriate are those methods consistent with a democratic sensibility that respects respondents as citizens and equals, that is, as rational, discursive, and self-interpreting beings rather than an aggregated mass to whom questions are administered and measures applied. A democratic methodology might also lead the researcher to assess critically the notion that he or she can (and should) move "beyond subjectivity" and strictly control or constrain the issues to which his or her subjects are invited to respond (Taylor 1985). In lieu of such a detached approach, the researcher might consider modes of inquiry that situate him or her within a context that allows for collective participation and leaves room for challenges to the research program itself. Methods that encourage wide-open, mutual discussion and debate and recognize the power of collective discussion as a mode of reaching political understanding not only serve to check the researcher's urge to order and control, they also approach democracy democratically, in its own spirit and with its own principles at work.

In this light, the approaches Conover et al. pursue in their study seem more democratic than many other methods, insofar as they give respondents the flexibility to cast political discourse about citizenship in their own terms and through freewheeling discussion. So, for example, instead of collecting an anonymous "representative" sample of subjects, the authors assembled four small focus groups in which citizens met face-to-face. Instead of administering written survey questionnaires, the authors organized structured, but nonetheless open-ended, group discussions that relied upon hypotheticals, dilemmas, and conceptual puzzles in order to elicit citizens' political ideas and self-understandings. They also pursued in-depth interviews with various individuals, in an effort to illuminate, rather than evade, the complexity of the political discourse of citizenship in the United States. In sum, integral to this study is an invitation to citizens to engage directly and democratically in dialogue about citizenship. Here, we might say, political science takes on the welcome but difficult task of actually *democratizing* the study of politics. In the process, political scientists are themselves not just the promoters but the beneficiaries of a civic education.

In Search of a Citizen Ethic

In his recent essay "The Communitarian Critique of Liberalism," Michael Walzer concludes that, communitarian hopes notwithstanding, in the United States there is no one "out there" but "rights-bearing, voluntarily associating, freely speaking liberal selves" (1990, 15). It is precisely this theoretical claim that Conover et al. want to examine and assess by probing the political discourse of ordinary citizens. The authors base their citizen profiles on a single conceptual guideline—rights versus duties—that they believe cuts the difference between liberals on the one hand and communitarians on the other. I argue, however, that "rights versus duties" does not adequately capture the difference between liberals (like Rawls) and communitarians (like Sandel and MacIntyre). As a result, and despite the otherwise substantial merits of their project, the authors' search for communitarians never gets off the ground. Indeed, given the misleading conceptual guide with which the authors begin, all we can possibly pick out in this thicket of political discourse is a colorful array of garden-variety liberals.

Before we venture into the field, however, we might review the way in which Conover et al. establish the citizen profiles that direct their study. The determination of who is "liberal" and who is "communitarian" rests heavily upon the responses individuals give to specific questions, hypotheticals, and dilemmas concerning the scope and content of collective, civic life. The questions, hypotheticals, and dilemmas are, in turn, structured according to a specific problematic: the tension between "privileges and responsibilities" that the authors also cast as analogous to the relation between "rights and duties." In determining what distinguishes some citizens from others, they focus on *which* rights and duties an individual takes as appropriate to citizenship, not *whether* "rights and duties" (as opposed to some other formulation) should, in fact, be the central focus of citizenship.

Not surprisingly, perhaps, the focus-group citizens exhibited a variety of understandings of rights, duties, and the meaning of being "an American." Some conceived of rights and duties more narrowly than others and hesitated to expand much beyond fundamental, or what Conover et al. call core, rights (including "speech, religion, movement, and freedom to become whatever one wants to become") and core duties (obedience to the law, paying taxes, serving on juries, and voting). Regardless of the scope of rights and duties, the authors found that core notions of rights and duties were common to *all* the citizens they interviewed. No one, in other words, challenged the very idea of rights as fundamental to citizenship or questioned the very idea of duties as integral to a democratic polity.

The telltale signs of communitarians, according to Conover et al., lie in the difference between those citizens who stop with core rights and duties and those who expand their articulation of each, but especially duties, to include "other types of citizen behavior." In the case of duties, this expansion includes public service, aid to the needy, political participation beyond voting, involvement in the local community, and an active concern for the land and its resources. The authors also suggest that communitarians cast their defense of duty in a distinctive vocabulary that stresses "obligation" rather than choice and gave greater weight to moral necessity than did their liberal counterparts. Behind the authors' claims about communitarians are two important assumptions: First, liberals have a narrowly articulated conception of duty that "demands no action *beyond those minimally required for the preservation of individual autonomy*" (emphasis added). Second, an "expansive" set of duties, tied to a language of moral obligation, transforms an ordinary liberal into a communitarian. Hence the authors' phrase, "duties make the difference."

In light of the authors' assumptions, we might first consider whether liberals are as inelastic or constricted in their views of rights and duties as the authors suggest, and in a way that can be uniformly characterized as "minimalist" and individualistic. As tempting as it may be to cast all liberals into such a common mold (with heavy emphasis on legality, formality, and "negativity"), I think it is hard to sustain this move with much theoretical or practical conviction. Indeed, its compelling quality quickly dissipates in the face of actual liberal theories that, despite their shared concern for individual right, seem to be more at odds than they are alike. Liberals differ enormously, for example, on the criteria through which rights and duties can be derived. Hence, to mention only a few examples from within the tradition of Western liberal thought, Kant defends the compulsion of a standard of justice superior to the individual, Jeremy Bentham establishes the utilitarian calculus of pleasure and pain, John Stuart Mill offers the standard of "self- and other-regarding actions," and John Rawls cites two minimal first principles of practical reason as the starting point for arriving at justice. All of these theorists are, in some sense, "liberal" insofar as they accept the centrality of questions of right. But in each of them we find decidedly different criteria—some more minimalist than others—according to which rights and duties are determined. Although all concede the priority of liberty and individual autonomy, these priorities are worked through vastly different and complex theories of self and society, public and private, some more "individualist" than others (the contrast between Rawls and Robert Nozick is instructive in this regard).

Early on, Conover et al. seem to recognize the problems their account of liberalism carries. They confess that theirs "is a rather terse, perhaps overly simplified, account of different liberal versions of the substantive content of rights, duties, and the relation between liberalism and democracy." Since an "overly simplified account" of complex political philosophies should probably never be the stock-in-trade of political scientists, I wish Conover et al. had resisted the temptation to reduce the "threnody of liberalism" (Hirsch 1986) to a single note.

Equally hard to sustain is the authors' more pointed claim that all liberals hold a rather grudging, legalistic, negative view of "duty" that eschews a vocabulary of moral obligation or necessity. Although there is no question that some liberal theorists place low relative weight upon the centrality of duty or altruism in political life (Bentham is one example), the world of liberalism—at least in the guise of political theory—is not exhausted by Benthamite sensibilities. For every liberal thinker for whom "duty is a four-letter word," there is another for whom it is integral to the exercise of liberty and morality. Consider Kant (an enlightenment liberal), who raised duty to the status of a heightened moral code and explicitly distinguished it from "self-serving" inclinations. T. H. Green (a liberal idealist) argued that rights can only be enjoyed within a civil community animated by a sense of civic duty and public-spiritedness. Rawls does not specify the nature of moral duty or the good life in his theory of justice, but the aim of his theory is to find principles that will make it possible for a society in which people disagree to deliberate and decide such issues fairly. Whether these principles limit or expand the scope of duties is an interesting but by no means settled question in Rawls studies. Finally, for even more explicit expressions of a moral duty deeply rooted in the language of social obligation, one might turn to numerous Protestant and Catholic twentieth-century liberals: Reinhold Niebuhr, Dorothy Day, Jacques Maritain, Martin Luther King, Jr., and Vaclav Havel, to name a few.

The ordinary language of political discourse also reminds us that the liberal is a slippery beast, neither easily captured nor contained. When we say "liberal," we might mean libertarians (who minimize duty) or "bleeding hearts" (who emphasize it). We refer to "welfare-state liberals" (who would expand social duties and the responsibilities of the state to its citizens) and to "laissez-faire liberals" (who place their faith, not in the state, but in the "free play" of the market). We would not, I suspect, have particular difficulty understanding as "liberal" both the eager activist who presses for community attention to social problems and the flinty Yankee who thinks fences make good neighbors—so long as they share other fundamentals: a language of individual rights, toleration, privacy, equality of opportunity, and the career open to talents (Walzer 1990). Upon these fundamentals, however—and on numerous levels of conceptual analysis—any number of distinctly different political edifices can be built and understandings of citizenship expressed. My point is that liberalism is perhaps best conceived of, as Don Herzog has put it, as a "family of disagreements" and not a single view (1986, 480). Thus, any attempt to reduce the family of disagreements to a theoretical party line on "duty," and the party line to a restrictive vocabulary, should probably be viewed skeptically, if not rejected altogether.

Nevertheless, we should not conclude that liberal theory is so hopelessly fraught with family disagreements that absolutely nothing distinguishes it or "liberals" themselves. The opposite assumption is, after all, what drives communitarian criticism and gives this research before us its purpose. What is it, then, that distinguishes liberals from communitarians?

The Right, the Good, and the Citizen

Despite the problems that plague the theoretical conception of liberalism from which Conover et al. operate, the focus-group discussions provide us with some interesting insights into the bedrock understandings that inform at least these citizens' conception of citizenship. To a person, all of the citizen-discussants shared "common understandings of the content, nature, and origins of rights" (especially civil rights) and a common schema with respect to duties. In interview material not included here, Conover et al. also report that all four focus groups emphasize the "same dominant theme"—freedom—and a fundamental sense of having important rights that ensure freedom. In summation the authors convincingly report, "It would appear that liberalism is the dominant discourse underpinning citizens' conceptions of their privileges qua citizens.

In other words, all of these citizens allow that individual rights or individual freedom are *core and essential* features of a healthy polity. None of them suggest that rights are, perhaps, tangential to a truly adequate understanding of citizenship or that respect for the individual is secondary to some higher common good or purpose. For all of these reasons, but primarily because they seem to give the notion of *individual rights* a lexical priority over other political values, these citizens merit the label "liberal."

Yet, if I understand the communitarian project correctly, this is precisely what communitarians do *not* do; they challenge, rather than endorse, the principle of rights and the sanctity of the (unencumbered) individual as central to an adequate conception of citizenship. For communitarians, the issue is not which rights and duties are appropriate to citizens, but what needs to preempt "rights and duties" as the central principle of political life. Despite their own family disagreements, almost all of the communitarian critics of liberalism share in this conclusion: when it comes to articulating the conditions of healthy political life, the principle of *the common good* outweighs the principle of individual rights and duties. Thus, when communitarians consider citizenship, they begin from a very different set of premises than their liberal counterparts.

To see this, let us return to the communitarian critics to whom Conover et al. refer. Sandel (1984a) argues that we should give up the "politics of rights" for a "politics of the common good"; MacIntyre

(1981) calls for "moral unity" and the construction of local forms of community in the face of the "liberal individualist world"; and Barber (1984) criticizes liberals for seeing political community as an instrumental rather than an "intrinsic" good. Although the communitarian critics are by no means a uniform bloc, they all reject a politics of "right over good" of the sort most often associated with Rawls. Such a politics, they argue, entails believing that justice takes priority over a conception of the good of the community as a whole (Gutmann 1985, 311). It is the priority of justice (or right) over good that the communitarian critics challenge in their attack on liberalism.

Now, neither Sandel nor MacIntyre have offered a programmatic conception of "the good," but both are certain that the concern for securing the rights of the individual has doomed modern liberalism to a perverse conception of the self and a hollow vision of society. Guiding both Sandel's and MacIntyre's work is the idea that our identities are constituted communally and derive from the "good" that guides the society to which we belong. Thus MacIntyre returns to Aristotle in order to defend the idea that "my good as a man is one and the same as the good of those others with whom I am bound up in human community" (1981, 212–13). In short, communitarian theorists like MacIntyre and Sandel privilege a conception of citizenship that emphasizes communal values and the good over one that emphasizes justice and core rights and duties. For Sandel, at least, justice is not "the first virtue" (1984a, 168). Its primacy, along with the conception of citizens as separate, rights-bearing individuals, is simply a sign of what we have lost: the community in which citizens know each other well enough to govern "by the common good alone" (Sandel 1984a, 175).

Exactly how this philosophical communitarianism translates into a political theory, and with what implications for liberty, individual autonomy, civil rights, and public policies, is not clear. (For this reason alone, it is difficult to know what positions count as "communitarian.") We might locate certain crucial human values within these antiliberal sentiments, however, and they include ties of love and friendship, social union, situatedness, association, a commitment to virtue over right, and the normative ideal of "community" over the individual. These are precisely the values that some of the citizen-discussants studied by Conover et al. extolled when they responded to questions about community participation with what the authors call "civic wisdom." So it is not surprising that Conover et al. are tempted to call these citizens communitarians. But we also need to recognize that central to communitarianism is more than just the laudatory expression of desirable civic behaviors or even a vocabulary of moral obligation or natural necessity. Underlying the communitarian displacement of justice and the rights-based individual in favor of the community is the notion that the common good *takes priority* over other political values. It is not a far step from this assumption to the claim that civic behaviors that foster the common good and the performance of duties that sustain the community itself take precedence over individual claims to privacy, separateness, independence, and liberty. The communitarian critics have not pushed the political side of their epistemological critique of liberalism thus far, but this does not mean that the implications simply go away. In any case, it is incumbent upon empirical researchers faced with citizen tributes to the common good or obligation to community to press this side of communitarianism to its logical conclusion, if only to see just how far defenders of the common good and obligation to community are willing to go.

I raise these points of communitarian criticism in order to suggest that "the right and the good contrasted," as Rawls indicates, and not "rights versus duties" as Conover et al. argue, is the real demarcation line between liberals and communitarians. But because they confine most of their framing questions and hypotheticals to the latter, the authors do not establish the discursive and conceptual conditions necessary for the discovery of communitarians. This is not to say the citizen-discussants who praised a notion of "common good," "collective responsibility," or obligation of a deep character to community were trading in incoherencies. As the authors report, a number of people raised these ideas in response to hypotheticals about helping victims of disaster, protecting public property, or as reasons for extending duty to encompass community involvement. Nevertheless, the litmus test of a communitarian is not *whether* citizens invoke the common good or speak an impassioned language of obligation to others, but what value relative to principles like individual liberty, personal happiness, or civil rights they place upon it. What counts in the discovery of communitarians, in other words, is whether individuals are willing to sacrifice or restrict other political goods—liberties foremost among them—in the pursuit of a "moral community." One might well imagine a citizen extolling the importance of, say, voluntary associations for an enlivened political community or acknowledging contractual debts to society or arguing that people have not just legal but moral obligations to others (as some of the citizens in these focus groups do). But one might also imagine the same citizen balking at the idea that the needs of "community" compel her or him consistently to sacrifice personal interests or rights for the common good, or rejecting the notion that activities that promote "sympathy and passion for others" can rightly be *required* of the individual by the community. These, however, are things we need to know if we are to conclude that there are communitarians in our midst. But the communitarians of North Carolina were not pressed on these matters. So we are left to wonder just how communitarian they really are.

In their search for communitarians, and drawing upon the guidance of communitarian critics, Conover et al. might have constructed hypotheticals and dilemmas for citizens to ponder framed by questions like these: In the interest of the common good, might it be acceptable to curtail or limit things we currently consider basic rights? If so, which rights and under what conditions? Are societies best governed when communities establish, as collectively obligatory, a single moral culture? What sorts of assumptions can we make about "persons" to guide our conception of a moral culture? Are we better off, as citizens, if we strictly control social and geographic mobility and encourage "bondedness, permanency, and proximity" to neighbor and kin? Should our schools be culture beds of civic virtue, community ethics, and patriotism—even if it means denouncing some habits, customs, and tastes (and perhaps individuals) as morally repugnant and pernicious to public lfe? Are censorship and the curtailment of free speech sometimes justifiable if they assist in the preservation of moral values and community standards of decency and virtue? In the interest of a healthy moral culture, might some individuals or institutions be empowered to enforce the performance of civic obligations (for example, assigning men to work in soup kitchens and women to build public housing) and perhaps curtail rights? Would you agree that you owe a "debt" to your community for giving you your very life, character, and personality? If so, what sort of "debt" is this, and how might a citizen be required to repay it in kind? Because we do not know how the focus groups would have responded to issues like these, I think we have to accept that Conover et al. are at least premature in concluding that they have found within the democratic discourse of their North Carolinians the sure echo of a communitarian ethic.

Conover et al. have found something important among their North Carolinians, however; it is perhaps truer to the complexity of ordinary political understandings than the analytical distinction between liberalism and communitarianism or the notion of two oppositional citizen ethics allows. For many of the citizens in this study, the vocabulary of community, civic responsibility, and collective good intermingles quite readily with and even amplifies the language of individual liberty. At the same time, the liberal vocabulary of "core rights" appears to frame basic notions of citizenship and provide a starting point for richer elaborations of political responsibility and community. Minimally, what the presence of these blended vocabularies suggests is that the relation between communitarianism and liberalism—at least within the ordinary political discourse of some citizens in the United States—is not one of mutual exclusivity or simple, stark opposition. Maximally, the presence of these blended vocabularies might lead us to question the sufficiency, if not the adequacy, of the categories "liberal" and "communitarian" as guides for understanding real citizens' discourse about democracy. For the moment, it is enough to appreciate that Conover et al. have contributed substantially to such reflection by bringing citizens back into the study of democratic discourse and by bringing citizens' discourse to the academic reaches of the liberal-communitarian debate.

References

Auerbach, Jerold. 1983. *Justice Without Law.* Oxford: Oxford University Press.

Barber, Benjamin. 1984. *Strong Democracy: Participatory Politics for a New Age.* Berkeley and Los Angeles: University of California Press.

Brown, Steven. 1980. *Political Subjectivity.* New Haven: Yale University Press.

Campbell, Angus, Phillip E. Converse, Warren E. Miller, and Donald E. Stokes. 1960. *The American Voter.* New York: Wiley.

Dworkin, Ronald. 1977. *Taking Rights Seriously.* Cambridge, Mass.: Harvard University Press.

Gutmann, Amy. 1985. "Communitarian Critics of Liberalism." *Philosophy and Public Affairs* 14:308–22.

Hartz, Louis. 1955. *The Liberal Tradition in America.* New York: Harcourt Brace Jovanovich.

Herzog, Don. 1986. "Some Questions for Republicans." *Political Theory* 14:473–93.

Hirsch, H. N. 1986. "The Threnody of Liberalism: Constitutional Liberty and the Renewal of Community." *Political Theory* 14:423–49.

MacIntyre, Alasdair. 1981. *After Virtue*. Notre Dame, Ind.: University of Notre Dame Press.

Mill, John Stuart. 1989. *On Liberty and Other Writings*. Cambridge: Cambridge University Press.

Rawls, John. 1971. *A Theory of Justice*. Cambridge, Mass.: Harvard University Press.

Ricci, David M. 1984. *The Tragedy of Political Science: Politics, Scholarship, and Democracy*. New Haven: Yale University Press.

Sandel, Michael. 1982. *Liberalism and the Limits of Justice*. Cambridge: Cambridge University Press.

———. 1984a. *Liberalism and Its Critics*. New York: New York University Press.

———. 1984b. "Morality and the Liberal Ideal," *New Republic*, 17 May, 15–17.

Taylor, Charles. 1985. "Interpretation and the Sciences of Man." In *Philosophy and the Human Sciences: Philosophical Papers Two*, 15–57. Cambridge: Cambridge University Press.

Walzer, Michael. 1983. *Spheres of Justice: A Defense of Pluralism and Equality*. New York: Basic Books.

———. 1990. "The Communitarian Critique of Liberalism." *Political Theory* 18:6–23.

9

Disjunction and Ambivalence in Citizens' Political Outlooks

Jennifer L. Hochschild

In the 1950s, political scientists and pundits rediscovered the question that so worried James Madison and his companions: Is the average citizen (or better, the aggregation of average citizens into the voting public) cognitively and emotionally capable of even the attenuated amount of self-government needed by a system of representative democracy and divided authority? Put rather more colloquially, is it true that "the masses are asses"? If so, what does that portend for democracy? Every student of American political science now knows the line of research stemming from those questions that shows the political judgments of most people to be unstable, poorly informed, inconsistent,

Thanks to the other authors of chapters in this volume, especially Hadley Arkes, George Marcus, Donald Moon, Virginia Sapiro, and David Tabb, for their generous help.

even nonexistent.[1] Such citizens make democracy, especially in its classical robust form of participatory, or republican, democracy, impossible or extremely dangerous (Kinder and Herzog, in this volume; Pateman 1970; Barber 1984; Nagel 1987). If citizens cannot understand and link arguments or will not expend the energy needed to find out a few key facts and decide their implications, democracies run the constant risk of disintegrating into tyranny or anarchy (Tocqueville [1835, 1840] 1969).

Recently, however, a note of cautious optimism has entered the discussion of democratic deliberation. "The miracle of aggregation" in electoral politics (Converse and Pierce 1986; Kinder and Herzog, in this volume) transforms unstable individual opinions into stable political views and policy proposals. Alternatively, over the *longue durée*, public opinion in the aggregate is remarkably stable and changes in intelligible, philosophically coherent ways (Jacobs and Shapiro 1989; Page and Shapiro, in this volume). In a third formulation, apparently inconsistent or ephemeral views actually result from the fact that people hold a cluster of beliefs among which they "sample" when responding to opinion surveys (Zaller and Feldman 1992). Qualitative interviews show that people hold political views that are as subtle and supple as—and often much more serviceable than—the views of political philosophers (Hochschild 1981; Gilligan 1982; Gilligan et al. 1988; Conover et al., in this volume). And in any case, "a democracy driven by diverse interests located within an extended republic does not demand or require ideological constraint in the electorate" (Marcus 1988, 31).

This cautious optimism contains different, even contradictory, claims: Although individual attitudes are inconsistent and incoherent, aggregated public opinion is nonetheless consistent and coherent. *Or* individuals are in fact consistent and coherent. *Or* conventional definitions of consistency and coherence are too narrow; under new definitions, individuals turn out to be consistent and coherent.

Adding philosophical concerns about democratic governance to these empirical claims about public opinion makes the discussion even more complex: Democracies thrive because citizens (individually or collectively) are consistent and coherent in their deliberations. *Or* democracies can thrive despite citizens' inconsistency and incoherence. (On these issues, see Moon, in this volume.)

1. This line of research began with Converse (1964); its development is traced in Kinder and Herzog (in this volume).

This chapter partakes of the new wave of cautious optimism but takes no position on any of these specific claims. It focuses on a different issue—systematic ways in which citizens are not consistent or coherent. That may sound like a contradiction; I hope to demonstrate how and why it is not and to suggest implications of that phenomenon for democratic deliberation.

Two cases inform the discussion. The first stems from my research into the old question Why is there no socialism in the United States? To an armchair Marxist, America's capitalist mode of production and unequal, alienating relations of production should generate a powerful working-class movement. Marx, of course, was no armchair Marxist, and he realized early on that the United States did not fit his model. Theorists and politicians have searched ever since for an explanation (Laslett and Lipset 1974; Foner 1984). I focused on citizens' beliefs about distributive justive and asked, "What norms of distributive justice do wealthy and poor Americans hold, and what do those norms imply for their beliefs about the redistribution of wealth?" (Hochschild 1981).

The second case is part of my current research on the effects of the changing class structure of African Americans on relations among races and within the black community. I seek most generally to examine the social consequences of the ideology of "the American dream"; here I am asking, "How do middle-class blacks, who supposedly exemplify the success of the dream, feel about it, about less successful African Americans, and about their white peers?"

The first project discovered, and the second began with an expectation of finding, that the respective research subjects felt disjunction and ambivalence. I define *disjunction* as a troublesome distinction drawn between two arenas of life. Most distinctions are not disjunctions; our mental life consists largely in drawing boundaries and creating categories, and to see them all as problematic would be absurd. It is when a boundary becomes problematic rather than useful that a distinction turns into a disjunction.

"Becomes problematic" is intentionally vague because it covers several cases. One common case occurs when people can no longer justify a distinction they have previously made. For example, if a person has assumed that women should stay home and care for children but men need not, then discovers that his assumption lacks a good reason, and becomes distressed by this lack, that person's distinction has become a disjunction. A second case occurs when people cannot persuade others of a distinction and are made uneasy by their inability to persuade or by the fact of standing alone. For example, a white Southerner may "know" that blacks are not as good as whites but understand that this is no longer a socially acceptable view and be disturbed by the implicit condemnation of a view she or he continues to hold. A third case moves partially out of the phenomenological realm of the subject and into the realm of the observer. An observer may see a "latent disjunction" in the subject that the subject is not (yet?) aware of. A latent disjunction is not simply a distinction that the observer does not understand or approve of, it must be a distinction that makes no sense within the subject's own context and that the subject him- or herself might find problematic if made aware of it. An example is a Latino raised to believe that however he acts at home, he must publicly deny his religious, linguistic, and cultural heritage in order to succeed in Anglo society. He feels no strain between his public and private selves, but an observer can plausibly expect him to feel a strain and predict that he will someday see his public-private split as undesirable or even untenable (Rodriguez 1982; Novak 1972).

The difference between a distinction and a disjunction is untidy for two reasons. It is conceptually not possible to identify precisely when a useful boundary between two concepts becomes problematic because the move from useful to problematic is an unbroken continuum rather than a sharp dichotomy. More important, the difference is itself politically, socially, and emotionally unstable; what seems clear and simple to one person, or in one mood, or in one social setting, or in one political context becomes disturbing and unsettled to another person, in another mood, in a different group of friends, or when political alliances dissolve in the face of new issues. The conceptual fuzziness is an unfortunate but inevitable constraint on my analysis, whereas the political instability—and its impact on democratic discourse—is largely the subject of my analysis.

Ambivalence is easier to define. It occurs when a person simultaneously holds several contradictory beliefs about the same issue. If I believe that I should grade students according to the quality of their exams and papers *and* according to how much they have learned in the course (regardless of the quality of their final product) *and* according to how hard they tried (regardless of what they learned and the quality of their final product), I am ambivalent about the criteria for grading. Ambivalence can also be latent, or in the eye of the beholder; the observation that a friend *ought* to feel more angry at her husband than she apparently does is common.

Like disjunction, the extent of ambivalence can be conceptually fuzzy (am I really caught between two grading criteria, or are they variations on the same goal?) or politically variable (does she become more angry at her husband as she becomes more aware of feminism?). The former is unfortunate but inevitable; the latter lies at the core of many of the most interesting analyses of political change (Merton and Barber 1963).

In short, disjunction addresses actually or potentially problematic boundaries between issues; ambivalence addresses actually or potentially contradictory impulses about the same issue.

Disjunction

To study citizens' norms of distributive justice, I devised a typology of theories of distributive justice ranging from a principle of equality to a principle of differentiation. The former principle begins with the assumption that people have equal value and can legitimately make equal claims on society. Differences in treatment must be justified. The latter principle assumes that people begin with different value and therefore can legitimately make different claims. Identical treatment must be justified. These two principles produce a continuum along which lie five more-specific norms of justice. These are (1) *strict equality*, which calls for giving identical amounts of goods to all; (2) *need*, which tries to ensure equal well-being to all; (3) *investment*, which makes rewards proportional to input; (4) *results*, which makes rewards proportional to output; and (5) *ascription*, which bases rewards on fixed characteristics such as race or gender. A final norm, *procedures*, can have either egalitarian or differentiating effects depending on the procedure chosen and the way it is played out.

I then conducted intensive interviews of about six hours duration with sixteen randomly selected white adults with incomes below $12,000 and twelve with incomes over $35,000 (in 1976 dollars). The topics of conversation included the distribution of money within the family, school, and workplace; views on family authority, fair incomes, the class structure, the electoral system, and government policies; and the meaning of justice, equality, and democracy. We discussed the idea of equalizing incomes and holdings several times. My questions sought perceptions, explanations, and evaluations of existing conditions as well as changes the respondent would make if he or she were "assistant God," as one woman put it. There were detailed probes, forced-choice questions, and opportunities for rambling anecdotes.

Respondents might plausibly have held several patterns of distributive norms. The Marxist would anticipate differences between classes or at least between those with the appropriate class consciousness; the poor should endorse greater equality and the rich greater differentiation. The student of Silvan Tomkins (1963) would anticipate differences between people with left-wing and right-wing orientations. The student of Robert Nozick (1974) would focus on the distinction between those who chose patterned end-state norms (the first five) and those who defined justice as fair procedures. The student of Philip Converse might expect no coherent ideology at all from most respondents.

I found none of these results. The dominant pattern of beliefs was systematic variation *within* individuals, *across* domains of life. That is, the modal respondent sought greater equality in the home and school, among friends and neighbors, in social and tax policies, in political authority, and in an imagined ideal society. The same person sought differentiation in the marketplace, workplace, and class structure. People should be equal in the personal and political realms, but unequal in the economic realm—so argued rich and poor, sophisticated and ignorant, Republican and Democrat.

I call this pattern of beliefs a *disjunction* across domains of life because it produced contradictory arguments, emotional distress for some respondents, and economic disadvantage for the poor. Thus, when respondents used a political perspective to consider the possibility of redistributing wealth, they often endorsed it. They wanted the government to make taxes more progressive, to enable at least the deserving poor to live with dignity and autonomy (often close to middle-class standards), to keep the "filthy rich" from acquiring too much. Some wanted the government to equalize incomes of all hard workers; most envisioned utopia as a community of moderately well-off equals.

But when the same respondents used an economic perspective to think about redistributing wealth, they usually opposed it. Doctors should make more than factory workers because they have more education, more responsibility, or more "headaches." Nelson Rockefeller should be able to bequeath his wealth to his children just as I hope to pass my savings account on to mine. A hierarchical class structure is natural and inevitable, even if not always desirable or just.

The most common consequence of simultaneously holding two such disjoint sets of views was political paralysis. When asked to juxtapose their egalitarian and differentiating norms—when asked to think about the *political* consequences of redistributing *economic* holdings—most respondents simply stammered apologetically and changed the subject. A few expressed more-active frustration; one man offered no solution except to rob a bank, and another proposed killing off everyone and starting over with "the perfect male—me—and the perfect female." Many of the poor even understood that their own norms, along with other Americans', left them with no apparently legitimate means to protest their condition and with only themselves to blame. They simply saw no recourse.

A few respondents, however, responded to their normative disjunction by taking a few steps toward a new political resolution. Several called, with varying degrees of sophistication and detail, for government provision of jobs for all. Such a program goes far toward reconciling differentiating economic and egalitarian political norms, and I was impressed with how many people came up with the idea on their own. Others talked about a high level of guaranteed incomes, institutions that would remove poor children from their homes and teach them self-sufficiency, or reforms in the legal system. What matters here is not the practicality, refinement, or political leanings of these proposals; what matters is the evidence that people can respond to disjunctions with creative ideas rather than paralysis.

Middle-class blacks manifest disjunction differently. Standard sociological theory predicts that as African Americans move up the socioeconomic ladder, they become more conservative than both those they leave behind and those whose class they are joining (Lipset and Zetterberg 1956; Lopreato 1967; but see Thompson 1971). Some anecdotal evidence and survey data support that theory. Corporate managers

> are a fundamentally new group among blacks. . . . As a condition for their advancement up the corporate ladder, black managers, like whites, must accommodate themselves to the corporate value system. But unlike whites, black managers have had difficulty justifying those corporate values. . . . They recognize them to be inconsistent with the set of views and values articulated by the

> traditional civil-rights leadership and accepted by the black community at large. So, they've been desperately searching for something which would give them and their views legitimacy in the black community. This black conservative ideology gives them something they can grab hold of. (Daniels 1981, 23)

A successful journalist is more blunt: "Guilt about the ghetto is passé. A lot of blacks won't admit that. But most of us have a lot of other things on our minds" (Brashler 1978, 140). Young blacks who perceived their personal financial situation to be improving led a dramatic increase in approval of President Reagan's job performance from 1984 to 1986 (Williams 1986, 4–7).[2] In 1986, black support for a second presidential campaign by Jesse Jackson declined as education, occupational status, and income rose (Harris and Williams 1986, 6). Similarly, support for President Bush was disproportionally strong among African Americans with high incomes and considerable education (Oresties 1990).

For every theory there is an equal but opposite theory. Many black scholars argue that racism's overwhelming force keeps middle-class and poor African Americans in the same boat: despite "some progress toward eliminating discriminatory barriers against blacks in the last half of the 1950s and the decade of the 1960s, . . . these actions failed largely because racial discrimination is deeply rooted in the structure of American institutions" (Pinkney 1984, 2). A 1978 resolution of the Association of Black Sociologists condemned an award to William Julius Wilson's book *The Declining Significance of Race* on the grounds that "the book clearly omits significant data regarding the continuing discrimination against blacks at all class levels. It . . . draws inferences that are contrary to the conclusions that other black and white scholars have reached with reference to the salience of race as a critical variable in American society" (cited in Pinkney 1984, 14–15).

This proposition too receives both anecdotal and systematic support. A now-successful black manager concludes an illuminating account of his rocky corporate initiation by claiming:

2. This survey gives contradictory results for direct measures of the relation between blacks' socioeconomic status and their support for President Reagan. Higher-income and better-educated blacks endorsed him more than poorer and less well educated blacks, but blue-collar workers gave him higher approval ratings than professional, business, or clerical workers. These results are all bivariate relations; to my knowledge, no regressions have been run on the data.

> What most white people do not understand or accept is the fact that skin color has such a pervasive impact on every black person's life that it subordinates considerations of education or class. . . . All blacks, regardless of status, are subjected to prejudice. I personally was not as disadvantaged as many other blacks, but to some extent all blacks are products of separate schools, neighborhoods, and subcultures. In short, black and white people not only look different but also come from different environments which condition them differently and make understanding and honest communication difficult to achieve. (Jones 1973, 114; see also Bell 1987, 140–61)

On surveys, higher-income blacks are most likely to say that they "feel closest to" other blacks, whereas higher-income whites identify more with members of their own class than those of their own race (Jackman and Jackman 1983, 45–53; see also Parent and Stekler 1985, 532). Middle-class blacks perceive more discrimination, have more dislike of whites, and perceive more racism among whites than do worse-off blacks (Lewis and Schneider 1983, 13; Bowman et al., n.d., table 4; Denton and Sussman 1981, A2; Colasanto and Williams 1987).[3] Blacks at all income and educational levels continue to experience residential segregation, lower economic returns to schooling (Farley and Allen 1987, 148–50, 303–6; Massey and Denton 1987), and employment discrimination (Ellwood 1986; Kirschenman and Neckerman 1991).

However, common sense as well as most evidence supports neither claim in its strongest form. What is most salient for middle-class blacks is that they are *both* middle-class *and* black. Thus their views are likely to be sometimes typical of the (predominantly white) middle class (that is, relatively conservative) and sometimes typical of African Americans (that is, relatively liberal)—making them a distinct group in their own right.

If the sparse and somewhat contradictory data can be trusted, that is in fact the case. Although African Americans overall remain more liberal than whites, in the past two decades middle-class blacks have become *more* liberal than poorer blacks on racial and civil rights issues but *less*

3. This finding reverses the pattern of the 1950s and 1960s, when (if the scant data can be trusted) well-off blacks were more optimistic about race relations than worse-off blacks (Banks 1950, 533; Brink and Harris 1966, 224–63 passim).

liberal on questions of social welfare policy. Thus, on the one hand, between 1968 and 1980 well-off, but not poor, blacks increasingly agreed that civil rights progress was too slow and denied that there had been "a lot" of civil rights change. On the other hand, during the 1970s, low- and high-income blacks increasingly diverged in their support for government intervention to give economic help to minorities and to guarantee jobs and incomes. Low-income blacks continued their strong support, but high-income blacks drastically reduced theirs (Parent and Stekler 1985, 529–33; see also Dawson 1993; Welch and Combs 1985; Welch and Foster 1987; Parent 1984; Lichter 1985; for mixed results, see Sigelman and Welch 1991; for disagreement, see Seltzer and Smith 1985).

What makes this increasing divergence between well-off and poor blacks a problematic disjunction rather than a simple distinction for people on both sides is its political context. Many poor blacks and veterans of the civil rights movement see well-off blacks as sellouts, Uncle Toms, Oreos—corrupted by their desire to get and retain the white man's wealth and power: "The new black middle class . . . is an *empty class* that has flowered into social prominence *without a clearly defined social mission*. . . . [It is] mindless of its own potential or else reticent to mobilize it. . . . It is an indulgent 'Me' generation . . . [with] puny . . . intellectual, scholarly, and creative output" (Cruse 1987, 389–90). Cruse excoriates the new black middle class precisely for its increasing split between strong support for political and civil rights and weakening support for economic and social equality—what he terms the NAACP's "debilitating leadership" in accord with "the guiding white philosophy of noneconomic liberalism" (79).

Middle-class African Americans worry about selling out. A Dow Jones executive begins a newspaper column, "We in the black middle class have failed to take care of our own people. Cubans in Miami take care of their own. So do Jews. So do Korean shopkeepers in New York. Why don't we?" (Logan 1986; see also Wilkins 1988; Raspberry 1985; Ifill and Maraniss 1986). As many well-off as poor black Atlantans (39 percent and 41 percent respectively) agreed in a 1981 survey that "non-poor blacks do not care about poor blacks in the city."[4] Nevertheless,

4. The same proportion of poor blacks (39 percent) felt that whites were uncaring; many more well-off blacks (51 percent) were willing to chastise whites. More poor than well-off blacks felt that "the City" and businesses had not done enough for poor blacks, and more poor than well-off blacks expected President Reagan's policies to hurt the poor. These findings all support my claim about well-off blacks' greater sensitivity to racial issues and lesser concern

well-off blacks have no intention of abjuring their new status and the views that often go along with it.

In short, as racial discrimination eases for some African Americans, increasingly well-off and integrated blacks are acquiring disjoint distributive norms analogous to those that most whites have held for a long time. But middle-class blacks bear a double burden of disjunction—not only in the growing disparity between their political and economic views but also in the growing disparity between their new views and the expectations and demands that poorer African Americans place on them.

Even this double burden of disjunction does not complete the picture of systematic inconsistency and incoherence that I initially proposed to examine. Let us turn to its other common form—ambivalence.

Ambivalence

Once the pattern of disjunction across domains became clear, my respondents' answers to interview questions about norms of distributive justice mostly fell into place. But not entirely. Even among those respondents who most clearly demonstrated the pattern of disjunction, there remained a lot of noise. That is, along with their normative distinctions *across* domains, respondents expressed a lot of apparently contradictory views *within* any one domain.

Thinking like most survey researchers, I first dismissed this noise as evidence of respondents' unclear thinking, my unclear questioning, or systematic variation whose cause remained outside the reach of my "independent variables." I came, however, to see intradomain contradiction, not as a problem to be submerged into the background, but as a finding that warranted the careful attention due a figure in the foreground. It could be analyzed and understood, and its role in respondents' belief systems was as important as their unambiguous normative statements were.

This point is best illustrated by an example. To the question "What role did luck play in your career?" one wealthy respondent answered:

---

about social welfare issues, compared to poor blacks (Center for Public and Urban Research 1981).

> You know, being happy. As I said years ago when I first started working, and I think everybody was healthy and all that. Oh, I wouldn't say "breaks"—I don't go by luck. Just felt that a lot of times, I mean, in business you gamble, and you do things, but we aren't business people, we aren't gamblers. But that's where you believe in Lady Luck and all that. But we just feel that if you've worked, then you should get. Well that's, I think, why I'm a little upset. (Hochschild 1981, 241–42)

This woman does not believe that luck should determine success, and she wants to believe in a norm of results. But because she knows that she has achieved a lot, if a norm of results obtains, she can attribute her own (perceived) lack of success only to bad luck—which she does not believe in. She is therefore driven into a flurry of confused, incomplete, vague phrases. So understood, this speech, incomprehensible in itself, became the key to understanding many of her other arguments that initially seemed merely inconsistent or churlish.

Other respondents gave similarly confused, contradictory, or vague responses that sorted ultimately into five patterns of ambivalence. Within a single domain, respondents would (1) attempt to answer a question either normatively or pragmatically, and then question that distinction or their placement of an issue on one side of it; (2) simultaneously hold strongly egalitarian and differentiating norms about a single issue, with no way of balancing them or giving priority to one; (3) feel torn between global differentiating beliefs they had been taught and specific egalitarian beliefs they derived from direct experience; (4) feel torn between global egalitarian beliefs and specific differentiating norms; or (5) permit economic concerns (which evoke differentiating norms) to impinge more than they wished on issues within the personal and political domains (which evoke egalitarian norms) (Hochschild 1981, 238–58).

Middle-class African Americans also demonstrate ambivalence. As was the case for disjunction, our knowledge is insufficient to categorize their views fully. But the published literature contains enough examples to suggest that middle-class blacks often feel deep internal conflict about their values, behaviors, and identity within a single sphere of life.

Two examples demonstrate black middle-class ambivalence. The first is an essay by the journalist Leanita McClain (1986), who rose from public-housing-project poverty to the editorial staff of the *Chicago*

Tribune. She committed suicide at age thirty-two, less than four years after writing the following:[5]

> I am a member of the black middle class who has had it with being patted on the head by white hands and slapped in the face by black hands for my success. . . . We have foresaken the revolution, we are told, we have sold out. . . . The truth is, we have not forgotten; we would not dare. We are simply fighting on different fronts and are no less war weary, and possibly more heartbroken, for we know the black and white worlds can meld. . . .
>
> My life abounds in incongruities. . . . Sometimes when I wait at the bus stop with my attache case, I meet my aunt getting off the bus with other cleaning ladies on their way to do my neighbors' floors. . . . But I am not ashamed. Black progress has surpassed our greatest expectations. . . .
>
> I have made it, but where? Racism still dogs my people. . . . I run a gauntlet between two worlds, and I am cursed and blessed by both. I travel, observe, and take part in both; I can also be used by both. I am a rope in a tug of war. If I am a token in my downtown office, so am I at my cousin's church tea. . . . I have a foot in each world, but I cannot fool myself about either. . . . I know how tenuous my grip on one way of life is, and how strangling the grip of the other way of life can be.

McClain's anguish contains at least two forms of ambivalence. Her feelings oscillate between optimism—"black progress has surpassed our greatest expectations"—and discouragement—"racism still dogs my people." In addition, her identity is split; she is always "being a rope in a tug of war" or "having a foot in both worlds." She is expected (and expects herself?) to be *either* black *or* middle-class, whereas she is of course both simultaneously.

The ambivalence of another successful black woman focuses more on her profession than on her social persona and self-understanding:

5. Originally in *Newsweek*, 13 October 1980, under the title "The Middle-class Black's Burden." For evidence that her suicide was partly due to despair over her dual identity, see Campbell 1984, Klose 1984, and Page 1986.

> The central dilemma of my professional training . . . [was]: I am a black child—one of the subjects whose behavior needed an alternative explanation [i.e., different from the social science "deficit theory" she had been taught but found unacceptable]. By enrolling in graduate school, I was embedding myself in an environment that denied the complexity of my experience. . . . I expected to develop new methods through activity that was based on the premises and methods of the very system I questioned. If I were successful, I might have to regard myself as a failure. (Mitchell 1982, 34)

Having become an academic, Jacqueline Mitchell's ambivalence has

> increased and intensified. New . . . [problems] have appeared. Most significantly, a role and identity conflict has crystallized: I am expected somehow to be an objective social scientist yet have a black perspective. This role is a contradiction, and I have begun to experience feelings of anxiety and futility, emotions that paralyze and inhibit my creativity and productivity. . . . It is of little consequence that we may be recognized and respected for our contributions and scholarship; our ever-present visibility never allows us to experience complete membership in white academia. At the same time, these marginal feelings begin to affect our ethnicity as well. We thus experience double marginality, belonging to and feeling a part of two worlds, yet never at home in either. (37–39)

Ultimately, Mitchell finds, "the ideologies of the two reference groups contradict and conflict. . . . We are in a no-win situation; if we 'sell out' and totally embrace the white system, we might enjoy some of its rewards, yet negate valued parts of ourselves. . . . Yet complete rejection of white academia may not be any better. . . . If we reject the system, we forfeit our opportunity to influence it in ways which will create a more receptive and responsive atmosphere for our input" (Mitchell 1982, 39).[6]

6. W.E.B. DuBois ([1903] 1986, 363–64) most famously described the "peculiar sensation, this double-consciousness, this sense of always looking at one's self through the eyes of others, of measuring one's soul by the tape of a world that looks on in amused contempt and pity. One ever feels his twoness,—an American, a Negro; two souls, two thoughts, two unreconciled

For respondents in *What's Fair?* ambivalence, like disjunction, most commonly resulted in political paralysis and emotional distress. One Jewish respondent exploded in anger at WASPs with "old money," whom he had been envying a moment earlier; another wealthy respondent was "a little bit of a Marxist" but could think of no circumstances in which the well-off should extend themselves to help people in need; a third engaged in an extended and fascinating debate with himself over confiscatory inheritance taxes, during which his views ranged from radically redistributive to radically social Darwinist. He concluded—correctly—that "I'm going around in circles here."

A few respondents, however, found creative resolutions to their ambivalence. These included an anxious mother's elaborate rules for an allocation of children's allowances that would simultaneously reward age, effort, and accomplishments; a devout Catholic's hard-won empathy with supporters of abortion rights; and a lawyer's carefully elaborated plan for guaranteeing incomes without condoning laziness. Although our knowledge in the second case is much less systematic, we can presume that middle-class blacks also respond to ambivalence with everything from paralytic distress to energetic creativity. Jacqueline Mitchell appears to be managing her ambivalence-generating circumstances actively and constructively;[7] Leanita McClain could not.[8]

The Context of Disjunction and Ambivalence

Earlier, I emphasized that social and political contexts are intrinsic to our understanding of disjunction and ambivalence. I mean by this four things.

---

strivings; two warring ideals in one dark body, whose dogged strength alone keeps it from being torn asunder."

7. Gilkes (1982) provides another example of how an individual's effort to resolve ambivalence can both help to forge a new personal identity and contribute to the creation of new institutions in the black community.

8. Like Leanita McClain, other African Americans can be paralyzed by the ambivalence induced in trying to succeed in the higher reaches of white corporate America. A black manager "never put[s] anything into the system that might be used against me"; another operates on the assumption that "they're just looking for something to hold against you, so you have to be very careful what you go public with. I don't even go to the same bathroom with my peers. . . . They've never seen me drink, smoke, or shit. I don't want them judging me." A third "tr[ies] to avoid saying anything personal. Whenever I'm around them I can tell they are keeping mental notes." (All quotes are from Davis and Watson 1985, 6; for similar sentiments from high school students, see Fordham 1988.)

First, as we saw above, disjunctions and ambivalence occur as individuals respond to their circumstances. Some disjunctions and ambivalences are surely idiosyncratic, or result from the internal psychological dynamics of particular individuals. As social scientists, however, we are most interested in the (more common?) case in which people express disjunctions and ambivalence because they are in a disjunctive situation (Merton and Barber 1963). For example, the bifurcation of norms into those of "public" behavior, which eschew violence, and those of "private" behavior, which have traditionally permitted a man physically to "discipline" his wife and children, is deeply embedded in American political culture, institutions, and practices. It is hardly surprising that some women, as well as many men, have difficulty deciding if a family conflict counts as rape and battery or not (Sapiro, in this volume). Ambivalence among middle-class African Americans illustrates the same analytic point. Middle-class white men typically are not in anguish about their dual roles, not because white men are inherently different from black men but because in the United States "black" and "middle class" have not, to put it mildly, traditionally been associated with one another.

Second, whether people can satisfactorily resolve their disjunctions and ambivalences depends largely on the institutions, ideas, and political movements available to them. Several *What's Fair?* respondents questioned the common American disjunction between political and personal equality and economic inequality. But they were unable to find a political leader or movement, a social group, or even other individuals who shared their doubts and with whom they could develop a systematic, satisfying alternative normative vision. So they were left hanging. Maria Pulaski, for example, waited until the tape recorder was turned off, after eight hours of conversation, to declare, "I only hope things get better, instead of what they are now. Change the government—no, I shouldn't say that, huh?" She made a few halting suggestions for reform, observed that "can't be just one person doing it, or two persons. You all gotta get together and go around, talking with the people, and try to let them understand things," but concluded, "But what can you do? Actually, you don't see anything like that happening though. Nope" (Hochschild 1981, 28–29). Some members of the black middle class work hard to create institutional and social supports, in part to resolve ambivalence and reinforce the new distinctions in their political attitudes. Contrast, for example, the relief expressed in one newspaper headline, "For Black Partners in Top Law Firms, Lunch Is Special" (Williams 1987) with the pessimism expressed by artist Gordon Parks (Moore 1989, 74): "I found myself on a plateau of loneliness, not knowing really where I belonged. In one world I was a social oddity. In the other I was almost a stranger. . . . Many times I wondered whether my achievement was worth the loneliness" (see also McCall 1988; Lacayo 1989, 62).

Extending the notion that "lunch is special" leads ultimately to the concept of political mobilization and incorporation (Tabb, in this volume). Creating or joining a coalition in which one can ally with like-minded others and jointly change political outcomes to accord with one's own views is surely the most rewarding way to overcome ambivalence or resolve disjunctions. However, the process is neither simple nor sure; as Bernice Reagon reminds us, coalitions sometimes require painful stretches of one's emotional and political capacities and may actually exacerbate ambivalence about new roles.[9] The recent history of the Chicago mayoralty illustrates both phenomena. Harold Washington was able to persuade African Americans and Latinos to overcome their ambivalence about one another and electoral politics and create a dominant coalition through political incorporation. But after his death, the tensions within the black community and between ethnic groups were too great, and the coalition fell apart (Starks and Preston 1990). The upshot may be an even greater disjunction in the minds of black Chicagoans between the political process and their own individual and collective desires.

Third, distinctions become disjunctive or disjunctions are eased into mere distinctions, and ambivalences are resolved or created, partly in response to changes in political and social circumstances. For many men during the 1960s, the comfortable distinction between rape and marital rights became the disconcerting disjunction associated with "marital rape"; for some women, the disjunction between marital duties and preferences about intercourse became the clear distinction between rape and consensual sex (Sapiro, in this volume). The same holds for ambiv-

9. "I feel as if I'm gonna keel over any minute and die. That is often what it feels like if you're *really* doing coalition work. Most of the time you feel threatened to the core and if you don't you're not really doing no coalescing. . . . You don't go into coalition because you just *like* it. The only reason you would consider trying to team up with somebody who could possibly kill you, is because that's the only way you can figure you can stay alive" (Reagon 1983, 356).

alence: In a gripping autobiography, Roger Wilkins (1982) traces the trajectory of moving from childhood innocence through the discovery of his anomalous status as a middle-class black to a slowly and painfully achieved psychological integration of the many facets of his character. Simple maturation was one cause of this trajectory. But another was Wilkins's and the United States' changing circumstances during the 1960s and 1970s, in which friends, ideologies, political climates, and institutions appeared and disappeared in ways that first heightened, then softened, the anomalies of his position.

Finally, a person's role in a given social setting has a lot to do with whether he or she feels disjunctions or ambivalence. Many men apparently feel comfortable with the current division of labor in their families, congratulating themselves that they have appropriately responded to their wives' new roles as salaried workers. Their wives, however, continue to feel deeply ambivalent about their household arrangements, often blaming themselves for not getting enough done while repressing anger at their husbands for not bearing their fair share of the work load (Hochschild 1989). Many whites are satisfied that the racial disjunction of the Jim Crow era and whites' corresponding ambivalence known as the "American dilemma" (Myrdal 1944) are behind us. They therefore cannot understand blacks' discontent. Most blacks, however, remain deeply ambivalent about whites and about their own place in American society (Hochschild 1990).

Thus, disjunction and ambivalence are more than traits of individual belief systems. They are clues to the ways that ideology papers over cracks in the social edifice (Geertz 1973, 203–20), entry points into the different perspectives of people in different power positions, and signposts to political and ideological changes over time. They are, in short, crucial elements of democratic deliberation.

Grounds for Cautious Optimism

Why, given so much political paralysis and emotional distress, do I claim that the systematic incoherencies and inconsistencies of disjunction and ambivalence are compatible with the new wave of cautious optimism about democratic deliberation? For four reasons.

At a minimum, disjunction and ambivalence demonstrate that "voters are not fools, . . . [that they are] moved by concern about central and relevant questions of public policy" (Key 1966, 7–8). Not all inconsistencies and incoherences demonstrate voters' intelligence and connectedness, of course. But those described here, and many others, do (see Conover et al., in this volume). Indeed, for members of the black middle class, *not* to be ambivalent about succeeding in the white man's world—and for workers, *not* to separate economic from political justice—would suggest either an astonishing degree of creative autonomy or an equally astonishing obliviousness to the world around them.

Cautious optimism is also warranted if one focuses on the implications of disjunction and ambivalence, not for their holders, but for the rest of society. People on the margins—who question, or whose behavior violates standard assumptions about "what goes with what"—enable or require others to avoid reifying what exists (Turner 1969; Norton 1988, 51–94; Kashima 1991). To be treated by a black doctor or given orders by a black supervisor challenges white Americans' assumptions about racial orderings. To be asked why the unemployed daughter of a rich man should have more money than the local garbage collector encourages Americans to rethink their beliefs about economic rights in the country where "all men are created equal."[10] Thus, although disjunction and ambivalence are costly to their holders, they are extremely valuable to a society that takes deliberation seriously.

Third, disjunctive and ambivalent situations—circumstances in which we do not know how people will act because they are torn in several directions—are politically crucial. Because one cannot predict whether people thinking about the *political* redistribution of *economic* goods will focus on political rights and the role of government (in which case they support it), on economic rights and the role of the market (in which case they oppose it), or on the contradiction between their two norms (in which case they may be paralyzed), there is room for persuasion, leadership, innovation. There is even room for someone to rethink the issue in a way that transcends the contradiction. Similarly, because middle-class African Americans can deal with their ambivalence in

10. In conversation, Hadley Arkes has observed that the appropriate resolution of disjunctions and ambivalence is not necessarily a movement to the left of the political spectrum. For example, people who support a woman's right to have an abortion but oppose the death penalty could resolve this discrepancy by endorsing the saving of "life" at all its stages. This example also illustrates an earlier point: the difference between a distinction and a disjunction is hardly clear-cut.

dramatically different ways—by simply living with it, by affirming one side and rejecting the other, or by transcending it in a new synthesis—ideas and arguments can play an important role in shaping relations across the races and within the black (and white) communities.

Finally, far from being a danger to democracy, as the most fearful writers of the 1950s might have claimed, disjunction and ambivalence are essential components of it.[11] A democracy composed of consistent, tranquil, attitudinally constrained citizens is a democracy full of smug people with no incentive and perhaps no ability to think beyond their own circumstances. They know who they are, how things fit together, and what follows from what—and woe betide anyone who questions or violates the standard pattern. Conversely, a democracy composed of citizens coping with disjunction and ambivalence is full of people who question their own rightness, who may entertain alternative viewpoints, and who, given the right conditions, are more driven to resolve problems than ignore them (Marcus 1988). The former democracy may be more content but is too brittle to survive for long; the latter one is less happy but stronger. If we could figure out how to transform, more often, the consequences of disjunction and ambivalence from political paralysis to empathy and creativity, the grounds for cautious optimism about democratic deliberation would indeed be solid.

References

Banks, W.S.M. 1950. "The Rank Order of Sensitivity to Discriminations of Negroes in Columbus, Ohio." *American Sociological Review* 15:529–34.

Barber, Benjamin. 1984. *Strong Democracy.* Berkeley and Los Angeles: University of California Press.

Bell, Derrick. 1987. *And We Are Not Saved.* New York: Basic Books.

Bowman, Phillip, Alida Quick, and Shirley Hatchett. N.d. "Social Psychological Status of the Black Population." University of Michigan, Ann Arbor. Unpublished paper.

11. People may seek to resolve their disjunctions and ambivalence by lurching to the certainty of one side or the other and rejecting alternative possibilities. Some of my respondents occasionally grasped for absolutes, and some uncompromising black radicals, or conservatives, may do the same. A demagogic leader can combine separate individual anxieties and rigidities into collective hysteria. Thus, disjunctions and ambivalence may be dangerous as well as salutory for a democracy, depending on the nature of its deliberations.

Brashler, William. 1978. "The Black Middle Class: Making It." *New York Times Magazine*, 3 December.
Brink, William, and Louis Harris. 1966. *Black and White*. New York: Simon & Schuster.
Campbell, Bebe. 1984. "To Be Black, Gifted, and Alone." *Savvy*, December, 67–74.
Center for Public and Urban Research, Georgia State University. 1981. "Selected Responses to a Survey Conducted in the Five-County Metro Area in July–August, 1981." Mimeo.
Colasanto, Diane, and Linda Williams. 1987. "The Changing Dynamics of Race and Class." *Public Opinion* 9 (5): 50–53.
Converse, Philip. 1964. "The Nature of Belief Systems in Mass Publics." In *Ideology and Discontent*, ed. David Apter, 206–61. New York: Free Press.
Converse, Philip E., and Roy Pierce. 1986. *Political Representation in France*. Cambridge, Mass.: Harvard University Press.
Cruse, Harold. 1987. *Plural but Equal*. New York: William Morrow.
Daniels, Lee. 1981. "The New Black Conservatives." *New York Times Magazine*, 4 October.
Davis, George, and Glegg Watson. 1985. *Black Life in Corporate America*. Garden City, N.Y.: Doubleday, Anchor Books.
Dawson, Michael. 1993. *Behind the Mule: Race and Class in African American Politics*. Princeton: Princeton University Press.
Denton, Herbert, and Barry Sussman. 1981. " 'Crossover Generation' of Blacks Express Most Distrust of Whites." *Washington Post*, 25 March, A1, A2.
Du Bois, W.E.B. [1903] 1986. *The Souls of Black Folk*. New York: Library of America.
Ellwood, David. 1986. "The Spatial Mismatch Hypothesis." In *The Black Youth Employment Crisis*, ed. Richard Freeman and Harry Holzer, 147–85. Chicago: University of Chicago Press.
Farley, Reynolds, and Walter Allen. 1987. *The Color Line and the Quality of Life in America*. New York: Russell Sage Foundation.
Foner, Eric. 1984. "Why Is There No Socialism in the United States?" *History Workshop* 17:57–80.
Fordham, Signithia. 1988. "Racelessness as a Factor in Black Students' School Success." *Harvard Educational Review* 58:54–84.
Geertz, Clifford. 1973. *Interpretation of Cultures*. New York: Basic Books.
Gilkes, Cheryl. 1982. "Successful Rebellious Professionals: The Black Woman's Professional Identity and Community Commitment." *Psychology of Women Quarterly* 6:289–311.
Gilligan, Carol. 1982. *In a Different Voice*. Cambridge, Mass.: Harvard University Press.
Gilligan, Carol, Jane Ward, and Jill Taylor, eds. 1988. *Mapping the Moral Domain*. Cambridge, Mass.: Center for the Study of Gender, Education, and Human Development.
Harris, Fredrick, and Linda Williams. 1986. "JCPS/Gallup Poll Reflects Changing Views on Political Issues." *Focus* (newsletter of the Joint Center for Political Studies, Washington, D.C.), vol. 14, no. 10.

Hochschild, Arlie. 1989. *The Second Shift*. New York: Viking.

Hochschild, Jennifer. 1981. *What's Fair?* Cambridge, Mass.: Harvard University Press.

———. 1990. " 'Yes, but . . .': Principles and Caveats in American Racial Attitudes." In *NOMOS XXXII: Majorities and Minorities*, ed. John Chapman and Alan Wertheimer, 308–35. New York: New York University Press.

Ifill, Gwen, and David Maraniss. 1986. "In Atlanta, Struggling with Success." *Washington Post*, 20 January, A1, A10.

Jackman, Mary, and Robert Jackman. 1983. *Class Awareness in the United States*. Berkeley and Los Angeles: University of California Press.

Jacobs, Lawrence, and Robert Shapiro. 1989. "Public Opinion and the New Social History." *Social Science History* 13:1–23.

Jones, Edward W., Jr. 1973. "What It's Like to Be a Black Manager." *Harvard Business Review* 51:108–16.

Kashima, Takako. 1991. *Anti-Structure: Rituals in Japanese Diet*. Princeton: Princeton University Press.

Key, V. O., with Milton Cummings. 1966. *The Responsible Electorate*. Cambridge, Mass.: Harvard University Press.

Kirschenman, Joleen, and Kathryn Neckerman. 1991. " 'We'd Love to Hire Them, but . . .': The Meaning of Race for Employers." In *The Urban Underclass*, ed. Christopher Jencks and Paul Peterson, 203–32. Washington, D.C.: Brookings Institution.

Klose, Kevin. 1984. "A Tormented Black Rising Star Dead by Her Own Hand." *Washington Post*, 5 August, C1, C2.

Lacayo, Richard. 1989. "Between Two Worlds." *Time Magazine*, 13 March, 58–68.

Laslett, John, and Seymour M. Lipset, eds. 1974. *Failure of a Dream?* Garden City, N.Y.: Doubleday, Anchor Books.

Lewis, I. A., and William Schneider. 1983. "Black Voting, Bloc Voting, and the Democrats." *Public Opinion* 6 (5): 12–15, 59.

Lichter, Linda. 1985. "Who Speaks for Black America?" *Public Opinion* 8 (4): 41–44, 58.

Lipset, Seymour M., and Hans Zetterberg. 1956. "A Theory of Social Mobility." *Transactions of the Third World Congress of Sociology* 2:155–77.

Logan, Harold. 1986. "Blacks Helping Blacks." *Washington Post*, 23 November, D5.

Lopreato, Joseph. 1967. "Upward Social Mobility and Political Orientation." *American Sociological Review* 32:586–92.

McCall, Nathan. 1988. "The Best Defense." *Black Enterprise*, April, 79–81.

McClain, Leanita. 1986. *A Foot in Each World*. Ed. Clarence Page. Evanston, Ill.: Northwestern University Press.

Marcus, George. 1988. "Democratic Theories and the Study of Public Opinion." *Polity* 21:25–44.

Massey, Douglas, and Nancy Denton. 1987. "Trends in the Residential Segregation of Blacks, Hispanics, and Asians: 1970–1980." *American Sociological Review* 52:802–25.

Merton, Robert, and Elinor Barber. 1963. "Sociological Ambivalence." In *Sociolog-*

ical Theory, Values, and Sociocultural Change, ed. Edward Tiryakian, 91–120. Glencoe, Ill.: Free Press.

Mitchell, Jacquelyn. 1982. "Reflections of a Black Social Scientist." *Harvard Educational Review* 52 (1): 27–44.

Moore, Deedee. 1989. "Shooting Straight: The Many Worlds of Gordon Parks." *Smithsonian Magazine*, April, 66–77.

Myrdal, Gunnar. 1944. *An American Dilemma*. New York: Harper & Brothers.

Nagel, Jack. 1987. *Participation*. Englewood Cliffs, N.J.: Prentice-Hall.

Norton, Anne. 1988. *Reflections on Political Identity*. Baltimore: Johns Hopkins University Press.

Novak, Michael. 1972. *The Rise of the Unmeltable Ethnics*. New York: Macmillan.

Nozick, Robert. 1974. *Anarchy, State, and Utopia*. New York: Basic Books.

Oresties, Michael. 1990. "Bush at G.O.P. High in Black Approval." *New York Times*, 13 April.

Page, Clarence. 1986. Introduction to *A Foot in Each World*, by Leanita McClain, ed. Clarence Page. Evanston, Ill.: Northwestern University Press.

Parent, Wayne. 1984. "Individual Explanations for Structural Problems: Blacks and Economic Redistribution Policy." Paper presented at the annual meeting of the Midwest Political Science Association, Chicago, April.

Parent, Wayne, and Paul Stekler. 1985. "The Political Implications of Economic Stratification in the Black Community." *Western Political Quarterly* 38:521–38.

Pateman, Carole. 1970. *Participation and Democratic Theory*. Cambridge: Cambridge University Press.

Pinkney, Alphonso. 1984. *The Myth of Black Progress*. Cambridge: Cambridge University Press.

Raspberry, William. 1985. "Will the Underclass Be Abandoned?" *Washington Post*, 24 May, A27.

Reagon, Bernice Johnson. 1983. "Coalition Politics: Turning the Century." In *Home Girls: A Black Feminist Anthology*, ed. Barbara Smith, 356–68. New York: Kitchen Table.

Rodriguez, Richard. 1982. *Hunger of Memory*. Boston: Godine.

Seltzer, Richard, and Robert Smith. 1985. "Race and Ideology." *Phylon* 46:98–105.

Sigleman, Lee, and Susan Welch. 1991. *Black Americans' Views of Racial Inequality*. Cambridge: Cambridge University Press.

Starks, Robert, and Michael Preston. 1990. "Harold Washington and the Politics of Reform in Chicago: 1983–1987." In *Racial Politics in American Cities*, ed. Rufus Browning, Dale Rogers Marshall, and David Tabb, 88–107. New York: Longman.

Thompson, Kenneth. 1971. "Upward Social Mobility and Political Orientation." *American Sociological Review* 36:223–35.

Tocqueville, Alexis de. [1835, 1840] 1969. *Democracy in America*. Trans. George Lawrence. Ed. J. P. Mayer. Garden City, N.Y.: Doubleday, Anchor Books.

Tomkins, Silvan. 1963. "Left and Right: A Basic Dimension of Ideology and Personality." In *The Study of Lives*, ed. Robert White, 388–411. New York: Atherton Press.

Turner, Victor. 1969. *The Ritual Process*. Ithaca, N.Y.: Cornell University Press.
Welch, Susan, and Michael Combs. 1985. "Intra-racial Differences in Attitudes of Blacks." *Phylon* 46:91–97.
Welch, Susan, and Lorn Foster. 1987. "Class and Conservatism in the Black Community." *American Politics Quarterly* 15:445–70.
Wilkins, Roger. 1982. *A Man's Life*. New York: Simon & Schuster.
———. 1988. "Dr. King's Unfinished Business." *Washington Post*, 17 January, C5.
Williams, Lena. 1987. "For Black Partners at Top Law Firms, Lunch Is Special." *New York Times*, 11 December, B8.
Williams, Linda. 1986. "1986 JCPS/Gallup Survey." Statement at the National Press Club, Washington, D.C., 14 October.
Zaller, John, and Stanley Feldman. 1992. "A Simple Theory of the Survey Response." *American Journal of Political Science* 36:579–616.

10

Theory, Citizenship, and Democracy

J. Donald Moon

Theorists, even theorists of democracy, tend to be hedgehogs: they seek to "relate everything to a single central vision, one system less or more coherent or articulate, in terms of which they understand, think and feel—a single, universal organizing principle in terms of which alone all that they are and say has significance" (Berlin 1979, 22). For hedgehogs, this is what it is to think. And to the extent that democratic citizens are supposed to think, then they should be hedgehogs as well. Their political behavior should be informed and directed by a more or less systematically unified set of ideas and beliefs, and the political process should function in such a way as to make the pattern and direction of public policy shift with changes in citizens' judgments. As citizens become more or less conservative or more or less internationalist, so should public policy move in the same direction.

Although something of a caricature, the sketch I have just given constitutes the conceptual background for the challenge to democratic theory posed by empirical studies of political, particularly electoral, behavior in the post–World War II period.[1] Citizens, however generously we treat the evidence, simply do not measure up to this ideal. Their shortcomings have often been seen as a failure of rationality; in some cases (e.g., Converse 1970), citizens' judgments are interpreted as reflecting a significant element of randomness in their responses to political issues and events. In her contribution to this volume, Jennifer Hochschild suggests that such explanations may be misleading. She argues that, paradoxically, there are "*systematic* ways in which citizens are not consistent" (emphasis added). On some issues they experience ambivalence, as they find themselves pulled in different directions by the different considerations that bear on them. In other cases, the distinctions they use to specify the domains within which certain values and principles are applicable become problematic, and so they experience (or become subject to the possibility of) disjunction. Her argument suggests that the inconsistencies and the lack of any organizing principle or "constraint" in their responses may reflect not simply randomness or thoughtlessness but a more complex, perhaps "foxlike," psychic world. Foxes, Isaiah Berlin tells us, "pursue many ends, often unrelated and even contradictory, connected, if at all, only in some *de facto* way, for some psychological or physiological cause, related by no moral or aesthetic principle" (Berlin 1979, 22). Instead of reflecting a failure to live up to the standards of rational thinking, ordinary democratic citizens may simply exhibit a different cognitive and personal style, with its own distinctive virtues and forms.

I do not wish to overstate the case here. Even if we allow that inconsistencies and incompleteness in citizens' beliefs do not necessarily show a rationality deficit, we cannot simply attribute a high level of "foxlike" cognitive functioning to citizens. Berlin classifies Shakespeare, Herodotus, Aristotle, Montaigne, Erasmus, Molière, Goethe, Pushkin, Balzac, and Joyce as foxes, and no one would want to argue that the thinking of ordinary citizens is at their level. Nonetheless, the possibility of an alternative, defensible cognitive style suggests the need to rethink the standard categories in terms of which the problem of citizen competence is conceived.

1. In their essay in this volume, Kinder and Herzog offer an account of the traditional expectations of citizens' cognitive abilities and of the empirical findings bearing on this issue.

The traditional formulation of the problem of citizen competence tacitly incorporates the view that the activity of citizenship and that of political theory or philosophy are in crucial respects the same. As private persons, we seek to make correct choices regarding the moral issues we face; as citizens, we seek to participate in deliberations on public issues to reach rational, well-reasoned judgments. Moral and political philosophers may have more time and training, and so can work out the answers in a more systematic way, but they are basically doing the same thing as ordinary moral actors and citizens do.

This view of political decision has led some to reject democracy, on the grounds that citizens are manifestly incapable of carrying out their role. Plato—the supreme hedgehog—comes to mind. Others, such as Kant or John Stuart Mill, who valued autonomy and disdained the "immaturity" of those who did not think for themselves, called for a public life through which citizens could be enlightened or "their virtue and intelligence" promoted. For them, philosophers should not be kings but should bring their "gifts," as Michael Walzer put it, to the people, contributing to and raising the level of public debate.

As long as we conceptualize the task of citizens, when deliberating on the public good and the direction their society should take, and the task of political theorists as similar, we face the challenge originally posed by Plato. As Walzer put it, "Truth is one, but the people have many opinions; truth is eternal, but the people continually change their minds. Here in its simplest form is the tension between philosophy and democracy" (1981, 383). This apparent dilemma leads some democrats to save democracy by driving a wedge between the kinds of knowledge and judgment required of citizens and that required of philosophers. Thus, Walzer argues that philosophical knowledge is universal in form, telling us "about the meaning and purpose of political association and the appropriate structure of the community (of every community) and its government." Political knowledge, by contrast, concerns "the meaning and purpose of *this* association" and "the appropriate structure of *our* community and government," for "political knowing is particular and pluralist in character" (393; emphasis in the original). There is an obvious difficulty here, for if there is an appropriate structure for *every* community, it must be the appropriate structure for *this* community as well. Either the philosophical project must fail, or there will be precious little for citizens to do.

Taking a more radical tack, Benjamin Barber has argued that political judgment is radically unlike philosophical analysis: "It is in essence political and not cognitive" (1988, 199). Barber laments the "conquest of politics" by philosophy, holding that philosophers are deeply mistaken in offering their theories as guides to political life, for "to be political is . . . to be free with a vengeance—to have to make judgments without guiding standards or determining norms, yet under ineluctable pressures to act" (206). Because political judgment is so different from philosophy, there is no need "to refine the mental faculties of the citizenry by teaching them philosophy so that they might emulate the wise" (211). For Barber, the philosophers do not offer the citizens "gifts" but are at best a massive irrelevancy—"the morticians but never the movers of a free state" (211).

I do not want to argue that the task of the theorist and that of the citizen are identical or that they call for exactly the same capacities; I would like to approach the problem of citizen competence from the other side—by questioning the model of "theory" employed in these analyses. There is something intuitively plausible in the idea that the work of philosophers who attend to questions of practice, to moral and political concerns, is at least continuous with the thinking of moral agents and citizens. At the risk of special pleading, it is hard to see what point political theory would otherwise have. Moreover, it is easy to find such continuity. It is illustrated, for example, in the early Socratic dialogues in which arguments about particular courses of action quickly pass over into self-consciously philosophical concerns, as well as in many of our ordinary moral and political activities. In the small, New England town in which I live, for example, there have recently been heated arguments at our town meetings over zoning and development policies in which the discussions have turned on arguments about property, rights, the integrity of the community, and other questions I regularly discuss with my classes at the university. The problem of citizen competence, I would like to suggest, is not so much that citizens fail to be theorists as it is that much of this discussion is premised on a mistaken conception of theory in which only a "hedgehog" style of theorizing is allowed.

There are, I think, two related aspects of this conception that have been important historically and that are attractive in their own right. The first is what might be called foundationalism, the expectation that our moral knowledge should be grounded in a way that provides a guarantee of its truth. This expectation is an aspect of what Dewey called the quest for certainty, and it takes the form of a demand for the *justification* of our moral beliefs by providing veridical foundations for them.

The second aspect is what might be called theoretical unification—the demand that discrete moral judgments should be "unified" by deriving them from more-general theoretical principles. These two demands of traditional theory are obviously related, in that the most general theoretical principles that unify discrete judgments may also serve as the "foundations" that justify these judgments. Nevertheless, they may vary independently. Classical intuitionism, for example, denies that ethical judgments can be unified in a theoretical system, while holding that such judgments can be justified by the direct apprehension of the moral properties of objects and situations. It is thus foundationalist without being unified. On the other hand, one could accept a theoretically unified system without believing that its fundamental axioms provided adequate guarantees of the "truth" of its theorems. Such a position is hinted at by Bentham when he defends the principle of utility not because of its "truth" but because no "moral sentiment" could be "justified on any other ground, by a person addressing himself to the community" (1948, 142).

This conception of theory as grounded and deductively unified arises naturally from what we might call the "skyhook" model of argumentation. According to this model, the request to justify a particular principle or moral judgment is answered by providing a more general, higher-level principle from which the first follows. This principle, in turn, is justified in the same way, in terms of a third, even more abstract and higher-level principle. And so it goes, until we reach the "skyhook," some (set of) ultimate principle(s) that constitutes the foundation for all of our particular judgments and that provides unity and coherence to our moral views. Our ultimate appeal might be to categorical imperatives that are dictates of pure practical reason or, perhaps, to the presuppositions of some ideal setting for discursively settling conflicting claims to truth. But if these principles are to provide an adequate foundation, they must be absolute, universal, and invariant.

It is easy to see the appeal of this model of argumentation and the associated view of theory as providing a foundation to and a unification of moral judgments. It makes moral knowledge akin to other kinds of knowledge, notably mathematics, which, since Plato, has often been taken to be paradigmatic of knowledge, as opposed to mere belief or opinion. By giving our moral judgments an objective structure akin to other branches of knowledge, it avoids the problem of subjectivism, with its threat of descent into nihilism. And by blazing sharply the distinction between what is allowable and what is not, it provides a check against self-deception and backsliding—constant temptations in murkier ethical worlds, where the genuine difficulty of distinguishing between shades of gray provides an opening for all kinds of rationalizations.

However attractive, the foundationalist project is widely conceded to have failed, at least in its most ambitious forms. In response, some thinkers have tried to put in its place a paler version of foundationalism. Fishkin (1984), for example, proposes what he calls minimal objectivism to replace it. It seems to me, however, that these solutions are often as problematic as foundationalism itself. Fishkin's minimal objectivism, for example, is too deeply affected by foundationalist thinking to do the job that he wants done. Indeed, the very term "minimal objectivism," which Fishkin places on a Gutman scale that begins with absolutism and ends with amoralism, shows it to be a kind of weak foundationalism. We cannot, Fishkin recognizes, have what we really want—principles that are absolute, that are demonstrably true, and that hold without exception. But we can have weak foundations for our judgments, foundations that are minimally objective.

But if we need foundations at all, we surely need strong ones. Weak foundations are simply not substitutes for strong ones. For weak, or minimally objective, foundations seem merely to push the problem of subjectivity back one step, to a choice among reasonable points of departure for making and justifying moral choices. To get around the problem of subjectivism, we need to see how we can dispense with foundations altogether.

To do so requires that we abandon the skyhook model of justificatory argument. It is this essentially deductive model of justification that is the root of the problem, leading us to think that, unless we can supply indubitable skyhooks for our beliefs, they are not really rational or objective, or are only weakly or minimally so. Thus, we must dispel the hold that this model of justification has upon us.

This is one place where empirical studies of citizens' beliefs and attitudes may play an important role in political and moral theorizing. As Hochschild argues, if we consider the actual nature of moral reasoning in specific contexts of choice and decision, we find that their arguments do not fit the skyhook model at all. Rather, they tend to be informal, making appeal to a variety of ideas, beliefs, values, and principles, in which the reasons offered for a judgment often do not strictly entail the judgment but lend varying degrees of cogency to it. Above all, these arguments are dialogic in structure; their purpose is not to anticipate and answer all possible objections, from whatever source, but rather to answer actual objections that are either raised by others or reflect the doubts, concerns, and uncertainties of the agent involved. Thus, these arguments are always contextual, presupposing a shared horizon of beliefs and values.

Unlike Habermas's ideal speech situation or the early versions of Rawls's original position, the arguments we actually make with and to each other are not intended to reach any and all rational agents but are directed to particular audiences. We should not think of ethical arguments as applications of general theories to particular cases, or of the theories themselves as dangling from first premises that serve as axioms. Rather, we should (following Quine and Ullian 1978) visualize them as "webs," in which different strands are linked to one another at a variety of points and in a variety of ways. Specific judgments, values, principles, or beliefs are supported by a range of others, and argumentation consists of clarifying and criticizing some of these strands, repairing holes that have occurred, stitching different ideas more closely together.

In addition to replacing the skyhook metaphor with the "web" metaphor, we must also reject the essentially static view of moral truth that is found in the traditional model of moral and political theory. If our fundamental axioms express practical truth, moral argumentation becomes the testing of specific decisions or judgments against these truths. But even as a regulative ideal, this is a distortion. No doubt, we sometimes, even often, simply apply general norms to new cases, but moral argumentation can also involve the use of new cases or specific judgments to reflect upon and criticize our existing values and principles. Moral argumentation can lead to the discovery of new moral knowledge, to new visions of how we can and should live our lives. As we give up the idea of discovering veridical foundations for our beliefs, we must also give up the idea of theory as capturing what is true and replace it with the idea of theorizing, of extending and developing our knowledge by criticizing and replacing inadequate beliefs and values.

The image I have been sketching of moral and political thinking is much more compatible with the data that Hochschild presents than with the traditional image. In particular, it takes its point of departure from ambivalence, from the experience of a host of partially conflicting considerations bearing upon an issue, tugging us in different ways. Instead of taking our beliefs as (ideally) unified in a rigorous system, it sees them as interconnected in various ways, some tightly and some loosely joined. Many of these interconnections will not be recognized until we confront particular cases or problems, and their recognition may lead us to alter our "initial" set of beliefs. In the absence of foundations and in the face of ambivalence, we will constantly face the necessity—and the exhilaration—of learning.

Ambivalence is pervasive, and sometimes it may also be radical. We may face conflicts that are so deep and so central to our lives that we become paralyzed by them. Sometimes they may destroy us. But they may also be occasions for moral discovery, for critical self-reflection leading to a transformation of our beliefs and values—and of our identities—in ways that overcome or at least mute such radical conflicts. By freeing ourselves from the static, overly rationalistic view of moral and political thought, we may find such creative responses to conflict easier to achieve.

This conception of theorizing helps to close the gap between theory and democracy, between philosophy and politics, from the side of theory. By changing our understanding of theory in this way, we can continue to accept the continuity between ordinary and philosophical reasoning regarding practical questions, without abandoning "philosophy" as pointless or undermining the possibility of a democratic politics by setting up an impossible standard for ordinary citizens. Under this conception of theory, political knowledge no longer need be seen as systematically unified, static, and forming an ideally closed system of propositions. The knowledge of foxes admits conflicting ideas and principles and allows for internal "strain" among beliefs and values; it is necessarily open; and the focus is dynamic, on learning and innovation.

Conceiving of theory as an activity of foxes rather than hedgehogs has important implications for substantive political values and principles. Specifically, I would argue that there is an internal connection between this model of theorizing and liberal democracy. Far from being threatened by the undermining of foundationalism, the recognition of the "messy indeterminacy" of our moral and political lives may support certain key tenets of liberal democracy. Further, this view of theorizing requires us to think about citizen competence in terms rather different from those of the traditional model.

The web model of argument I have sketched provides a nonskeptical basis for moral diversity or moral pluralism. As different individuals wrestle with the conflicting values and principles bearing on specific questions, they will inevitably arrive at different solutions. The failure of the foundationalist project means that there can be no expectation of a unique, harmonious, rational ordering of the values and principles, of the identities and aspirations, that provide meaning and direction to our lives. Different decisions will reflect different weightings of these values, weightings rooted in different life experiences, perceptions, abilities to tolerate ambiguity and uncertainty, and a host of other factors. These decisions, it should be stressed, are rationally defensible and defeasible. With good will and enough time, rational discussion could even lead to significant convergence among judgments. But even in principle there is no reason to expect full or complete consensus. An adequate political theory, then, must begin with the fact of moral pluralism and the possibility of conflicting moral positions. From this perspective, the task of politics is to seek norms that everyone could accept, even given their significant and continuing disagreements. If these disagreements are too deep, this project may not succeed. But the alternative to free agreement is the unilateral imposition of the choices of some onto others, an imposition based on force or manipulation and for which we could offer no compelling, rational justification.

The problem I have just sketched is what might be called the "liberal problematic." Liberal political theory can be interpreted as an effort to answer the question How can people who disagree on important and enduring questions regarding the ends and purposes of life come to live together under rules that they can all accept as just and reasonable? This question originally presented itself during the religious conflict of the seventeenth century, when a strategy for dealing with pluralism without resort to repression became increasingly urgent. The basic liberal response was to remove religious issues from the scope of authoritative decision, that is, to erect a separation between the public sphere, in which matters are subject to collective, authoritative decision and control, and the private sphere, in which individuals are free to control and direct their own behavior.[2]

2. There are numerous uses of the terms "public" and "private" in political theory, and my

This response leads to the possibility of what Hochschild calls "disjunction," since it requires that we hold apparently contradictory views in different domains. Indeed, the whole point of this strategy is to establish different domains in order to make it possible to act on different principles or norms in each. In my religious association I may feel it incumbent upon me to insist upon doctrinal purity and so to expel those with unorthodox or heretical views. But in public life, I recognize an obligation to tolerate the same individuals. And I can simultaneously be intolerant and tolerant because the spheres within which these attitudes are appropriate are separate and (more or less) well defined. The separation of domains is a strategy for managing ambivalence by providing scope, as it were, for conflicting values. At the same time, however, pressures for consistency and the need to justify the boundaries we set up may lead to disjunction as the distinctions we make are called into question.

Conceiving of politics as the discovery and development of principles of association acceptable in a pluralist world not only leads to religious toleration but also supports a host of distinctive tenets of liberal democracy, including negative liberty, individual rights, equality, and political participation. I do not have the space to spell this argument out here, but the intuitive connection should be fairly evident. The most obvious is that it undermines the kind of authority that philosophy has sometimes claimed, an authority that Walzer and Barber see as threatening to democratic participation. More positively, the open, dynamic, and dialogic character of theorizing legitimates conflict, which is a necessary condition of democracy. And the premium it places upon discovering bases of agreement among opposed positions requires a democratic politics in which all citizens and all points of view can be heard.[3]

This view of theorizing also suggests a somewhat, though not totally, different list of the virtues we should seek in democratic citizens.[4] We should not, in this view, demand a high level of constraint in citizens' belief systems. Ideological consistency is not a necessary feature of

usage here is significantly different from that of Sapiro in her contribution to this volume. For a comparison of the "separate spheres" and "liberal" uses, see Moon, n.d., chap. 7.

3. For interpretations of liberalism along these lines, see Larmore 1987, Rawls 1985, and Moon, n.d.

4. The virtues I discuss here are (broadly) "intellectual"; the role of a democratic citizen requires a host of other virtues as well. See the discussion in the chapter by Conover et al. (in this volume).

rational and attentive concern with public affairs. Rather, openness and tolerance of alternative points of view, a capacity to entertain ambivalence and conflicting perspectives, and a willingness and ability to learn, to change one's views upon reflection, become crucial. These are the skills that contribute to the "democratic discussion" that Donald Kinder and Don Herzog place at the center of democratic theory. Once we accept the impossibility of rational closure and aspire to a politics premised upon the search for areas of agreement, we can see serious dangers in citizens' holding systematically unified systems of belief. For, as Marcus has argued, "coherent and stringent ideologies are not conducive to democracies" (1988, 43). The very rigidity they introduce makes citizens less open to persuasion and reduces both the incentive and ability of political actors to develop policies that can command widespread support. The creation of such policies involves a twin process of, first, adjusting proposals to incorporate a wide range of interests, perspectives, and values and, second, providing information and arguments that lead citizens to change their views as they come to grapple with the issues.

These virtues—tolerance, capacity to cope with ambivalence, openness, and willingness to learn—are suggested by the conception of theory I sketched above, but they are obviously not purely "cognitive" virtues. They involve emotional and affective traits as well. One of the deficiencies of the traditional view of theory is that it encourages us to separate cognitive and emotional issues too sharply. If we think of knowledge as organized into well-integrated structures, it is easy to separate these structures of cognition from the rest of a person's life, treating them as self-standing constructions. That is harder to do for the knowledge of foxes, whose "ends, often unrelated and contradictory," may be "connected" only by "some psychological or [even] physiological cause" (Berlin 1979, 22). The cognitive world of a fox cannot be divorced from its noncognitive elements—the capacity to tolerate ambiguity or ambivalence, the salience of different ideas and values, the affect with which certain ends and symbols are invested, and so on. The study of democratic citizenship must be centrally concerned with the kinds of emotional and affective factors addressed in the other chapters in this volume (particularly Chapters 12, 14, 15, and 16).

The argument that has been sketched here does not, and is not intended to, settle the question of citizen competence. What I have attempted to do is to offer an analysis drawn from a theoretical perspective that complements Hochschild's empirical work in rethinking this problem by reconceptualizing the terms in which it is cast. Like Hochschild's work, this analysis provides "grounds for cautious optimism," at least in the sense that the lack of ideological sophistication on the part of mass electorates does not appear to be as serious, from the perspective developed here, as it did before. Of course, before we can offer more than cautious optimism, further work is required to determine how citizens actually think about themselves and their place in the political world, an issue that has been addressed by several papers in this volume, including those by Hochschild, Sapiro, Conover et al., and Kinder and Herzog. And even if we find that our optimism is in order, it will still be true that this perspective places different demands on citizens, demands that may in some ways be even more difficult for them to meet. But democracy has always been a risky and difficult project—no theory can change that. But we can hope to clarify what the risks are and what we can do to overcome the difficulties.

References

Barber, Benjamin. 1988. *The Conquest of Politics*. Princeton: Princeton University Press.

Bentham, Jeremy. 1948. *An Introduction to the Principles of Morals and Legislation*. Oxford: Basil Blackwell.

Berlin, Isaiah. 1979. *Russian Thinkers*. New York: Penguin.

Converse, Philip. 1970. "Attitudes and Non-attitudes: Continuation of a Dialogue." In *The Quantitative Analysis of Social Problems*, ed. Edward R. Tufte, 168–89. Reading, Mass.: Addison-Wesley.

Fishkin, James. 1984. *Beyond Subjective Morality*. New Haven: Yale University Press.

Larmore, Charles E. 1987. *Patterns of Moral Complexity*. New York: Cambridge University Press.

Marcus, George. 1988. "Democratic Theories and the Study of Public Opinion." *Polity* 21:25–44.

Moon, J. Donald. N.d. *Thin Selves, Rich Lives, Tragic Conflicts: Moral Pluralism and the Creation of Political Community*. Princeton: Princeton University Press. Forthcoming.

Quine, W.V.O., and J. S. Ullian. 1978. *The Web of Belief*. 2d ed. New York: Random House.

Rawls, John. 1985. "Justice as Fairness—Political, Not Metaphysical." *Philosophy and Public Affairs* 14:223–51.

Walzer, Michael. 1981. "Philosophy and Politics." *Political Theory* 9:379–400.

III

Passion and Politics

11

Thinking About Political Tolerance, More or Less, with More or Less Information

James H. Kuklinski
Ellen Riggle
Victor Ottati
Norbert Schwarz
Robert S. Wyer, Jr.

This chapter scarcely resembles the manuscript we originally wrote for this volume, thanks in great part to the critical comments of those who participated in the Democratic Theory Symposium at Williams College. The substantive domain, political tolerance, remains intact,[1] but for

1. In the long run, we intend to consider a variety of political domains. Political tolerance offers a good starting point. It represents an arena in which the idea of deliberative thought

reasons explicated below, we no longer focus solely or even principally on the relative influence of cognition and affect on political judgments. Instead, we explore—and it is *explore*—whether *thinking* about political tolerance increases it. The simplicity of this question, it will become evident, belies the challenge of answering it. Citizens think about democratic values, more or less, with more or less information.

Although this chapter centers on a particular domain, about which we hope to offer a few new insights, our long-term goal is to elucidate how different types and levels of thinking about politics, under a set of varying conditions, affects the quality of the final judgments. If our examination of political tolerance has shown us anything, it is that our dependent variable, "quality of judgment," defies quick and easy definition.

Gut-Level Reaction Versus Deliberation: A Wrong Assumption? A False Dichotomy?

We have all heard the words; many of us have spoken them. "Don't make a final decision until you've given the matter more thought"; "You're not using your head"; "If you reflected on what you're doing, you would act differently." "Think, think what you're doing to me" are the words with which rhythm and blues singer Aretha Franklin begins one of her top hits. Each of these statements captures, in everyday language, a theme that scholars have been advancing for centuries: the more that people deliberate before reaching their decisions, the better decisions they will make.

---

makes some sense. Sizable majorities of the U.S. citizenry may know little about technical and complex policy debates taking place in Congress, but most can say something worthwhile about democratic principles such as the right to free speech and freedom of religion. Second, political tolerance has everyday meaning. Few aspects of political life so directly and immediately touch upon the daily lives of common citizens as their willingness to put up with each other's behavior. In the words of McClosky and Brill (1983, 15), "The attitudes and beliefs of the American public on questions of tolerance, freedom, and control are often as important to know, sometimes more important, in fact, than the opinions of governing officials. . . . [M]any forms of intimidation and human oppression occur not only at the level of political decision and enforcement but at the level of the neighborhood, the community, and the reference group. Men and women often pay more attention to the opinions of their peers and neighbors than they do to the attitudes or potential actions of their rulers."

In the realm of public affairs, prescriptions for a deliberative citizenry have dominated writing at least since the Enlightenment. The oft-cited words of Berelson et al. (1954, 309) pretty much say it all: "The democratic citizen is expected to have arrived at his [judgments] by reason and to have considered rationally the implications and alleged consequences." Gut-level reactions will not do, and a democracy in which citizens evaluate politics with their hearts instead of their minds leaves much to be desired.

It all sounds rather simple; in fact, it is not.

The Assumption: Thinking Leads to Better Judgments

Underlying the time-honored prescription for a reasoning and thoughtful citizenry is the seemingly warranted assumption that deliberation improves political judgments. Thinking, a more active mode of decision making than (often automatic) visceral response, presumably enhances recognition of the complexity of political phenomena, thus encouraging greater balance and sophistication in dealing with them. Conversely, reliance on feelings leads to oversimplification and often projects more about our inner states than about the objective world we wish to understand and evaluate. "Passion blinds us" goes the argument in one of its stronger and more familiar versions.

Although there has always been a writer or two to challenge this dominant perspective, only recently has a chorus of critics emerged (Lyons 1980; Rorty 1980; de Sousa 1987). The criticisms take several forms, not the least of which is that rational thinking often fails to produce a unique outcome. To take a close-to-home example, political science research in the logical-positivism tradition has fallen short of its original promise, leaving most questions of "fact" unresolved. Policymakers employ an increasingly sophisticated arsenal of rational techniques and still find themselves disagreeing about the nature of society and the economy. And even if citizens possess the intellectual ability to reason logically from cause to effect, the complexity of national politics severely limits what they can know (Carmines and Kuklinski 1990); indeterminancy may be the most compelling fact of political life.

If pure reason often leads to deadlock, intuition, or going with one's gut feelings, can break it. This itself hardly recommends knee-jerk judgments, however, especially if they lead to the wrong choices.

Apparently they often do not. Social psychologists have begun to accumulate impressive evidence that feelings serve as valuable sources of information about the world (Frijda 1987; Schwarz 1992; Schwarz and Clore 1983; Wyer and Srull 1989).[2] In one of the most revealing experiments to date, Wilson and Schooler (1991) demonstrate that thinking can lead to worse decisions, objectively defined, than those arrived at through intuition. Asked to identify bank robbers and rank foods in accordance with experts' opinions, subjects in the study did better when they made quick judgments than when they listed reasons for their choices. The authors conclude that "implicit," or "tacit," knowledge warrants a prominent place on the scholarly mantel.

This recent literature surely will not lead scholars to advocate *less* thinking on the part of citizens. But it does underline the importance of turning a crucial assumption into an empirical question: Does deliberation produce better political choices than gut reactions?

The Dichotomy: Thinking Versus Feeling

The meaningfulness of the preceding question depends on the validity of the assumption that thinking and feeling truly represent alternative pathways to political judgments. We noted earlier that philosophers long have taken the dichotomy as given, and contemporary investigators continue to frame their research around it. Students of voting behavior can point to a series of articles proclaiming the rationality of citizen choice in presidential elections (Riker and Ordeshook 1968; Ferejohn and Fiorina 1974; Frohlich et al. 1978; Fishbein and Ajzen 1981) or to an equally long line of research showing that people commonly choose among candidates on the basis of gut-level reactions to factors only remotely related to presidential performance (Campbell et al. 1960; Markus and Converse 1979; for an interpretation that places higher value on knee-jerk reactions, see Miller et al. 1986). In a similar vein, studies of the connection between economic conditions and vote preferences fall into two camps: those that assume or purportedly show people to make

2. Schwarz and Clore (1983) demonstrate that people frequently simplify complex judgmental tasks by asking themselves, "How do I feel about it?"—using their apparent affective reaction to the object of judgment as a basis for evaluation. This process results in more favorable evaluations when the target stimulus elicits positive feelings than when it elicits negative feelings.

systematic evaluations of the economy and then vote accordingly (Kramer 1971; Kinder and Kiewiet 1979; Kuklinski and West 1981) and those that identify a "mad-as-hell" syndrome, whereby individuals' votes represent strong emotional expressions of discontent about the health of the economy or their own financial conditions (Conover and Feldman 1986). Finally, scholars continue to be embroiled in controversy about the true nature of racial attitudes. Does the lack of support for government intervention on behalf of blacks reflect gut-level prejudice (Sears et al. 1979; Sears et al. 1980; Kinder and Sears 1981; Kinder 1986) or does it arise largely from a considered political philosophy (conservatism) and basic values (especially individualism) that have little to do directly with feelings toward blacks (Sniderman et al. 1984; Sniderman with Hagen 1985; Sniderman and Tetlock 1986)?

Two chapters in this volume present the strongest evidence to date in support of the idea that citizens react viscerally to political situations (see also Marcus 1988). Sullivan and Masters's imaginative research demonstrates conclusively that people react, strongly and unconsciously, to political leaders' facial expressions. Using both self-reports and physiological measures, the authors trace the effects of facial displays on episodic emotions, which in turn influence attitudes toward politicians. Theiss-Morse et al. turn our original design, discussed in study one below, into a more complex and more sophisticated one. Threatening situations, they find, evoke negative emotions that reduce tolerance of group activities, whereas reassuring ones activate emotions that increase tolerance.

Should one need to be convinced that feelings and emotions play a big role in mass politics, these two studies do the job. Yet the question remains, How far can we take the affect-cognition distinction? As we write, psychologists continue to disagree about the true nature of the relation between the two. Some, most notably Zajonc (1980, 1984), contend that affect and cognition function as independent systems. Others argue otherwise, proposing either that cognition precedes affect, that affect precedes cognition, or that each simultaneously influences the other (Fiske and Pavelchak 1986; Lazarus 1982, 1984; Mandler 1975; Ortony et al. 1988; Schachter and Singer 1962). Unfortunately, the kind of single-shot experiments that psychologists typically conduct preclude examining whether people first think about something and, once having reached a conclusion, henceforth just respond from the gut, or, alternatively, react emotionally to something and then subsequently think about it (or neither).[3]

What, then, to do? Frankly, we are a bit less sanguine now than we were earlier (in a study reported elsewhere [Kuklinski et al. 1991] and summarized below) about the prospects of identifying and measuring the independent effects of cognition and affect on political judgments, given current research methodologies.[4] Not that we consider the distinction trivial; to the contrary, it may prove to be one of the most important in all of the social sciences.

Rather than take yet another step into the fray, we have opted to propose and test some tentative ideas about political thinking. This cop-out, as the reader is about to learn, did not lead us down the easier path we expected.

A Few Thoughts on Political Thinking

All of us deliberate about one thing or another: Should we marry or just continue to live together? Should we buy a new sports car or a used station wagon? Should our department implement a new set of required graduate courses? Why has race once again become such a burning issue in American politics? Should the United States move to a system of private schools?

Now, when thinking about these and millions of other items, we can think a lot or not much at all.[5] Most of us can point to friends who decided to marry "on the spur of the moment" and to others who seemingly took forever to make a decision (we cannot say, on the basis of casual observation, that the latter have fared better). Similarly, some

3. Much of the literature advocating deliberative thought (such as work on issue voting) implicitly assumes that people begin from a neutral posture. In the area of politics, especially, it is highly unlikely that people approach an issue or candidate without some gut feeling. Many of the political arguments to which we are exposed and that fall under the guise of rational debate appear to be designed to support already-drawn conclusions presumably based in part on feelings.

4. We continue to assume here that feelings play a proportionately greater role in quick, or knee-jerk, judgments than in deliberated judgments. Given the current intellectual flux about the affect-cognition nexus, even this assumption may be proven wrong.

5. Admittedly, we are rather cavalier in our approach to the concept of thinking, especially in light of the sophisticated work in cognitive psychology.

people write books and articles about the nature of racial conflict, others never give the issue a moment's thought.

More importantly, and we see this as a critical distinction that deserves more treatment than we give it here, people contemplate this or that subject with more or less information at their disposal. His emergence as a presidential candidate, for example, has led many potential voters to ponder a potential Perot presidency. Some undoubtedly have done so with little factual information about the man and his past actions, whereas others have searched out whatever statements the press and other sources have made available. "I think" need not imply or require "I know."

Our argument thus far, then, is that thinking and information represent independent dimensions, such that thinking can (or cannot) occur with different amounts of relevant information. The most useful political information, we further believe, presents both sides of an issue or other choice situation about which citizens must decide (see Kuhn 1991). Classic debates fit the bill especially well: members of the audience hear the best arguments each side has to offer and then cast a vote for the side they find more persuasive. Berelson et al. had this very process in mind when they offered the normative prescription that we cited earlier; it also underlies calls for representative democracies in which elected officials fully deliberate policy options.

Distinguishing between thinking about and mere exposure to relevant information raises the possibility that people who think about a political phenomenon but lack access to the full complement of arguments reach different choices than those who do not share that lack. In other words, the critical variable may not be thinking but, rather, information availability or some combination of the two factors. This might be especially true when arguments on the one side take a concrete form—"this action will raise my taxes"—and on the other take an abstract and less directly relevant form—"this action will protect democratic rights." That is, in the absence of information dissemination, it is conceivable that citizens naturally base their judgments on the immediate and easily recognized consequences of an action.

Figure 11.1 summarizes our main points and also serves as a guide for the empirical studies reported below. From this schematic, we derive three questions: (1) When faced with political choices, do people tend to think about them or do they principally react from the gut? (2) Do thinking and visceral response lead to qualitatively different choices?

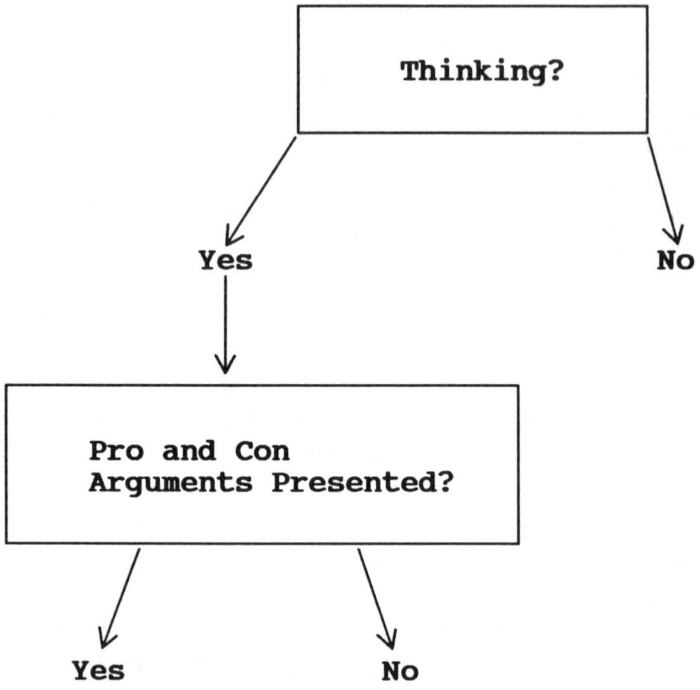

Fig. 11.1. A proposed schematic for the study of thinking

(3) In situations where people do deliberate, does the availability of information affect the final judgments? To answer these questions we must first define—or more correctly, try to define—a good political judgment.

The Qualitative Dimension of Political Judgments

There would be no reason to recommend thinking as a means by which to improve the quality of political choices if some judgments were not preferable to others. A fundamental question, therefore, is, What makes some decisions better than others? Despite the prominence of the thinking-improves-political-judgment assumption, we found no compelling answer to this question; few empirical researchers even explicitly address it. In retrospect, we understand why. As long as the thinking-improves-judgment assumption is just that—assumption—writers can unwittingly fall into tautological reasoning: good decisions involve thought; when people think before they decide, they make good decisions. Turn the assumption into hypothesis, as we proposed earlier, and the tautology becomes apparent, for we now see that a "good" decision is explicitly defined in terms of the very criterion that serves as the independent variable in the hypothesis.

"Good" must be defined independently of thinking. But how? Since our own thoughts about this critical definitional issue are in their infancy, we refrain from any sweeping statements and instead focus more specifically on political tolerance. For within this domain, researchers have displayed near consensus in their definition: more tolerance is better than less. It is an operational definition that we adopt here, which in turn leads to the hypothesis that thinking increases tolerance.

Although our equating decisional quality with increased tolerance draws on a long tradition and greatly facilitates our empirical work, by no means do we construe the definition as unproblematic. Throughout the analyses that follow, we allow our subjects themselves to speak directly to the idea that a tolerant posture is always preferable to an intolerant one, and, in the concluding section, consider more fully the place of political tolerance in democratic societies.

Study One: Thinking Versus Knee-Jerk Reaction

During the fall of 1986, we conducted a survey of 553 undergraduates who were enrolled in an introductory American politics course at the University of Illinois. Its purpose was to address two of the three questions that we posed above: (1) What appears to drive judgments about political tolerance, gut-level feelings or considered thought? (2) Does asking people to think about tolerance increase it?

The following analysis focuses on five statements of general values, each accompanied by two specific applications of it. One real-world example included a group that people generally like, the other a group that most dislike (as determined by normative data collected prior to the study itself). All respondents answered the general items; those exposed to one specific application did not receive the other.

One-third of the students (henceforth labeled the F, or feelings, group) received these instructions:

> We are interested in the attitudes and opinions of college students concerning contemporary social and political issues. On the following pages, you will find a series of propositions. Read each statement, and then indicate your agreement or disagreement with it by circling a number along the scale below it. Note that the scale ranges from −5 (disagree strongly) to +5 (agree strongly). You may circle any number you wish along the scale that best represents your opinion.
>
> Note: We have found that people's attitudes and opinions are reported most accurately when they do not think carefully about the statements but, rather, simply base their judgments on the feelings or emotional reactions they experience when they read the statement. Therefore, in evaluating each of the propositions you will read, try to base your responses on your feelings or the emotions you experience when you read the statement, rather than think carefully about all of its possible consequences.

A second group (the C, or consequence, group) were given the same first paragraph but a very different second one:

> Note: We have found that people's opinions about statements are often most accurate when they think about the consequences of the action or event that is described in the statement. Therefore, in evaluating each of the propositions you will read, think about what consequences it would have if the proposition advocated in the statement were adopted or if the event described were to occur, and base your judgment on the desirability of these consequences.

The remaining students (the NI, or no instruction, group) read only the first paragraph.

The logic of this first study consists in comparing the responses of the NI group to those of the two instructed groups. If political tolerance judgments are largely knee-jerk reactions, then the mean response of the former should be significantly different from that of the C group but not from that of the F group. Just the opposite pattern would suggest that individuals expend at least a modicum of thought when asked about their willingness to tolerate the behavior of others. All of this assumes, of course, that visceral reaction and reflection differentially affect attitudes toward political tolerance, which in fact proved to be the case.

We have reported the results of the study in detail elsewhere (Kuklinski et al. 1991) and thus merely summarize them here. We found that (1) subjects voiced considerable support for democratic values in the abstract, (2) the NI group appeared to respond to both the broad principles and specific applications more out of gut-level feelings than considered thought, and (3) explicitly asking respondents to contemplate consequences *reduced* tolerance, as we measured it, on both the abstract and applied levels. A replication involving nonstudents confirmed these results and also provided evidence that our experimental manipulations worked as we intended.

To understand why thinking might reduce tolerance, a counterintuitive and unexpected finding, we probed into what people think about when they "deliberate the possible consequences" of allowing this or that act, especially when a specific group is not even mentioned. Among those respondents who evaluated either of two general statements—"People should have the freedom to express their own opinions publicly" or "Groups should not be prevented from holding public meetings"—we randomly selected a subset and instructed them to record, as precisely as they could, what came to mind as they read. Political scientists writing about democratic principles almost invariably begin with the assumption that they must be upheld if democracy is to survive, indeed, to exist. Ordinary citizens, if we are to believe their self-reports, think in considerably less lofty, and more myopic, terms. Although a few of our respondents echoed the concerns of democratic theorists ("Stop one person from speaking out and soon no one will be able to speak out"; "American government guarantees that everyone can say what is on his mind"; "Can you imagine what would happen to our basic freedom were people to be told that they could not live in a particular neighborhood?"), most expressed fears about close-to-home threats. "Many groups, if allowed to say whatever they want, would brainwash our children"; "Our government is far from perfect, but we don't need radicals going around advocating communism and socialism"; "Lose control over who enters your neighborhood and soon property values will reduce to nothing"—these statements more closely reflect the modal thought of American citizens. When people think about consequences, even with regard to general principles, they typically dwell on immediate and close-to-home consequences; many of these consequences happen to be negative.

But why the emphasis on the negative (if such is the right term)?[6] One possibility, raised by Elizabeth Theiss-Morse, George Marcus, and John Sullivan (in this volume), is that the term "consequences" biases subjects' thoughts in a negative direction. In other studies, however, we substituted the term "outcomes" for "consequences" and found little change in the results. Although the problem of proper question wording deserves further probing, we are inclined to look elsewhere for clues.

Consider, as a partial explanation, that our C respondents were especially inclined to express negative thoughts about a general value when the immediately preceding item applied the same principle to an "unfavorable" group. Thus, for example, people who evaluated free speech in the abstract, after they had evaluated whether Nazis should be allowed to state their views publicly, expressed more fears and concerns than did those who first pondered the desirability of Roman Catholic church officials speaking publicly. Apparently, individuals retrieved the concerns that thinking about a group-specific behavior activated and, out of context, used them to assess the general proposition (in psychological parlance, they assimilated). Presumably those instructed to react quickly and from the gut did not have time to assimilate.

We also asked selected C respondents to express what "went through their heads" when they contemplated whether homosexuals should have an equal opportunity to be hired for jobs for which they are qualified. Others did the same in response to the proposition that the Ku Klux Klan should not be prevented from publishing materials in newspapers. Among the former, the modal comment, by far (nine of twelve), was an expression of wariness about homosexuals teaching in elementary and secondary schools. On the question of tolerating Ku Klux Klan publications, nearly every respondent (eight of ten) offered one or more of these general comments: "They represent a threat to the *freedom* of blacks"; "They stand for *hatred* and *violence*"; "They operate outside the confines of the *law*." The most frequently offered comment was more personal in nature: "I know some black people, and they should not have to put up with such insults." In one instance, then, thinking

6. For more general treatments of negativity effects, see Lau 1982, 1985.

brought a personally and immediately relevant consequence to the fore; in the other, both a personal concern and a variety of democratic values, including many that conflict with the notion of granting total freedom.

Study Two: Justifying Political Choices

Although the widespread use of surveys has helped us learn much about the political preferences people hold,[7] we know considerably less about why they hold them (for one important and notable exception, see Zaller and Feldman 1992). Typical survey questions do not ask citizens to justify their choices. To the contrary, they encourage quick responses that may or may not be based on prior thought about the issue.

Our second study was designed to ascertain whether motivating people to think—really think—about issues of political tolerance affected their choices.[8] Unlike the first experiment, which merely asked subjects to think about consequences, study two instructed everyone to write down justifications for their choices, which subjects purportedly would discuss openly upon completion of the questionnaire.[9] A priori, we were not sure what to expect. On the one hand, the "thought motivation" manipulation in study two is analogous to the "consequences" manipulation in study one, which leads to the expectation of no difference in results. Alternatively, increased motivation "to think" could encourage subjects to consider a wider range of issues surrounding political tolerance than they had in study one, especially those related to the maintenance of democratic freedom. We then would predict higher levels of tolerance under the "thought motivation" condition.

The results in table 11.1, which are based on nine of the fifteen items included in study one, send a fairly clear message. In only two of nine instances are the means significantly higher in study two than they were

7. Subjects for this and the subsequent studies consist of nonstudent adults from the Champaign-Urbana area. Although all segments of the general population are represented, the subjects were not randomly selected.

8. Until very recently, psychologists and, thus, political scientists have given short shrift to motivation. See Sorrentino and Higgins 1986 for an excellent collection of emerging work.

9. Subjects completed the questionnaires as members of small groups (five to seven people per group) and anticipated that they would justify their answers to the whole group.

Table 11.1 Effects of "Motivated Thinking" on Political Tolerance Judgments

Statement	Study One			Study Two
	No Instruction Condition	Feelings Condition	Consequences Condition	"Motivated Thinking" Condition
People should have the freedom to express their own opinions publicly.	4.19 (n = 40)	4.23 (n = 39)	2.48 (n = 39)	2.61 (n = 32)
Representatives of the Roman Catholic church should be allowed to state their views in public.	3.72 (n = 21)	3.99 (n = 19)	2.01 (n = 20)	3.97[a] (n = 18)
Representatives of the American Nazi party should be allowed to state their views in public.	1.11 (n = 19)	1.16 (n = 19)	0.38 (n = 19)	0.44 (n = 14)
People should be guaranteed equal opportunity for employment in jobs for which they are qualified.	4.23 (n = 39)	4.01 (n = 39)	2.01 (n = 40)	3.28[a] (n = 34)
Disabled veterans should have equal opportunity to be hired for jobs for which they are qualified.	4.86 (n = 19)	4.52 (n = 19)	2.18 (n = 20)	2.42 (n = 16)
Homosexuals should have equal opportunity to be hired for jobs for which they are qualified.	1.98 (n = 20)	2.06 (n = 19)	−1.15 (n = 19)	−1.04 (n = 18)
The government should not have the right to censor published materials.	1.55 (n = 39)	2.01 (n = 40)	1.11 (n = 40)	1.23 (n = 33)
The American Civil Liberties Union should not be prevented from publishing materials in the newspapers.	2.16 (n = 20)	2.46 (n = 19)	0.07 (n = 20)	1.98[a] (n = 18)
The Ku Klux Klan should not be prevented from publishing materials in the newspapers.	−0.38 (n = 19)	−1.07 (n = 20)	−1.11 (n = 20)	−1.14 (n = 15)

NOTE: Entries are means derived from scales ranging from −5 to +5; positive numbers indicate greater tolerance.

[a]Indicates that study two mean differs significantly from "consequences" group mean in study one.

in the C condition in study one. Both instances involve groups that people view relatively favorably: the Roman Catholic church and the American Civil Liberties Union. Otherwise, our (admittedly limited) experiments show that motivating people to give concentrated thought to political tolerance does *not* enhance their willingness to extend democratic principles to various groups.

Why this is so becomes readily evident upon reading subjects' justifications of their positions. As we found in our replication of study one, what undergirds people's relative intolerance are their immediate fears and concerns—"Homosexuals will indoctrinate our children," for example—and additionally, in the case of the Ku Klux Klan, their strong sense that the group represents a real threat to black people.

Study Three: Knowing the Arguments

Even when compelled to justify their support for or opposition to democratic principles, people, we have found thus far, rarely argue for tolerance on the grounds that its absence can undermine basic freedoms for everyone. Either ordinary citizens reject the grand ideas to which political scientists so frequently pay homage or they simply do not come to mind. Which explanation obtains is a matter of some consequence: in the latter case, people will be open to the kinds of arguments that favor political tolerance; in the former case, they will not.

In an exploratory effort to understand what is going on, we asked a group of subjects to evaluate the statement (from study one) that "the Ku Klux Klan should not be prevented from publishing materials in the newspapers." Before completing this task, all subjects read and reflected on two arguments in favor of tolerance and two arguments in favor of intolerance:[10]

> *Arguments for tolerance*
>
> If members of the Ku Klux Klan are prevented from publishing materials, it is a small step to preventing members of other groups

10. Of course, there is nothing magical about these particular statements.

> from publishing as well. Once censorship begins, it is hard to stop—witness the McCarthy era. It is far better to let an obnoxious group have its say than to endanger the principle of freedom of speech.
>
> Even though the Ku Klux Klan is known for making insulting and inflammatory statements about black people, the law protects blacks from harassment and bodily harm. There is no reason to believe that KKK rhetoric will endanger black people's lives. Moreover, it is good to let the KKK reveal themselves for what they are.
>
> *Arguments for intolerance*
>
> The Ku Klux Klan exists only for one reason: to harass and harm blacks. To allow the Ku Klux Klan to publish inflammatory materials can serve no good purpose in a country that values equality and dignity.
>
> To allow the Ku Klux Klan to publish hate material in newspapers will only encourage even more dangerous groups to lash out at innocent citizens.

A second group of subjects evaluated the statement that "representatives of the American Nazi party should be allowed to speak their views in public." Before expressing a judgment, they also read two statements on each side of the issue.

Table 11.2 reports the means of this study, as well as the means from studies one and two that serve as bases of comparison. There are three plausible explanations of the patterns reported there, two methodological and one substantive. Unfortunately, we cannot confidently reject the former. First, the small number of subjects in each study raises questions of reliability. The small coefficients of variability in all three studies reduce, but do not eliminate, the possibility of the patterns arising from random fluctuations.[11] Second, we conducted the studies at different points in time. To our knowledge, nothing happened to raise or lower the overall level of political tolerance, but the fact remains that our studies do not meet the strictest standards of experimental design.

11. All of the coefficients were under .75.

Table 11.2 Effects of "Informed Thinking" on Political Tolerance Judgments

Statement	Consequences Condition (Study One)	"Motivated Thinking" Condition (Study Two)	"Informed Thinking" Condition (Study Three)
Representatives of the American Nazi party should be allowed to state their views in public.	0.38 (n = 19)	0.44 (n = 14)	2.62[a] (n = 26)
The Ku Klux Klan should not be prevented from publishing materials in the newspaper.	−1.11 (n = 20)	−1.14 (n = 15)	1.38[a] (n = 24)

NOTE: Entries are means derived from scales ranging from −5 to +5; positive numbers indicate greater tolerance.

[a]Indicates that study three mean differs significantly from study one ("consequences" group) and study two means.

These cautions duly noted, let us now consider the substantive story. Recall that subjects in the "think about consequences" group in study one expressed less tolerance than those in the "feelings" group. When told that they would be asked to justify their choices (study two), subjects remained relatively intolerant, offering the same kinds of explanations that subjects in study one offered—those related to everyday living rather than to the preservation of democratic life. The means in the last column of table 11.2 suggest that enumerating arguments for and against tolerance affects the choices people make. Exposure to both sides of the tolerance issue increases willingness to accept specific applications of democratic principles. But why?

The best clue lies with our earlier studies, which found that people often do not consider the long-range concerns that motivate, say, the American Civil Liberties Union; once aware of them, however, they incorporate such considerations into their political judgments, while keeping the more proximal, and often more negative, concerns close at hand.[12]

Interestingly, although "informed thinking" leads to more tolerance than "just thinking," it does not increase it beyond that resulting from knee-jerk judgments. Perhaps formal schooling inculcates tolerant atti-

12. The higher level of tolerance in this study, compared to studies one and two, is attributable to a higher proportion of people expressing somewhat more tolerant attitudes, rather than to a few espousing much greater tolerance.

tudes such that when asked simply to react from the gut, people echo what they have learned. But when they truly think about tolerating this or that group activity (something they may rarely do), negative consequences come to mind.

Thinking, Feeling, and the Quality of Political Judgments

Students of democracy impose tough standards on the citizens they study. Ordinary people should be rational, deliberative thinkers who eschew their gut feelings and intuitions. And they must be tolerant. They may not like this or that group, but nonetheless they must support its members' rights to speak publicly, teach in schools, hold public rallies, and run for president. Presumably the one condition, tolerance, follows directly from the other, deliberation. Thinking, so goes the argument, will increase people's willingness to extend basic rights even to members of groups they dislike.

Our admittedly exploratory analyses found that citizens fall short of both expectations. Not only are they relatively intolerant, but they tend to make quick judgments, presumably based largely on feelings. It seemingly follows that were they to be more thoughtful, all would be well. Not necessarily. When asked explicitly to think about consequences, our subjects actually voiced less tolerance, on whole, than did those who reacted from the gut. Advising subjects that they would be asked to justify their choices presumably increased their motivation to think about the ramifications of their choices; it did not increase their tolerance. Only when we exposed subjects to a range of arguments, including those about guaranteeing freedom in the long-run, did thinking result in a level of tolerance equivalent to that found in the "feeling" condition in study one. We underline "equivalent"—not greater than, but the same.

Is there then a good case to be made in favor of people making political judgments on the basis of their gut reactions? This is a provocative idea about which, unfortunately, we can say less than we would like. Although our studies build upon one another, they do not constitute a single, integrated experiment. Moreover, they lack the kind of iterative fine tuning necessary to build confidence in the results. Taking respondents out of their real world contexts raises the inevitable concern about external validity. Moreover, our premise that feelings undergird knee-jerk judgments more than deliberated ones could prove to be wrong, as we acknowledged earlier.

Temporarily casting these caveats and qualifications aside, what about the suggestion that prescriptions for a deliberative citizenry may be ill-directed? Our (firm!) conclusion: not necessarily. We did find, after all, that contemplation causes people to consider simultaneously a variety of democratic values, of which political tolerance is only one. Thus, we found that our subjects' intolerance of Ku Klux Klan activities (and note that all recent studies report the Ku Klux Klan to be by far the most popular target of intolerance) stems largely from a perception that the group's central objective is to limit the freedom and liberties of another social group—blacks. We are not implying that two negatives, intolerance of intolerance, result in a positive, tolerance. Nor are we insensitive to the possibility of rationalization, especially when the true potential of one group to restrict the freedom of another is a matter of interpretation. If, as Gibson has discovered (in this volume), many people willingly restrict their own freedoms, why should they not be inclined to do the same to others?

Nonetheless, our subjects communicated a valuable message: political tolerance alone does not equal democracy (see also Hanson's comments, in this volume). The latter consists of an amalgam of values, some inherently in conflict. The truly critical test for citizens of democratic societies may lie with their ability to recognize complexity and deal with it in a balanced, flexible, and evenhanded manner. Contemplation absent the whole gamut of arguments, pro and con, may not always enhance tolerance, but presumably it does foster perspective, and perhaps self-control. If nothing else, a moment of reflection should remind one that intolerant behavior can bring down the wrath of fellow citizens, let alone the hand of the law.

This leads us directly to the issue that we raised and then skirted earlier: What is a good political decision? Is more of any given democratic value always better than less? Until we can come to grips with the definition of good, we will be stymied in our efforts to evaluate the effects of thinking on political judgments.

This unresolved and thorny problem aside, if we believe the results of our third study, the task is to get citizens not simply to think about political phenomena but to think in a relatively informed way. How might this be achieved in the real world?

Many writers look to increased formal education, although a verdict on its true effect remains outstanding (Jackman 1978; Kuklinski et al. 1982; Sniderman et al. 1984; Sullivan et al. 1982). Alternatively, and especially in contemporary societies characterized by rapid, nationwide communication, political elites can and often do set the agenda and tenor of political debate (Gibson 1988). Is it with these actors, then, that the best chance of an informed, deliberative citizenry lies?

Whatever the answer in the abstract, the reality is that elites, enmeshed in a political battle of win or lose, have little incentive to encourage informed and systematic citizen evaluation of political phenomena. To the contrary, it is appeal to emotions that proves most effective in the battle for public support. Equally important, the president and members of Congress themselves display feeling—often impassioned—when they deal with one another. When Edward Kennedy proposes new civil rights legislation, Jesse Helms, we suspect, does not undertake a complete reading of the bill before deciding where he stands; his gut reaction serves him equally well. Surely it cannot be rationality alone that consistently pits liberal Democrats against conservative Republicans. Moreover, we uncovered evidence that most people find it easier to evaluate politics in terms of the likely short-run effects on their lives than in terms of broad, abstract criteria. One serious implication is that elected officials, who knew this already, may not feel compelled to dwell on the latter.

Should we want a deliberative citizenry? That is the question we have been addressing. If the answer is yes, then two other questions naturally follow: What will motivate ordinary people to think about important political choices? How can representative democracies best provide the kinds of information citizens need to make thoughtful *and* informed decisions?

Perhaps, however, we have misstated the original question. Only an antidemocrat would reject the idea of a reflective, thoughtful citizenry. Whether we should prescribe a deliberative, and *only* deliberative, citizenry is another matter. We, along with other authors in this volume, have demonstrated that relying on feelings and intuitions does not fare as poorly as most writers would have us believe.

In her *Living in the Light*, author Shakti Gawain (1986) posits that all of us have a male and female energy. The former clamors for absolute clarity, truth, and decisive action; the latter stresses feelings and intuition. Historically, Gawain argues, men have drawn on only their male energy, women on only their female energy. Consequently, both men and women have functioned as less than total persons.

So it may be with a nation's citizenry. One that limits itself to searching for final truths through rational deliberation alone, if such a citizenry can exist, may find itself misguided and increasingly devoid of the human element. Granted, the case for an intuitive citizenry, one whose individual members sometimes use their gut feelings as sources of information, has yet to be made. But so does a convincing case against it.

References

Berelson, Bernard R., Paul F. Lazarsfeld, and William N. McPhee. 1954. *Voting: A Study of Public Opinion Formation in a Presidential Campaign*. Chicago: University of Chicago Press.

Bloom, Howard S., and H. Douglas Price. 1975. "Voter Response to Short-term Economic Conditions: The Asymmetric Effect of Prosperity and Recession." *American Political Science Review* 69:1240–54.

Campbell, Angus, Philip E. Converse, Warren E. Miller, and Donald E. Stokes. 1960. *The American Voter*. New York: Wiley.

Carmines, Edward G., and James H. Kuklinski. 1990. "Incentives, Opportunities, and the Logic of Public Opinion in American Political Representation." In *Information and Democratic Processes*, ed. John A. Ferejohn and James H. Kuklinski, 240–68. Urbana: University of Illinois Press.

Conover, Pamela J., and Stanley Feldman. 1986. "Emotional Reactions to the Economy: I'm Mad as Hell and I'm Not Going to Take It Anymore." *American Journal of Political Science* 30:50–78.

de Sousa, Ronald. 1987. *The Rationality of Emotions*. Cambridge, Mass.: MIT Press.

Ferejohn, John A., and Morris P. Fiorina. 1974. "The Paradox of Not Voting: A Decision Theoretic Analysis." *American Political Science Review* 67:525–36.

Fishbein, Martin, and Icek Ajzen. 1981. *Belief, Intention, and Behavior: An Introduction to Theory and Research*. Reading, Mass.: Addison-Wesley.

Fiske, Susan T., and Mark A. Pavelchak. 1986. "Category-Based Versus Piecemeal-Based Affective Responses: Developments in Schema-Triggered Affect." In *Handbook of Motivation and Cognition: Foundations of Social Behavior*, ed. Richard M. Sorrentino and E. Tory Higgins, 167–203. New York: Guilford Press.

Frijda, Nico J. 1987. *The Emotions*. New York: Cambridge University Press.

Frohlich, Norman, Joe A. Oppenheimer, Jeffrey Smith, and Oran R. Young. 1978.

"A Test of Downsian Voter Rationality: 1964 Presidential Voting." *American Political Science Review* 72:178–97.
Gawain, Shakti. 1986. *Living in the Light.* San Rafael, Calif.: New World Library.
Gibson, James L. 1988. "Political Intolerance and Political Repression During the McCarthy Red Scare." *American Political Science Review* 82:511–30.
Jackman, Mary R. 1978. "General and Applied Tolerance: Does Education Increase Commitment to Racial Integration?" *American Journal of Political Science* 22:302–24.
Kinder, Donald R. 1986. "The Continuing American Dilemma: White Resistance to Racial Change Forty Years After Myrdal." *Journal of Social Issues* 42:151–71.
Kinder, Donald R., and D. Roderick Kiewiet. 1979. "Economic Discontent and Political Behavior: The Role of Personal Grievances and Collective Economic Judgments in Congressional Voting." *American Journal of Political Science* 23:495–527.
Kinder, Donald R., and David O. Sears. 1981. "Prejudice and Politics: Symbolic Racism Versus Racial Threats to the Good Life." *Journal of Personality and Social Psychology* 40:414–31.
Kramer, Gerald H. 1971. "Short-term Fluctuations in U.S. Voting Behavior." *American Political Science Review* 65:131–43.
Kuhn, Deanna. 1991. *The Skills of Argument.* New York: Cambridge University Press.
Kuklinski, James H., Daniel S. Metlay, and W. D. Kay. 1982. "Citizen Knowledge and Choices on the Complex Issue of Nuclear Energy." *American Journal of Political Science* 26:615–42.
Kuklinski, James H., Ellen Riggle, Victor Ottati, Norbert Schwarz, and Robert S. Wyer, Jr. 1991. "The Cognitive and Affective Bases of Political Tolerance Judgments." *American Journal of Political Science* 35:1–27.
Kuklinski, James H., and Darrell M. West. 1981. "Economic Expectations and Voting Behavior in United States House and Senate Elections." *American Political Science Review* 75:436–47.
Lau, Richard R. 1982. "Negativity in Political Perception." *Political Behavior* 4:353–77.
———. 1985. "Two Explanations for Negativity Effects in Political Behavior." *American Journal of Political Science* 29:119–38.
Lazarus, R. S. 1982. "Thoughts on the Relations Between Emotion and Cognition." *American Psychologist* 37:1019–24.
———. 1984. "On the Primacy of Cognition." *American Psychologist* 39:124–29.
Lyons, William. 1980. *Emotion.* New York: Cambridge University Press.
McClosky, Herbert, and Alida Brill. 1983. *Dimensions of Tolerance.* New York: Russell Sage Foundation.
Mandler, George. 1975. *Mind and Emotion.* New York: Wiley.
Marcus, George E. 1988. "The Structure of Emotional Response: 1984 Presidential Candidates." *American Political Science Review* 82:737–62.
Markus, Gregory B., and Philip E. Converse. 1979. "A Dynamic Simultaneous Equation Model of Electoral Choice." *American Political Science Review* 73:1055–70.

Miller, Arthur H., Martin P. Wattenberg, and Olesana Malanchuk. 1986. "Schematic Assessments of Presidential Candidates." *American Political Science Review* 80:521–40.

Ortony, Andrew, Gerald L. Clore, and Allan Collins. 1988. *The Cognitive Structure of Emotions*. New York: Cambridge University Press.

Riker, William H., and Peter C. Ordeshook. 1968. "A Theory of the Calculus of Voting." *American Political Science Review* 62:25–42.

Rorty, Amelie Oksenberg. 1980. *Explaining Emotions*. Berkeley and Los Angeles: University of California Press.

Schachter, S., and J. E. Singer. 1962. "Cognitive, Social, and Physiological Determinants of Emotional State." *Psychological Review* 69:378–99.

Schwarz, Norbert. 1992. "Feelings as Information: Informational and Motivational Functions of Affective States." In *Handbook of Motivation and Cognition: Foundations of Social Behavior*, 2d ed., ed. E. Tory Higgins and Richard Sorrentino. New York: Guilford.

Schwarz, Norbert, and Gerald L. Clore. 1983. "Mood, Misattribution, and Judgments of Well-being: Information and Directive Functions of Affective States." *Journal of Personality and Social Psychology* 45:513–23.

Sears, David O., Carl P. Hensler, and Leslie K. Speer. 1979. "Whites' Opposition to 'Busing': Self-Interest or Symbolic Politics?" *American Political Science Review* 73:369–84.

Sears, David O., Richard R. Lau, Tom R. Tyler, and Harris M. Allen, Jr. 1980. "Self-Interest vs. Symbolic Politics in Policy Attitudes and Presidential Voting." *American Political Science Review* 74:670–84.

Sniderman, Paul M., Richard A. Brody, and James H. Kuklinski. 1984. "Policy Reasoning and Political Values: The Problem of Racial Equality." *American Journal of Political Science* 28:75–94.

Sniderman, Paul M., with Michael Hagen. 1985. *Race and Inequality: A Study in American Values*. New York: Chatham House.

Sniderman, Paul M., and Philip E. Tetlock. 1986. "Symbolic Racism: Problems of Motivation in Political Analysis." *Journal of Social Issues* 42:129–50.

Sorrentino, Richard M., and E. Tory Higgins. 1986. *Handbook of Motivation and Cognition: Foundations of Social Behavior*. New York: Guilford.

Sullivan, John L., James Piereson, and George E. Marcus. 1982. *Political Tolerance and American Democracy*. Chicago: University of Chicago Press.

Wilson, T. D., and J. W. Schooler, 1991. "Thinking Too Much: Introspection Can Reduce the Quality of Preferences and Decisions." *Journal of Personality and Social Psychology* 60:181–92.

Wyer, Robert S., Jr., and Thomas K. Srull. 1989. *Memory and Cognition in Its Social Context*. Hillsdale, N.J.: Lawrence Erlbaum.

Zajonc, Robert B. 1980. "Feeling and Thinking: Preferences Need No Inferences." *American Psychologist* 35:151–75.

———. 1984. "On the Primacy of Affect." *American Psychologist* 39:117–23.

Zaller, John R., and Stanley Feldman. 1992. "A Simple Theory of the Survey Response: Answering Questions Versus Revealing Preferences." *American Journal of Political Science* 36:579–616.

12

Passion and Reason in Political Life: The Organization of Affect and Cognition and Political Tolerance

Elizabeth Theiss-Morse
George E. Marcus
John L. Sullivan

Perhaps no debate has been more enduring than that between those who proclaim and foresee the elevation of the public to full sovereignty, mainly through the enlightening accomplishments of education and the development of reason, and those who see greater value in the public's sentimental attachments to core values.[1] Immanuel Kant and John Stuart Mill readily come to mind as exemplars of those who espouse the value

1. For a full and thorough review, see Halebsky 1976.

of reason, whereas Gustave Le Bon, Edmund Burke, and Joseph de Maistre are representative of those who find virtue in the role of sentiment.[2]

The debate presumes two states of mind, one governed by reason and the other by passion. Max Weber describes these two states very well. According to Weber, the first state, instrumental rationality, is the basis of free action because it is capable of freeing one from the second state of mind, the enchaining grip of custom, religion, and tradition:

> With its clarity of self-consciousness and freedom from subjective scruples, instrumental rationality is the polar antithesis of every sort of unthinking acquiescence in customary ways as well as of devotion to norms consciously accepted as values. . . . One of the most important aspects of the process of "rationalization" of action is the substitution for the unthinking acceptance of ancient custom, of deliberate adaptation to situations in terms of self-interest. (Weber 1978, 1:30)

It is not surprising that those who subscribe to the values enunciated in liberal democratic thought see progress and the growth of individual autonomy and freedom as contingent upon the reduced role of passion and the enhanced and elevated role of reason. Hadley Arkes (in this volume) strongly argues this position, with some passion, as do political scientists who subscribe to the public-choice, or rational-choice, school, whereas those of the symbolic-politics school have found the empirical support for these expectations wanting (an excellent review can be found in Sears and Funk 1990).

The empirical work we report here suggests a reformulation of this debate, namely, that citizenship requires combined reliance on passion and reason. In our research on the impact of threat on political tolerance, we wish to explore the role of both affect and cognition in order to determine their unique roles and also to assess how they jointly affect perceptions of threat and, subsequently, tolerance.[3] We suggest that

2. Indeed the history of the evolution of liberal political thought, from Hobbes to Rawls, has been a story of the rise of the place of reason and the decline of the valued role of passion. Hobbes, the seminal author of liberal thought, took the position that sentiment is the cause of action and that reason provides a calculating ability that helps achieve the goals defined by the sentiments. But, after Hobbes, reason emerges in Locke as the ascendant and crowning achievement of personal liberty and autonomy, and the principal and proper basis of action. This presumption is most fully endorsed by the utilitarians Bentham and John Mill.

3. A word or two about language is required at this juncture. The political philosophers

citizens must rely on both reason and passion if they are to perform suitably their citizenly duties.

The Affective and Cognitive Sources of Intolerance

Political intolerance has a central place in the debate about the role of reason and passion in politics. Previous studies on tolerance and intolerance have identified both cognitive and affective sources. For example, support for general democratic norms enhances levels of tolerance even in the presence of high levels of perceived threat, and this support seems to be largely cognitive (McClosky and Brill 1983; Sullivan et al. 1982). On the other hand, affective characteristics, such as feelings of low self-esteem, increase intolerance even in the presence of support for general democratic norms (Sniderman 1975; Sullivan et al. 1982). Thus, tolerance has been presumed to be the proper consequence of the use of reason, and intolerance has been presumed to be a natural result of prejudice and emotion.

However, another powerful force that can reduce levels of tolerance is the degree of threat presented by disliked and unpopular groups (McClosky and Brill 1983; Stouffer 1955; Sullivan et al. 1982; Sullivan et al. 1985). Yet perceptions of threat are not clearly cognitively or affectively based. Perceptions of threat can be interpreted as a primarily affective reaction—people may simply rely on their feelings and prejudices about certain groups. Alternatively, these perceptions can be interpreted as a reaction that is primarily cognitive—people may gauge the realistic threat posed by the group to their own values and to the regime itself.

Our conceptualization of tolerance requires some measure of forbearance. Our previous studies of tolerance therefore developed a methodology that would ascertain which group, if any, individuals found most

discussed at the beginning of this chapter use the terms "reason" and "passion" to refer to broad forces governing human affairs. Modern social scientists use the terms "cognition" and "affect" to refer to individuals' thoughts and perceptions, on the one hand, and their surface feelings, on the other. They use the term "emotion" to refer to deeper states of arousal, such as anger, love, hatred, and so on. In the experiment described in this chapter, we rely on the language of social science. Readers should be aware that the language of the philosophers quoted at the beginning of this chapter and that of social scientists, used in the later sections, are not isomorphic.

objectionable. To assess the importance of the perceived threat evoked by respondents' least-liked groups, we asked them to describe these groups using a series of polar adjectives: strong-weak, dishonest-honest, trustworthy-untrustworthy, predictable-unpredictable, dangerous-safe, important-unimportant, violent-nonviolent, and good-bad. Of course, there are many other features that could be described, but on balance these represent fundamental dimensions of human perception (Osgood et al. 1957).[4] In addition, we included a question that asked respondents to assess how likely it was that their least-liked group would become more popular in the future.[5]

As was previously reported (Sullivan et al. 1982), six adjective pairs were strongly related to political tolerance.[6] The correlations ranged from −.24 to −.34. Three of these adjective pairs—violent-nonviolent, dangerous-safe, and good-bad—measured the extent to which the least-liked group was perceived to be bellicose and belligerent. Three others—trustworthy-untrustworthy, predictable-unpredictable, and honest-dishonest—measured the extent to which the least-liked group was perceived to be treacherous.[7] It is likely that perceptions of belligerence and treachery evoke powerful negative emotional reactions in most people.

Two adjectives—strong-weak, important-unimportant—and the question asking how likely the least-liked group was to become popular, initiating a primarily cognitive process, gauged perceptions of the least-liked group's strength. Because these measures report perceptions of potency, they should, as a matter of judgment, play a significant role in determining levels of tolerance. However, they were not correlated with tolerance (Sullivan et al. 1982). As noted earlier, similar findings have been reported in the area of racial tolerance, where measures based principally on support for racial integration were not related to percep-

4. Polar terms were presented on a seven-point scale. The first pair of adjectives presented was strong-weak, with 1 anchoring weak and 7 anchoring strong.

5. The response options provided were *very likely, somewhat likely,* or *very unlikely.*

6. Political tolerance is measured here by six statements concerning the political rights that should be extended to each respondent's least-liked group. See footnote 15 below.

7. A Lisrel analysis of these six items requires a two-dimensional solution, with items loading in two groups as described above. Each of these dimensions, belligerence and treachery, has an independent effect on political tolerance, although they are positively correlated with each other. A recent study of how Americans perceive the Soviet Union revealed two dimensions, trust and belligerence (Hurwitz and Peffley 1990). We take this as further confirmation that threat is defined by these two dimensions.

tions that a particular consequence would actually occur (Kinder and Sears 1981).

Psychologist Jeffrey Gray (1987a, 1987b, 1988) has developed a theory of emotional arousal that explains these findings. This theory implies that reactions to political groups are based on sensory information provided by the current environment and on affective processing of that information. Thus, feelings provide a constant stream of reports—as changes in mood—thereby monitoring the state of contemporary affairs. Gray's model of emotional arousal identifies two systems of sensory monitoring. One, called the behavioral inhibition system, is specifically concerned with signals of threat and sudden unexpected intrusion. Mood changes, from calm to anxious and from anxious to calm, reflect the appearance or disappearance of threatening stimuli (Gray 1981). Affective reactions to threat therefore chronicle specific contemporary occurrences that violate the norms of trustworthiness and proper orderly behavior. Research has shown that affective responses are strongly related to immediately threatening circumstances (Lazarus et al. 1965).

Gray's work, along with that of other psychologists (Moreland and Zajonc 1979; Zajonc and Markus 1984; Zajonc 1980, 1984), suggests a substantial disjunction between cognition and affect—between attending to thoughts and attending to feelings.[8] This theory suggests a perspective not presented in the debate between the public-choice school and the symbolic-politics school. Emotional arousal may serve to provide contemporary assessments of the state of the environment while cognition supports detached reflection and introspection.

Study Design

Our discussion has identified three factors that might influence how threat affects levels of tolerance. The first is people's states of mind—whether they are attending to their thoughts or feelings. If affect serves to monitor the environment for the appearance of threat, then attending to feelings should increase wariness. Wariness has two characteristics:

8. The claim of disjunction is actively rejected by many cognitive psychologists (Lazarus 1982, 1984) where the dominant approach has been to account for affect as subservient to cognitive processes (Fiske 1981; Fiske and Pavelchak 1986).

(1) guarding against danger or deception and (2) being alert to the world. The opposite of the first is reassurance, and of the second, inattentiveness. To the extent that people are in a heightened state of wariness, evidence of threat will produce greater intolerance and attention to the environment. To the extent that people are encouraged to ignore their feelings and to concentrate on their thoughts, they should be more tolerant because they are less attentive to signals of threat and to strategic features of the environment.

The second factor is cognitive appraisal of the probability that a noxious group will become powerful. When the probability is high, individuals will become more intolerant. The third factor is affective appraisal of treachery and belligerence. These appraisals often arouse feelings of anxiety. To the extent that disliked groups evoke these feelings, individuals will become more intolerant. We designed an experiment to examine these three distinct factors.[9]

The experiment consisted of two stages. Subjects were first given a pretest to establish which groups they most disliked. Two weeks later they were given a posttest that included a scenario about a hypothetical group, and that scenario contained the randomly assigned experimental manipulations. In order to disguise the true purpose of the experiment, subjects were told at the beginning of the posttest that the researchers were interested in social networks and wished to discover where individuals obtain their political information and who influences their political values and beliefs.[10]

The pretest questionnaire was administered to students in five introductory American government classes at the University of Nebraska in the spring of 1989. Since every student entering the University of Nebraska must take a humanities or social science elective, of which the introductory American government course is one option, the students in these classes represented a broad range of interests and backgrounds. Two hundred and nineteen students completed both the pretest and the posttest.

9. We have conducted a number of additional experiments similar to the study reported here. In the interest of space, we defer describing these additional studies except to say that we report findings here that have been replicated across these additional experiments. This series of experiments was stimulated by earlier reports of the work of James Kuklinski and his colleagues (1991, and the chapter in this volume).

10. After the experiment, students were debriefed and told the true purpose of the study. None of them had discerned the true purpose of the experiment.

Students were presented with a list of eleven extremist political groups and were asked, among other things, to indicate how much they liked or disliked each group and to select the group they most disliked. One group, those who oppose prayer in public schools, was not chosen by anyone. The Ku Klux Klan, on the other hand, was chosen by about half of the students.

Based on the least-liked target group chosen in the pretest, each student read a scenario about a hypothetical group coming to power in the United States. Table 12.1 shows the least-liked groups that were selected and the hypothetical groups designated to correspond to each target group.

For example, students who chose the Ku Klux Klan as their most disliked group in the pretest read a scenario about a hypothetical group called the White Supremacist Faction (WSF) in the posttest. Similarly, students who chose feminists read a scenario about a group called

Table 12.1 Target Groups and Corresponding Hypothetical Groups

Least-Liked Group Selected	Number of Students Selecting Least-Liked Group	Scenario Assigned
Religious fundamentalists	4	Christians in Politics (CP)
Pro-life on abortion issue	3	Christians in Politics (CP)
American Communists	15	New Movement for America (NMA)
Socialists	1	New Movement for America (NMA)
Ku Klux Klan	108	White Supremacist Faction (WSF)
American racists	37	White Supremacist Faction (WSF)
American Nazis	37	Nationalist Party of America (NPA)
Pro-choice on abortion issue	5	Women for Justice (WJ)
Feminists	4	Women for Justice (WJ)
Oppose nuclear weapons/ foreign policy	5	Americans Against the Military (AAM)
Oppose prayer in public schools	0	

Women for Justice, and so on. Thus, each student read a scenario about a group he or she was especially opposed to, thereby controlling the level of opposition to a group. This procedure also ensured that students did not read a scenario depicting a group they might support.[11]

Each scenario began with a description of the beliefs held by the hypothetical group; the second and third paragraphs outlined actions the group proposed to take to implement their beliefs. The first section of the White Supremacist Faction scenario is presented below:[12]

> Now we would like you to read the following scenario about a hypothetical group that has organized in the United States. While you read the scenario, please think about how you and the people in your social network would react to such a group.
>
> Suppose it is the late 1990s and a new political group has been formed in the United States. It is an extremist group that evolved from the Ku Klux Klan of the 1980s. This group—the White Supremacist Faction (WSF)—has pledged to rid the United States of Black influence which they believe has grown too great. They believe that Blacks have been favored by liberal government policies and have taken advantage of the system. Recent evidence of this, they believe, is the massive affirmative action efforts of recent decades and the various special job training programs in Black neighborhoods and communities, as well as the attempts to integrate schools. They believe that American society has lowered its standards, and blame Blacks for this. They are also beginning to worry more and more about the power and influence of Catholics as well but have decided to concentrate for now on Blacks.
>
> The WSF has not been very specific about the actions they propose to take, but there are hints that they would like to restrict the economic and political rights of Blacks and perhaps even Catholics. They would like to keep Blacks out of public office, and have stated that they would like to screen other candidates to make sure they do not support programs designed

11. Since our definition of tolerance requires a demonstration of forbearance, this design ensures that students will be confronted with a group they find objectionable.

12. The text of the other scenarios is available from the authors. Subsequent analysis showed no difference in the overall responses by scenario. Thus, the variation in responses is due to factors other than the particular target group selected by the respondent.

> to help disadvantaged minorities. They would like to restrict welfare programs, and have mentioned eliminating many job and welfare programs. They have stated that they will not use violence to achieve their aim of limiting Black influence in America.
>
> Another part of the WSF program seems to be in favor of restricting entry into colleges and universities, largely because they perceive them to be the major training ground for the Black middle classes and liberal intellectuals. These Blacks and intellectuals have masterminded the decay of white middle-class values and have assisted in creating and maintaining the Black and liberal stranglehold on the political system in the United States. The WSF would like to restrict the college experience to small denominational, Christian institutions and to do away with the large research universities across the country. They want to ensure that only the physically and intellectually "fit" are allowed to attend college and to become part of the governing classes in the U.S. Although they have not explicitly said so, it appears likely they would institute a screening program to weed out dangerous college professors.

The instructions and the format of the other five scenarios were identical. The scenarios differed only in the name of the group and the group's beliefs and specific goals. Following these paragraphs were two additional paragraphs that contained two of the principal experimental manipulations. One paragraph was concerned with the probability of the group coming to power and the other with the treachery and belligerence of the group (i.e., violations of the norms of trustworthiness and proper orderly behavior).

Each paragraph had two versions. The *probability-of-power paragraph* had high and low versions:

> *High Probability Paragraph*
>
> The WSF has already amassed large sums of money for a sophisticated and subtle advertising campaign. Public opinion polls show that although they are not likely to win any major national elections soon, more and more people—particularly young people—are beginning to listen to their message and to find some value in it. Most people do not agree with everything they say, but do find some points appealing. This is evidenced by

some electoral gains that the WSF has begun to register in local elections in some parts of the country, particularly Chicago, Southern California, and parts of the South. Some public opinion polls indicate that as much as 10% of the public feels sympathy for the WSF and its point of view, and the percentage appears to be on the rise. Several Black organizations, including the NAACP, are taking the threat very seriously indeed and have begun an urgent campaign to combat the WSF.

Low Probability Paragraph

The WSF has tried raising money for an advertising campaign, but public opinion polls show that few people are paying much attention to them. In fact, many people find their views objectionable, and most people are apathetic about the group and its agenda. The group has grown some in recent years, but most political analysts have classified it as another in a long line of extremist groups in the U.S. that simply do not appeal to the bulk of the moderate American public. Analysts agree that they might indeed do harm to some Black groups and individuals but they have little chance of gaining any significant political power.

These paragraphs systematically differ in their statements about the effectiveness of fund raising and the degree of public responsiveness to the group's appeals.[13] They also differ in the group's electoral success and the significance accorded to it by appropriate monitoring organizations. We would describe this manipulation as primarily cognitive because it provides significant information about the danger presented by the hypothetical group. If threat perceptions are primarily based upon a rational and pragmatic assessment of the group's potential for gaining real power, then those who read the high-probability paragraph ought to be less tolerant than those who read the low-probability paragraph. We are, in other words, manipulating information about the group—

13. In order to keep the manipulation credible, we created two versions that would not be so implausible as to risk incredulity among the subjects. In an unpublished study by Professor Michal Shamir of Israel, a parallel experiment using a more powerful and believable "high" probability paragraph was used. Her results on the impact of the probability paragraph are identical to ours.

information designed to provoke primarily cognitive rather than affective processing.

The second manipulation was achieved by creating two versions of a paragraph that varied in the degree to which the description of the group and its actions was affectively evocative. We called this the *normative-violations paragraph* and it had a threatening and a reassuring version.

Threatening Paragraph

> The WSF has begun to hold public rallies to generate support for their cause. Before their rallies, they refused to cooperate with the police and local authorities but did promise to have peaceful demonstrations according to the conditions of their parade permits. However, they have not always marched along the designated routes and have gotten enmeshed with counter demonstrators and the police. As a result violence has broken out at some of the rallies. Fist fights and rock throwing have resulted in spectators, demonstrators and some police getting hurt. Members of the WSF have shouted, "Whites only, down with the Blacks" and "First get the dirty blacks, then Catholics." At the rallies and demonstrations, leaders of the WSF have asked their supporters to take bold actions to pursue their cause.

Reassuring Paragraph

> The WSF has begun to hold public rallies to generate support for their cause. Before their rallies, they cooperated with the police and local authorities and promised to have peaceful demonstrations according to the conditions of their parade permits. They have marched along the designated routes and did not cause any trouble with counter demonstrators, spectators or the police. At the rallies and demonstrations, leaders of the WSF have asked their supporters to act vigorously but as lawfully as possible to pursue their cause.

These paragraphs differ in their use of emotionally charged language. The threatening paragraph portrays the group as uncooperative with the police and devious with regard to their demonstration plans. They were also portrayed as involved in violence and using inflammatory language.[14] This paragraph was gauged to invoke feelings of treachery and belligerence, thereby alerting subjects to the presence of a threat. The reassuring paragraph portrays the group as cooperative, trustworthy, and peaceful, thereby alerting subjects that threat was minimal. If affective processing is threat monitoring, the first paragraph should produce intolerance, whereas the second paragraph should produce tolerance.

After reading the scenario, subjects responded to tolerance statements specifically related to the hypothetical group. For example, if the students read a scenario about the Christians in Politics, one of the tolerance statements they responded to was "Members of the Christians in Politics should be allowed to make a public speech." The posttest tolerance scale was created from six statements about the hypothetical group.[15]

In order to be confident that we could properly interpret the findings from this experiment, we randomly alternated the order of presentation of the two sets of paragraphs. Half of the time the probability paragraph preceded the normative-violations paragraph, and half of the time it followed the normative-violations paragraph. Thus, the scenarios set the stage for three experimental manipulations: the subjects read (1) a high- or low-probability paragraph, (2) a threatening or reassuring normative-violations paragraph, and (3) the probability and normative-violations paragraphs in varied order.

After reading their scenarios, subjects read, preceding the tolerance statements, an instruction set that told them to pay attention to their feelings or to their thoughts. Previous research has shown that manipulating instructions in this way leads people to process information differently (Ottati et al. 1989; Kuklinski et al. 1991; Millar and Tesser 1986; Wilson et al. 1989). It is important to note that we use the same affective instruction as James Kuklinski and his colleagues (in this

14. While this paragraph does note that violence occurs, it does not depict the group engaged in illegal actions or as the cause of the violence.

15. The statements that make up the tolerance scale are as follows: Members of the [White Supremacist Faction] should be banned from running for public office in the United States. Members of the [White Supremacist Faction] should be allowed to teach in public schools. [The White Supremacist Faction] should be outlawed. Members of the [White Supremacist Faction] should be allowed to make a public speech. The [White Supremacist Faction] should have their phones tapped by our government. The [White Supremacist Faction] should be allowed to hold public rallies. The groups listed on the right-hand side of table 12.1 were inserted between the brackets according to respondents' selection of the least-liked group.

volume) but that we replaced the cognitive instruction to "think about the consequence." The instructions read as follows:

> *Affective State of Mind*
>
> *Instructions*: We have found that people's attitudes and opinions are reported most accurately when they do not think carefully about the statements. It is more accurate for people to simply base their judgments on the feelings, or emotional reactions they experience when they read the statement. Therefore, in evaluating each of the propositions you will read, try to base your responses on your *feelings*, or emotions, not your thoughts.
>
> *Cognitive State of Mind*
>
> *Instructions*: We have found that people's attitudes and opinions are reported most accurately when they ignore the feelings, or emotional reactions they experience when they read the statement. It is more accurate for people to simply think carefully and base their judgments on the thoughts they have when they read the statements. Therefore, in evaluating each of the propositions you will read, try to base your responses on your *thoughts*, not your feelings.

The instruction set occurs after reading the scenarios and therefore cannot influence how the subjects regarded that information.[16]

The full design of this experiment is a four-way between-subjects analysis of variance. Simply put, each of our experimental variables has two levels. The design of the experiment enables us to evaluate whether exposure to each manipulation prods most individuals to become either tolerant or intolerant. These manipulations should reveal whether (1) information about the probability of power is a crucial factor, (2) describing the group in reassuring or threatening language is a crucial factor, (3) the primacy of the information is a crucial factor, and (4) state of mind (thoughts versus feelings) influences levels of tolerance. The

16. Previous work has suggested that when subjects are given no instructions with respect to thoughts or feelings, they respond in the same way they would if given the affective instruction set (Kuklinski et al. 1991). For this reason, we did not add a control group to this already rather complex design.

design also enables us to examine any possible interactions among these main effects.

Findings

The tolerance scale ranges in value from 6 to 30.[17] The mean scale score is 17.8. This means that the average response, for the six statements, was "uncertain"—the middle option of the five possible responses.

Two of the four main effects are not statistically significant. Respondents who read the low-probability paragraph were no more tolerant than those who read the high-probability paragraph (mean of 18.0 versus mean of 17.5; p = .52). Similarly, the order of presentation of the two paragraphs made no difference (when the normative-violations paragraph was first, the mean was 18.0; when it was second, the mean was 17.5; p = .39).

The instruction set, which cues individuals to attend to their feelings or to their thoughts, has a significant impact on tolerance (p = .001). Those who were told to pay attention to their thoughts gave more tolerant responses. Their mean score, 19.0, is over one point above the midpoint of the scale. Those paying attention to their feelings were almost one and a half points below the midpoint (16.4). This result suggests that people are more wary when they attend to their feelings than when they attend to their thoughts.

The paragraphs designed to vary normative violations also had a significant influence on political tolerance (p = .05). Those who read the more disturbing description of their target group as belligerent and treacherous were more than a point below the midpoint (16.7). On the other hand, those who read the reassuring description of their target group were above the midpoint (18.7).

Reactions to emotionally evocative language appear to play a more powerful role than information about the group's power in explaining how perceptions of threat affect tolerance. In particular, manipulating the likelihood that the target group will become more powerful does not have a unique effect on political tolerance. If threat were primarily the

17. Each tolerance statement had five responses listed, from *strongly agree* to *strongly disagree*. The most tolerant response was assigned a 5 and the least tolerant response a 1.

result of a purely cognitive appraisal of the group, then this manipulation would surely have produced a significant effect. However, there are two significant interaction effects that add considerable insight and power to this interpretation.

The only significant second-order interaction is between the normative-violations paragraph and the order of presentation, which means that the main effect of the normative-violations paragraph is not the entire story.[18] When the normative-violations paragraph is presented before the probability paragraph there is no difference between the tolerance scores of those exposed to the threatening and the affectively reassuring versions (mean of 18.0 in both conditions). However, when the normative-violations paragraph appears last in the scenario then the impact of this information is substantial and significant ($p = .02$). When affective stimuli are threatening, the mean tolerance score is 15.5, more than two points on the intolerant side of the midpoint. When the affective stimuli are reassuring, the mean tolerance score is 19.4, over one point on the tolerant side of the midpoint.

This finding suggests a number of possibilities. First, affective responses may not be long-lived. Second, unless affective stimuli are sufficiently prominent (i.e., presented last) they may not activate the threat-monitoring system. This interaction effect doubles the main effect of the normative-violations paragraphs or it eliminates it altogether. It is important to reinforce the point that affective stimuli can be either reassuring, yielding tolerance, or threatening, yielding intolerance.

It is worthwhile to consider the way in which all four experimental factors interact. When affective stimuli are presented before the cognitive stimuli, none of the differences within or between the probability and the normative-violations manipulations are statistically significant. This is true whether respondents have been told to attend to their thoughts or their feelings before answering the tolerance questions.

When affective stimuli are presented after the cognitive stimuli the probability and normative-violations manipulations have significant effects. These interactions produced significant differences ($p = .05$), presented in figures 12.1 and 12.2.

Figure 12.1 shows the results for people who were told to pay attention to their feelings in the instruction set and who received the

18. As with all interactions, this means that the impact on the dependent variable is defined by two or more factors working together rather than separately.

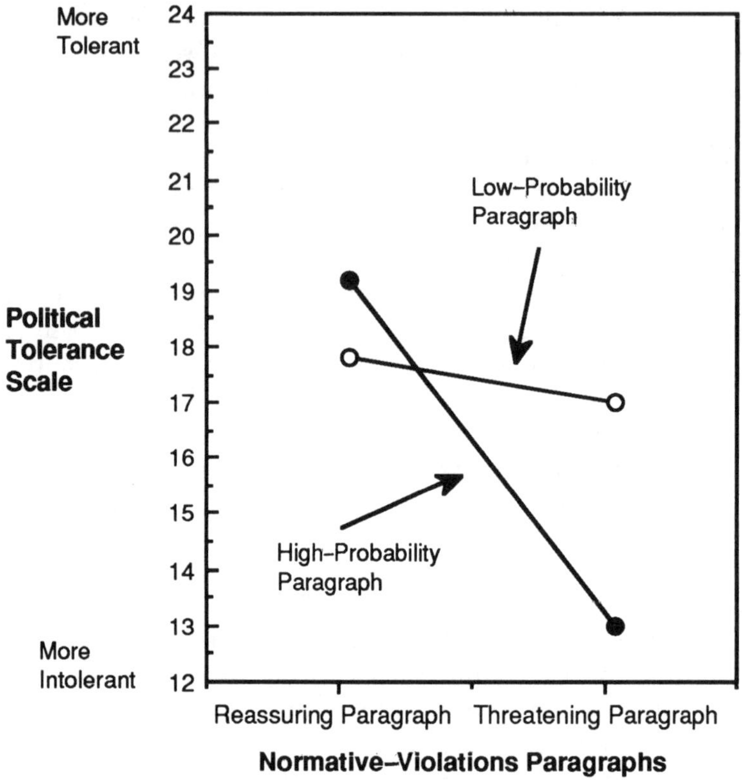

Fig. 12.1. Fourth-order interaction effects: attending to feelings—normative-violations paragraph is last

normative-violations paragraph just prior to answering the political tolerance questions. These are the conditions that heighten the influence of feelings on judgment. Clearly, the probability information mediates the impact of the normative-violations paragraph on tolerance. When the target group was presented as likely to become more powerful, levels of tolerance plummeted to a low of 12.8, an average drop of more than 6 points on the tolerance scale. In other words, the threatening normative-violations paragraph, in conjunction with the high-probability paragraph and the affective cue, moved respondents from a neutral to an intolerant position across each of the six statements (the difference between the low- and high-probability paragraphs, in this instance, is significant at $p < .04$). When the state of mind is affective—when people are encouraged to attend to their feelings—the normative-violations

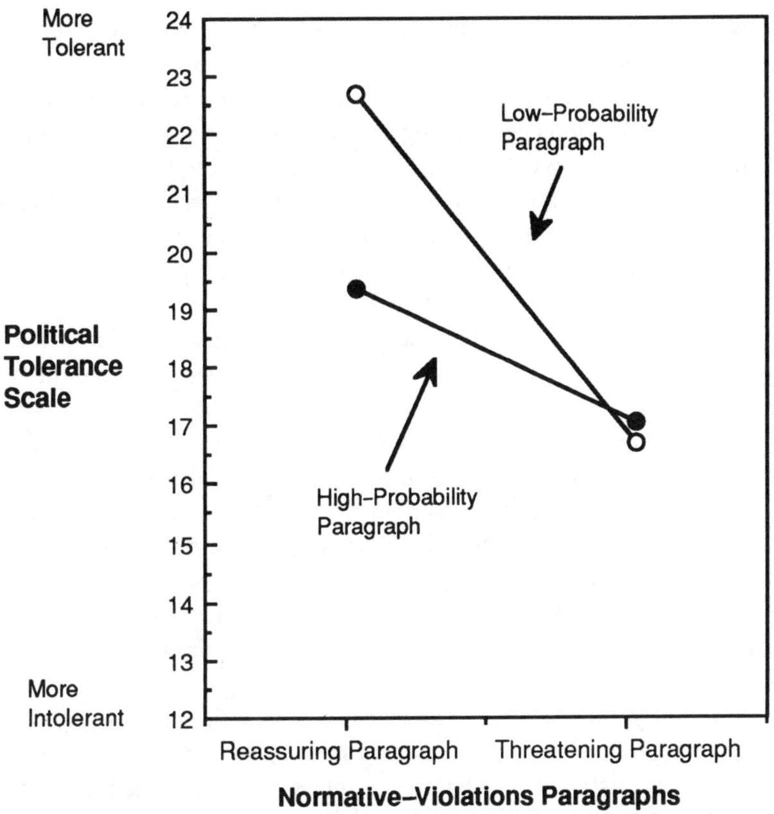

Fig. 12.2. Fourth-order interaction effects: attending to thoughts—normative-violations paragraph is last

stimuli are most influential when they are corroborated by cognitive content. In this sense, affect and cognition work together in influencing levels of tolerance.

Figure 12.2 shows the results for people who were told to pay attention to their thoughts and, as in figure 12.1, received the normative-violations paragraph just prior to the tolerance questions. Here the probability information is not influential (none of the differences are significant). Figure 12.2 does show that the threatening normative-violations paragraph does cause an increase in wariness. It is interesting to note that probability information is taken into account, but only when respondents are attending to feelings and only when they feel that normative violations are serious.

Thus, contrary to the general presumption that emotions interfere with effective use of reason, we find that attention to one's feelings can enhance the use of reason. In this instance, people are attentive to the probability of a noxious event being serious *only* when they are attentive to their feelings. When they are attentive to their thoughts, they are not responsive to the probability information. Finally, even when instructed to attend to their feelings, people do not utilize the probability information when they are reassured. They attend to the probability information only when they feel threatened.

What then are the conditions that produce the greatest tolerance and the greatest intolerance? Among the conditions we examined in our experiment, tolerance requires both affective and cognitive reassurance and it also requires attention to thoughts. When all of these conditions are met, the mean tolerance score is 22.5 (fig. 12.2). Intolerance occurs when affective and cognitive content is threatening and attention is directed to one's feelings. When all of these conditions are met, the mean tolerance score is 12.8 (fig. 12.1). The magnitude of the difference between these extremes is equivalent to the difference between agreeing with the tolerant response to all six questions and disagreeing with the tolerant response to all six.

We have not yet discussed the instruction-set manipulation—the states of mind. We pointed out above that a threat system, to be strategically effective, must also ensure that alert and wary individuals are more capable of noticing salient features of their environment. This requirement leads us to expect that those given the instruction to attend to their feelings would be more attuned to the salient strategic differences located among the various experimental treatments, whereas those told to attend to their thoughts would be less mindful of these differences. More precisely, we can predict that those given the affective instruction would have a less tolerant mean response, as they do, and would have a greater dispersion of results—reflecting the strategic differences between reassuring, low-probability information and threatening, high-probability information contained in the experimental treatments. Similarly, those given the cognitive instruction would be less attentive to external information and would be less influenced by the differences embedded in the scenarios.

Indeed, there is greater variance in the tolerance judgments in the group given the affective instruction than in the group given the thoughts instruction (about 10 percent more variance).[19] Inviting people to attend to their thoughts makes them less influenced by either threatening or reassuring information and less influenced by probability information. Put more simply, when instructed to attend to their thoughts, people are less responsive to environmental stimuli before them.

The results we have presented, though complex, convey two stories, one familiar and one that challenges prevailing ideas. The familiar story is that arousing emotions is an effective way to gain people's attention. To that we can add that normative violation or normative compliance, in matters of tolerance, appears to be at the heart of feeling threatened or feeling reassured. When emotions are not aroused—that is, when people attend to their thoughts and when the normative violations are placed earlier in the scenarios—people are more tolerant. Encouraging people to deliberate, to attend to their thoughts, may, in effect, short-circuit the emotional arousal system (Wilson et al. 1989).

This story has a corollary that is less congruent with prevailing opinion regarding reason and passion. The familiar contention is that being emotional diminishes accurate comprehension of the state of the world. From this premise it is often suggested that we ought to be rational and, therefore, clear-headed and clear-sighted (Janis 1982; Janis and Mann 1977). The experiment described above suggests an important revision of this presumption, namely, that affective reactions play an important role in enabling people to evaluate their current environment. People appear best able to notice and react to both affective stimuli and cognitive information about their least-liked group when they pay attention to their feelings and when they affectively process information about the group's treachery and untrustworthiness. Under all other conditions, information about the likely success of a noxious group's quest for power (the probability paragraph) does not systematically influence how people respond to the group.[20] Thus, the familiar story

19. We have conducted two other experiments that find exactly this same pattern—a 10 percent greater variance in the group instructed to attend to their feelings compared to the group instructed to attend to their thoughts. In this case, the difference is not statistically significant, but the two replications show this result to be robust and not likely to be a sampling artifact. The standard test for equal variances, the F-test, requires a ratio of difference between the variances to be greater than 2 to 1. A difference of that magnitude is hardly likely, particularly given such mild stimuli.

20. One should bear in mind that our subjects are college students and that different results

has a surprising conclusion: feelings enable people to attend and respond to the state of the world before them.

Indeed, the virtue of introspection, thinking about things carefully and deliberately, is that we can set aside, at least for the moment, the onrush of attention-demanding contemporary stimuli. It is precisely because we sometimes do not wish to be goaded into action that attending to thoughts, as Hadley Arkes's argument invites, is so often endorsed. But humans have to act as well as contemplate, and attending to feelings provides additional information about the world precisely because the limbic system relies on considerable cognitive processing to evaluate sensory stimuli as feelings (Gray 1987b).

The second, more complex, story concerns the ways in which thoughts and feelings work together. When people attend to their circumstances, affective and cognitive processes most often work in conjunction. However, although affect and cognition work together, we should emphasize that they do so while maintaining some distinct orientations. All else being equal, when people are asked to pay attention to their thoughts, they are in fact more tolerant than when they are asked to pay attention to their feelings.

Kuklinski et al. (in this volume) show that when asked to pay attention to the consequences, people are less tolerant than when instructed to attend to their feelings. Both sets of findings, theirs and ours, have been replicated. Clearly, then, the impact of the instruction "pay attention to consequences" is not the same as that of the instruction "pay attention to thoughts."

In our view, the claim that emotions are dangerous—in this case leading more easily to intolerance—ought to be taken seriously. Yet we find that threat leads to greater intolerance when affective processing occurs in conjunction with cognitive information.

However, our results also show that attending to feelings, while making people more wary, does not necessarily lead to intolerance. We have discovered that affective reactions can be reassuring. All else being equal, when people read emotionally evocative language describing their least-liked group as breaking the norms of trust and proper behavior,

---

might obtain with a more diverse or differently constituted subject population. However, insofar as college students are a select group and presumably more cognitively oriented and cognitively adept than the population at large, we would expect that our findings—if they are biased by subject selection—are slanted toward greater cognitive influence. We have recently completed a replication with adult subjects, and the findings are similar to those reported here.

they are likely to provide an intolerant response to that group. On the other hand, when people read emotionally reassuring language describing their least-liked group as conforming to the norms of trust and proper behavior, they are likely to be more tolerant.

The paragraph designed to trigger threatening affect emphasized the potential treachery and belligerence of the least-liked group and presumably evoked affective threat reactions in many people. The paragraph designed to be less threatening did not present highly positive and warm descriptions of the least-liked group, but it did present such language as "cooperative," "did not cause any trouble," "act . . . as lawfully as possible." One presumes this language evoked some degree of emotional reassurance in most people, particularly when the affective stimulus was corroborated by cognitive information.

What, then, ought one to conclude about the classic debate over the role of emotion and reason in political life? It seems clear that to ignore the powerful role of emotion is to negate much of what motivates political thought and action. The best empirical evidence shows that emotion—or passion, if you will—affects human behavior at least as much as, if not more than, cognition.[21] This conclusion is corroborated by the experiments conducted by Kuklinski et al. (in this volume) and Sullivan and Masters (in this volume) as well as by survey research studies (Abelson et al. 1982; Marcus 1988).

Indeed, we found that people are most discerning when attending to their feelings, when emotionally charged information is prominent, and when relevant cognitive information is available. If one were to encourage citizens to eschew their emotions—as a state of mind and as relevant information—what would be the result? At least with respect to threat and tolerance, citizens so instructed would ignore instrumentally relevant descriptions of the noxious group before them.

We should close on a measure of caution. Critical faculties—for example, contemplation, reflection, and prudence—are usually advanced to ensure that private deliberation is brought to bear on the reasons and ideas put forward for collective determination. As Hadley Arkes notes,

21. It might be questioned whether we have appropriately matched cognition against affect in this study. There are, after all, other relevant cognitions that might be manipulated. Indeed, this is so. However, we have selected those features, cognitive and affective, that have been given the greatest prominence by theorists and researchers. Therefore we think it likely that our conclusion, the greater influence of affect, would not be greatly modified had we used different cognitive manipulations. But this is a possibility that bears more study.

these critical faculties require sustained education and nurturing. Kinder and Herzog (in this volume) and Page and Shapiro (in this volume) review considerable evidence that supports their claims that the American electorate does display sufficient deliberative capabilities.

However, as Arkes also notes, people display emotions with great vigor, whether in Filene's basement or at Fenway Park. People have many things they can care about—for example, family, sports, career, and community. People need not, and do not, care about all of these things. If we wish citizens to pay attention to the world of politics, their feelings must be engaged, as every teacher and as every politician quickly comprehends. Citizens who attempt to eschew their political passions will likely become inattentive and unresponsive to their political environment. Absent some minimal compelling political passion, people have little motivation to engage in political reasoning or citizenship.

References

Abelson, Robert P., Donald R. Kinder, Mark D. Peters, and Susan T. Fiske. 1982. "Affective and Semantic Components in Political Person Perception." *Journal of Personality and Social Psychology* 42:619–30.

Fiske, Susan. 1981. "Social Cognition and Affect." In *Cognition, Social Behavior, and the Environment*, ed. John H. Harvey, 227–64. Hillsdale, N.J.: Lawrence Erlbaum.

Fiske, Susan, and Mark Pavelchak. 1986. "Category-Based Versus Piecemeal-Based Affective Responses: Developments in Schema-Triggered Affect." In *Handbook of Motivation and Cognition: Foundations of Social Behavior*, ed. Richard Sorrentino and E. Tory Higgins, 167–203. New York: Guilford Press.

Gray, Jeffrey. 1981. "The Psychophysiology of Anxiety." In *Dimensions of Personality: Papers in Honour of H. J. Eysenck*, ed. Richard Lynn, 233–52. New York: Pergamon Press.

———. 1987a. "The Neuropsychology of Emotion and Personality." In *Cognitive Neurochemistry*, ed. S. M. Stahl, S. D. Iversen, and E. C. Goodman, 171–90. Oxford: Oxford University Press.

———. 1987b. *The Psychology of Fear and Stress*. 2d ed. Cambridge: Cambridge University Press.

———. 1988. "Anxiety and Personality." In *Handbook of Anxiety*, vol. 1, *Biological, Clinical, and Cultural Perspectives*, ed. Sir Martin Roth, Russell Noyes, Jr., and G. D. Burrows, 231–57. New York: Elsevier.

Halebsky, Sandor. 1976. *Mass Society and Political Conflict*. Cambridge: Cambridge University Press.

Hurwitz, Jon, and Mark Peffley. 1990. "Public Images of the Soviet Union: The Impact on Foreign Policy Attitudes." *Journal of Politics* 52:3–28.
Janis, Irving L. 1982. *Groupthink*. 2d ed. Boston: Houghton Mifflin.
Janis, Irving L., and Leon Mann. 1977. *Decision Making*. New York: Free Press.
Kinder, Donald, and David Sears. 1981. "Prejudice and Politics: Symbolic Racism Versus Racial Threat to the Good Life." *Journal of Personality and Social Psychology* 40:414–31.
Kuklinski, James H., Ellen Riggle, Victor Ottati, Norbert Schwarz, and Robert S. Wyer, Jr. 1991. "The Cognitive and Affective Bases of Political Tolerance Judgments." *American Journal of Political Science* 35:1–27.
Lazarus, Richard. 1982. "Thoughts on the Relations of Emotion and Cognition." *American Psychologist* 37:1019–24.
———. 1984. "On the Primacy of Cognition." *American Psychologist* 39:124–29.
Lazarus, Richard, Edward Opton, Markellos Nomikos, and Neil Rankin. 1965. "The Principle of Short-circuiting of Threat: Further Evidence." *Journal of Personality* 33:622–35.
McClosky, Herbert, and Alida Brill. 1983. *Dimensions of Tolerance*. New York: Russell Sage Foundation.
Marcus, George E. 1988. "The Structure of Emotional Response: 1984 Presidential Candidates." *American Political Science Review* 82:735–61.
Millar, Murray G., and Abraham Tesser. 1986. "Effects of Affective and Cognitive Focus on the Attitude-Behavior Relation." *Journal of Personality and Social Psychology* 51:270–76.
Moreland, Richard L., and Robert B. Zajonc. 1979. "Exposure Effects May Not Depend on Stimulus Recognition." *Journal of Personality and Social Psychology* 37:1085–89.
Osgood, Charles E., George J. Suci, and Percy H. Tannenbaum. 1957. *The Measurement of Meaning*. Urbana: University of Illinois Press.
Ottati, Victor C., Ellen J. Riggle, Robert S. Wyer, Jr., Norbert Schwarz, and James Kuklinski. 1989. "Cognitive and Affective Bases of Opinion Survey Responses." *Journal of Personality and Social Psychology* 57:404–15.
Rogers, Ronald W. 1983. "Cognitive and Physiological Processes in Fear Appeals and Attitude Change: A Revised Theory of Protection Motivation." In *Social Psychophysiology: A Source Book*, ed. J. T. Cacioppo and R. E. Petty, 153–76. New York: Guilford Press.
Sears, David O., and Carolyn L. Funk. 1990. "Self-Interest in Americans' Public Opinions." In *Beyond Self-Interest*, ed. Jane J. Mansbridge, 147–70. Chicago: University of Chicago Press.
Sniderman, Paul. 1975. *Personality and Democratic Politics*. Berkeley and Los Angeles: University of California Press.
Stouffer, Samuel. 1955. *Communism, Conformity, and Civil Liberties*. New York: Doubleday.
Sullivan, John L., James Piereson, and George E. Marcus. 1982. *Political Tolerance and American Democracy*. Chicago: University of Chicago Press.
Sullivan, John L., Michal Shamir, Patrick Walsh, and Nigel S. Roberts. 1985. *Political Tolerance in Context*. Boulder, Colo.: Westview Press.

Weber, Max. 1978. *Economy and Society.* 3 vols. Ed. Guenther Roth and Claus Wittich. Berkeley and Los Angeles: University of California Press.

Wilson, Timothy D., Dana S. Dunn, Dolores Kraft, and Douglas J. Lisle. 1989. "Introspection, Attitude Change, and Attitude-Behavior Consistency: The Disruptive Effects of Explaining Why We Feel the Way We Do." *Advances in Experimental Social Psychology* 22:287–343.

Zajonc, Robert B. 1980. "Feeling and Thinking: Preferences Need No Inferences." *American Psychologist* 5:151–75.

———. 1984. "On the Primacy of Affect." *American Psychologist* 39:117–23.

Zajonc, Robert B., and Hazel Markus. 1984. "Affect and Cognition: The Hard Interface." In *Emotions, Cognition, and Behavior*, ed. Carroll E. Izard, Jerome Kagan, and Robert Zajonc. New York: Cambridge University Press.

13

Deliberation, Tolerance, and Democracy

Russell L. Hanson

Over the past thirty years, scholars have amply documented the democratic shortcomings of ordinary American citizens. They have shown that many citizens know little—and care less—about politics. Barely a majority of the eligible population bothers to vote in presidential elections, and only a tiny fraction is involved in more-demanding forms of political activity. Moreover, an alarming number of individuals seem weakly committed to tolerance and other practices deemed central to democratic politics. The need for revised theories of democracy, based on a realistic assessment of citizens' dispositions, seems obvious to those who find this evidence compelling.

Yet previous research may underestimate citizens' capacity for deliberation. Recent studies by James Kuklinski and his colleagues Ellen

Riggle, Victor Ottati, Norbert Schwarz, and Robert Wyer, Jr., and by Elizabeth Theiss-Morse and her colleagues George Marcus and John Sullivan show that citizens are capable of political deliberation, which would seem to support democratic theorists who resist the move toward realism in democratic theory. At the same time, however, these investigations challenge the assumption that deliberation produces the felicitous results generally attributed to it by advocates of participatory democracy. They suggest that deliberation does not always lead to greater tolerance of others and may even decrease tolerance by focusing attention on the negative consequences of tolerating dangerous or unpopular groups. As such, these studies fundamentally challenge democratic theorists to show not only that citizens are capable of thinking about politics but that deliberation will produce decisions and actions consistent with democratic ideals.

Because it questions the value of deliberation, and not just its prevalence in the citizenry, this challenge is potentially more damaging than criticisms leveled by an earlier generation of revisionists. I say "potentially" because I do not believe that either Theiss-Morse et al. or Kuklinski et al. have provided compelling evidence that deliberation does not, or cannot, have the positive effects generally attributed to it by democratic theorists. My doubts arise partly from reservations about the investigators' conceptualization of deliberation and their methods of assessing its effects: instructing respondents to think about tolerance does not capture all, or even most, of the possibilities for enlightenment so often ascribed to debate and other styles of collective deliberation.

However, my chief complaint is that both teams of scholars equate a lack of tolerance with intolerance, glossing over a highly significant difference. Most people refrain from intolerant actions, even though they harbor less-than-tolerant attitudes. They may disavow the right of, say, the Ku Klux Klan to march in places like Skokie, but they do little or nothing to prevent such marches from occurring. This forbearance is extremely important, insofar as it calls attention to the potentially moderating influence of political institutions and practices so familiar to those interested in democratic regimes, not just democratic character.

Researchers' neglect of institutions' role in fostering forbearance betrays a tendency to identify the fates of democracy and tolerance. This move should be resisted; the connection between democracy and tolerance may be strong, but the two are not the same. So important is this point that I will for the moment assume that Kuklinski et al. and Theiss-

Morse et al. have produced incontrovertible evidence of a depressing effect of deliberation on levels of tolerance, in order to expose the questionable relevance of this finding to the conclusion that deliberation undermines democracy.

The Value of Tolerance

The general alarm sounded by Kuklinski and his colleagues stems from their inference that democracy may be ill served by citizens who react deliberatively where rights and liberties are at stake. Kuklinski et al. conclude that "cold reason" need not always yield a more tolerant, just, or fair society. To the contrary, when people explicitly consider the consequences, they tend to focus on immediate and negative ones and thus find justification for increased intolerance. This is especially true where individuals or groups are disliked, so positive affect toward others is the best hope for sustaining democracy—a point echoed by Theiss-Morse et al.

This conclusion, if warranted, would require major changes in contemporary democratic theory. Before we undertake those changes, however, we should inquire if the conclusion on which they would be based stems from an understandable, but nevertheless troublesome, simplification. Much empirical research on tolerance equates the fate of democracy with the willingness of citizens to abide others. In this identification of democracy with tolerance, anything that contributes to the latter necessarily enhances the former—or, to put it negatively, as is more often done, anything that inhibits tolerance lessens democracy. And since deliberation undermines tolerance, it diminishes democracy—Q.E.D.

This position is not unreasonable; in the absence of tolerance it *is* difficult to imagine how democracy might originate or be sustained for any length of time. But the difficulty arises less from any necessary connection between tolerance and democracy than it does from liberal democratic values that infuse research in this area. To make this point, it is enough to recall that tolerance plays a much different, and significantly less important, role in nonliberal conceptions of democracy than it does in our own. Consider, for example, leftists' indictment of "repressive tolerance" and their refusal to accord tolerance pride of place in discussions of American democracy. Consider, too, the small role that tolerance plays in social democratic thought, where considerations of solidarity and equity are at the center of discussion. Unless we are prepared to dismiss these positions as undemocratic, we must concede the nonidentity of tolerance and democracy.

Even within the liberal democratic tradition it is hard to find unqualified support for tolerance, except perhaps among libertarians, as Larry Preston notes elsewhere in this volume. Despite their preoccupation with individual freedom, theorists and practitioners of liberal democracy have always countenanced certain forms of intolerance. Thus, neither John Locke nor John Stuart Mill believed all groups deserved tolerance, and liberal democratic jurisprudence is replete with exceptions to and qualifications upon the civil liberties that figure so prominently in tolerance studies. So, for example, rights of speech and assembly have been abridged regularly during times of war and national emergency, and even during normal times these rights are restricted by other concerns, for example, public order or national security. In these and many other instances, limitations on individuals' actions are widely viewed as both necessary and desirable and are seldom held to be undemocratic.

This is especially true when the actions in question are those of intolerant people, for example, racists or religious bigots; liberal democrats, or at least many of them, do not tolerate intolerance, nor do they believe they should. In that sense, liberal democrats are not absolutists when it comes to rights and liberties, and neither are they committed to the maximization of tolerance in the name of democracy. Thus, a diminution of tolerance is not necessarily a reduction in democracy, *unless we assume that tolerance is the greater (or only) part of democratic rule*—a proposition that is rather difficult to defend, since it makes "democracy" superfluous.

Still, is it not reasonable to worry about the diminution of tolerance, and hence the partial degradation of democracy, even if tolerance is not all of what we mean by democracy? Should we not be suspicious, or at least circumspect, about deliberation, if it diminishes such an important part of democracy as tolerance?

That all depends on what deliberation means, and the fact that democracy involves considerations other than tolerance—for example, equality and majority rule—suggests that deliberation is highly complex. If citizens are truly deliberating in the way that Kuklinski et al. aver, they may weigh competing or even contradictory values: does freedom of expression mean that wealthy individuals are entitled to spend enormous amounts of money to influence election outcomes and policy choices, overcoming the opposition of large numbers of ordinary citizens and possibly defeating the principle of political equality? These are momentous decisions involving several values, and "trade-offs" seem both unavoidable and desirable. Surely this works against the maximization of any single value, including tolerance. It would be more surprising, therefore, if upon reflection individuals *did not* qualify their judgments and show less commitment to principles of tolerance. That would raise doubts about people's ability or willingness to reason about complex matters.

Furthermore, even the rare and uncomplicated case in which only a single value, tolerance, is at stake may require sophisticated reasoning. What if the requirements of tolerance in specific circumstances are not very obvious? For example, is it intolerant to deny rights of free speech and assembly to intolerant groups, for example, racists who seek to propagate their hateful messages and deny others' rights? If so, under many circumstances an unconditional commitment to tolerance may be self-defeating for democrats, depending on the power and influence of intolerant groups. If one purpose—and hence justification—of tolerance is to promote diversity, then the application of this value to specific cases must weigh the long-term consequences for diversity of being tolerant (or intolerant) of certain groups.

In the face of such uncertainty, an unyielding commitment to the maximization of tolerance is surely evidence of a lack of deliberation, and not the product of reasoned consideration. Yet this is precisely what seems to be required of respondents if they are to be considered "tolerant" in the two studies in question. Consider, for instance, the way in which deliberation operates in the experiment of Kuklinski et al. Deliberation, or rather cogitation, on consequences leads people to qualify their endorsement of tolerance in principle, and even more in practice, when the identity of groups and nature of their actions are known. (I use the term "qualify" to mean both that people limit their willingness to tolerate others and that their conclusions are based on considerations that may be quite reasonable and informed by knowledge and experience.)

There is something odd about this conclusion, however. Ordinarily, we expect the two senses of "qualification" to go hand in hand: reasoning works against extreme positions, whether maximalist or minimalist.

Interestingly enough, the clear implication of Kuklinski et al.'s charge against deliberation is that moderation is no virtue where tolerance is concerned: truly democratic citizens ought to remain firmly committed to tolerance, no matter which groups or actions are involved. Otherwise, the fact that deliberation produces lower levels of tolerance could not be construed as being *necessarily* harmful to democracy.

But if moderation is no virtue where tolerance is concerned, then tolerance risks being repressive. An abstract or pure conception of tolerance that refrains from taking sides implicitly assumes that liberty already prevails and that it is no longer necessary to be intolerant of institutions, practices, and groups that are discriminatory or oppressive. Perhaps we can now afford to tolerate contemporary white supremacists, who seem to pose little risk to others. That was surely not true for most of American history, nor is it obvious that all other institutions in contemporary society have been rendered nondiscriminatory. When intolerant institutions exert a powerful influence over individuals' lives, they must be abolished, not tolerated, according to some democrats' way of thinking.

Thus, citizens who express only qualified support for civil liberties (this being the operational test of "tolerance") are not necessarily a threat to democracy. They may instead be exhibiting an appreciation for the complexities of democratic governance and the need to balance tolerance against other significant concerns and considerations. It is only from the standpoint of "pure tolerance" that these citizens appear dangerous, but pure tolerance itself may threaten democratic progress if it is opposed to the legitimate interests of a majority in overturning slavery, gender discrimination, or other institutions that abridge citizens' freedom.

Passion and Tolerance

So far I have assumed that the results presented by Kuklinski et al. and Theiss-Morse et al. are valid, in order to question the authors' conclusions vis-à-vis democratic theory. In fact, the new findings about the value of deliberation are rather inconclusive. Indeed, the two studies in question are not in agreement on the actual impact of deliberation on respondents' expressions of tolerance. Consequently, the empirical premise of the overall argument—that thinking does not generally enhance tolerance—is as much in doubt as the theoretical claim that the fates of tolerance and democracy are indistinguishable.

Kuklinski et al. state their findings most starkly. They discover that affect—or people's feelings toward various groups—influences tolerance, measured by individuals' willingness to extend basic civil liberties to members of the groups in question. The impact of affect on tolerance is complex; it bears mainly on the oft-noted slippage in support for specific applications of general principles of tolerance. Kuklinski et al. show that this slippage is minimized when esteemed groups are involved; indeed, in some cases, a willingness to tolerate a specific group may be greater than support for the general principle involved. Thus, "equal opportunity" for disabled veterans receives more support than the abstract (and anonymous) principle that "people should be guaranteed equal opportunity for employment in jobs for which they are qualified."

The second finding is that untutored cogitation about the consequences of tolerance produces less tolerance, contrary claims about the "enlightening" effects of reason notwithstanding. When respondents were instructed to think about consequences, many trimmed their support for tolerance, apparently because they feared that undesirable effects would follow from allowing the Palestine Liberation Organization to use a community's hall for public meetings, for example. Nor is this effect restricted only to groups that are negatively viewed. Among respondents who were asked to evaluate consequences, support diminished for groups held in high esteem and also for the very principles of tolerance themselves. In short, the depressing effects of deliberation on tolerance are quite general, raising the possibility that reflection undermines democracy.

Theiss-Morse et al. are not so pessimistic. They agree that emotions affect people's willingness to tolerate others, but they further argue that emotions enable individuals to cogitate more effectively by focusing attention. This may actually increase tolerance if the emotional cues about least-liked groups are reassuring; on the other hand, threatening cues produce lower levels of tolerance. However, Theiss-Morse et al.'s main conclusion is that "all else being equal, when people are asked to pay attention to their thoughts, they are in fact more tolerant than when they are asked to pay attention to their feelings"—which seems to contradict the findings of Kuklinski et al.

This is actually more of a qualification than a contradiction; Theiss-

Morse et al. observe that cognitive reactions produce higher levels of tolerance, *but only under relatively restricted conditions.* Among those who attend to their thoughts, who deliberate, tolerance for least-liked groups is highest when such groups engage in nonthreatening actions and are unlikely to assume power over respondents—relatively easy cases to tolerate. Tolerance is lower when such groups have a greater chance of coming to power and is lower still when least-liked groups engage in threatening actions, regardless of the power potential of the group in question. In the last case, levels of tolerance are no higher than they are for people who respond affectively to groups with little chance of coming to power.

This discrepancy between the two studies on the impact of cognition on tolerance may be explained in any number of ways. It might reflect sampling differences. It might be due to the research teams' use of different instruments, in a setting where such differences are presumed to matter. Or it may be the result of different constructions of the faculty of deliberation itself. For Kuklinski et al., deliberation involves weighing the consequences of tolerating certain acts, and judging their desirability. But for Theiss-Morse et al., deliberation involves assessing the probability that a group might amass power, presenting a real threat to public order.

However, the most likely reason for the divergent findings is that Theiss-Morse et al. first ascertain each respondent's least-liked group and then use that group or a surrogate in subsequent efforts to compare the effects of affect and cognition on tolerance. Kuklinski et al. omit the first step; they simply present respondents with fixed pairs of groups, one of which is generally esteemed, the other of which is generally despised. Respondents are then asked if they would tolerate a specific act by each member of the pair of groups. In that sense the effect of affect is more heavily constrained by investigators' decisions in the Kuklinski et al. study than it is in the inquiry conducted by Theiss-Morse et al.

If Theiss-Morse et al. are right, Kuklinski et al. have not properly measured affect, and their conclusions about the relative impacts of affect and deliberation are suspect, although of course the differences between the control group and the group asked to deliberate would still stand. Even that difference can be questioned, however. Kuklinski et al. fail to attend to the different consequences of different acts. To suggest, as they do, that the anticipation of negative consequences depresses levels of tolerance certainly implies that especially negative consequences will lead to unusually low levels of tolerance. An obvious way to examine the impact of consequential reasoning would involve presentation of a variety of acts, each with different consequences, perhaps measured in terms of their severity, immediacy, and so forth. If severe consequences have especially depressing effects on levels of toleration, that would constitute strong evidence of the impact of thinking about consequences.

Although Kuklinski et al. do not systematically vary the consequences of tolerance, Theiss-Morse et al. approximate this effect by manipulating the "normative-situations" paragraph in hypothetical scenarios that were presented to respondents. The manipulation "varied the degree to which the description of the group and its actions was affectively evocative." But the information contained in the paragraphs contrasts violent and nonviolent actions, and so it implicitly varies the degree to which least-liked groups are seen as threatening. This might plausibly be construed as an invitation to reason, since the evaluation of groups and their actions clearly has a strong cognitive component. To insist that it is an emotional reaction seems arbitrary.

This suggests that future survey experiments must allow respondents to identify the consequences they find most disturbing, as well as the groups they like least, in order to provide a better test of the relative impact of cognition and affect on tolerance. Such a strategy also demands that we reject the assumption that affect is only or primarily directed toward groups, whereas cognition is only or primarily about the consequences of actions that groups undertake—an unduly restrictive assumption common to both studies. People react affectively to behavior they find especially offensive, for example, flag burning as an exercise of free speech. Just as surely, people cogitate about groups, especially those which trigger intense emotional reactions; thoughtful citizens very reasonably attach different consequences to peaceful and violent demonstrations, for example.

In light of these objections, what may we conclude about the effects of deliberation on tolerance? Unsurprisingly, the answer is "not much." Questions surrounding the empirical claims of Kuklinski et al. and Theiss-Morse et al. prevent us from inferring that reason does not generally improve tolerance or, more strongly, that it undermines tolerance. On the other hand, it would be foolish to *assume* that deliberation has a positive impact on tolerance, as we have in the past. At the very least these two studies suggest how inappropriate that assumption may be. That is an important accomplishment, and it means that we are actually making progress by admitting that we cannot now conclude anything certain about the enlightening effect of thinking on tolerance.

Intolerance and Forbearance

Having qualified the indictment against reason and its impact on tolerance, I now want to consider the relation between tolerance and intolerance. Kuklinski et al. and Theiss-Morse et al. proceed as if this relation were very straightforward: respondents who are unwilling to grant civil liberties to disliked groups are considered less tolerant than respondents who would extend these liberties. Less tolerant respondents are then presumed to be intolerant, in varying degrees. Thus, a lack of tolerance is associated with intolerance, making the empirical findings obviously relevant to democratic theory.

Kuklinski et al. report an interesting example of intolerance, so defined. In their study, respondents who deliberate support a white family's right to move into an all-black neighborhood that opposes the move, and they do so to a much higher degree than they support the general proposition that "people should have the right to live in any neighborhood they want, if they can afford it." On the other hand, the slippage in support is very large when respondents are asked to think about the consequences of a black family moving into an all-white neighborhood. Respondents do not support that act, presumably because they imagine dire consequences will follow, consequences that are not associated with whites moving into black neighborhoods.

Similar examples of intolerant attitudes appear in the study by Theiss-Morse et al., and in fact both teams of authors report rather low levels of tolerance, even among an educated elite. However, this finding is strongly conditioned by the type of research design employed by the investigators. Both of the studies in question present subjects with tolerance scenarios, that is, situations that invite respondents to embrace tolerance. However, tolerance scenarios are probably biased toward finding intolerance; if intolerance were taken as the reference point, a more favorable reading of citizens' willingness to tolerate others might unfold.

To see this, imagine that respondents were presented with intolerance scenarios. These might include a "Howard Beach scenario," along with other situations involving intolerant behavior directed toward least-liked groups. Such scenarios invite respondents to reject intolerance, and those who did would be exhibiting tolerance. Although we can only speculate, it seems likely that many people would accept that invitation, either because they abhorred intolerance or because they were too ashamed to admit that they did not oppose intolerance. If many people rejected intolerance, then our conclusion would be that people are reasonably tolerant—and that they pose no great threat to democracy.

Interestingly, Kuklinski et al. report that a few respondents in their second study voluntarily wondered "what would happen to our basic freedom were people to be told that they could not live in a particular neighborhood" or expressed other thoughts about the consequences of intolerance. Mostly these consequences were systemic in orientation; they had little to do with "close to home" effects upon respondents themselves, as was apparently the case when the negative consequences of tolerance were weighed. But it is easy to imagine consequences of intolerance that might directly affect individuals and perhaps cause them to exhibit higher levels of tolerance in order to avoid suffering those effects: as one respondent put it, "Stop one person from speaking out and soon no one will be able to speak out," a classic defense of tolerance.

Concern about the consequences of intolerance helps make sense of a puzzle left unsolved by Kuklinski et al. and Theiss-Morse et al. Neither team of investigators suggests that citizens frequently *act* in ways that are intolerant; they merely observe that many people have intolerant attitudes when presented with hypothetical scenarios involving suspect groups. In fact, relatively few people do act upon their darker sentiments. For whatever reason, most people act tolerantly, even if they do not think or feel tolerant. That is not to say that ours is a tolerant society—far from it. Racial, religious, and ethnic minorities are, and have always been, frequent targets of intolerant behavior, as are women, homosexuals, and other minorities. Yet collective life would probably be impossible, or at least unspeakably dreadful, if all who hold intolerant attitudes behaved accordingly.

From the standpoint of democratic theory, this forbearance requires explanation. Why is it that most people, most of the time, exhibit tolerant behavior, even when they hold intolerant attitudes? Could it be that deliberation plays a large role in short-circuiting the connection between attitude and action where intolerance is concerned? Might the consequences of intolerant action be a part of citizens' deliberations, in the same way that Kuklinski et al. argue that the consequences of tolerant actions figure in individual calculations?

The possibility that individuals consider the consequences of intolerance raises important questions about the role of sanctions in deterring people from acting on intolerant attitudes. A particularly important calculation faces individuals who are deciding whether they will commit intolerant acts. For them, deliberation may center on systemic consequences, but more likely it focuses on the personal costs that might be incurred by someone who actually tried to prevent Nazis from marching, the ACLU from publishing, blacks from moving, and so forth. Those personal costs might involve physical harm, economic retaliation, incarceration, prosecution, and public condemnation. In addition, the benefits of tolerance mentioned by those who participated in the study conducted by Kuklinski et al. would also be lost.

With these costs in mind, it is not to hard to construct "rational-actor" models that predict inaction fairly well. Presumably, forbearance occurs when sanctions for intolerant behavior are widely known and well understood. In addition, the sanctions must levy serious penalties, and transgressors must believe that they are very likely to suffer these consequences if they engage in acts of intolerance. Otherwise, it is hard to imagine how someone who held intolerant views would be deterred from acting intolerantly out of concern for consequences that might befall them.

Such models of forbearance have clear policy implications. In order to ensure tolerant behavior, effective sanctions must be promulgated and enforced. But this is problematic in a democracy, as Madison well knew. Under a popular government, it is the majority that must consent to these sanctions, but that same majority is itself likely to act intolerantly. By what act of considerable deliberation will a majority agree to restrain itself, even to the point of accepting penalties for using the power at its disposal to abuse the rights and liberties of minorities or to oppress those who hold unusual opinions or lead unconventional lives? To such constitutional questions I now turn.

The Constitution of Tolerance

A staple feature of much contemporary work on tolerance is a nearly exclusive focus on the character of the democratic citizen. The unstated, but guiding, assumption underlying this research is that a strong correspondence exists between the requisites of a democratic system of governance and the virtues of individual citizens. Thus, it is often assumed that citizens must be tolerant of others if democracy is to survive, since one of the characteristics of democracy is tolerance.

This simply does not follow. The characteristics of a political system are not the orientations of its citizens writ large, for the simple reason that political institutions and organizations are also part of what we mean by a "political system." These institutions and organizations shape citizen orientations or hold them at bay, or both—often in complex ways that we do not yet understand, and perhaps never will. However, it is at least possible that a democratic regime may be sustained if individuals either of their own volition do not act on their intolerant orientations or are prevented from doing so by social, political, and legal authorities. If so, a properly constituted democracy may survive the shortcomings of its citizenry.

Seen from this perspective, the distinguishing feature of a democratic regime may be its capacity to prevent citizens from acting on their worst opinions or attitudes. Political elites undoubtedly play a crucial role in this process, and in fact there is a well-established line of empirical research on the different political interests and capacities of masses and elites as they bear on tolerance. The most interesting conclusion of this approach is that democracy does *not* depend on the existence of high levels of tolerance among the masses. So long as elites defend against intolerance, a democratic system may persist and even function smoothly in spite of intolerant attitudes among the masses.

A variety of preventive measures are available to authorities interested in promoting forbearance among intolerant citizens. If they so choose, political authorities may use the coercive powers of the state to protect the rights and liberties of the weak and unpopular or to infiltrate and destroy intolerant organizations, for example, violent white supremacists. Legal actions may restrain those who seek to abridge the liberties of others, and civil and criminal penalties may be imposed on individuals or groups who succeed in unfairly limiting those liberties. Finally, moral suasion may be exercised by religious leaders, civic groups, and organizations such as the ACLU, all of whom may urge forbearance.

Leaders who urge restraint and practice it themselves perform an educational function that is crucial for democracy. As Theiss-Morse et al. note, this "instruction" may require education in the proper use of emotions, as well as reason, if emotions are as important as these investigations suggest. Of course, this assumes that elites are willing to combat intolerance, that elites are the "carriers of the democratic creed." Not all elites are unequivocally committed to tolerance, however. Demagogic appeals are not unknown in American politics, and we must admit that elites can be dangerous to democracy, too. Elites who lack tolerance or are intolerant do not encourage forbearance by citizens; what is worse, these elites may have opportunities to translate their intolerant sentiments into policy.

Thus, where elites are not strongly committed to tolerance, democracy may well be at risk—or at least that part of democracy related to tolerance. Kuklinski et al. conclude that contemporary elites have little motivation to foster tolerance among citizens; if so, there is a pressing need to elaborate political institutions and practices to remedy this defect. Surely that project deserves attention from all who are concerned about the vitality of contemporary democracy.

14

Can Emotion Supply the Place of Reason? Comments on the Chapters on Passion and Tolerance

Hadley Arkes

I find in these chapters some reflections of my earlier life, when I trafficked almost daily in the findings of survey research. I find myself in the position of that character of Henry James, a woman who professed to have washed her hands of her former husband, but who was nevertheless willing to offer precise, extended critiques of the man to anyone with the remotest interest in the subject. James had his narrator remark of this woman that if, indeed, she had washed her hands of her former husband, she had evidently "preserved the water of this ablution and . . . handed it about for inspection" ("The Coxon Fund"). I moved away, early, from survey research, for some of the reasons that brought forth this conference: it seemed to me that the questions shaping that research did not make contact with any questions of philosophic substance, which is another way of saying that the surveys did not make contact with any questions worth addressing.

Behind most of the questionnaires was an understanding that reduced politics to some of the cruder models of behavioral psychology. It was not merely that the surveys sought to confirm a "psychological" explanation for political conduct, but that the notion of the "psychological" was radically diminished and truncated. I have had the benefit, for many years, of a close friend who professed neuropsychology and contributed some fourscore papers on problems of vision and neural processes. He was also one of that rare species, a psychologist fluent in Greek and Latin. I learned from him years ago that the study of "psychology"—the study of ψυχη, or the soul, in the Greek root—encompassed the study of our understanding. Therefore, it did not merely study the behavior that is "caused" by operant conditioning or by the laws of nature. It made a place also for the study of "reasons" and principles as the objects of understanding and the ground of motivation. With the advantage of this tutoring, I was cautioned years ago to understand that, if we gave a man Shakespeare's "reinforcement schedule," we might produce a fellow with a taste for English mutton and beer, but we would not necessarily produce the writer of *King Lear*. And even if we could have recorded rather precisely the pattern of electrical activity in the brain of John Marshall, nothing in that record could possibly offer an "account" of Marshall's reasoning in *Marbury* v. *Madison*.

But the vice we find in so many works in survey research is that the writers do indeed try to reduce reasons to causes: instead of trying to understand the reasons, or the principles, that may govern the judgments of people, they find it more persuasive to find the springs of "behavior" in nonrational motives. The chapters written by Elizabeth Theiss-Morse and her colleagues George Marcus and John Sullivan and by James Kuklinski and his colleagues Ellen Riggle, Victor Ottati, Norbert Schwarz, and Robert Wyer, Jr., have the advantage of designs produced by artful, subtle minds. But in this case, I fear that my friends and colleagues might have been overcome, in the end, by a tendency that is simply endemic in their field. As thoughtful as they are, I wonder if they have not been drawn into a tendency to reduce the political to the nonpolitical, and the rational to the nonrational.

After all, if Kuklinski and his colleagues turned out to be correct in their argument, they would urge upon us this curious notion: that people are more likely to respect the rights of others—they are more likely to affect the habits of "good citizens" in a democracy—if they do not reflect too strenuously on the grounds that make it "good" or "justified" to be tolerant of others. Apparently, without an overly strenuous reflection on the point, the writers have been willing simply to stipulate "tolerance" as a "good," or a "virtue," perhaps even the cardinal virtue that marks a citizen in a democracy. And then they suggest that this tolerance is more likely to flourish if it springs from our feelings—if we permit our sympathies to be engaged, our sentiments to flow, rather than constrain these feelings through the cold uses of reason. But anyone who has encountered the votaries of "tolerance" will soon discover that they have no patience, or tolerance, for the intolerant. And for that reflex there are good reasons. By its very logic, the ethic of tolerance must rule out intolerance. When our sentiments are recruited to our judgment, it stands to reason that the proponents of racial tolerance will despise the racists and the Ku Klux Klan. But clearly, nothing in these reactions flows from the mere temper of tolerance. It is not in the nature of an affable tolerance to condemn and despise. It is quite natural, however, to despise what is hateful and condemn what is evil. Those reactions naturally flow from a moral passion, which is to say, a passion that is guided by a reasoned judgment on the things that merit our approval or disapproval, our admiration or repugnance.

But when we trace our reactions back in this way to the reasoned ground of our judgments, we would realize that there is nothing in the logic of democratic government that would designate "tolerance" as the chief virtue in a democracy. One might as plausibly argue that the democratic citizen ought to be marked, first, by a moral persuasion about the goodness, in principle, of popular government. That moral conviction must impress the citizen with an intolerance for any group, like the Nazis or the Communists, that would deny the claim of human beings to be ruled only by a government of their own consent. Nevertheless, the writers are willing to suppose, for a while, that "tolerance" stands as a "good," without any moral shadings or qualifications. And they would have us believe that people are more likely to take on this wholesome cast of mind if they can be insulated from any extended deliberation about the grounds on which tolerance can be shown to be warranted or justified. To put it another way, we are urged to absorb this odd proposition: that if we wish to produce good or moral people, we should not try to teach them the principles of goodness or justice. We should not seek to teach them what there is about a republican government that merits their reverence. But rather, we should try to enlist their sentiments in support of certain virtues (such as "tolerance"), or we should summon their beliefs in support of a "good" political regime, whose goodness, however, we cannot explain or justify.

The chapter offered by Theiss-Morse et al. has the advantage of a design even more subtly wrought, but it is vulnerable in the end to objections of the same kind. In a more diffident phase of their argument, the writers claim merely to have shown "that emotion—or passion . . . —affects human behavior at least as much as, if not more than, cognition." Now, anyone who has seen a crowd at Bloomingdales on a Saturday, anyone who has seen the fans in New York tear up the turf after their team has won the pennant, anyone who has seen or read the accounts of lynchings, knows that emotion has a powerful effect on behavior. That could not have been the question that inspired the clever design of this research. The writers have evidently been reaching for something far more striking, which they cannot quite bring themselves to claim. In an earlier version of their chapter, they suggested this import for their findings:

> Democratic citizens require education in the proper use of their emotions at least as much as in the proper use of their reason because the former *better enables cognition to play its role* and because affective reactions *seem particularly attuned* to the normative enactment of public policy. . . . If we wish to understand how to encourage the development of a democratic citizenry, we would do well to . . . understand the role that affect, particularly in combination with cognition, plays in defining and sustaining codes of tolerant behavior. (Emphasis added)

The suggestion in this passage is not merely that emotion may have an effect on conduct. The claim, rather, is that emotion may lead, direct, improve the cognition, or understanding, that forms our moral judgments. And those judgments about the things that are right and wrong, just and unjust, furnish the ground for the "normative enactment of public policy." The writers seem to have backed away from that explicit statement of their claims, but the strands of those claims still seem to be present, though muted and scattered:

> Inviting people to attend to their thoughts makes them less influenced by either threatening or reassuring information and less influenced by probability information. Put more simply, when instructed to attend to their thoughts, people are less responsive to the stimuli before them.
>
> People appear best able to notice and react to both affective stimuli and cognitive information about their least-liked group when they pay attention to their feelings and when they affectively process information about the group's treachery and untrustworthiness. . . . *[F]eelings enable people to attend and respond to the state of the world before them.* (Emphasis added)
>
> [O]ur results also show that attending to feelings, while making people more wary, does not necessarily lead to intolerance. We have discovered that affective reactions can be reassuring. All else being equal, when people read emotionally evocative language describing their least-liked group as breaking the norms of trust and proper behavior, they are likely to provide an intolerant response to that group. On the other hand, when people read emotionally reassuring language describing their least-liked group as conforming to the norms of trust and proper behavior, they are likely to be more tolerant.

When we begin to collect these strands and make these claims more explicit, the question posed in the chapter does in fact become more noticeably astounding: Might emotion actually have a *rival* claim, against reason, in governing our conduct? The writers suggest that "feelings" may be a better guide than reason in helping people "attend to the state of the world before them." And by that, they presumably mean attend aptly, rightly, wisely to the world before them. But is it on the basis of *feelings* that we know the difference between just and unjust feelings? That difference surely cannot turn on "feelings"; it must depend instead on the principles that establish the things that are "justified" or "unjustified." In the same way, it cannot be on the basis of "emotions" that citizens are instructed on the "proper use of their emotions." Emotions themselves cannot instruct us on the difference between their "proper" and "improper" ends. That difference can be known only through an understanding of the ends that are proper and improper. What needs to be known are the principles, or the standards, of moral judgment, and we would ordinarily call the knowledge of these things a "moral understanding." And yet, the writers suggest that emotion may guide our acts in a good or justified way; that emotion may actually take the place of reason as a source of understanding the ends that are justified or unjustified, right or wrong.

But when the problem is framed in that way, there is a serious philosophical question that must arise at once. For the question would seem to be crystallized in this manner: Is there a nonrational way of knowing what is good or just—and *knowing* that we know it? The answer is, briefly, no. Nothing turned up in the survey could affect the answer to that question, because the question, cast in this form, does not offer an empirical problem. It is, as we used to say, a point in logic. To know something is to know something *truly,* or to know the difference between knowing and not-knowing. Or, to put it another way, it is to grasp the difference between true and false claims to know. As Gottlob Frege remarked on this point, "Truth is not a quality that answers to a particular kind of sense-impression. So it is sharply distinguished from the qualities we call by the names 'red,' 'bitter,' 'lilac-smelling.' . . . That the sun has risen is recognized to be true on the basis of sense-impressions. But being true is not a sensible, perceptible property" (Frege [1918] 1977, 5).

It is not through our smell, or even our hearing, that we know the truth of *propositions*. Nor is it through our emotions or our feelings. As Thomas Reid once observed, "A feeling must be agreeable, or uneasy, or indifferent. It may be weak or strong. . . . [But] it implies neither affirmation nor negation; and therefore cannot have the qualities of true or false, which distinguish propositions from all other forms of speech, and judgments from all other acts of the mind." We may experience, quite vividly, the sensations of a toothache or a headache, "but to say that they express a judgment would be ridiculous" (Reid [1788] 1969, 459).

We may fancy, in any case, that we can "smell" a lie, but we are being metaphorical; the truth of propositions can be known to us only through our reason. When the writers gave directions to the students in their experiment, they told the youngsters to make a distinction between their "thoughts" and their "feelings." But these directions were not imparted to the students through their feelings. The writers did not try to provide guidance to the students by offering knowing glances, accompanied by suggestive noises. They conveyed explicit directions, which were accessible through the faculty of reason. They told some of the students to be governed mainly by their thoughts, some by their feelings; but they appealed to their *thoughts* as the medium for gaining access to their understanding. Implicitly, they recognized what they have been reluctant to acknowledge in the survey: namely, that thought, or reason, does claim a critical sovereignty in these matters—the matters that lend themselves to conversation, discussion, judgment.

We might imagine, in this vein, a simple thought-experiment. Let us suppose that we had a corps of judges who would simply hand down their verdicts and say, persistently, "We cannot tell you why we think this is the right or just decision; it is simply the way we feel about it." As Thomas Reid remarked about an earlier expression of this same state of mind, the person animated by this understanding could not claim the name of "judge," for he would bear the title absurdly: he ought to be called, instead, "a feeler" (see Reid [1788] 1969, 442).

The writers contend that, when the students were instructed to attend to their thoughts, they became more attentive to "their interior subjective concerns" and less attentive to "the state of the world before them." Here, I am afraid, the writers have been swept by their own imagination, for nothing in this study could gauge the capacity of the subjects to "attend to the state of the world before them." The writers seem to have forgotten that the students were not being asked to respond to any real state of affairs cast before them. There were no real squads of racists, bedecked with polyester and bad grammar, crashing in on their communities. The students were responding only to a series of fictive scenes, involving fictive groups. The "stimuli" to which they were invited to respond consisted of a series of descriptions of these groups, cast either as law-abiding or as lawless. The students were asked to engage their imaginations—and then they were criticized by the writers for resorting to "interior subjective concerns." But in forming their judgments, the students latched on to items of information that were hardly "subjective." These items of description were put forth by the writers precisely because they could be grasped, quite commonly, as strands of evidence, which bore on the character of these racist groups. The students evidently treated these descriptions as items of evidence that could form the ground of their judgments. But for some reason, the writers seem to have trouble in acknowledging that these reactions were something more than subjective, and that these judgments were indeed responsive to the "world" placed before the students. I would suggest that the problem here arises from the fact that the writers have not been quite accurate in sorting out the components of "cognition" and "affect" in the cases they offered to the students. Nor have they been especially interested in the difference between a judgment grounded in principle and a judgment that is merely responsive to what they call "probability information."

Delivered, serenely, from the concern for that difference, the writers are able to affect surprise when they discover that their respondents do not show significantly different levels of tolerance depending on whether there is an imminent likelihood, or only a faint possibility, that a threatening group may come to power. These calculations, concerning the imminence of the threat, are attributed by the writers to the domain of "cognition." As the writers put it, "Inviting people to attend to their thoughts makes them less influenced by either threatening or reassuring information and less influenced by probability information." When the subjects allowed themselves to be guided by their emotions, they could be either more or less tolerant; but either way, as the writers claim, they were more responsive to the facts of the situation. In that event, emotion may be more decisive than cognition as a guide to judgment on matters of tolerance. And yet, the question is just how many of these "facts" in the case can properly claim to affect, or control, the judgment reached by citizens. On this point the writers may simply be ignoring the logical implication of a commitment, or a concern, grounded in principle. If there *is* such a concern, say, for the Nazis or the KKK, that concern must be utterly unaffected by any showing that the Nazis are commanding 8 percent—or 48 percent—of the vote.

A dozen years ago I happened to participate, as a writer and a speaker, in the controversy over the Nazis marching in Skokie, in a community containing many survivors of the Holocaust. I think I made it clear, from the beginning, that I never regarded as a serious political threat that ragtag handful of misfits—probably not even a dozen in number—who were pleased to call themselves the American Nazis. My opposition to them was not affected by any emotional turbulence or fright generated by these bootless characters. And it certainly was not affected by any estimate that these characters had even the remotest chance of gaining political power. What was far more frightening, I thought, were the implications in principle of the argument we were asked to incorporate in our constitutional law, in our public philosophy, as the ground for protecting the Nazis. Far more ominous to me was the corruption of understanding on the part of our political class—the kind of corruption that Lincoln encountered in an earlier day, during the crisis of our "house divided." In the debate between Lincoln and Douglas, Douglas insisted that he did not "care" whether slavery was voted up or down, so long as it was done in a democratic way, in a manner that would respect the principle of popular sovereignty. But Lincoln thought that this was a corruption of democracy: to say that in a democracy it did not matter what was chosen in substance, so long as the choice was made in a formally democratic way, as though democracy was entirely a matter of forms with no implications about substance. And now, over a hundred years later, David Hamlin of the ACLU was arguing that we must be free to hear the Nazis because *we must be free to choose the Nazis*. In other words, the meaning of democracy was that there were no interests that could be regarded as illegitimate, no interests that a free people were morally obliged to forgo if they respected the premises of their own freedom. But in this replay of Stephen Douglas, we heard that the American people must be free to choose Nazism or slavery. The substance did not matter, as long as we preserved the principle of free choice. And the principle of "choice" now seemed to rest on this understanding: that there was, in the end, no moral or political truth, and therefore no grounds on which to say that one set of ends in politics was less legitimate or decent than any other.

But if I respect the moral claim for democracy, if I understand that government by consent is in principle better than Nazism, then I cannot coherently claim a "right" to choose Nazism for myself or others. And therefore, I cannot be asked, rightly, to "tolerate" the Nazis as a "legitimate" party without calling into serious question the grounds on which we regard government by consent as morally superior to a despotism.

The point then is this: If I hold to this commitment in principle, then my judgment cannot be altered by the fact that the danger posed by the Nazis is imminent or remote. Whether the American Nazis have a claim to be tolerated, or regarded as legitimate, cannot hinge on the question of whether their prospects for attaining power are serious or laughable. Therefore it should not be a matter of surprise—or criticism—that the judgments made by the students, on the tolerance of racist parties, were not very responsive to differences in the "probability" that the racists would succeed.

If some of the students in the sample had understood the problem in this way, they could not have been reproached for obtuseness or for a failure to be responsive to "the world before them." But without exploring these implications, the writers move to the conclusion that the reactions of the students were founded on emotion rather than cognition, or reason. Consider, in this vein, the examples collected under the "manipulation," as the writers put it, that was "affectively evocative." The students were offered two different scenes under the heading of "normative violations." One descriptive paragraph was characterized as "threatening" and the other as "reassuring." But if we consider the descriptions contained in these paragraphs, the difference between them cannot be characterized as merely emotional. The ingredients contained in these distinctions have a moral significance, precisely because they mark off practices that reflect the character of a constitutional order. For example, in the description of the White Supremacist Faction, in the more benign, or low-trigger, account, we find these features: The leaders have cooperated with the police and promised to have peaceful demonstrations, according to the conditions of their parade permits. At their rallies, they have asked their supporters to act vigorously but as lawfully as possible. In other words, we are told that the leaders respect the law that deals in permits for parades, that they are asking their followers to pursue their ends within a framework of commitment to lawful procedures.

But why would these points be described as "affective" rather than "cognitive," or as a "trigger threatening affect" rather than as points of information that may affect the grounds of our reasoned judgment? We may remind ourselves here of Lincoln's point, that there were important, substantive implications bound up with the respect for lawfulness. Those who would rule others by force would have no motive to respect a law that is not of their own making. And when we avoid a politics of force, we sustain a politics of reasoned discourse in a framework of lawfulness. Candidates and parties offer reasons to the public and seek support when they are acting within a politics of peaceful process rather than a politics of coups d'état.

But when we grasp these rudimentary points, we understand more readily that we are not faced here simply with emotional triggers when we are informed, in several ways, that this white supremacist group shows an elementary commitment to the premises of lawfulness. To say that people respect a regime of law is to say that they are willing to respect a law outside themselves and their own interests. It is to begin filling in details of moral consequence in giving an account of their character. And when the writers filled in details of this kind about this political faction, they touched the ingredients that made me more inclined to tolerate this party. They supplied here a critical item of *cognition* that was necessary to the forming of a judgment. And as a result, I became willing to accord to this faction a certain presumption of legitimacy, even though I had no emotional engagement with this fictive group.

In short, my criticism here is that the writers have not moved with a sure hand as they have assigned items to the domains of cognition or emotion, and the result must be to cast the most serious doubts over the contentions they would offer, both new and striking, about the relation between cognition and emotion. I think the misstep they make here is the one described by Frege when he warned of that tendency to mistake the properties of a proposition with the constituents that make up the thought. As Frege wrote, "I can indeed have the idea of a green field; but this is not green, for there are no green ideas. . . . [I]f a missile were my idea, it would have no weight. I can have an idea of a heavy missile. This then contains the idea of weight as a constituent idea. But this constituent idea is not a property of the whole idea" (Frege [1918] 1977, 19).

The writers may think that they are appealing to emotions when they describe, in various ways, the lawlessness or the lawfulness of these white supremacist groups. But what they are articulating, in the end, is *still a thought or a proposition*. And that proposition must be reckoned or judged in the way we deal with other propositions: it engages the reason; it is assessed with principles of judgment; and it may produce then the same conclusion, even among people who differ widely in their emotional reactions to these bands of yahoos.

My main complaint, then, is that the writers have been too quick to enfold, in the range of "emotion," ingredients that properly belong to "cognition" and to the province of reasoned judgment on moral questions. In this respect, they may be mirroring some of the bewilderment that has entered the literature and our public discourse on the meaning of "cognition." This confusion has found a powerful and disturbing expression in the courts of law, in the tests of "cognitive and sapient" states. And there the misunderstanding of cognition has served as a device for ending the lives of silent patients.[1] The corrective may be found in that seminal chapter on "cognition" (chap. 4), in Daniel Robinson's book *Systems of Psychology.* To put it mildly, Robinson managed to show in that inspired piece that cognition ran well beyond the matter of perception. Men from Mars, seeing a Stop sign, might well be able to see and reproduce an octagonal figure. But they may still not understand its significance as a Stop sign. The children in the experiment by Piaget had no trouble in perceiving the beads poured from a tall, thin beaker into a low, wide container. The youngsters did not understand that the amount of beads had remained the same throughout these changes in their state. The youngsters did not have "cognition" of the event, because they had not yet grasped the principle of the conservation of matter or the "law of identity" (Socrates sitting is the same as Socrates standing; the beads in the tall beaker are the same beads in the low, wide container). As Robinson advanced in this way, he led the reader quite deftly to the understanding that "cognition" finally involves the grasp of certain "rules of thought."

If that is the case, the rules of thought that form the ground of our moral judgment must belong far more clearly to the domain of reason and cognition than to the province of emotion and "affect." When we say that "people may not be held blameworthy or responsible for acts, or attributes, they are powerless to affect," we are stating a moral axiom, utterly necessary to our moral judgments. The proposition has the standing of an axiom, or a necessary truth, because we would find ourselves falling into contradiction if we sought to deny it. On the strength of this proposition, we may go on to explain many understandings in our law, from the insanity defense to the wrong of racial discrimination. Tutored by propositions of this kind, we may understand, securely, the wrong of creating disabilities for people on the basis of race, and with that ground of conviction, we may cultivate the passion that condemns racism in all of its forms. But our conviction is grounded in this axiom of our moral reasoning; it is grounded, that is, in logic, and we can know it only through our reason. Therefore, it holds out this advantage: The logical ground of our conviction would remain, even if our passions altered overnight. Even if most people in the country suddenly developed a revulsion for black people, the ground of our

1. On this misuse of "cognition" in the courts, see Arkes 1987, 421–33.

policy would remain the same, for the wrongness of racial discrimination would be established now in an understanding that would not be altered by any shifts in the public mood or by the vagaries of our feelings from one moment to the next.

There is a hard, logical difference here, which cannot be effaced. And the sufficient test for us should come in a case of this kind: we see people animated by passion, or emotion, for different causes in our politics. We see people coming out, evidently with a sincere emotion, to march for the Ku Klux Klan or participate in drawing swastikas on the walls of synagogues. But we also see other people, animated by passion, drawn out into the street to resist the Ku Klux Klan or support civil rights. If we took passion, or emotion, to measure the plausibility of these interests, then we might not be able to make any moral distinctions among them. But obviously we do not use passion or emotion as the ground of our judgment. We reach a judgment, on different grounds, about the kinds of ends that are just or unjust, right or wrong, And we esteem people, not on the basis of whether they are motivated by a sincere passion, but on the ground of whether their passions are directed to ends that are just or unjust. In the face of passions corrupted by indecent ends, our reflex has been to restrain the passion, not to honor it. Beyond that, we may wish that these people could be instructed in the kinds of political ends that properly *merit* the commitment of their passions.

H. L. Mencken once warned us of those people who are inclined to think that if we are reluctant to buy the cancer salve, it must be because we want Uncle Julius to die. I trust I have said enough now to make it clear that I am not an enemy of passion. I have not been making the case here for the life of cold reason, utterly detached from emotion and feeling. I hope that our people will cultivate a passion for justice and a sense of moral outrage for the things that truly merit outrage. That is to say, I hope people will come to love what is admirable and despise what is base. But my point is that our passions must be recruited and instructed by our moral understanding; our moral understandings cannot plausibly be directed or governed by our feelings.

Beyond that, I have not been suggesting that we are incapable of "knowing" things through our emotions or that we cannot know, or sense, certain things apart from our reason. Professor Gilbert Ryle rendered the distinct service of dislodging us from the casual assumption that the seat of our knowing, or the powers of "mind," must be located in the "head" (see Ryle 1949). We have a richness of examples, from athletes, dancers, surgeons, of the many reflexes, or understandings, that seem to be contained, as the saying goes, in our "body memory." It used to be said of Joe DiMaggio that he could tell, at the sound of the bat against the ball, the direction of the fly ball, and he would begin to move at once in the right direction. Quite evidently, DiMaggio did not engage any syllogistic mode of reasoning before he would determine the course of his own reactions. The story could be told in many forms, by concert pianists or dancers, who can remember an intricate pattern of moves, with their fingers or legs. The moves are too quick to be remembered, or reproduced, one at a time. What is remembered is obviously a pattern or ensemble of moves, and it is not at all clear that it is remembered in our heads. Yet, DiMaggio truly "knew" the outfield in Yankee Stadium, and Vladimir Horowitz truly knew Beethoven's Sonata in F.

There are also cases in which our emotions clearly indicate a level of "knowing" that is not always evident to our reason. A woman leaves a man, and suddenly, that night, he feels a tightening in his chest, or a shortness of breath, in fact a certain difficulty in breathing. Does he suddenly realize, in a way he had not quite grasped before, just what it would mean to be without her? The epiphany, the discovery, does not apparently spring from his suddenly reasoning anew. But rather, something in his feelings alerts his reason, urges him to look again at a record of relations he might not have seen with a clear eye or understood rightly.

Through her feelings, Ingrid Bergman may come to *know* that she never stopped loving Humphrey Bogart, and that she will not leave Casablanca without him. None of this would I deny. But what I contend is that she "knows" this in a radically different way from the way in which we "know," say, that $E = mc^2$ or that "moral agents, who can give and understand reasons, deserve to be ruled with the rendering of reasons, in a government of consent."

The knowledge of these kinds of things is the knowledge of propositions. Judgments on rightness and wrongness imply a standard for measuring true or false claims, and therefore, as Thomas Reid taught us, they must depend on the affirming or denying of propositions. My contention here is that citizenship in a democracy requires the understanding of "propositions." As Lincoln said, in his Gettysburg Address, this nation was founded on "a proposition," a proposition that Lincoln regarded as "the father of all principles" among us. That was, of course, the proposition articulated in the Declaration of Independence as a necessary, or self-evident, truth: that "all men are created equal." The distinguishing mark of America was that our citizenship would not be found in a common nationality or race but in our common dedication to a central "proposition." Anyone knew enough to be a good citizen in America if he could understand that central proposition, which formed the ground of all of our rights. If he could grasp the ground of his equal rights, he could also grasp his duty to respect the equal rights of others. He understood then the rational ground of his tolerance. At the same time, he would understand that he had no right to deprive people of their equal rights by voting for a totalitarian party and closing down a regime of consent. He could be properly, radically, intolerant of the political factions that rejected the truth that "all men are created equal." He would understand, then, the rational ground for withdrawing his tolerance. And he would understand the rational ground on which he would be justified in committing his passions. He could properly love a free society, and he could rightly despise all of the enemies who would destroy a free society, from the Right or the Left. He could summon his passion to the support of a government by consent, but it would be, again, a passion directed by his moral understanding.

But the tendency in our own time is not to connect reason and passion, judgment and emotion, in this way. The tendency has been to separate them by identifying moral questions with "emotional" issues—and then removing these emotional, moral questions from the domain of reasoned argument. We have become familiar with this translation in recent years as it has been carried out on the issue of abortion: the "moral" issue is readily converted into the "emotional" because the question of abortion stirs controversy and ignites outrage. But that conversion places the question beyond the range of reasoned argument, and in the next step, the question is removed altogether from the arena of legislation: since we cannot truly deliberate on this question with reason—since it engages too many personal beliefs and passions—then it is not a subject on which one set of people may properly legislate for others.

The controversy over abortion may actually provide a far more significant and apt test for the writers, as they seek to make the case for emotion in political life. When an attempt is made to show pictures of unborn children in the womb—say, a fetus of a few months, sucking its thumb—the argument is usually made that these kinds of displays are "emotional" and therefore illegitimate as a part of political discussion. Television stations will not run pictures of this kind, and the respectable press condemns this style of presentation. Apparently, abortion is too "emotional" to lend itself to rational debate, and appeals to pictures are branded, for some reason, as "emotional" or unfit for political discourse. These pictures are tagged as "emotional" because they bring into view the object of the abortion, and that "object" becomes instantly recognizable as a baby. It ceases then to be an object, or a fetus, or a piece of tissue. It cannot be named any longer with the terms that are used to disguise the things that would be plain to our senses. The "vice" in these pictures is that they break through the fog of euphemism and make visible to us the facts about this victim. What, then, is "emotional" about this presentation? What it brings into view are facts, realities, not sentiments or emotions. And why should it be illegitimate, in political life, to bring forth more facts about the beings who may stand as victims? The pictures can be classified as "emotional" only because they make a profound appeal to our sentiments. But in that event, they would seem to sustain the claims of the writers in these papers: the engagement of our sentiments may merely excite our interest in the "cognitive" material. We may be encouraged, then, or even obliged, to face the array of facts, cast up in rich detail by embryology, about the nature of the child in the womb. In that case, would the writers count this appeal to our sympathies as a legitimate part of political discourse? And would they count themselves then as critics of those people who would screen this information from the public—actually block its dissemination in the media—on the ground that appeals of this kind to our sentiments are illegitimate in political discourse?[2]

2. In a recent column on Thurgood Marshall, Edwin Yoder took Marshall's side in associating the cause of rights with a certain disdain for "victim impact" statements. Yoder's complaint was that statements of this kind would have the effect of inflaming the sentiments of a jury. Apparently, it is a matter of indifference to Yoder whether people are inflamed by an appeal to their moral outrage or to their rank prejudice. Yoder noted that in a recent case "a Tennessee grandmother had been permitted to describe how her bereaved grandson 'cries for his mom,' the victim of a heinous murder. After so horrible a crime, public sympathy for the defendant is surely slight. But that is neither here nor there. It is easy to imagine how opening the gates to 'victim impact' stories and tales could bring all sorts of inflammatory and prejudicial, but immaterial, 'evidence' into the courtroom." But why is the account "immaterial," or irrelevant to an assessment of the wrong that was suffered? The evident purpose of

A case of this kind has the advantage of showing, more precisely, the points at which moral judgments do come to depend on sympathy or on a sensitivity to feeling. We may be reminded that the threshold of moral judgment begins, after all, with our awareness of a hurt or an injury. It is when we are in the presence of a hurt that we ask for justifications. When we judge the reasons, or justifications, we judge with the canons of reason and the rigors of the syllogism. But before that discipline of judgment becomes engaged, we must have some awareness that we have crossed a threshold of moral significance, that we are in the presence of an act that calls out for justification.

If we consider only the "material" at stake, there is little difference between a burning shoe box and a burning cross. The first does not strike us as a wrong or as a disturbing act, in need of justification. The second is stamped with the meaning of an assault because this gesture of burning a cross has been invested, in our experience, with the meaning of an assault or an act of intimidation. But many hurts, we know, are subtle, and they may have no material component. There are the emotional hurts, the signs saying, No Irish need apply; Gentiles only; No Negroes served here. In some cases, it may require a certain imagination, or sensitivity, to become aware of a hurt. Of course, as Hobbes reminded us, the root of "injury" is "in jus"—without a justification. Not all hurts are injuries. A dentist may hurt us, but it may be with our permission, in a procedure directed to our benefit. Before a harm is converted into an injury, a judgment needs to be made that a hurt was inflicted with or without a justification. Still, as I say, it may require no small imagination to explain, in the first place, just how we become aware of a hurt. And it would be worthy of our most imaginative scholars, doing survey research and political psychology, to illuminate this question of how people come to recognize a hurt emotionally if they do not respond to empirical evidence, the evidence of their senses.

---

these "victim impact" statements is to break through the artificial cast of a trial, in which the defendant may be seen as a relatively weak, isolated person, a "victim," held up against the powers of the state. But what is lost from sight in this setting is the real victim, the one whose injury brought forth the prosecution in the first place. When the victim is dead, it may take the testimony of those closest to him to remind the onlookers of the depth of the loss and the sorrow that was suffered. I would suggest that Theiss-Morse and her colleagues would find an apt field of research for themselves in the mind of the Yoders among us: to explain why Yoder, and so many commentators on the law, can declare with such conviction that appeals to the suffering of the victim are "immaterial" to any assessment of innocence and guilt. See Yoder 1991, C5.

To revert for a moment to the example of abortion, it has been about two hundred years since we had the first substantial work on the neuroanatomy of the human fetus. And with the advance of embryology over the last thirty years, it could hardly be said that we know less about the nature of this organism than we did in the past. But in our own time the notion has been treated, with ever more seriousness, even by people in medicine, that the scientific facts have no bearing, that we really cannot speak with any certitude about the nature of the being in the womb. What they mean, of course, is that they have reached a judgment about the "right to an abortion," and in the face of that right, they are prepared to screen out even the most obvious evidence about the nature of fetuses and to resist, adamantly, this appeal to their senses.

At the beginning of *Huckleberry Finn*, there is a report on a steam engine blowing up. The question was asked, "Anyone hurt?" And the answer was, "No, just a couple niggers killed." My own suspicion is that, as we try to give an account of the change in sensibility, reason and evidence may turn out to be far more important than we might suspect: at a certain point, the observer recognizes, as Lincoln said, that the black man is indeed a man, that we cannot "estimate him only as the equal of the hog" (speech in Peoria, 16 October 1854). And that recognition may open the way to a flood of emotional reactions.

But perhaps the circuit runs the other way, and it would be no trifling work to map out that path of understanding: our principles of judgment do not tell us when we are in the presence of a hurt. The threshold of moral argument begins with the awareness of harms, but our awareness of harms may be rendered all the more sensitive and acute when our sentiments have been awakened by our imaginations and our emotions. A sensibility cultivated by a wider sympathy may help to avoid that dullness of moral wit that prevents people from seeing. It may help to steer us then to the path of serious reflection, where our judgment becomes engaged, where syllogisms can do their wholesome work.

To chart the path of this understanding, from our emotion to our reason, would require nothing less than the powers of the writers who have joined in this study. I would simply enter a plea, then, to summon those powers to a project even more powerful yet.

References

Arkes, Hadley. 1987. " 'Autonomy' and the 'Quality of Life': The Dismantling of Moral Terms." *Issues in Law and Medicine* 2:421–33.

Frege, Gottlob. [1918] 1977. "Thoughts." In *Logical Investigations*. Trans. P. T. Geach and R. H. Stoothoff. New Haven: Yale University Press.
Reid, Thomas. [1788] 1969. *Essays on the Active Powers of the Human Mind.* Cambridge, Mass.: MIT Press.
Robinson, Daniel. 1978. *Systems of Psychology*. New York: Columbia University Press.
Ryle, Gilbert. 1949. *The Concept of Mind*. London: Hutchinson's University Library.
Yoder, Edwin. 1991. "The Radical Agenda of a Triumphant Chief Justice." *Washington Post*, 30 June, C5.

15

Nonverbal Behavior, Emotions, and Democratic Leadership

Denis G. Sullivan
Roger D. Masters

Democratic political theory during the twentieth century has had a paradoxical attitude toward the role of emotion in politics. Political philosophers from Plato to Rousseau and Madison emphasized the necessary and, within limits, beneficial role of feelings or passions in political life. In contrast, contemporary theories typically deal with political behavior as if it could be understood as a purely rational or

The research here was supported by grants from the Rockefeller Center for the Social Sciences, Dartmouth College. Earlier phases of the studies reported here were supported by grants from the Harry Frank Guggenheim Foundation, National Science Foundation, and Maison des Sciences de l'Homme (Paris). We thank our colleagues and students at Dartmouth College for invaluable assistance in the development and execution of experimental studies.

cognitive assessment of costs and benefits or interests and opinions (e.g., Dahl and Lindblom 1953; Dahl 1956; Key 1961; Rawls 1971). In the last generation, this characteristic has been most obvious in the predominant role played by rational-choice theories, in which models from game theory or economics are used to predict and explain outcomes (e.g., Downs 1957; Olson 1965; Axelrod 1983; Hirschleifer 1987).[1]

For the major political philosophers in the Western tradition, passions or emotions are often of central importance in understanding the behavior of citizens. According to Plato, for example, reason can only control the appetites if it is allied with *thymos*, the emotions associated with honor, pride, and guilt (*Republic* 4.434d–445a [1968, 113–25]). For Rousseau, not only are feelings of patriotism necessary if the free citizen is to be attached to his country (*Political Economy* 1978, 217–24), but attempts to base virtue on reason and philosophy alone are corrupt and bound to fail (*First Discourse* 1964, 39–47, 56–58; *Second Discourse* 1964, 132). Madison teaches that factions arising in the passions are not merely inevitable but—when properly channeled—beneficial to a free, or constitutional, form of government (*The Federalist* No. 10). In the study of electoral politics, on the other hand, contemporary theories have, until the last few years, paid relatively little attention to the way emotion interacts with attitudes and interests in the judgments and behavior of citizens (for exceptions that prove the rule, see Marcus 1988 and several of the contributions to this volume).[2]

A similar paradox arises in the study of the behavior of leaders. In the Western tradition, leadership was assumed to involve, among other

1. The remarks that follow should not be viewed as a criticism of rational-choice theories, which have contributed greatly to our understanding of politics; quite the contrary, for as Frank (1988) has brilliantly shown, a game theoretic model like the prisoners' dilemma can provide an extraordinarily rich way of showing the role of feeling and expressing emotions in human social behavior. The difference between Frank's approach to the prisoners' dilemma and that of most political scientists (notably Axelrod [1983]) illustrates, however, the tendency to interpret choice theories without reference to feelings and nonverbal communication. Nor should it be forgotten that many contemporary democratic theorists have had a clear understanding of the importance of affect (e.g., Almond and Verba 1965, esp. 354–57). At issue is a tendency to underestimate the complexity of emotion and to relegate it to a secondary role in theories of the relations between leaders and citizens.

2. This contemporary tendency to emphasize rational calculus and understate the importance of emotion has by no means been limited to political science; in philosophy since Kant the analysis of moral behavior has tended to focus on rational calculation, thereby ignoring the much richer understanding of past thinkers (see Baier 1987).

things, an understanding of the emotions and of nonverbal displays that serve as social cues. Training in nonverbal behavior, and especially in facial display, was once an integral part of teaching rhetoric (Courtine and Harouche 1988); as a result, textbooks in public speaking often included detailed instructions for expressing emotions in a way that would influence audiences in the desired way (for an example said to have been used by Lincoln, among others, see Scott 1820). Western literature provides ample evidence that leaders actually attended to such behavior in establishing and maintaining dominant status (e.g., Shakespeare, *III Henry VI*, 3.3.168–95; *Henry V*, 4.1.103–11; Milton, *Paradise Lost*, 2.302–9). Since such cues play a direct role in social interaction among nonhuman primates and human children (Hinde 1982; Kagan 1988; Chance 1989), it is not surprising that traditional political theorists like Mandeville (1924, 2:286–87) and Rousseau (1978, 122–23) considered an understanding of nonverbal behavior essential to a science of human politics.[3] Here too, however, contemporary theories and assessments of leadership tend to stress the cognitive, or rational, elements of rhetoric, strategy, or personality while paying relatively little attention to the role of nonverbal behavior and emotion (e.g., Burns 1978; Barber 1985; Kalb and Hertzberg 1988).

Because television seems to have increased the impact of the nonverbal behavior of leaders and the emotional responses they elicit in followers, it is paradoxical that phenomena once emphasized by political theorists as natural or passionate forms of communication have recently been minimized or ignored by most political scientists. At a time when citizens have the opportunity to see close-up images of leaders on a daily basis, it is particularly important to understand the dynamic relations between the visible behavior of rivals for power and the mass of the citizenry. On this point, as in other respects, recent empirical work may help enrich democratic theory and improve our understanding of the way citizens relate to leaders and to the political system more broadly.

Over the last several years, we have been studying the effects of leaders' facial displays on emotions and attitudes by showing videotapes of regular television coverage under controlled conditions (for a review, see Lanzetta et al. 1985). In this chapter, we outline a theoretical explanation of the effects of leaders' nonverbal cues and present experi-

3. For a contemporary assessment of the relevance of nonverbal behavior for political philosophy, see Masters 1989a, chap. 2.

mental evidence of the way emotional responses elicited by such displays can shape popular attitudes toward rivals for power. By comparing new data on the American presidential candidates in 1988 with similar studies in 1984, moreover, we show that the effects of nonverbal communication are sensitive to differences of the leader's personal style, of the political context, and of the viewer's attitudes. Nonverbal displays and emotional responses, though traditionally described as a "natural language," thus form a complex system in which there is great individual and cultural variability. Once the complex interactions between cognition and emotion have been understood, many otherwise puzzling features of modern democratic politics may be easier to understand.

Facial Displays as Leadership Behavior

How do political leaders and candidates evoke emotions and impressions that modify attitudes toward them? Obviously the process is complex. First, those in office are held accountable for the perceived consequences of their past actions: incumbents seek "credit" for beneficial outcomes, whereas rivals seek to hold them responsible for past "failures." In recent years, research has burgeoned on theories of "retrospective voting," in which vote choice is determined by cognitions about and emotional responses to the recent political past, rather than prospectively by what candidates promise (Fiorina 1981). Second, the rhetoric of different candidates can lead voters to associate them more or less strongly with particular issues (Lodge et al. 1989; Zullow and Seligman 1990). Third, political leaders can elicit emotions and convey impressions by their nonverbal style, including voice quality and facial expressions (Frey et al. 1983; Atkinson 1984; Roseman et al. 1986). In focusing on the third of these factors, our studies are of course intended to complement findings of other lines of research and do not pretend to have a unique and global explanation of all political outcomes.

In a series of experiments carried out from 1982 through 1988, we explored how a leader's facial displays seen on television influence viewers' impressions, emotions, and political attitudes (Lanzetta et al. 1985; Masters et al. 1986; Sullivan and Masters 1988; Sullivan et al. 1991). Our theoretical approach combines the perspectives of ethology and social psychology with current work on the role of impressions and emotions in shaping political attitudes. Research on the social behavior of nonhuman primates and human children emphasizes the importance of facial displays signaling attack, flight, or submission in regulating status and power relations (Van Hooff 1969, 1973; de Waal 1982; Goodall 1986; Montagner et al. 1988). Human facial displays corresponding to these three functional categories—happiness/reassurance (H/R), anger/threat (A/T), and fear/evasion (F/E)—were defined according to objective criteria (Masters et al. 1986; Sullivan et al. 1991). Because such displays play a role in social interaction among all human groups, exemplars were plentiful in videotaped archives of national television coverage of press conferences, party rallies, nominating conventions, and speeches in American politics (Masters et al. 1987).

In describing these displays, ethologists have used Charles Darwin's insight that "antithetical" cues are likely to become salient through the process of natural selection (Darwin [1872] 1965, 50–65). In human happiness/reassurance displays, for example, eyebrows are likely to be raised (in contrast to the lowered brows in anger/threat), body movement to be smooth (in contrast to abrupt movements of flight or attack), and head tilted (in contrast to the rigid and forward motion of the head in signaling attack). In a similar way, it is possible to specify objectively the features of anger/threat or fear/evasion and to show that they function as "unconditioned stimuli" in responses to others (e.g., Ekman and Oster 1979; Lanzetta and Orr 1980; Orr and Lanzetta 1980).

These three gestures are of special interest because ethological research shows their effects to depend on the power relations and affective bonds between the emitter and the observer (Lorenz and Leyhausen 1973; de Waal 1982, 1991). Moreover, the observer's response, in addition to being dependent on the leadership status of the emitter, may feed back in a way that either enhances or weakens the leader's position (Chase 1982; McGuire and Raleigh 1986; Raleigh and McGuire 1986; Masters and Carlotti 1993). As a result, these nonverbal cues may be important factors mediating the response of the electorate to leaders and their rhetoric.

Previous work in social psychology showed that human viewers distinguish the three types of facial display accurately (Ekman and Oster 1979) and that each display elicits different psychophysiological responses associated with self-reports of emotional experience (Schwartz et al. 1976). Our own studies confirm these findings in responses to displays of known and unknown political leaders in both the United

States and France (Vaughan and Lanzetta 1980; Englis et al. 1982; McHugo et al. 1985; Masters et al. 1986; Masters and Sullivan, 1989a, 1989b; Sullivan and Masters 1993; McHugo et al. 1991). The verbal self-reports of episodic emotion thus appear to be solidly validated responses.

This experimental finding is important because survey research has shown that emotions are important determinants of political attitude toward presidential candidates (Abelson et al. 1982; Marcus 1988). In the Abelson study, positive and negative emotional response scales were constructed from voter recall of specific emotion-evoking episodes for each candidate; these scales included the positive emotions of hope, happiness, pride, and sympathy and the negative emotions of anger, disgust, fear, and uneasiness. This study showed that responses toward the candidate on the two emotional scales and on trait attributions were roughly equal in weight and that both played a stronger role in predicting attitude than did the traditional variables of party identification or issue position. More-recent research has replicated and reinforced many of the Abelson findings (Marcus 1988).

Because facial displays play such a central role in all primate social behavior, it is likely that these stimuli are significant determinants of viewers' attribution of traits and their emotional reactions to leaders. When television shows close-up, full-face images of politicians who often rely on simple, stereotyped emotional gestures for communicative purposes (Masters et al. 1987), viewers should interpret their meaning accurately (Masters and Sullivan 1989a, 1989b; Sullivan and Masters 1988). More particularly, whenever viewers have minimal information or commitment, these "natural" cues are likely to be used as the basis of attitude change. We also predict, however, that these effects on attitude will be most likely when they are congruent with cultural or individual expectations: whereas dissonant cues imply that a leader is not capable of appropriate social behavior and hence not completely in control of the situation, expected behavior can provide an effective positive reinforcement, particularly if the leaders' record or rhetoric is to be associated with outcomes valued by the voter. Finally, context should matter: because a leader is more likely to serve as the focus of public attention when he or she is generally perceived as successful or dominant (Chance 1976), even identical display behavior should vary in its effects depending on the political situation or status of the leader being seen.

Attitudes and Emotional Responses Elicited by Leaders

As Marcus (1988) has pointed out, there is a disjuncture between research on emotions and studies of political attitudes. Research on voting behavior has usually treated the emotional component of attitude as a unidimensional continuum ranging from negative to positive. In using a term made popular by Kurt Lewin in the 1940s, Marcus has labeled this a "valence theory" of emotions. Yet the subjective experience of emotion seems to entail the discrete categories of happiness, anger, disgust, fear, sadness, and surprise, leading many theorists to array the emotions in clusters or multiple dimensions (Plutchik 1980). The task for political science is to explain the process by which these apparently distinct emotional responses can be elicited by each political leader's issue positions, policy outcomes, rhetoric, and gestural style and then be integrated into attitudes and ultimately to political behavior.

The viewers' integration of cognition and emotion when choosing between candidates is at least a two-stage process: immediate or episodic experiences in which diverse emotions are felt must be integrated into a single accessible opinion or attitude. It is important to capture precisely the dimensions of emotional responses to leaders' facial displays that may later be cognitively adjusted in shaping attitudes toward them. While feelings may be classified as discrete states or reactions, research has revealed that the different emotional reactions can be arrayed along two independent dimensions, one positive and the other negative (Marcus 1988; Warr et al. 1983; Abelson et al. 1982; Masters and Sullivan 1989b). The emotions of anger, disgust, and fear are negative, whereas happiness, interest, and sympathy are positive. Therefore, whether emotions are viewed as discrete categories or as experiences arrayed along dimensions, it is not appropriate to assume that affect forms the single, unidimensional valence from positive to negative that has been used by political scientists.

The first step in reconceptualizing the problem is to understand the relation between emotional experience and the evidence that has been conventionally used to measure it. Embedding a question about citizens' emotional responses to a leader in the attitudinal questionnaire given to voters during an election campaign requires that the respondent perform a very specific task. Given the election context in which the attitude question is normally asked, it is perhaps reasonable to expect respondents to sum up their complex emotional feelings about candidates on a single dimension of "warm," or positive, versus "cold," or negative.

The phrasing of the conventional question requires the voter to hide any ambivalence when reducing the discrete emotions of happiness, interest, anger, fear, disgust, surprise, and sympathy into one dimension. That is, cognitive work has already taken place in integrating emotions in a manner appropriate for the choice process. As a consequence, such a measure confounds emotion and cognition and is interchangeable with vote intention. Despite its obvious predictive value, therefore, the conventional unidimensional conception of emotion embedded in attitude measures may be theoretically misleading.

Can the voter's emotional responses be separated from a subsequent process of cognitive assessment and judgment of a leader? To solve this problem in the context of a presidential election survey, Abelson et al. (1982) sought to measure the unfiltered emotional response by asking respondents to recall episodes in which they felt a particular emotion toward a candidate.[4] "The episodic nature of affective experience can explain how the frequent co-occurrence of good and bad affect mentions . . . can leave . . . different traces without any necessity to 'reconcile' them" (Abelson et al. 1982, 628). A factor analysis of the emotional response scales reveals two correlated factors (Abelson et al. 1982; cf. Marcus 1988). Although our research revealed orthogonal factors, it confirms that of Abelson and Marcus in finding a two-dimensional factor structure of emotional responses in both France and the United States (Sullivan and Masters 1988; Masters and Sullivan 1989b).

Facial Display, Emotion, and Attitude

Because episodic responses differ from habitual feelings, our experimental approach is particularly well-suited for an exploration of the way emotion and cognition interact in the formation and maintenance of voters' attitudes toward the leaders of a democratic polity. Although the experiments in our series have varied in some details, all have been based

4. Cognitive neuroscientists have confirmed the role of such episodic memories in learning (e.g., Mishkin and Appenzeller 1987).

on the same fundamental paradigm. Excerpts of nationally known political leaders, in both the United States and France, have been selected from routinely shown television coverage of political events. Videotape segments of 20 to 120 seconds in length were chosen on the basis of the facial display cues shown, with every effort made to minimize interference from other visible cues like hand movements; excerpts were chosen that had an intelligible verbal message from the leader, so that subjects could be shown the same material in sound-plus-image or image-only media conditions.

Broadly speaking, these experimental studies have demonstrated three main features of the way viewers respond to the experience of watching nationally known leaders on television. First, the emotionally arousing effects of nonverbal displays are real: each of the three types of display is accurately described by viewers in France as well as in the United States, each elicits a different pattern of psychophysiological response, and each is described has having produced different emotions in the viewers (Lanzetta et al. 1985; McHugo et al. 1985; Masters and Mouchon 1986; McHugo et al. 1991). Second, in both France and the United States, verbal self-reports of emotional response have the same two-dimensional structure found in analyzing voter's emotions in survey research data (Abelson et al. 1982; Marcus 1988); as a result, affect does indeed seem to be a phenomenon that is theoretically distinct from political attitude. Finally, the type of display that has been seen sometimes interacts with prior attitude in eliciting emotional response—and whether or not this is the case, the emotions felt while watching the excerpts sometimes change the viewer's attitude toward a leader.

It has often been objected that emotion is merely a surrogate for the viewer's prior attitude toward a leader. According to this interpretation, the pressure to cognitive consistency may lead viewers to adjust their self-reported emotional response to match their previously established attitude toward the leader. Regardless of the kind of display, the reported emotional response would be made consistent with attitude. In this model, the stimulus excerpt activates a cognitive process that leads to an adjustment of emotional response to attitude. If emotional responses to a leader's facial displays reflected nothing beyond the attitude toward them, however, their structure should be unidimensional, mirroring the emotional component of attitude. If, on the other hand, emotional responses to the nonverbal gestures of a leader can be independent of attitude toward the leader, their factor structure should be two-dimensional.

When viewers in our studies see selected displays of leaders, emotional response scores reflect two factors, one positive, or "hedonic," and the other negative, or "agonic" (table 15.1). Similar dimensions are found from separate analysis by media condition (Masters et al. 1986), and the specific weightings on these factors resemble those found in survey research (Abelson et al. 1982; Marcus 1988; Sullivan and Masters 1988). The structure underlying these episodic emotions is, moreover, parallel to that found in more-lasting emotional responses in another experimental design (Sullivan et al. 1984; Sullivan and Masters, n.d.), when viewers reported feelings toward Reagan twenty-four hours after having seen a series of newscasts over a two-day period (table 15.2).

Although every study reveals the difference between the positive and negative emotional responses to significant political stimuli, these emotions are powerfully affected by the viewer's previous attitudes. As a

Table 15.1 Factor Structure of Emotional Responses to Happiness/Reassurance, Anger/Threat, and Fear/Evasion Displays in France and the United States (All Media Conditions Combined) (N: United States = 145, France = 65)

	Reagan		Chirac		Fabius	
Scale	Positive	Negative	Positive	Negative	Positive	Negative
Joyful	.65	−.44	.79	−.08	.83	−.11
Interested	.81	−.07	.61	−.28	.64	−.16
Comforted	.82	−.31	.89	−.09	.88	−.10
Inspired	.83	−.22	.85	−.21	.84	−.24
Angry	−.07	.83	−.36	.68	−.30	.73
Fearful	−.12	.81	−.06	.84	.06	.77
Disgusted	−.25	.79	−.35	.76	−.21	.78
Confused	−.20	.59	−.03	.67	−.18	.63

SOURCES: Emotional responses to Fabius and Chirac: experiment at Université de Nanterre (Masters and Sullivan 1986); emotional responses to Reagan: experiment no. 2 at Dartmouth College (Masters et al. 1986). For the comparable factors for the French data when emotional responses to Le Pen are included along with Chirac and Fabius, see Masters and Sullivan 1989b.

NOTE: Cell entries are factor loadings from principal components factor analysis retaining and rotating by Varimax factors with eigenvalues > 1. The negative factor accounts for 33 percent of the total variance for Reagan and 32 percent for Chirac and Fabius; the positive factor accounts for 32 percent for Reagan and 34 percent for Fabius and 35 percent for Chirac. Underlined scales are used to interpret the factor.

Table 15.2 Factor Structure of Emotional Responses When Thinking About Reagan One Day After the Newscasts

	Emotional Response Factor	
Emotional Response Scale	Negative	Positive
Angry	−.825	−.344
Hopeful	.397	.744
Fearful	−.819	−.184
Proud	.422	.765
Disgusted	−.784	−.371
Sympathetic	.030	.760
Uneasy	−.866	−.199
Happy	.459	.729

NOTE: Principal components factor analysis retaining and rotating factors with eigenvalues > 1. The negative factor accounts for 41 percent and the positive factor for 32 percent of the total variance.

result, the existence of two independent factors of emotion hardly resolves the question of how attitude toward a leader shapes emotional responses to that leader's appearance on television. Do verbal self-reports of emotion actually measure episodic emotion—or are they merely a different form of cognition, verbalized in terms associated with feelings? Before using the subject's report of an emotional response as an indication that feelings or passions have really been evoked, clearly it is necessary to confirm the difference between cognitions—whether verbalized or not—and emotions.[5] To address this issue, videotapes of leaders can be used as stimuli while continuously measuring physiological responses known to be associated with what is generally accepted as an emotional experience (Petty and Cacioppo 1981).

The "gut reactions" to which politicians refer when speaking of emotion are, in fact, associated with changes in bodily response—autonomic reactions (heart rate and skin conductance) and facial electromyographic (EMG) reactions. Emotional responses activate the facial muscles associated with the corresponding display behavior, even though the result need not be a visible facial expression (Fridlund and Izard

5. The need to make this distinction is reinforced by evidence of the "parallel distributed processing" of stimuli due to the "modular" organization of the brain (Gazzaniga 1985)—and especially by the role of nonverbal "mental images" (e.g., Kosslyn 1988; Masters 1989a, 253–54). A verbal self-report of emotion need not, therefore, be an emotion at all—it could as well be a "projection" of attitude into verbal terms.

1983; Schwartz et al. 1976; Cacioppo and Petty 1979; Vaughan and Lanzetta 1980; Englis et al. 1982). As Schwartz et al. (1976) found, for example, when experimental subjects are asked to imagine they are happy, the cheek muscle (zygomatic muscle) producing the smile is activated; the muscle that lowers the eyebrows (corrugator) is most likely to be active when a subject is asked to imagine he is angry, although this muscle is activated to some extent whenever attention is being focused.

This approach makes it possible to compare verbal self-reports of emotion with immediate psychophysiological reactions during the experience. In one experiment, subjects saw eight excerpts of President Reagan—four displays (neutral, happiness/reassurance, anger/threat, and fear/evasion) in each of two media conditions, image only and sound plus image—while autonomic activity (changes in heart rate and skin resistance) and facial expressive behavior (corrugator supercilli [brow] and zygomaticus major [cheek/mouth] EMG) were being recorded; after the presentation of each facial display, verbal self-reports of emotion were obtained. (For a full description of the experimental methods and the findings, see McHugo et al. 1985.)

The results (fig. 15.1) not only confirm the two-dimensional structure underlying emotions but show that the immediate responses to the experience of watching leaders are not merely reflections of verbal opinions or attitudes. In the sound-plus-image condition, the different effects of the three displays are also evident (McHugo et al. 1985). All

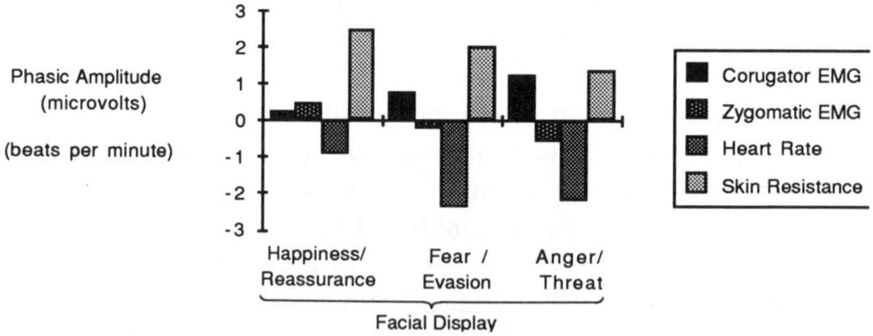

The facial EMG and autonomic response are measured as change from a pretape baseline. The skin response scale is in kilohms.

Fig. 15.1. Autonomic changes during exposure to Reagan's facial displays: image only

the stimuli activate the corrugator muscles to some degree, reflecting the lowering of the eyebrows associated with focusing visual attention, but this reaction is strongest in reactions to anger/threat displays. In contrast, the zygomatic muscles are activated in response to seeing happiness/reassurance excerpts but relaxed after seeing excerpts of either anger/threat or fear/evasion. When the same displays were seen without the sound, the psychophysiological effects were similar but greatly amplified. Although the displays also produce significantly different effects on heart rate and skin resistance, activation of the facial muscles associated with emotional motor response is especially good evidence that the television presentation of leaders' facial displays actually elicit the physiological substrates of emotional experience.

On the physiological level, when viewers saw the three types of facial displays of President Reagan in a single study, measures of emotional experience were quite independent of attitude toward Reagan; there were no attitude effects on facial EMG and autonomic responses during exposure to the displays (even though, after each display, attitude did affect self-reports of emotion). As a result it is clear that display behavior *can* elicit an affective response independent of prior attitude, even though subsequent self-reports of emotion may then be adjusted in terms of these cognitions.[6]

These findings show that self-reports of emotion do indeed reflect real experiences but that there is a complex relation between the nonverbal display and the viewer's prior attitudes. The strong effects of prior attitude on verbal self-reports, combined with the absence of comparable effects of prior attitude on the physiological level, suggest that subjects modified their initial emotional responses to the expressive displays over the viewing period. The attenuated amplitude of facial EMG responses in the sound-plus-image condition is consistent with this possibility insofar as a stimulus that combines a verbal message with a facial display should activate cognitive processes and dampen immediate emotional reactions, whereas an image-only stimulus may be processed first as an

6. In a subsequent experiment designed to heighten the partisan context by showing displays of President Reagan and presidential candidate Hart, attitude toward the leader did affect facial EMGs and autonomic responses (McHugo et al. 1991). Although a highly partisan context may increase the impact of attitude on emotional responses, all the evidence reviewed thus far suggests that the emotional responses elicited by a leader's facial displays are partially independent of attitude toward him.

emotionally evocative cue and only subsequently compared to relevant cognitive schemas involving prior attitudes (cf. McHugo et al. 1991).

Displays, Emotional Responses, and Attitude Change in U.S. Presidential Elections

The presidential elections of 1984 and 1988 gave us an ideal opportunity to explore the integration of cognition and emotion. During both election campaigns, a set of naturally occurring expressive displays of the presidential candidates as well as of President Reagan was shown to subjects at an Ivy League university. In each study, two excerpts—one neutral and one including the clearest happiness/reassurance facial display available—were used for the leading candidates in that year's campaign; to compare effects due to the political context, the same happiness/reassurance and neutral displays of Reagan and Hart were used in both years.[7]

Each year's set of videotapes was shown to two comparable groups of subjects, one at the start of the election campaign and the other at its end. The first phase of the experiment in both years took place in early spring, before the Iowa caucus and the first primaries, when some of the candidates were still unknown to many citizens. The second phase of the experiment was conducted shortly before election day, by which time voters were more likely to be following the election and to be familiar with at least those candidates who had been relatively successful.

The theoretical expectations concerning the effect that viewers' emotional responses to candidate displays have on their attitudes toward the

7. In 1984, we selected one neutral and one H/R excerpt of all the Democratic candidates (Mondale, Hart, Jackson, Glenn, Askew, Cranston, McGovern, and Hollings); since an individual subject saw one-half of the excerpts with sound plus image and the other half in image-only media condition, to balance the design we selected two neutral and two H/R excerpts of President Reagan (Sullivan and Masters 1988). Media condition was controlled by making two videotapes, each having half of the excerpts in image-only condition and the other half with sound plus image. For every sample, subjects were randomly assigned to see one of the two videotapes. For the 1988 study, we used the same procedure, selecting one neutral and one H/R display of the leading Democratic and Republican contenders (Dukakis, Jackson, Gephardt, Bush, Dole, Robertson), with a single mixed display of the remaining candidates (Simon, DuPont, Kemp, and Gore), along with the neutral and the H/R excerpts of Hart and Reagan that had been used in 1984 (for the 1988 experimental design, see Carlotti 1988).

candidates are as follows. First, candidate differences in display behavior should affect support during campaigns. Second, these effects should be mediated by the viewer's emotional responses, themselves a function of both the displays observed and the viewer's prior attitude toward each candidate. Third, changes in candidate status should modify the effect of emotional responses on attitude toward the candidate.

Viewers were told that we were studying the effects of the media in politics; although our interest in the effects of watching television on political opinions had to be explicit, no reference was made to our focus on the relations among nonverbal cues, emotional response, and political attitudes.[8] Before subjects saw the videotapes, they reported their party identification, attention to the media, attitude toward each of the leaders on the traditional 0–100 point "thermometer" scale, agreement with each leader on the issues on a 0–7 scale, and an assessment of leadership ability on a 0–7 scale. After each excerpt, subjects were asked both to describe the emotions exhibited by the candidates and to report on their own emotional responses on 0–6 unipolar scales. Each feeling—joy, comfort, anger, or fear—was identified by a triad of adjectives. A composite emotional scale has been formed by subtracting the values of the negative emotional responses (anger plus fear) from the positive (joy plus comfort).[9] After viewing all the excerpts, subjects again rated the leaders on the 0–100 "thermometer" scale.

Since our stimuli had been shown on network television during the early phase of the 1984 and 1988 campaigns, the reactions elicited by these videotape segments should provide a clue to the way seeing various candidates affected voters at two phases of each election year. Given the role of reassurance gestures in primate dominance behavior (see, e.g., de

8. Anonymous critics of our earlier papers have often expressed concern about "demand characteristics" in our experimental design. We were attentive to this danger (in postexperimental briefings, very few subjects had detected the purpose of our studies), but in any event, such a factor can have no bearing on *within-subject* differences in response.

9. The use of a summary scale of "net warmth" (combining positive and negative dimensions of emotion) does not contradict the emphasis on the two factors underlying emotional responses: in the conversion of episodic emotion to a change in more lasting attitude, some cognitive processing, or "interpreting," of experience is obviously necessary, as Gazzaniga (1985) has shown empirically. Particularly in response to seeing other people, this process must provide some measure of the costs and benefits of interacting with the person being seen (Frank 1988). As a result, it should not be surprising that the sum of positive and negative emotion is often a significant predictor of attitude change (Sullivan and Masters 1988; and below).

Waal 1982), a candidate's communication of his own joy to viewers should evoke powerful feelings of happiness and reassurance that could influence cognitive attitudes. In particular, candidates whose displays are not successful in communicating positive emotion should have more difficulty in translating their campaign rhetoric into effective voter support.

The intensity of emotional response to the leading candidates is summarized in table 15.3 as the net warmth of the viewer's self-reported feelings while watching each display. To show the differences between candidates in the capacity to elicit favorable emotions in viewers, as well as the impact changes in the political context have on the effectiveness of the same videotape excerpts, we show the results for Reagan and Hart in both years, for Mondale in 1984, and for Bush and Dukakis in 1988. As is evident, different candidates elicited quite distinct emotional responses both in neutral and in happiness/reassurance excerpts, and—except for Bush[10]—the happiness/reassurance displays of the leaders elicited more positive emotion than did their neutral displays.

Table 15.3 "Net Warmth" of Emotional Responses to Candidate's Displays

	Emotional Response to							
	Happiness/Reassurance Display				Neutral Display			
	1984		1988		1984		1988	
	Winter	Fall	Winter	Fall	Winter	Fall	Winter	Fall
Reagan	**3.33**	**5.36**	**3.83**	**5.24**	**1.68**	**3.05**	**2.35**	**1.70**
Mondale	**1.36**	**1.11**			**−.05**	**−.76**		
Hart	**4.21**	**4.81**	**2.08**	2.30	**−.92**	**−.73**	**−1.34**	**−1.13**
Bush			1.15	.69			1.88	.56
Dukakis			**2.45**	1.89			**1.36**	.32

NOTE: The table represents self-reported emotional responses of subjects in 1984 and 1988. Cell entries measure "net warmth" as (joy + comfort) − (anger + fear). Statistically significant differences between preprimary or winter samples and preelection or fall samples ($p < .05$) are underlined, and those between the emotional responses to the candidate's H/R and neutral displays in a particular month are in bold.

10. Our stimulus material had to be selected in the fall of each election year. Although we chose the best exemplar of happiness/reassurance we could find for each candidate, our Bush display was described by viewers as exhibiting a considerable degree of fear (Carlotti 1988; Masters and Carlotti 1993). This feature of Bush's display behavior was, of course, the subject

Differences in the net warmth elicited by the different leaders are striking. Mondale, Bush, and Dukakis were all dramatically less successful in transmitting warm emotions to viewers, particularly with happiness/reassurance displays, than were Reagan (and Hart in 1984). But political context also sometimes had a significant effect: for Reagan, the activation of political interest in the course of each election year seems to have increased the evocative potential of his happiness/reassurance display; a similar tendency, though not significant, occurred for Hart. Changes in political context also seem to account for the decline in emotional response to the displays of Hart after he was forced to withdraw from the race due to the Donna Rice affair early in 1988 (Masters and Carlotti 1993).

To assess the effects of these episodic emotions on attitude, in table 15.4 we present selected results from the same multiple regression model previously reported in our study of the 1984 data, together with responses to several of the main leaders studied in 1988. In both samples of our 1984 experiment, postexposure attitude was significantly influenced by the viewer's "net warmth" when watching the happiness/reassurance display of all leaders except Mondale (Sullivan and Masters 1988). A similar effect was observed in 1988 for Jackson, Gephardt, and Dole.

In addition, table 15.4 shows two striking findings. First, the results for Bush and Dukakis reflect the general impression that neither was a "charismatic" leader whose presence on television was as effective as President Reagan had been in 1980 and 1984. The relatively weak emotional responses elicited by the happiness/reassurance displays of both Bush and Dukakis did not significantly affect postexposure attitude toward either of them; these results for Bush and Dukakis are similar to those for Mondale in 1984. And as was the case for Mondale in 1984, the emotional response to the neutral image of Bush and Dukakis did have a marginally significant effect on postexposure attitude toward them. For the type of leader who would be popularly characterized as lacking "charisma," for whom the ability to communicate warmth through nonverbal display behavior seems to be lacking, it is the sight of the face exhibiting neutral behavior that triggers positive affect and favorable attitude change.

---

of considerable press coverage prior to the transformation of his image at the time of the Republican National Convention (e.g., Suplee 1988; Barnes 1988).

Table 15.4 Influence of Viewers' Pretest Attitudes and Emotional Responses on Their Posttest Attitudes at Outset and Conclusion of Campaign

Candidate		Pretest Attitude	Emotional Response to: Happiness/ Reassurance Display	Emotional Response to: Neutral Display	Party Identi- fication	Issue Agree- ment	Assessed Leader- ship Ability	R^2
		Preprimary Sample (January 1984, February 1988)						
Reagan	'84	.52	1.22	.90	−3.45	3.91	−2.00	.84
Reagan	'88	.48	.67	.79	−1.50	3.14	1.39	.75
Bush	'88	.53	−.19	1.02	−1.30	3.51	2.22	.75
Mondale	'84	.64	.48	.99	.73	1.73	−.92	.69
Dukakis	'88	.49	.16	−.45	−3.40	−4.90	3.00	.35
Hart	'84	.45	1.21	1.22	−.64	.90	1.11	.43
Hart	'88	.57	.41	.55	2.06	.26	5.74	.79
Jackson	'84	.39	1.50	.47	−.80	4.21	.44	.78
Jackson	'88	.58	1.29	.27	−1.73	3.26	−.64	.79
		Preelection Sample (October 1984, November 1988)						
Reagan	'84	.22	2.01	.41	−.75	3.56	.41	.76
Reagan	'88	.32	.08	1.08	.57	3.94	2.91	.86
Bush	'88	.46	.36	.34	−.51	4.16	.87	.76
Mondale	'84	.54	.55	1.00	−1.06	1.77	.60	.76
Dukakis	'88	.48	.65	.81	1.29	2.86	2.80	.83
Hart	'84	.61	1.43	−.45	−.05	2.96	.19	.69
Hart	'88	.31	.36	1.55	.80	7.31	.04	.59
Jackson	'84	.32	1.83	−.08	.07	2.63	3.53	.83
Jackson	'88	.64	.81	1.02	−.17	−.41	.65	.79

NOTE: The table represents multiple regression analysis of posttest attitude to each candidate on 0–100 "thermometer" scale, combining responses to sound-plus-image and image-only presentation of displays. Relative weight of pretest attitudes and emotional responses were measured by unstandardized partial regression coefficients. Statistically significant coefficients ($p < .05$) are underlined. Independent variables: pretest attitude (0–100 scale), "net warmth" of emotional response ([joy + comfort] − [anger + fear]) to each type of display, strength of self-reported party identification, issue agreement with leader, and assessment of candidate's leadership ability (on 0–6 scales).

Second, the results for Reagan and Hart show that the effectiveness of a charismatic leader may be to some extent mediated by popular attitudes and political context.[11] The effects of emotional reactions to the happiness/reassurance displays of Reagan and Hart in 1984 and 1988 confirm the role of status in translating episodic emotional responses into attitudes of support. In 1984, viewers' emotional reactions to the happiness/reassurance displays of Reagan and Hart had powerful effects on postexposure attitude. In 1988, when we showed exactly the same videotapes of Reagan and Hart to comparable viewers, the displays elicited a similar pattern of emotional reactions—but these emotional responses had no effect on postexposure political attitude toward either leader.[12]

The results in table 15.4 suggest other ways in which our study can contribute to a better understanding of the relation between leaders and followers. As has been noted, the different effect of emotional responses to a leader's neutral versus happiness/reassurance excerpt seems to provide an empirical way of measuring what is popularly described as "charisma." Equally interesting, the full regression model suggests that the sight of a leader may in varied ways activate such cognitive variables as the viewer's party identification, issue agreement, or assessment of leadership ability.[13] In addition, the difference between responses to a given candidate at the start and at the end of the campaign (the two waves each year) provide a measure of the effects of a political campaign in activating political interest and awareness. Since the value of R^2 ranges from .35 to .86, for example, by comparing the different variance in

11. The results for some of the other candidates are also instructive as evidence of the effect of a leader's political situation on the emotions evoked by his displays. In the 1988 preprimary sample, Dole's H/R display was highly evocative and significantly affected posttest attitudes ($B = 1.22$, $p < .02$); at this time, Dole was Bush's principal Republican rival. More unusual is the finding that the joy viewers reported in response to Pat Robertson's H/R display made their attitude toward him significantly less positive ($B = -1.16$, $p < .05$); this is an interesting instance of "counterempathy," perhaps reflecting the hostility of our Ivy League sample to a candidate with Robertson's background.

12. In Reagan's case, his situation as a "lame duck"—i.e., the realization that his power of incumbency was virtually at an end—may have been combined with changes in popularity and perceived effectiveness to reduce the impact of episodic emotion on attitude; for Hart, the Donna Rice affair and its consequences provide an obvious explanation for similar results. An analysis comparing male and female responses in 1984 and in the preprimary sample in 1988 shows that these context effects for both candidates seem to have been stronger for women than for men (Masters and Carlotti 1993).

13. For example, in the preelection sample of 1988, the experience of seeing Jackson and Hart seems to have activated issue agreement more effectively than seeing Dukakis.

posttest attitudes that is explained by the same equation, one has a measure of the stability or predictability of responses to each leader.[14] Although a fuller report on the 1988 study will appear subsequently, it is obvious that experimental research is able to clarify the precise and varying way in which emotions and cognitions interact in the relation between leaders and citizens in a modern democratic regime.

The experiments described above indicate that selected facial displays of a political leader can have important effects on television viewers. Studies of the facial images of candidates shown in the print media reveal emotive variations among candidates as well as over the course of an election campaign (Masters 1981, 1989a). Videotape monitoring of television news during the 1984 American presidential election also indicates differences in the images shown of each candidate (Masters et al. 1987; Joslyn and Ross 1986). These differences in media coverage matter, moreover, because—as media specialists like Roger Ailes have discovered—they can influence the emotional and cognitive reactions of viewers (Suplee 1988).

As Larry Preston indicates, critics of our approach consider it dangerous to admit that politicians' nonverbal behaviors could elicit emotional responses that may interfere with reasoned deliberation. It is, however, both natural and inevitable that voters respond to leaders by integrating from nonverbal as well as verbal cues. The gestures of politicians, as Jane Mansbridge has commented, are part of the presentation of a political self, showing clearly to the public the nature of a leader's commitment. In addition to communicating the nature of emotion expressed to the viewer, they signal the moral values to which the political leader is committed (Marcus 1988).

Humans use a variety of channels—nonverbal as well as verbal—to process information. Voters respond not only to the issues as articulated by rival leaders but to their power and presence as well. Although an individual's emotional responses will vary in intensity depending on the candidate's identity or behavior, these emotions are also subject to changes in the salience of gestural information for the viewer's attitude and belief system. The effects of nonverbal displays are thus extremely

14. For example, the explanatory power of the regression model for Dukakis in February 1988, when he was only one candidate among many, is only .35, whereas the R^2 jumps to .83 just before the election, when Dukakis is the Democratic standard-bearer.

complex, depending on such diverse factors as the kind of display observed; the performance style of the individual leader; the congruence between the display and the verbal message; the attitudes, personality, and gender of the viewer; the cultural and social context; the media condition in which the event is observed; and the popularity or power of the leader.

Nonverbal cues may be particularly relevant as a means of communicating information about rivals during electoral campaigns. As two of the candidates move closer to nomination as their parties' candidates, the increase in their status makes their verbal and nonverbal behavior more important in organizing the voters' attitudes and belief systems. Events and candidate characteristics that were of little importance before the candidates approached power may now become part of the focus of attention (Sullivan et al. 1974). As a consequence, episodic emotional responses to gestures at salient moments such as the Kennedy-Nixon debate or Bush's address to the 1988 Republican Convention may be converted into more generalized attitudes and feelings toward candidates. It follows that the system of responses studied here may play an important role in election outcomes.

This view of the way leaders' nonverbal behavior can influence the citizen does not presume that the presence of powerful emotional elements in political behavior is, in itself, a bad thing. It is both natural and inevitable that voters respond to leaders by integrating information from nonverbal as well as verbal cues. Even more to the point, as research in the structure of the human brain demonstrates (Gazzaniga 1985; Kling 1986; Mishkin and Appenzeller 1987), it is folly to assume that emotion could be absent from political thinking. As traditional political theorists insisted, citizenship rests on an appropriate articulation between the feelings and the judgments of both leaders and led—not on a disembodied calculus of costs and benefits by an unfeeling computer.

These findings do suggest, however, that television has increased the danger of public apathy and greatly reinforced the need for an informed electorate. Our experimental evidence confirms that it is viewers with little information and weak political commitment who are most likely to be swayed by nonverbal cues or journalistic interpretations of what they have seen (Newton et al. 1987; Sullivan and Masters 1993). Precisely because emotions are so powerful and easily manipulated, in the media age a democratic electorate needs more than ever to be well informed and clearly focused on the issues. Yet insofar as journalists themselves become victims of a politics of image and style, the media often make the problem worse. The main practical conclusion from our experiments is thus the value of an active, educated, and committed citizenry. There is no substitute for what was traditionally called civic virtue.

References

Abelson, Robert, Donald Kinder, Mark Peters, and Susan Fiske. 1982. "Affective and Semantic Components in Political Person Perception." *Journal of Personality and Social Psychology* 42:619-30.

Almond, Gabriel A., and Verba, Sidney. 1965. *The Civic Culture*. Boston: Little, Brown.

Atkinson, Max. 1984. *Our Master's Voices: The Language and Body Language of Politics*. London: Methuen.

Axelrod, Robert. 1983. *The Evolution of Cooperation*. Cambridge, Mass.: Harvard University Press.

Baier, Annette C. 1987. "Getting in Touch with Our Feelings." *Topoi* 6:89–97.

Barber, James D. 1985. *The Presidential Character: Predicting Performance in the White House*. 4th ed. Englewood Cliffs, N.J.: Prentice-Hall.

Barnes, Fred. 1988. "Campaign '88: A Fine Romance." *New Republic*, 11 July, 10–12.

Burns, James MacGregor. 1978. *Leadership*. New York: Harper & Row.

Cacioppo, John T., and Richard E. Petty. 1979. "Attitudes and Cognitive Response: An Electrophysiological Approach." *Journal of Personality and Social Psychology* 37:2181–99.

Carlotti, Stephen J., Jr. 1988. "The Faces of the Presidency: Individual Differences in Responses to Nonverbal Behavior of American Leaders." Senior fellowship thesis, Dartmouth College.

Chance, Michael R. A. 1976. "The Organization of Attention in Groups." In *Methods of Inference from Animal to Human Behavior*, ed. Mario von Cranach, 213–35. The Hague: Mouton.

———. 1989. *Social Fabrics of the Mind*. Hillsdale, N.J.: Lawrence Erlbaum.

Chase, Ivan D. 1982. "Behavioral Sequences During Dominance Hierarchy Formation in Chickens." *Science* 216:439–40.

Courtine, Jean-Jacques, and Claudine Harouche. 1988. *Histoire du visage: Exprimer et taire ses emotions, XVIe—début XIXe siècle*. Paris: Rivages.

Dahl, Robert. 1956. *A Preface to Democratic Theory*. Chicago: University of Chicago Press.

Dahl, Robert, and Charles E. Lindblom. 1953. *Politics, Economics, and Welfare*. New York: Harper & Row.

Darwin, Charles. [1872] 1965. *The Expression of the Emotions in Man and Animals.* Chicago: University of Chicago Press.

de Waal, Frans. 1982. *Chimpanzee Politics.* London: Jonathan Cape.

———. 1991. "Sex Differences in the Formation of Coalitions Among Chimpanzees." In *Primate Politics*, ed. Glendon Schubert and Roger D. Masters, 138–60. Carbondale: Southern Illinois University Press.

Downs, Anthony. 1957. *An Economic Theory of Democracy.* New York: Harpers.

Ekman, Paul, and Harriet Oster. 1979. "Facial Expressions of Emotion." *Annual Review of Psychology* 30:527–54.

Englis, Basil G., Katherine B. Vaughan, and John T. Lanzetta. 1982. "Conditioning of Counter-empathetic Emotional Responses." *Journal of Experimental Social Psychology* 18:375–91.

Fiorina, Morris P. 1981. *Retrospective Voting in American National Elections.* New Haven: Yale University Press.

Frank, Robert. 1988. *Passions Within Reason.* New York: W. W. Norton.

Frey, Siegfried, Hans-Peter Hirsbrunner, Annemarie Beiri-Frolin, Walid Daw, and Robert Crawford. 1983. "A Unified Approach to the Investigation of Nonverbal and Verbal Behavior in Communication Research." In *Current Issues in European Social Psychology,* ed. W. Doise and S. Moscovici, 143–97. Cambridge: Cambridge University Press.

Fridlund, A. J., and Carroll E. Izard. 1983. "Electromyographic Studies of Facial Expressions of Emotions and Patterns of Emotion." In *Social Psychophysiology: A Sourcebook*, ed. J. T. Cacioppo and R. E. Petty, 243–86. New York: Guilford Press.

Gaxie, Pierre, ed. 1985. *Explication du vote.* Paris: Presses de la Fondation Nationale des Sciences Politiques.

Gazzaniga, Michael. 1985. *The Social Brain.* New York: Basic Books.

Goodall, Jane. 1986. *The Chimpanzees of Gombe.* Cambridge, Mass.: Harvard University Press.

Hinde, Robert. 1982. *Ethology.* Glasgow: Collins.

Hirschleifer, Jack. 1987. *Economic Behavior in Adversity.* Chicago: University of Chicago Press.

Joslyn, Richard, and Marc H. Ross. 1986. "Television News Coverage and Public Opinion in the 1984 Primaries." Paper presented at the annual meeting of the American Political Science Association, Washington, D.C.

Kagan, Jerome. 1988. "Biological Bases of Childhood Shyness." *Science* 240:167–71.

Kalb, Marvin, and Hendrik Hertzberg. 1988. *Candidates '88.* Dover, Mass.: Auburn House.

Key, V. O., Jr. 1961. *Public Opinion and American Democracy.* New York: Knopf.

Kling, Arthur. 1986. "Neurological Correlates of Social Behavior." In *Ostracism: A Social and Biological Phenomenon,* ed. Margaret Gruter and Roger Masters, 27–38. New York: Elsevier.

Kosslyn, Stephen M. 1988. "Aspects of Cognitive Neuroscience of Mental Imagery." *Science* 240:1621–26.

Lanzetta, John T., and Scott P. Orr. 1980. "Influence of Facial Expressions on the

Classical Conditioning of Fear." *Journal of Personality and Social Psychology* 39:1081–87.

Lanzetta, John T., Denis G. Sullivan, Roger D. Masters, and Gregory J. McHugo. 1985. "Emotional and Cognitive Responses to Televised Images of Political Leaders." In *Mass Media and Political Thought*, ed. Sidney Kraus and Richard E. Perloff, 85–116. Beverly Hills, Calif.: Sage Publications.

Lau, Richard. 1985. "Political Schemas, Candidate Evaluations, and Voting Behavior." In *Political Cognition*, ed. Richard Lau and David Sears, 95–126. Hillsdale, N.J.: Lawrence Erlbaum.

Lazarus, Richard. 1984. "On the Primacy of Cognition." *American Psychologist* 39:124–29.

Lodge, Milton, Kathleen M. McGraw, and Patrick Stroh. 1989. "An Impression-Driven Model of Candidate Evaluation." *American Political Science Review* 83:399–419.

Lorenz, Konrad Z., and Paul Leyhausen. 1973. *Motivation of Human and Animal Behavior*. New York: Van Nostrand Reinhold.

McGuire, Michael, and Michael T. Raleigh. 1986. "Behavioral and Physiological Correlates of Ostracism." In *Ostracism: A Social and Biological Phenomenon*, ed. Margaret Gruter and Roger D. Masters, 39–52. New York: Elsevier.

McHugo, Gregory J., John T. Lanzetta, and Lauren Bush. 1991. "The Effect of Attitudes on Emotional Reactions to Expressive Displays of a Political Leader." *Journal of Nonverbal Behavior* 15:19–41.

McHugo, Gregory J., John T. Lanzetta, Denis G. Sullivan, Roger D. Masters, and Basil G. Englis. 1985. "Emotional Reactions to Expressive Displays of a Political Leader." *Journal of Personality and Social Psychology* 490:1513–29.

Mandeville, Bernard. 1924. *The Fable of the Bees*. 2 vols. Oxford: Clarendon Press.

Mandler, George. 1975. *Mind and Emotion*. New York: Wiley.

Marcus, George. 1988. "The Structure of Emotional Appraisal: 1984 Presidential Candidates." *American Political Science Review* 82:737–62.

Masters, Roger D. 1981. "Linking Ethology and Political Science: Photographs, Political Attention, and Presidential Elections." In *Biopolitics: Ethological and Physiological Approaches*, ed. M. W. Watts, 61–80. New Directions for Methodology of Social and Behavioral Science, no. 7. San Francisco: Jossey-Bass.

———. 1989a. *The Nature of Politics*. New Haven: Yale University Press.

———. 1989b. "Gender and Political Cognition." *Politics and the Life Sciences* 8:3–39.

Masters, Roger D., and Stephen J. Carlotti, Jr. 1993. "Gender Differences in Responses to Political Leaders." In *Social Stratification and Socioeconomic Inequality*, ed. Lee Ellis. Westport, Conn.: Praeger.

Masters, Roger D., and Jean Mouchon. 1986. "Les gestes et la vie politique." In *Le Français dans le monde*, no. 203, 85–87. Paris: Hachette.

Masters, Roger D., and Denis G. Sullivan. 1989a. "Facial Displays and Political Leadership in France." *Behavioural Processes* 19:1–30.

———. 1989b. "Nonverbal Displays and Political Leadership in France and the United States." *Political Behavior* 11:121–53.

Masters, Roger D., Denis G. Sullivan, Alice Feola, and Gregory J. McHugo. 1987. "Television Coverage of Candidates' Display Behavior During the 1984 Democratic Primaries in the United States." *International Political Science Review* 8:121–30.

Masters, Roger D., Denis G. Sullivan, John T. Lanzetta, Gregory J. McHugo, and Basil G. Englis. 1986. "The Facial Displays of Leaders: Toward an Ethology of Human Politics." *Journal of Social and Biological Structures* 9:319–43.

Mishkin, Mortimer, and Thomas Appenzeller. 1987. "The Anatomy of Memory." *Scientific American* 256:80–89.

Montagner, Hubert. 1977. "Silent Speech." *Horizon—BBC2*, 28 July, Videotape.

Montagner, Hubert, A. Restoin, D. Rodriguez, and F. Kontar. 1988. "Aspects fonctionels et ontogénétiques des interactions de l'enfant avec ses pairs au cours des trois premières années." *Psychiatrie de L'enfant* 31:173–278.

Newton, James, Roger D. Masters, Gregory J. McHugo, and Denis G. Sullivan. 1987. "Making Up Our Minds: Effects of Network Coverage on Viewer Impressions of Leaders." *Polity* 20:226–46.

Olson, Mancur, Jr. 1965. *The Logic of Collective Action*. Cambridge, Mass.: Harvard University Press.

Orr, Scott P., and John T. Lanzetta. 1980. "Facial Expressions of Emotion as Conditioned Stimuli for Human Autonomic Responses." *Journal of Personality and Social Psychology* 38:278–82.

Petty, Richard E., and John T. Cacioppo. 1981. *Attitudes and Persuasion: Classic and Contemporary Approaches*. Dubuque, Iowa: William Brown.

Plato. 1968. *Republic*. Ed. Allan Bloom. New York: Basic Books.

Plutchik, Robert. 1980. *Emotion: A Psychoevolutionary Synthesis*. New York: Harper & Row.

Raleigh, Michael J., and Michael T. McGuire. 1986. "Animal Analogues of Ostracism: Biological Mechanisms and Social Consequences." In *Ostracism: A Social and Biological Phenomenon*, ed. Margaret Gruter and Roger Masters, 53–66. New York: Elsevier.

Rawls, John. 1971. *A Theory of Justice*. Cambridge, Mass.: Harvard University Press.

Roseman, Ira, Robert Abelson, and Michael Ewing. 1986. "Emotions and Political Cognition: Emotional Appeals in Political Communication." In *Political Cognition*, ed. Richard Lau and David Sears, 279–94. Hillsdale, N.J.: Lawrence Erlbaum.

Rousseau, Jean-Jacques. 1964. *The First and Second Discourses*. Ed. Roger D. Masters. New York: St. Martin's Press.

———. 1978. *The Social Contract, with Geneva Manuscript and Political Economy*. Ed. Roger D. Masters. New York: St. Martin's Press.

Schwartz, G. E., P. L. Fair, P. Salt, M. R. Mandel, and G. L. Klerman. 1976. "Facial Muscle Patterning to Affective Imagery in Depressed and Nondepressed Subjects." *Science* 192:489–91.

Scott, William. 1820. *Lessons in Elocution; or, A Selection of Pieces in Prose and Verse for the Improvement of Youth in Reading and Speaking*. Leicester: Hori Brown.

Sullivan, Denis G., and Roger D. Masters. 1988. " 'Happy Warriors': Leaders' Facial

Displays, Viewers' Emotions, and Political Support." *American Journal of Political Science* 32:345–68.
———. 1993. "Nonverbal Cues, Emotions, and Trait Attributions in the Evaluation of Political Leaders: The Contribution of Biopolitics to the Study of Media and Politics." In *Research in Biopolitics*, ed. Albert O. Somit and Steven A. Peterson. Greenwich, Conn.: JAI Press.
Sullivan, Denis G., Roger D. Masters, John T. Lanzetta, Basil G. Englis, and Gregory J. McHugo. 1984. "The Effect of President Reagan's Facial Displays on Observers' Attitudes, Impressions, and Feelings About Him." Paper presented to the annual meeting of the American Political Science Association, Washington, D.C.
Sullivan, Denis G., Roger D. Masters, John T. Lanzetta, Gregory J. McHugo, Basil G. Englis, and Elise F. Plate. 1991. "Facial Displays and Political Leadership: Some Experimental Findings." In *Primate Politics*, ed. Glendon Schubert and Roger D. Masters, 188–206. Carbondale: Southern Illinois University Press.
Sullivan, Denis G., Jeffery Pressman, Benjamin I. Page, and John D. Lyons. 1974. *The Politics of Representation*. New York: St. Martin's Press.
Suplee, Curt. 1988. "Sorry, George, but the Image Needs Work." *Washington Post*, 10 July, C1, C4.
Tranel, Daniel, and Antonio R. Damasio. 1985. "Learning Without Awareness: An Autonomic Index of Facial Recognition by Prosopagnosics." *Science* 228:1453–54.
Van Hooff, Jan A.R.A.M. 1969. "The Facial Displays of Catyrrhine Monkeys and Apes." In *Primate Ethology*, ed. Desmond Morris, 9–81. New York: Doubleday, Anchor Books.
———. 1973. "A Structural Analysis of the Social Behavior of a Semi-captive Group of Chimpanzees." In *Social Communication and Movement*, ed. Mario von Cranach and Ian Vine. New York: Academic Press.
Vaughan, K. B., and John T. Lanzetta. 1980. "Vicarious Instigation and Conditioning of Facial Expressive and Autonomic Responses to a Model's Expressive Display of Pain." *Journal of Personality and Social Psychology* 38:909–23.
Warr, Peter, Joanna Barter, and Garry Brownbridge. 1983. "On the Independence of Positive and Negative Affect." *Journal of Personality and Social Psychology* 44:644-51.
Zajonc, Robert. 1982. "On the Primacy of Affect." *American Psychologist* 39:117–23.
Zullow, Harold, and Martin E. P. Seligman. 1990. "Pessimistic Rumination Predicts Defeat of Presidential Candidates, 1900–1984." *Psychological Inquiry* 1:52–85.

16

Democratic Leadership, Reason, and Emotion

Larry M. Preston

As practiced in contemporary democracies, citizens' fundamental civic responsibility is to select competent leaders in free elections. And political leaders' basic democratic responsibility is to compete for the electorate's vote in open and fairly contested campaigns. This identifying feature of contemporary Western democracies was made explicit by Joseph Schumpeter almost fifty years ago. "The democratic method is that institutional arrangement for arriving at political decisions in which individuals acquire the power to decide by means of a competitive struggle for the people's vote" (1943, 269).

Unlike earlier models, real and imagined, contemporary democracy assigns to elected leaders the authority to govern in the fullest sense of this term: they discern from the mosaic of interests and contending values those issues and ideals that define the public interest, their policy initiatives focus and direct the policy process, and they largely shape the public's sense of policy successes and failures.[1] Effective government and social stability as well as bona fide control and accountability are typically thought to accompany this modern, pluralist polity. Although it is not *all* true, there is much truth in this picture, and for this reason it is a picture worth keeping in place. Still, its claim to represent a process of *democratic* governance rests primarily on the connections that exist between elected leaders and individual citizens—especially, the connections that operate within the arena of electoral campaigns.

All of this is implicit in Denis Sullivan and Roger Master's study of presidential candidates' nonverbal communication to voters as presented within televised campaign messages. Indeed, their work is important precisely because they examine the electoral linkage between citizens and political leaders—a linkage that is increasingly mediated through television. For better or worse, the democratic requirement that leaders be sensitive to the needs of citizens and accountable to citizens for their actions is (or is not) met during those critical months when millions of citizens turn on their television sets in the evenings and watch interviews, speeches, paid announcements, and press conferences that feature the presidential candidates.

Sullivan and Masters are surely right to insist that much more attends presidential candidates' messages on television than a rational effort to clarify issues and state policy positions. Accompanying such cognitive appeals and perhaps projecting a more captivating image is the silent but ever-present guest of honor: emotion. Sullivan and Masters are also right in claiming, contrary to contractarian and economistic interpretations of the electoral process, that emotion has long been recognized as an

1. This expansive role for central, elected leadership provides the basis for much of the critique of modern electoral democracies. The other face of assigning a heightened position to leaders is that ordinary citizens play a radically diminished part in democratic governance. And this, of course, is problematic. Carole Pateman (1970, 1986), Benjamin Barber (1984), and Peter Bachrach (1967) have offered eloquent arguments challenging the view of Joseph Schumpeter and other proponents of "elitist" democracy that citizens' basic democratic role is to select their leaders. Equally problematic is the tendency to restrict concerns about democracy to the arena of government. Even Robert Dahl (1986) argues in his more recent work that democracy is quite empty unless carried into economic institutions. I find much that is compelling in these critiques. Yet we also need to examine the prospects for democracy within our prevailing practices. In any case, we start from here. Given this, some attention needs to be paid to keeping "here" within reasonable democratic boundaries.

inevitable and potentially salutary component of politics. Yet there are limits to the role that emotional appeals can play in an electoral process that can claim, without doing violence to the term, to be substantially democratic.[2] It is well to have some reasonably clear sense of these limits before assessing whether Sullivan and Masters's findings bode well or ill for contemporary electoral democracy.

Communication, Emotion, and Democratic Leadership

It is certainly true, as Sullivan and Masters note in their introductory remarks, that emotion has been a recognized and legitimate part of both political theory and practice from the time of Plato and continuing through Rousseau and Madison. I will add Joseph Schumpeter to the list, given his importance in formulating the contemporary electoral theory of democracy. But these theorists and others (even Machiavelli comes to mind) were rather precise about the specific boundaries within which emotion should operate in a properly constituted politics. It is not a matter, as Sullivan and Masters appear to assume, that those who inject emotion into the electoral process will also be motivated by (or constrained by) democratic purposes. The images presented by the selective, one-way lens of television provide too many opportunities for manipulation; emotions are potentially too powerful; and in a democratic polity, the need for reason to assume an important place in political discourse is too essential to view emotional appeals with an uncritical eye.

Certainly, as urged by James Madison in *The Federalist* No. 10 ([1787] 1961), the liberty that republican politics is intended to nourish and protect requires the broadest possible interplay between reason and emotion. But Madison as well as other republican theorists clearly believed that there were quite definite and important boundaries this interplay had to respect. Grounded in the democratic ideal of consent of

2. I will use the terms "democracy" and "republic" interchangeably—with the understanding that I have in mind an indirect, representative form of democratic governance. There are other ingredients of republican government—civility, tolerance, community, and so on—that are discussed at some length in other contributions to this volume.

the governed, these boundaries exist for all varieties of democratic theory and practice. It is well to have them in mind as a basis for analyzing the findings presented in the study by Sullivan and Masters.

Major republican theorists have proposed that political leaders may use emotion (1) to gain support for policies that reflect the basic, legitimate ideals of a community; (2) to create and strengthen a sense of community and commitment to the common good so that public deliberations will focus on shared rather than particular interests; and (3) to reflect and give expression to a wide range of individual or partisan interests. With respect to the theorists mentioned earlier, Plato and Schumpeter hold most closely to the first position, Rousseau argues for the second, and Madison proposes the third.

In elaborating these requirements, I will focus on Madison and Schumpeter because they have the greatest relevance within the context of contemporary democratic politics. Schumpeter emphasizes that political leaders are generally free to use whatever appeals they find effective as they engage in the competition for votes. Notably, this competition "does not exclude the cases that are strikingly analogous to the economic phenomena we label 'unfair' or 'fraudulent' competition or restraint of competition. And we cannot exclude them because if we did we should be left with a completely unrealistic ideal" (1943, 271).

In this, Schumpeter agrees with Madison that political leaders must have the greatest possible freedom to pursue interests that are passionately held and to seek them through passionate appeals. He also recognizes, however, that "as in the economic field, *some* restrictions are implicit in the legal and moral principles of the community" (1943, 271 n. 5; emphasis in the original).[3] Schumpeter's formulation gives would-be leaders wide latitude in their efforts to win the votes of electors. Yet he realized that the disinclination of republican politics to restrict the types of appeals and measures used to gain power means that "there is a continuous range of variation within which the democratic method of government shades off into the autocratic one by imperceptible steps" (1943, 271). As those concerned with understanding the character of

3. Madison and Schumpeter generally assume the existence, as well as the viability, of a liberal republic; consequently, their focus is on how it should function so as to be faithful to its principles and ideals. Plato and Rousseau shared this concern, yet they also engaged in the conversation at an earlier stage and were concerned with understanding the proper role of emotion and reason in creating and maintaining the moral principles of a properly constituted republic.

democratic politics, we are obliged to identify, insofar as possible, when a "range of variation" is taken that clearly challenges the fabric of a democratic polity.

Madison is more explicit regarding the character of the underlying principles that bind political leaders in their efforts to achieve power and regarding the boundaries implied by those principles. As we all know, Madison's world of republican politics is driven by the competition of interests, and interests are both attached to deep emotions and fought for through emotional appeals. Thus, we have the famous phrase in *The Federalist* No. 10: "By a faction, I understand a number of citizens, whether amounting to a majority or minority of the whole, who are united and actuated by some common impulse of passion, or of interest, adverse to the rights of other citizens, or to the permanent and aggregate interests of the community" ([1787] 1961, 17).

The political assumptions built into Madison's conception of emotion and its role in political life are clear. First, interests and emotions are attached to deeply held individual and partisan values or purposes. Second, the number and diversity of interests that a free people will come to hold is virtually endless. Third, Madison assumes that efforts to effect a governmental response to particular demands will be generated by partisan interests or desires that are held in common by a substantial number of people. (Indeed, his primary concern is that an interest passionately held by a majority may impel government to act in ways that threaten important rights or sound policy.) Finally, and perhaps most important for my purposes here, Madison assumes that leaders hold and are themselves concerned with pursuing certain passionately held desires or interests—desires or interests that are shared by (some) other citizens and by rather clearly identifiable partisan groups. As they seek electoral victory, would-be leaders in a republic are presumed to be motivated by reasons and emotions connected to genuine interests that they share with their actual and potential supporters. It is this shared commitment to common desires and interests that forms the critical moral linkage between leaders and those who support them; it is the strength and vitality of this commitment that lies at the heart of contemporary democratic governance.

Schumpeter recognizes the importance of this shared commitment; for him, it provides the legitimate boundary within which the competition for votes in a free election should occur. The moral principle built into this competition is that leaders do not seek power only for its own sake; rather, they seek power, in part, to further reasonably clear and bona fide interests that they and the constituents to whom they appeal hold with considerable conviction. The obvious implication for democratic political communication is that emotional appeals should not be used by political leaders simply as a vehicle for gaining power independent of these common desires and interests. Appeals to emotion should not be contrived, they should not be matters of appearance only, and they should not be used primarily as instruments of manipulation. It is from within this framework that I suggest we consider the implications of Sullivan and Masters's study for contemporary republican politics.

Emotion, Elections, and Nonverbal Cues

The critical question with respect to the findings presented in Sullivan and Masters's study is this: Does the use of emotional appeals by candidates in recent election campaigns help voters identify the deeply held values and interests that would-be leaders represent? There is no clear answer. Their evidence is somewhat difficult to place within the context of democratic communication, and the interpretations that may be given to their data are mixed and open. Still, some leap of faith is required to interpret the evidence they offer as reassuring.

The most troubling uncertainty is whether the underlying emotional appeals that attend candidates' facial gestures represent ideals and policy positions that they and their constituents hold—or whether such displays reflect carefully orchestrated, psychological posturing for the sole purpose of manipulating electors' emotions and attitudes. Certainly, Sullivan and Masters provide strong evidence that citizens' attitudes are often influenced by the emotional dimensions associated with candidates' facial expressions as presented in televised speeches. In particular, facial expressions that exhibit warmth (happiness/reassurance displays) foster positive attitudes toward candidates, whereas threatening, angry, or fearful expressions tend to generate negative attitudes toward them. These nonverbal, emotional influences have an especially powerful impact on those individuals who have no strong prior attitudes regarding the candidates and relatively little information about them. Sullivan and Masters generally interpret such evidence as revealing new information about the interplay of cognition and emotion in the electoral process and as consistent with viewing that process in democratic terms. One of their most important conclusions is that a politician's gestures "are part of the presentation of a political self, showing clearly to the public the nature of a leader's commitment."

If true, this is precisely the connection between reason and emotion implicit in Schumpeter's view and explicit in Madison's presumption of leaders' passionate attachment to their own (and their followers') deeply held values and interests. If true, this conclusion confirms an association between emotional appeals and accountability that is the truest test of a democratic process that rests on competition for citizens' votes in free elections. The strength of this conclusion depends on two factors that Sullivan and Masters find mediating the role of emotion: prior attitudes and learning, and political context. In their interpretation, the emotional influences they discovered had the weakest impact on attitudes when their subjects had clear prior attitudes and notable preexisting information regarding the candidates. Under these circumstances, the emotional influence was short-lived and rather quickly revised to fit with prior attitudes. This is important because it suggests that emotional influences are not always, by themselves, the controlling influence in shaping individuals' attitudes toward candidates.

Given the subjects of their study (students at an Ivy League university), however, this conclusion is problematic. It is doubtful that the strength of prior attitudes and store of political information of these students are generally replicated in the majority of the American electorate.[4] In any case, some evidence to this effect is needed before conclu-

4. Obviously, there are important and perfectly reasonable practical grounds for using students in experimental research. Students are readily available, often eager to participate, and so on. With respect to political attitudes and political life generally, however, extreme caution needs to be exercised in extending conclusions based on a study of students—especially when using the exceptional students who attend Ivy League universities—to draw conclusions about the general public. It is intuitively unlikely that students' attitudes and responses will reflect those of the public at large. Roger Masters has suggested in a letter to me that in a somewhat similar study (Newton et al. 1987) using adults drawn from outside the university, the pattern of emotional responses to televised political messages was similar to that of the students in this study. But the respondents in the related study were "drawn from the middle to upper middle-class community of Hanover" and do "not accurately reflect American society at large." While Newton and his coauthors suggest that other studies have produced similar results using "viewers of different ages" (1987, 244), there is also serious uncertainty whether respondents in these studies reasonably reflect those of a broad audience. The problem remains: students, affluent and well-educated citizens, or others who have the time, leisure, and inclination to participate in experimental studies are problematic stand-ins for the general public.

sions based on this parallel can be made. My own suspicion is that those who constitute the broader public are generally less informed, have less firmly held attitudes with respect to candidates, and are therefore considerably more subject to underlying emotional messages than the students of Sullivan and Masters's study. If so, there are not likely to be countervailing influences that mediate the impact of these messages.

There is even greater difficulty finding evidence to support Sullivan and Masters's interpretation of the role that context plays in mediating the impact of candidates' underlying emotional appeals on voters' attitudes. Undeniably, they demonstrate that the impact of facial displays that exhibit precisely the same underlying emotional appeals varies with the situation. Displays may have considerable impact within one situation and little or none under other circumstances. Two interesting instances are given. Ronald Reagan's and Gary Hart's reassuring facial displays engendered considerable support in 1984; these same messages had little impact in 1988. Sullivan and Masters suggest that the quite different context in 1988 explains the declining influence of Reagan's and Hart's emotional appeals. This changed context is explained in the following manner. "In Reagan's case, his situation as a 'lame duck'—i.e., the realization that his power of incumbency was virtually at an end—may have been combined with changes in popularity and perceived effectiveness to reduce the impact of episodic emotion on attitude; for Hart, the Donna Rice affair and its consequences provide an obvious explanation for similar results."

As a second instance, Sullivan and Masters suggest that context helps to explain George Bush's (initially) unsuccessful effort to send reassuring messages to the electorate—these messages, in fact, elicited a fearful response. The authors note that this result was observed "prior to the transformation of his image at the time of the Republican National Convention." Presumably, Bush's efforts to instill positive emotions by means of reassuring nonverbal cues became more successful after this transformation. Different context, different emotional impact.

Again, there are difficulties with the proffered interpretation. It is possible, as Sullivan and Masters suggest, that rational considerations led to a changed context that in turn lessened the impact of Reagan's and Hart's emotional appeals in 1988. It is also possible that the "real" George Bush came forth at the Republican convention, that voters learned this, and that their subsequent emotional and rational assessment of him changed accordingly. If so, of course, the democratic requirements of political communication were alive and well—even as voters' attitudes were partially shaped by the emotional appeals embedded in candidates' facial gestures.[5]

But this positive interpretation of these actual and presumed transformations is highly speculative. No specific information is offered that would explain the basis of the changes. Against Sullivan and Masters's account, it is entirely possible that the transformations were fueled by a complex network of emotional appeals that had little or nothing to do with the creation of a context in which voters had an improved understanding of the candidates. In particular, did voters in 1988 have more relevant information regarding Reagan and Hart, or were they responding to the altered emotional cues presented by television newscasters? Given the central importance of emotional cues, as suggested by Sullivan and Masters, it may be that television correspondents' underlying emotionally laden messages were the primary source of the new assessments on the part of viewers—that is, such reporters may have gone from exhibiting reassuring emotional messages to messages that were fearful and threatening as they reported on the activities of Reagan and Hart. The obverse may have happened with respect to Bush.

We also need to know far more about the relative role of emotion and reason in accounting for the transformations undergone by recent presidential candidates. Sullivan and Masters provide an insufficient basis for interpreting these changes in ways that conform to the requirements of electoral democracy. It is very difficult to fit the notion of an overnight "transformation" (such as Bush's) into the requirements of democratic communication discussed earlier. True transformation on the part of political leaders, like molting, is a long and arduous process. It would represent, as Schumpeter and Madison assume, a change in commitment with respect to the deeply held values and interests of a candidate and those with whom she or he identifies—a change accompanied by passion and emotion, to be sure, but perceived accurately nonetheless by the citizenry. The essentially overnight transformation of Bush from a candidate perceived as weak to one who was viewed as confident and

5. There are numerous historical accounts, of course, of essentially unbridled emotional appeals in politics. From Sophocles' *Antigone* to Machiavelli's *Prince* and Hobbes's *Leviathan*, widespread use of emotion has been both recounted and recommended. But the regimes and theories that have placed no identifiable limits on leaders' use of emotion cannot properly be called democratic. It is the use of emotion by leaders within the framework of *democratic* principles and practices that above all needs to be understood.

strong, though perhaps instrumental in securing his election, would seem to have woefully little to do with a (revised) commitment on his part to a new set of important values or interests. Unfortunately, the more intuitive interpretation is that this transformation was entirely the result of long hours of coaching for the purpose of presenting a new image. Such images and image transformations would seem to have an uncertain connection to the commitments, values, and interests of either candidates or voters.

While I have doubts about the conclusions they draw, it is important to emphasize the value of Sullivan and Masters's pioneering work. Most important, their study reminds us that the Dionysian side of the human character continues to have its say in politics. It is an important reminder. The psychological, emotional dimension of human motivation is almost entirely absent from recent theorizing that argues that political life in a democracy is simply grounded in ethical (John Rawls, Ronald Dworkin, William Galston, et al.) or rational (public-choice) calculations. Emotion is nowhere to be found.

Yet the chances are that emotion is everywhere in our social and political lives—deeply shaping our political principles, our political institutions and practices, our ideals and our efforts to realize them. Sullivan and Masters have given us a glimpse of the way in which emotion enters into the electoral arena that is the very heart of contemporary democratic politics. There is a long way to go before we have a reasonably complete picture of the way in which emotion informs either elections or other dimensions of political life. Whether that picture will reveal a viable democratic politics remains to be seen.

References

Bachrach, Peter. 1967. *The Theory of Democratic Elitism*. Boston: Little, Brown.

Barber, Benjamin R. 1984. *Strong Democracy*. Berkeley and Los Angeles: University of California Press.

Buchanan, James M., and Gordon Tullock. 1962. *The Calculus of Consent*. Ann Arbor: University of Michigan Press.

Dahl, Robert A. 1956. *A Preface to Democratic Theory*. Chicago: University of Chicago Press.

———. 1986. *Democracy, Liberty, and Equality*. Oslo: Norwegian University Press.

Madison, James. [1787] 1961. *The Federalist* No. 10. In *The Federalist Papers*, ed. Roy P. Fairfield, 16–23. Baltimore: Johns Hopkins University Press.
Newton, James S., Roger D. Masters, Gregory J. McHugo, and Denis G. Sullivan. 1987. "Making Up Our Minds: Effects of Network Coverage on Viewer Impressions of Leaders." *Polity* 20:226–46.
Pateman, Carol. 1970. *Participation and Democratic Theory*. New York: Cambridge University Press.
———. 1986. *The Problem of Political Obligation*. Berkeley and Los Angeles: University of California Press.
Schattschneider, E. E. 1960. *The Semi-sovereign People*. New York: Holt, Rinehart & Winston.
Schumpeter, Joseph A. 1943. *Capitalism, Socialism, and Democracy*. London: George Allen & Unwin.
Spragens, Thomas A., Jr. 1990. *Reason and Democracy*. Durham, N.C.: Duke University Press.

IV

Democracy and Diversity

17

Democratic Discussion

Donald R. Kinder
Don Herzog

"Democracy," remarked H. L. Mencken, "is the theory that the common people know what they want, and deserve to get it good and hard." Mencken found American politics a droll spectacle and showered contempt on the dullards he named "the booboisie." Plenty of other intelligent and perceptive observers have concluded that ordinary citizens are flatly incapable of shouldering the burdens of democracy. Uninformed and uninterested, absorbed in the pressing business of private life, unable to trace out the consequences of political action, citizens possess neither the skills nor the resources required for what Walter Bagehot pithily named "government by discussion."

We thank Judith Ottmar for impeccable help in preparing the manuscript and Janet Weiss for good advice.

In this light, democratic theorists might appear hopelessly naive or romantic, bent on promoting a politics we haven't seen yet, and likely never will. We want here to take the challenge of antidemocratic thought seriously, particularly on the question of the intelligence of democratic discussion. Our aim is to assess the quality of the political conversations that go on between the American public and American leaders. Our special interest is in what citizens have to say, both to each other and to their elected representatives. But assessing the quality of such discussions requires an assessment not only of the skills and interests of citizens but of the political environment in which citizens find themselves: the "opportunities for political learning" and the "quality of political information" (Page and Shapiro 1988, 13) that are made available to them. And we want to evaluate both where we are now and where we might be in the future, not in some utopian and unrealizable rendition of American society, but in a foreseeable one. We begin by summarizing Mill's vision of democracy, which accords discussion a central place. Next we review the attack on the possibility of democratic discussion implicitly mounted in recent American survey research, especially as set out in the authoritative and influential writings of Philip Converse. Then, in the heart of the chapter, we examine several different lines of argument and evidence that offer the possibility of modifying Converse's melancholy conclusions. Democratic discussion may be more than just a romantic dream. We needn't be breathless and starry-eyed—determined "to see some blue sky in the midst of clouds of disillusioning facts" (Schumpeter 1942, 256)—to resist the thesis that voters are invincibly ignorant.[1]

Mill's Vision of Democracy

John Stuart Mill would have had no patience for any economistic concept of democracy as a system of preference aggregation; nor for that matter would he have relished any pluralistic conception focusing on the struggles among interest groups.[2] Instead, Mill placed debate over the

1. We are deliberately vague about exactly what kind of discussion we have in mind. For an argument that genuine democratic discussion should follow the form of testimony, not deliberation, see Sanders, n.d.

2. This isn't the place for laborious textual exegesis, so we will present a bald summary account of Mill's conception of democracy, drawn from the *Considerations on Representative Government*, *On Liberty*, and some of the journalism.

common good at the heart of democracy. Even majority rule, often thought to be a signally important feature of democracy, faded into the background in his treatment. The majority's vote is important not because it has any right to rule but because it's our best way of seeing what seems the most reasonable view at the moment:

> Unless opinions favourable to democracy and to aristocracy, to property and to equality, to co-operation and to competition, to luxury and to abstinence, to sociality and individuality, to liberty and discipline, and all the other standing antagonisms of practical life, are expressed with equal freedom, and enforced and defended with equal talent and energy, there is no chance of both elements obtaining their due; one scale is sure to go up, and the other down. Truth, in the great practical concerns of life, is so much a question of the reconciling and combining of opposites, that very few have minds sufficiently capacious and impartial to make the adjustment with an approach to correctness, and it has to be made by the rough process of a struggle between combatants fighting under hostile banners. (Mill [1859] 1951b, 28)

The more wide-ranging, the more vibrant, the more well-informed the debate, the better. Only in a richly diverse debate can we have any confidence that emerging views have any rational warrant. That's one reason Mill struggled in and out of Parliament to extend the franchise to workers and women (a campaign giving him a reputation as a crazy radical). Members of Parliament, he urged, could talk all day about the interests of the working class, but they'd never really understand those interests until workers themselves could present them. (Mill had other reasons for extending the franchise, chief among them the pregnant thought that being a citizen, not a subject, is partly constitutive of dignity and equality. However important elsewhere, though, these themes don't cut directly into our topic.)

Critics of liberal democracy have often savaged it as mindless chatter and celebrated instead the cult of action, the heroic leader who firmly grasps what needs to be done. Mill's theory explains why we should want there to be endless talk, in and out of the legislature, and especially between legislators and citizens. We simply can't grasp what might be worth doing and why—we can't learn from our previous mistakes and seek to correct them—without that talk:

> There must be discussion, to show how experience is to be interpreted. Wrong opinions and practices gradually yield to fact and argument: but facts and arguments, to produce any effect on the mind, must be brought before it. Very few facts are able to tell their own story, without comments to bring out their meaning. The whole strength and value, then, of human judgement, depending on the one property, that it can be set right when it is wrong, reliance can be placed on it only when the means of setting it right are kept constantly at hand. (Mill [1859] 1951b, 27)

For other theories of democracy, all that talk poses an explanatory mystery. We needn't talk a lot to register our preferences or to estimate the pressure of competing interest groups. Economists should explain why we don't literally auction off legislation. Pluralists should explain why legislators don't play tug of war in the chamber, why lobbyists don't hire sumo wrestlers to compete on the floor.

The more talk, the more intelligent the talk, the better. Mill here offers an exhilarating contrast to Rousseau, who, weirdly, is still routinely embraced by self-styled ardent democrats. Rousseau's citizens are zealots, enthusiasts for politics who fly to the public assembly. But when they get there, what do they do? Apparently, they participate in a largely silent ritual of communal affirmation. Long debates, Rousseau warns portentously, are a sign of decline in the state, and he adds proudly that his citizens are too stupid to fall for clever and deceptive arguments. Democracy is a capacious enough concept or tradition to include Rousseau, but we see no reason to embrace his vision as any kind of ideal.

No doubt there are important failings in Mill's views. Mill wanted to rig the popular discussion by giving the intelligent plural votes; worse yet, he was willing to entertain taking occupation and wealth as proxies for intelligence. He thought the popularly elected legislature shouldn't be in the business of actually drafting legislation but should tell some career experts what sort of bill they wanted. He tended to underplay the hustle and bustle and crass manipulation of democratic politics, casting it instead as a bloodless debate among intellectually scrupulous citizens bent on getting the right answer. Most important, perhaps, Mill's quasi-utilitarianism sometimes led him to think that political questions are just complicated technical questions, that there's a correct answer to the question what policy would maximize the greatest happiness.

These are genuine defects, and we have no interest in whitewashing Mill. Still, the insight that democracy is government by discussion remains attractive even after we scrap Mill's errors. As Mill knew full well, however, there are lots of prerequisites to fruitful discussion. If democratic debate is to go well, what has to be true?

Converse and the Improbability of Discussion

Democratic discussion might seem to require what Walter Lippmann (1922) once called the "omnicompetent citizen," who is attentive to and informed about the persons and problems that animate public life, familiar with the policies and philosophies that divide rival parties and candidates, and in possession of coherent and wide-ranging ideas about government and society. If so, government by discussion is in deep trouble. For it was the omnicompetent citizen that Philip Converse (1964) effectively demolished in his celebrated essay "The Nature of Belief Systems in Mass Publics."

Converse did the job with evidence. Based on a detailed analysis of national surveys carried out in 1956, 1958, and 1960, Converse concluded that qualitative, perhaps unbridgeable differences distinguished the political thinking of elites from the political thinking of ordinary citizens. Imagine a triangle, with elites occupying the apex and the vast majority of citizens crowding into the base. As one descends from the pinnacle of American society to the all too ordinary depths, two striking transformations take place in political comprehension, according to Converse:

> First, the contextual grasp of "standard" political belief systems fades out very rapidly, almost before one has passed beyond the 10% of the American population that in the 1950s had completed standard college training. Increasingly, simpler forms of information about "what goes with what" (or even information about the simple identity of objects) turn up missing. The net result, as one moves downward, is that constraint declines across the universe of idea-elements, and that the range of relevant belief

> systems becomes narrower and narrower. Instead of a few wide-ranging belief systems that organize large amounts of specific information, one would expect to find a proliferation of clusters of ideas among which little constraint is felt, even, quite often, in instances of sheer logical constraint.
>
> [Second,] the character of the objects that are central in a belief system undergoes systematic change. These objects shift from the remote, generic, and abstract to the increasingly simple, concrete, or "close to home." Where potential political objects are concerned, this progression tends to be from abstract "ideological" principles to the more obviously recognizable social groupings or charismatic leaders and finally to such objects of immediate experience as family, job, and immediate associates. (1964, 213)

Together, these two changes pose a challenge to the very possibility of democratic discussion. They suggest not only that leaders and citizens think about public life in fundamentally different ways, they also question whether citizens are capable of participating in democratic discussion at all. As Converse put it, the fragmentation and concretization of everyday political thinking "are not a pathology limited to a thin and disorganized bottom layer of the *lumpenproletariat*; they are immediately relevant in understanding the bulk of mass political behavior" (213).

Converse came to his gloomy conclusions in part because of Americans' utter unfamiliarity with standard ideological concepts like liberalism and conservatism. Practically nobody relied on such concepts when they commented on what they liked and disliked about the major parties and candidates. Converse also found that although positions on a variety of pressing domestic and foreign policy issues taken by candidates for the United States House of Representatives revealed clear ideological inclinations, the views expressed by the general public on the same issues did not. Candidates were consistently liberal or conservative; citizens scattered all over the place. Moreover, when citizens were questioned in a series of interviews, their opinions appeared to wobble back and forth randomly, liberal on one occasion, conservative on the next. Some citizens seemed to possess genuine opinions and hold on to them tenaciously, but they appeared to be substantially outnumbered by those who either confessed their ignorance outright or, when nudged, invented a "nonattitude" on the spot (Converse 1970). Nor, finally, did ordinary

Americans seem to know very much about politics. Imposing fractions of the general public do not know whether the Contras were Communist, how William Rehnquist makes a living, who exactly represents them in the United States Senate: the dreary litany goes on and on. In Converse's analysis, "staggering" and "astronomical" differences in knowledge set the leadership echelon apart from the public. "Very little information 'trickles down' very far" (Converse 1964, 212).[3]

All in all, quite an unpretty picture. Most Americans glance at the political world innocent of ideology and information: indifferent to standard ideological concepts, lacking a consistent perspective on public policy, in possession of authentic opinions on only a few policy questions, and knowing precious little. Democratic discussion would seem to be out of reach—and not only here and now. We should keep in mind that Converse's conclusions are directed at an American public that in historical and comparative perspective is remarkably affluent, extraordinarily well educated, and virtually bombarded with news. What, if anything, can we say in response?

It Ain't So

Much of Converse's analysis hangs on the contrast between the actual responses of Americans and the hypothetical responses of a "sophisticated observer." But we can doubt the sophistication of this observer; that is, we can wonder if Americans have to fit this particular preconceived model in order to think intelligently about politics. Converse's sophisticated observer, for instance, would have strong views about whether utilities should be publicly owned or not, but we know of no evidence that this was pressing business on the public agenda in 1958. Citizens absorbed in the question

3. Estimates of political knowledge, which are unrelievedly depressing, no doubt fail to tell the grimmer truth. Even the very best sample surveys—like the National Election Study or the General Social Survey—successfully interview only about 75 percent of the targeted sample. Those who refuse to be questioned, like those who simply are never contacted in the first place, are unrepresentative of the public as a whole: they fall disproportionately among those totally disengaged from politics. Were we to correct for such selection bias, we would discover that the American public is even less well informed than the reported figures suggest (Brehm 1989).

might well have struck their friends and neighbors as quaint. More generally, citizens who proceeded in the way recommended by Converse's sophisticated observer could be described not as informed and intelligent but as single-minded and doctrinaire.

Converse emphasizes the advantages of ideology and therefore laments its absence. From his perspective, an ideological framework provides the citizen with a deeper, richer understanding of politics than is available through other means. In part this longing for ideology reflects Converse's disdain for these "other means": remember that to Converse, the bulk of the American public thinks about public life in ways that should be regarded as *pathological.* But more than that, Converse believes that ideological frameworks provide an economical and useful way for citizens to make sense of the "swarming confusion of problems" (Lippmann 1925) that constitutes the world of politics. To the ideologically inclined, "new political events have more meaning, retention of political information from the past is far more adequate, and political behavior increasingly approximates that of sophisticated 'rational' models" (Converse 1964, 227).

But as a mode of thinking, ideology also has its disadvantages. Robert Lane (1973), Converse's most persistent critic over the years, worries in particular that ideological thinking is not only economical but also dogmatic and intolerant: "Reference to an ideological posture would not only 'constrain' policy thinking but would confine it. There are meanings of the term *ideology* that suggest defensive postures (Rokeach 1960) such that the main objective of ideological policy thinking is to defend an ideological commitment, not to explore alternative policies" (104). That people don't think the way Converse stipulated they should doesn't necessarily show there's anything wrong with people. It might just show there was something wrong, or at least incomplete, about Converse's specifications (more on this later).

The most devastating element in Converse's original indictment, however, is the nonattitude thesis, the claim that few citizens possess real views on pressing matters of public policy. Because the nonattitude result presupposes nothing about what counts as a valid structure or approach in political deliberation, it would seem to make serious trouble for the wide-ranging discussion that democracy requires.

Fortunately for the prospects of democratic discussion, the nonattitude thesis now seems less persuasive, in light of empirical work of two sorts that has followed in Converse's wake. In the first place, unstable opinions, we now know, are a reflection not only of vague and confused citizens, as Converse would have it, but of vague and confused *questions*, as well; instability is, in part, a product of the very imperfect way survey questions are put to citizens (Achen 1975; Erikson 1979; Brody 1986; and for a review of the evidence, Smith 1984). Second, the political events of the last twenty-five years have made clear that issue publics need not be confined to minuscule fractions of the public as a whole. Most Americans developed real attitudes toward racial busing, capital punishment, abortion, the war in Vietnam, affirmative action, and more (see, e.g., Converse and Markus 1979; Kinder and Rhodebeck 1982; Luker 1984). When policy issues become entangled with moral, racial, religious, and nationalist loyalties, the nonattitude problem appears much less problematic.

These developments leave us somewhat more confident in the public's capacity to develop genuine political commitments than where Converse left things a quarter century ago. Still, what we have said so far does no damage to the contention that Americans know astonishingly little about the political world that whirls around them. Perhaps democratic discussion doesn't require that citizens know more (see below), but nothing we have said to this point gets around the finding of profound and widespread ignorance.

It Ain't Necessarily So

Converse clearly understood himself as uncovering not a particular historical contingency but something deeply essential: thus tags like "the nature" of mass publics, and thus his relishing similar findings from France (Converse and Pierce 1986). Now, forty million Frenchmen may be wrong—they may even be empty-headed—but it doesn't follow that all "mass publics" everywhere, even counterfactual mass publics, are or would be wrong and empty-headed.

Like Converse, Lippmann thought his findings depended on nothing but some elementary considerations of psychology. In *The Public and Its Problems* (1927), a veiled response to this part of Lippmann's case, John Dewey suggested that instead of seeing human nature as the cause of political ignorance we should see contingent social practices. Change the practices, and people would become intelligent, acute, incisive.[4]

4. This, we suggest, is one thrust of some rather murky Hegelian passages about the public coming to know itself.

Typically allergic to thinking of psychological predicates as irreducibly "in the head," Dewey emphasized instead the sociological nature of intelligence. The ancient Greeks did a wretched job of economic calculation; we do a surpassingly good job. What explains the difference? Not, surely, that we're brighter than they were. It's that we have a series of social practices and conceptual tools available to us that they didn't have: we have markets, double-entry bookkeeping, the idea of capital depreciation, and the like. Or again: Mark Twain's Connecticut Yankee amazes the gawking yokels of King Arthur's Court, not because he is smarter, but because modern science and technology enable him to do things they can't do.

In a Deweyan view, then, we're not necessarily stuck with the bleak findings of Lippmann and Converse. Change the world, reform our practices, and we can improve the intelligence of citizens. Dewey's argument is the right context for considering the cascade of leftist indictments and reforms offered in recent years. American "democracy," we've been told, is nothing but a spectator sport, a beauty contest, in which voters are systematically distracted from genuinely pressing issues of public policy and fed stupid television advertisements, canned "debates" guaranteeing no real confrontation of competing views, and so on. Or again: a capitalist workplace, a consumerist culture, and the rest explain why the working-class men of Eastport interviewed at length by Robert Lane (1962) were so concerned with buying and selling, so little concerned with social justice and elections. Such critics of liberal democracy as Benjamin Barber (1984) and Joshua Cohen and Joel Rogers (1983) have plenty of antecedents—among them, we note, John Stuart Mill, who himself urged at length that the modern workplace ought to be run democratically and who pressed for unbelievably low spending limits on campaigns.

When Lippmann tells us that politics looms awfully remote on the horizon of the ordinary citizen, he must be talking about social distance, not physical distance. But social distance depends in part on personal identity. Because they identify with Israel, many American Jews know and care a lot about Israeli politics, which (short of intercontinental flights) they can't even participate in. It's flatly implausible to view personal identity as any kind of brute fact: it too depends on contingent social practices, cultural norms, and the like. Americans could think of themselves as citizens concerned with politics; if they did in part have that identity, political issues would no longer be far away.

Remember that we want to keep the conterfactuals reasonably close to the actual world. Some critics of American democracy seem to take perverse pride in insisting that only heroically radical changes could make America truly democratic. One could dispute their programs on the merits, of course, but one could also note that those radical changes just don't seem to be in the cards, not now anyway. We prefer to think about available changes in the name of making America more democratic, even if not fully and ideally democratic according to someone's stern standards.[5] So, for instance, changes in journalism might not have the dramatic implications some attribute to democratic socialism, but those changes are still worth pursuing. If this counts as bourgeois reformism, we are happy to plead guilty.

And if appeals to counterfactual worlds seem unscientifically speculative, consider two real examples pointing in the same direction. In 1964, Senator Goldwater spoke forcefully against the intrusions of national government and for states' rights, making no secret of his staunch opposition to the Civil Rights Act. In this respect, Goldwater was unusual: on matters of policy, American presidential candidates typically seek the safety of ambiguity (Page 1978). When they do not, when they offer clear and distinctive proposals, public confusion and ignorance can diminish, sometimes precipitously. By election day in 1964, more than three quarters of the public claimed some familiarity with the Civil Rights Act, and of those, practically everyone knew that Goldwater opposed the act and that Johnson favored it (RePass 1971). These are extraordinary figures: public perceptions are seldom so clear, and the electoral hazards of clarity—Goldwater *was* slaughtered—have not been lost on the consultants and pollsters who seem increasingly to be in charge of campaigns (and administrations) these days. Still, it is worth keeping in mind that if candidates can be coaxed (or compelled) into presenting their differences, a significant fraction of the public seems capable of appreciating them.

A second example concerns public understanding of congressional candidates, who, compared to their colleagues competing for the presidency, toil for the most part in utter darkness. Immediately following midterm elections, for example, fewer than one in four Americans can recall something about the major party candidates that have just run for the House in their district (Pierce and Converse 1981). That's the way

5. Keeping in mind that what counts as an available change is in part up for political grabs.

things usually are. But every now and then, things can be quite different. A case in point is the 1958 campaign in the Fifth District of Arkansas. There the incumbent representative had become entangled in the federal government's effort to resolve the Little Rock school desegregation crisis. Hardly an integrationist, the incumbent was nevertheless effectively portrayed as soft on civil rights and was defeated in a write-in campaign by a local hero of Southern resistance. In the Fifth District in 1958, *every* voter claimed to know *both* candidates (Miller and Stokes 1966).

Thus, the melancholy indictment of the American public as "wretchedly informed" need not hold always, everywhere. Whatever hurdles stand in the way of informing the public can be overcome, given the right set of circumstances. Of course, the right set of circumstances may not come along very often. And what voters do with the information once it is in their possession is another matter. In the Fifth District in 1958, they swept a racist into office. This is democracy at work, a discussion (we can presume) really took place, the people got what they wanted (i.e., those who were eligible to vote, in part because of the pale color of their skin). Somehow, though, it is an episode hard to celebrate. Discussion is a necessary but insufficient condition for democratic practice.

What about the claim of ideological innocence, which we regard as a less serious liability for democratic discussion? Many critics argued that Converse's conclusions ignored politics, that his analysis paid too little attention to the nature of campaigns and public debate. According to this line of criticism, the quality and sophistication of citizens' understanding of politics mirrors the quality and sophistication of the public debate that they witness. Furnish Americans with a conspicuously ideological politics, and they are perfectly capable of responding in kind.

Certainly the critics have had time on their side. Surely Converse's conclusions reflected in part the comparatively tranquil Eisenhower years, a period of political recovery from the intense ideological debates of the New Deal and from the collective trauma of the Great Depression and world war. Surely the original claim must be modified given the events that have shattered national tranquillity since.

The short answer is no. The long answer is long and complicated, and we have neither the time nor the heart to plow through all the details (for the details, see Kinder 1983; Luskin 1987; Smith 1989). Suffice it to say here that Converse's original claim of ideological innocence stands up reasonably well, both to detailed reanalysis and to political change. Indeed, in some respects, the claim is strengthened. *Despite* the boisterous events, panoramic changes, and ideological debates that have punctuated American politics over the last quarter century, most citizens continue to be mystified by or at least indifferent to standard ideological terminology; most continue, as Lane put it, to "morselize" the items and fragments of political life (Lane 1962, 353). We turn, then, to another question. Does ideological innocence preclude rational democratic discussion? Or is there room for rationality even if we concede the lion's share of Converse's case?

Enough Already About Ideology

The great debate over ideology, which took over the study of American public opinion over the last twenty-five years, has taught us more about how Americans *do not* think about politics than about how they *do*. This is a lesson of basic importance for our understanding of public opinion, and one with real practical application. It leads us, for example, to doubt sweeping claims about the American public's embrace of liberalism in the 1960s or the public's supposedly sharp movement to the right during the Reagan years. Detailed and careful investigations reveal, as we would expect, that public opinion actually moved in various ideological directions at once (Gold 1992; Schuman et al. 1985). Although ideological innocence is an important conclusion (especially in light of newly elected leaders' persistence in claiming an ideological mandate), it does not tell us anything in detail about how Americans do in fact participate in democratic discussion.

From this vantage point, a welcome recent development in the study of public opinion has been the investigation of foundations for political belief other than ideology. In the absence of ideological principles, perhaps everyday thinking about politics is determined by the pursuit of self-interest or by the perception of group conflict or by various prejudices and solidarities or by the values Americans embrace, the belief in equality or individualism or limited government. Much of this research follows directly in Converse's footsteps, in the sense that the proper subject of investigation is taken to be the nature of belief systems as a whole. The difference, of course, is that in place of ideology is substituted some other "master idea"—individualism, say. Another and complementary line of empirical analysis attempts to understand public opinion not in general terms but in a particular domain, on a particular topic. By abandoning an analysis of belief *systems*, this approach is necessarily less panoramic and sweeping than the analysis Converse provided. Such work includes research on Americans' willingness to extend political rights to groups they despise (Sullivan et al. 1982), on the American public's view toward relations with the Soviet Union (Hurwitz and Peffley 1987), and on Americans' reactions to affirmative action policies (Kinder and Sanders 1987, 1990). In each of these quite different cases, empirical work has been able to uncover a solid foundation for opinion. The discovery here is not of nonattitudes but of real attitudes, reasonably structured and well embedded in a set of relevant considerations. Public opinion on affirmative action, for example, appears to reflect in systematic ways views on equality and individualism, the expected consequences of affirmative action for family and group, and strongly felt prejudice against affirmative action's intended beneficiaries. Such findings go some distance toward relieving the gloominess that surrounded Converse's original conclusion.

But if public opinion is more intelligible and better structured than Converse's analysis implied, some of the considerations that provide the intelligibility and structure are deplorable. For example, political intolerance has its roots in personal distress and insecurity—in the "psychological burdens of freedom," as Lane (1962) put it. For example, the American public's view toward the Soviet Union was powerfully conditioned by an informationally impoverished response to the symbol of Communism. An important ingredient in whites' opposition to affirmative action programs, probably the most important, is racial prejudice. That public opinion is real does not make it, or the democratic form of government that it shapes, necessarily laudable.

Furthermore, the view of public opinion that we are promoting here—public opinion as a systematic reflection of interests, social attachments and hatreds, and American values—carries with it two potential problems for democratic discussion. First is the problem of *diversity*. Virtually all the empirical results on public opinion assume and address that most hypothetical of creatures, "the average American." Research on political tolerance, like research on U.S.-Soviet relations or on affirmative action, tells just one story, with a single protagonist. This inclination in public opinion research to treat Americans as if they were homogeneous and interchangeable, which is of great statistical convenience, should be resisted. Average results may be quite misleading, disguising "population heterogeneity in much the same way census averages describing the 'average' family as having 2.5 children do: one has trouble finding an average family" (Rivers 1988).

Whether diversity is taken into account in research or, as is more often the case, obliterated, the sheer fact of diversity could spell trouble for democratic discussion. If Americans turned out to be vastly different from one another in ways that were consequential for how they arrived at their views on public issues, then democratic discussion might prove impossible. At the extreme, each of us would possess a private language of politics. We might all be speaking to the same topic—whether government restrictions on abortion should be tightened or relaxed, say—but in ways that our fellow citizens would find quite incomprehensible.

This goes too far. Americans are amazingly diverse, but not all differences count for politics. If this were the case, our "average" results would not be as systematic or powerful as they are. Such results are incompatible with the strong version of diversity: namely, that the American public consists of millions of individual citizens, each operating off an idiosyncratic logic. Moreover, those (regrettably few) studies that have directly investigated the possibility that different kinds of Americans come to their views on politics in fundamentally different ways, often conclude that they do not. Differences marked by education or information or social class or ideas about how the economy works generally do not require a proliferation of qualitatively different models of public opinion. This line of research typically uncovers differences of degree, not kind (see, e.g., Feldman 1982; Stimson 1975; Rivers 1988; Kinder and Mebane 1983; Zaller 1992). Such results, provisional as they are, seem from our angle to be good news: we see no evidence to indicate that diversity precludes democratic discussion.

A companion to the problem of diversity is the problem of *complexity*. If, as we maintain, public opinion is structured by a complex amalgam of interests, attachments, hatreds, and values, is democratic conversation impossible? Does such complexity mean that elites and masses are doomed to talk past each other, the former employing an ideological vocabulary destined to sail past the latter?

Not necessarily. Consider the work of Gamson and his colleagues (Gamson and Lasch 1983; Gamson and Modigliani 1987) on the concept of frame, which holds out both a promise and a threat to democratic conversation. In their account of the public discourse that surrounds political issues, Gamson and Modigliani (1987, 143) portray a frame as "a central organizing idea or story line that provides meaning to an unfolding strip of events, weaving a connection among them. The frame suggests what the controversy is about, the essence of the issue." Frames consist of metaphors, exemplars, catchphrases, depictions, and visual images; they often include a rudimentary causal analysis and appeals to honored principles. We believe that frames lead a double life: that they are structures of the mind that impose order and meaning on the problems of society and that they are interpretive structures embedded in political discourse (Kinder and Sanders 1990). At both levels, frames provide narrations for social problems. Frames tell stories about how problems come to be and what (if anything) needs to be done about them.

The good news here is that frames appear to provide a common vocabulary, one that enables elites and citizens to speak clearly to one another. Take, for example, the controversial issue of affirmative action. Gamson and Modigliani (1987) describe how elites in the United States have framed the debate on affirmative action and how the debate has evolved over the past fifteen years. To identify elite frames, they examined the opinions of Supreme Court justices in pivotal cases, *amicus curiae* briefs, speeches and statements delivered by prominent public officials, and the views expressed in various political journals. Gamson and Modigliani then went on to trace changes in each frame's prominence from 1969 to 1984 by examining national news magazines, network news programs, editorial cartoons, and syndicated opinion columns. According to Gamson and Modigliani's analysis, supporters of affirmative action have typically defended their position throughout this period by referring to the need for "remedial action." Under this frame, race-conscious programs are required to offset the continuing pernicious effects of America's long history of racial discrimination. On the other side of the issue, opponents of affirmative action began by arguing that affirmative action constituted "unfair advantage." This frame questions whether rewards should be allocated on the basis of race and expresses the particular concern that blacks are being handed advantages that they do not deserve. Unfair advantage has gradually given way among elite opponents of affirmative action to "reverse discrimination." Like unfair advantage, reverse discrimination questions whether rewards should be allocated on the basis of race, but this time by raising the particular concern whether the rights of whites must be sacrificed in order to advance the interests of blacks. The important and in certain respects, uplifting point here is that elite frames are widely comprehensible to mass publics: they were created, in part, with this aim explicitly in mind. Through frames, democratic discussion between leaders and citizens seems quite unproblematic.

On the other hand, the creation of artful frames enhances the possibility for manipulation. By sponsoring and promoting rival opinion frames, political elites may alter how issues are understood and, as a consequence, what opinion turns out to be (Kinder and Sanders 1990). We don't mean to suggest that *either* democratic discussion is bloodless, gentlemanly, and overintellectualized *or else* it's passionate, manipulative, and irrational. The introduction of a symbol, even a deliberately created symbol, doesn't itself show that something has gone wrong. Nor does the presence of passion, even stridency. Symbols and emotions aren't the enemies of cognition, or anyway, they aren't necessarily its enemies. Typically democratic discussion is at once rational and emotional, at once a matter of the manipulations of interest and the sorting out of sensible positions on public policy. And that's fine. Our worry about the nefarious possibilities of framing is just that they can become freewheeling exercises in pure manipulation.

Elections as Government by Discussion

Elections do not a democracy make—not even free, fair, and frequent elections. But we need not repeat Schumpeter's (1942) mistake to insist that elections play a special role in democracy and so deserve special attention here. The campaigns that lead up to election day constitute an opportunity for candidates and parties to make their case to the voters. And on election day itself, voters are provided the opportunity to "talk back." What can we say here about how voters make up their minds that bears on the quality of democratic conversation?

It should come as no surprise to learn that voting is seldom driven by ideological concerns. This discovery, like the parallel discovery in the study of public opinion, is no ground for democratic despair. Moreover, recent developments in scholarship on voters and elections suggest several grounds for optimism. We take up three here: the ongoing reassessment of the meaning of party identification, the apparent resurgence of issue-based voting, and the powerful inclination among voters to punish incumbents when things go bad.

Party identification revisited. According to *The American Voter*, identification with one of the major parties typically begins in childhood. Such identifications grow stronger but rarely change through the course of adult life. To Campbell et al. (1960), party identification was a standing commitment, a "persistent adherence," one that lent order and stability to a complicated and ever-changing political world:

> To the average person the affairs of government are remote and complex, and yet the average citizen is asked periodically to formulate opinions about these affairs. At the very least he has to decide how he will vote, what choice he will make between candidates offering different programs and very different versions of contemporary political events. In this dilemma, having the party symbol stamped on certain candidates, certain issue positions, certain interpretations of political reality is of great psychological convenience. (Stokes 1966a, 126–27)

This may be convenient for the individual citizen, and it may even mean that democratic discussion is fixed to familiar anchoring points—those provided by the parties. But the preeminence of party identification in the voter's calculus is also troubling for democratic discussion. Mechanical attachment to a party, formed in childhood, seems on the face of it rather discouraging to democratic prospects. It suggests that insofar as campaigns are discussions, no one is really listening: virtually everyone made up their minds long ago.

But this interpretation of party identification has in recent years been vigorously challenged. The central theme here is that party identification should be regarded not as a standing decision, a residue of childhood learning, but, as Fiorina (1977, 618) put it, a "running balance sheet on the two parties." As it happens, party identification is not immovable. The loyalty citizens invest in the parties is at least partly conditioned by what the parties *do*. The Democratic and Republican parties are judged by the candidates they nominate (Markus and Converse 1979; Jennings and Markus 1984); the policy proposals they promote (Jackson 1975;

Franklin and Jackson 1983); the peace, prosperity, and domestic tranquillity that they manage to deliver (Fiorina 1981; Kinder and Kiewiet 1981); and the company they keep, as in the political realignment of the American South over the last quarter century (Grofman et al. 1988). Party identification is not merely a blind attachment left over from childhood; it has real political content; it accommodates history.

We should not press this too far, however. Although party identification does respond to the grand events of the day, it does so sluggishly. A deep and sustained "Democratic recession" may weaken the loyalties of the rank and file, but very few will actually abandon their party and cross over to the other side. In this respect, the metaphor of the running balance sheet is misleading. Party identification remains a durable attachment, one not easily relinquished and one that presumably operates both to curtail democratic discussion and to fix it to familiar anchoring points.

The possibility of issue-based voting. Citizens who weigh public policy in their electoral decisions are often commended for their civic responsibility. By supporting candidates whose views on public policy most resemble their own, such citizens supposedly contribute to the formation of policy itself. But according to Converse's diagnosis, the typical voter seemed ill prepared to make such a contribution. Remember that many citizens confessed to having no opinion on policy questions, and some substantial fraction of those who claimed to have an opinion seemed to do so capriciously. Moreover, as revealed in *The American Voter*, few seemed to know current government policy; many thought the parties did not differ appreciably in the policies they advocated. In light of these results, Campbell et al. (1960) concluded that opinions on specific matters of policy ordinarily play a modest role in presidential elections.

This conclusion provoked a strong reaction. Beginning with V. O. Key's posthumously published volume, *The Responsible Electorate* (1966), a major preoccupation of research on voting has been to rehabilitate the ordinary citizen by demonstrating that policy voting is in fact more widespread than originally alleged in *The American Voter*. Succinctly put, Key's argument was that voters were no more foolish than the political choices they confronted; if provided clear alternatives, voters were perfectly capable of being "moved by concern about central and relevant questions of public policy" (1966, 7–8).

And so they are. Clarity about policy differences in the voter's mind does indeed depend on the clarity of the choices available (Pomper 1972). More important, when confronted with real differences, voters take them into account. Policy voting waxes and wanes according to the clarity and aggressiveness with which rival candidates push alternative programs (Nie et al. 1979; Rosenstone 1983).

A clinching demonstration of this point—and its limitations—is provided by Page and Brody's (1972) analysis of the 1968 presidential campaign. They discovered that late in the campaign, opinions on Vietnam policy correlated trivially with voters' comparative assessment of the major party candidates. Page and Brody blamed this result not on voters but on Hubert Humphrey and Richard Nixon's near total failure to articulate alternative policies for voters to choose between. In contrast, voting in a hypothetical election pitting Eugene McCarthy against George Wallace reflected voters' opinions on Vietnam policy much more faithfully (see also Converse et al. 1969). However—and here is evidence on the limits to policy voting—despite the clarity and extremity of the positions on Vietnam staked out by McCarthy and Wallace, confusion on these matters in the general public was nonetheless widespread. In mid-August, only about two-thirds of the public were able to assign positions to McCarthy and to Wallace, of whom less than one-half placed McCarthy to the left of Wallace. Thus, rival candidates who differ on important matters and say so clearly and conspicuously will certainly encourage policy voting—but many voters will never notice.

Throwing the rascals out. This brings us at last to those voters who, when times go bad, seem quite willing to evict incumbents from office. Bad things happen to incumbents who preside over recessions, scandals, international humiliations, domestic turmoil, and the like. Presidents, senators, and governors seeking reelection have much to fear from the voters' inclination to throw the rascals out (see, e.g., Chubb 1988; Fiorina 1981; Kramer 1971; Tufte 1978; Rosenstone 1983).[6]

At first glance, this seems a welcome result: elections become a device, though a crude and retrospective one, for shaping government action.

6. Incumbent members of the U.S. House are another matter. It is not that House incumbents are immune to national tides (see, e.g., Kramer 1971; Tufte 1978); it is that incumbent members of the House, when faced with national tides running against them, can compensate through their ability to monopolize resources and deliver benefits to their district. These days, House incumbents are virtually undefeatable (Jacobson 1987).

Public officials bent on reelection then "have strong incentives to anticipate their constituents' reactions to the social and economic conditions that result from government actions" (Fiorina 1981, 201). Of course, voters asserting that they don't like what's happened during the preceding administration is not the same thing as giving detailed instructions on what the new administration should do. But such imprecision actually has a certain advantage, as Fiorina points out, "It lays no policy constraint on the governing administration; rather, the government is free to innovate, knowing that it will be judged on the results of its actions rather than their specifics. In a word, the accountability generated by a retrospective voting electorate and reaction anticipating politicians provides latitude for political leadership" (Fiorina 1981, 201).

The pervasiveness of this simple reward-punish calculus leaves wide open the important questions how and how *well* voters decide whether a government's record has been glorious or abysmal or merely ordinary. One possible answer is supplied by the self-interest hypothesis: perhaps voters examine their own circumstances first. Voters motivated by self-interest support candidates and parties that have advanced their own interests and reject candidates and parties that have impeded their own interests. A political calculus based entirely on such private calculations would of course substantially reduce the costs that are normally incurred by becoming informed about the world of politics—costs that Lippmann, Downs, Converse, and many others insist the voter is very reluctant to pay.[7]

The self-interest answer is appealing to many—but not to Mill. Mill would have reviled the "realistic" thought that voters are out to maximize their self-interest. Market rationality isn't what Mill's conception requires. The news that voters are out to maximize their self-interest would have struck him as a fatal blow to democratic politics; voters must pursue instead the common good or sound public policy.

Thus, Mill would have welcomed the news that the self-interest hypothesis has fared poorly in a variety of empirical tests. The electoral effects associated with personal economic well-being appear to be quite modest and seem confined for the most part to that usually small

7. Why concede so readily that learning about politics counts as a cost? It's odd for political scientists, who themselves pore over daily newspapers and the like, to talk—and think—this way. Here again, we would insist on the prior place of identity and social practices; given other attachments, other practices, people might see learning about politics as a calling, not a chore.

minority of voters who see a connection between their own economic predicament and broader economic trends in the country as a whole (e.g., Feldman 1982; Fiorina 1981; Kinder and Kiewiet 1981; Kinder et al. 1989; Lewis-Beck 1988; Sears et al. 1980; Markus 1988).[8]

A second possibility is that voters pay attention not so much to their own problems and achievements when they reach their political decisions as to the problems and achievements of the country—the "sociotropic hypothesis" (Kinder and Kiewiet 1981). Whereas self-interested voters ask the incumbent, What have you done for *me* lately? sociotropic voters ask, What have you done for the *nation* lately? Voters seem in fact to resemble this sociotropic creature, responding to changes in general economic conditions much more than to changes in the circumstances of personal economic life, in the United States and in Western Europe alike (see, e.g., Feldman 1982; Kinder and Kiewiet 1981; Kinder et al. 1989; Lewis-Beck 1988).

At one level, the sociotropic result can be construed to mean that some significant portion of the electorate is sensible (perhaps even rational). That is, in making political decisions, citizens tend to rely on information about the economy as a whole, instead of information about their own idiosyncratic experiences. But how well do they do this? Perhaps voters can be bamboozled about the real state of the country. They may know very well what has happened to themselves and their families, but as we've seen, such clear-eyed perceptions seem not to matter very much for their political decisions. Assessments of the nation's vitality do not have the same grounding in everyday experience. Edelman (1988) for one, contends that the public's beliefs about government success and failure are among the most arbitrary of political constructions: "Assessing governmental performance is not at all like evaluating the plumber by checking whether the faucet still drips. Officials construct tests that show success, just as their opponents construct other tests that show failure. The higher the office the more certain that judgments of performance depend upon efforts to influence interpretations by suggesting which observations are pertinent, which irrelevant, and what both mean" (41). Edelman reminds us that the sociotropic calculus is subject to manipulation and distortion, that there

8. If voters were motivated by self-interest alone, it would of course never occur to them to vote. That millions do so in the face of this strong prediction is a perpetual embarrassment to economic styles of explanation, as Barry (1970) noted many years ago.

is no necessary correspondence between the public's diagnosis and the actual health and vitality of the nation.

That voters are sociotropic is promising: it means they may be capable of shouldering Mill's burden of relegating concern with mere self-interest and thinking about (something like) the common good. But we'd like to know more. Given a more detailed account of sociotropic voting, will Mill's account be adequate? Or (as we suspect) will it need sharpening, recasting, more nuance? Perhaps we should emphasize yet again that it is not appropriate to adjust our normative standards so they fit whatever the facts are. Maybe it will turn out that current sociotropic voters aren't good enough.

The Miracle of Aggregation

If the public is "that miscellaneous collection of a few wise and many foolish individuals," as Mill maintained, the public *as a whole* may behave quite wisely. This can happen in part through the sheer mechanical process of statistical aggregation, the law of large numbers applied to public opinion. Aggregating from individuals to the public as a whole drives out the noisiness that is so visible to analysts of individual opinion. The signal that emerges from the miracle of aggregation, as Converse calls it, may be determined disproportionately by the relative handful of citizens who are paying careful attention. Thus, it is quite possible "to arrive at a highly rational system performance on the backs of voters most of whom are remarkably ill-informed much of the time" (Converse 1990; see also Converse 1975, 135; McKelvey and Ordeshook 1990).

The citizenry may behave wisely, even if made up largely of foolish citizens, also because of what Page and Shapiro call *social aggregation*, a phrase that is meant to point to the division of political labor in society:

> Experts and researchers and government officials learn new things about the political world. They make discoveries and analyze and interpret new events. These analysts pass along their ideas and interpretations to commentators and other opinion leaders, who in turn communicate with the general public directly through newspapers, magazines, and television and indirectly through

> social networks of families, friends, and coworkers. Members of the public think and talk among themselves and often talk back to elites, questioning, criticizing, and selecting ideas that are useful. Most citizens never acquire much detailed information about politics, but they do pay attention to and think about media reports and friends' accounts of what commentators, officials, and trusted experts are saying the government should do. And they tend to form and change their policy preferences accordingly.
>
> As a result, new information and ideas can affect collective public opinion even when most members of the public have no detailed knowledge of them. Even when most individuals are ill informed, collective public opinion can react fully and sensibly to events, ideas, or discoveries. (this volume, 42)

If this seems Panglossian, it is. Are experts and officials really so determined to turn up the "truth"? Is it reasonable to assume that most members of the public who know so little nevertheless hang on the words of friends for advice about what the government should do? Even in a society featuring an efficient division of political labor, can the public really be expected to react *fully* to new information? Well, no.

Still, statistical and social aggregation together can work wonders. A particularly illuminating illustration of this can be found in research devoted to explaining fluctuations in public support for the president. This is an important topic, not least because popular support is a vital political resource, perhaps the president's single most important base of power (Neustadt 1960; Rivers and Rose 1985; Ostrom and Simon 1985). We now know that a president's support depends upon the prevailing economic, social, and political conditions of the times. Unemployment, inflation, economic growth, flagrant violations of public trust, the human toll of war, international crises, dramatic displays of presidential authority—all these affect the president's standing in the public at large (Hibbs et al. 1982a, 1982b; Kernell 1978; MacKuen 1983; Ostrom and Simon 1985). These results suggest a certain reasonableness of public opinion *in the aggregate* to conspicuous events on the national and international stage.

Much the same conclusion emerges from the study of elections. Although the typical voter seems ill informed, the typical *electorate* seems to behave as if it were well informed. For example, Feld and

Grofman (1988) have shown that the electorate can express preferences among candidates exactly congruent with an ideological ordering, despite the fact that a large fraction of the voters who constitute the electorate express preferences that are ideologically incoherent. This result—ideological consistency as a collective phenomenon, a kind of Arrow's paradox running in the opposite direction—may hold not only for the electorate as a whole but for most major social groups as well. Feld and Grofman argue that "it is a 'fallacy of composition' to believe that collective decision making will be ideological *only* when all or most members of the collectivity, as individuals, are ideological" (774).

Change in electoral outcomes from one contest to the next—again, an aggregate phenomenon—displays the same kind of coherence. Such change seems provoked primarily by the emergence of new candidates and by alterations in national circumstances (see, e.g., Stokes 1966b; Popkin et al. 1976; Rosenstone 1983; Markus 1988; Kramer 1971). The overriding point for our purposes is that electoral change appears to be both intelligible—see especially Rosenstone's (1983) model's ability to *predict* presidential election outcomes months before they happen—and sensible. Voters in the aggregate behave as though a real discussion had taken place.[9]

The results on presidential popularity and on election outcome are quite representative of the empirical returns from a wide range of inquiry into the dynamics of public opinion taken as a collectivity. During the last fifteen years, there has been an explosion of research of this sort: on the American public's attachment to political parties (Converse 1976), support for racial integration (Schuman et al. 1985), opposition to war (Mueller 1973), support for government policy (Page and Shapiro 1988), assessments of the national economy (Markus and Kinder 1988), and more. A very general conclusion across such investigations is how finely responsive public opinion is to social, economic, and political change. Viewed from this vantage point, public opinion looks extremely sensible, reasonable, perhaps even rational (Page and Shapiro 1989).

The construction of a rational public in this fashion is certainly possible, but not foolproof. The claim for aggregation has an illustrious

9. This kind of intelligibility, we grant, can also be taken as a threat to democratic debate. For it can be (mis-?)read as suggesting that campaigns make no difference, that all that talk is surface blather, obscuring our view of the deep causal mechanisms, like economic growth, that really drive election outcomes.

history: roughly parallel arguments litter the history of political thought. The miracle of aggregation is reminiscent of Condorcet's jury theorem. It may well be what Rousseau had in mind in a notoriously obscure passage in *The Social Contract* about the pluses and minuses canceling out in voting. And it must be what Madison was hoping for in thinking that after public opinion was refined and filtered by large districts, indirect elections, and the like, republican devotion to the common good would outweigh the din of faction.

Like their modern counterparts, these arguments are tempting, but they're all a bit too convenient. Put in terms of signal and noise, the essential problem is that the noise we want to drown out may not be random; it may instead be systematic, structured by cynical television advertisements, appeals to racism, and the like. There's no reason a priori to expect that these various forces will neatly cancel themselves out. In fact, the noise may add up to a tightly unified signal that will drown the signal we're interested in. It is—no surprise here—an empirical question how often aggregation produces miracles. Perhaps the answer is frequently. But it is wise to remember that aggregation is no magical mechanism that somehow guarantees systematic rationality on the backs of ignorant and confused voters.

Blue Sky and Clouds of Disillusioning Facts

"Democracy," wrote Mencken, "is the art and science of running the circus from the monkey-cage." Or, for those who like their theory formal, "If x is the population of the United States and y is the degree of imbecility of the average American, then democracy is the theory that $x \times y$ is less than y." Such sentiments tempt not just cynics but those anguished by the undeniable shortcomings of the American citizen—and of American politics. But are they justified?

Not completely. Granted, there is much that Americans just flatly don't know about politics, and their ignorance does indeed threaten the very possibility of government by discussion. The bleak results of Converse and others can't be lightly dismissed. But as we've discovered here, citizens are capable of expressing real opinions on government policy, opinions that are systematically rooted in their interests, social attachments, and political values. Citizens sometimes think sensibly about politics, and in the right context, they can learn quite a bit, quite rapidly, about the candidates who compete for their support. Broadly speaking, many voters seem to behave in reasonable ways, given the discourse and choices they are presented: they reassess their attachments to party in light of political, economic, and social change; they select the candidate that more closely resembles their own views on policy, the more so on those comparatively rare occasions when opposing candidates actually stake out alternative positions; and they are quite prepared to evict incumbents from office when, as they see it, things have run downhill on their watch. And however ill informed and eccentric individual voters may seem, through the miracle of aggregation, the public as a whole may often behave quite sensibly.

Those content with bleak conclusions seem to us sadly mistaken about the problems and possibilities of democratic politics. Theories of democracy that focus on preference aggregation or the pluralistic clash of interests are portraits of a polity in trouble, not any kind of ideal worth affirming. The real hope lies in reforming our politics and practices, not in lowering our aspirations. Given what passes for democratic debate these days, we shouldn't be too surprised by the bleak empirical findings—by the clouds of disillusioning facts. Still, it is not difficult to discern patches of blue sky, and not utopian to press for more.

References

Achen, Christopher H. 1975. "Mass Political Attitudes and the Survey Response." *American Political Science Review* 69:1218–31.

Barber, Benjamin. 1984. *Strong Democracy.* Berkeley and Los Angeles: University of California Press.

Barry, Brian. 1970. *Sociologists, Economists, and Democracy.* Chicago: University of Chicago Press.

Brehm, John. 1989. "How Survey Nonresponse Damages Political Analysis." Paper presented at the annual meeting of the American Political Science Association, Atlanta, Georgia.

Brody, Charles J. 1986. "Things Are Rarely Black and White: Admitting Gray into the Converse Model of Attitude Stability." *American Journal of Sociology* 92:657–77.

Campbell, Angus, Philip E. Converse, Warren E. Miller, and Donald E. Stokes. 1960. *The American Voter.* New York: Wiley.

Chubb, John E. 1988. "Institutions, the Economy, and the Dynamics of State Elections." *American Political Science Review* 82:133–54.

Cohen, Joshua, and Joel Rogers. 1983. *On Democracy*. New York: Penguin.

Converse, Philip E. 1964. "The Nature of Belief Systems in Mass Publics." In *Ideology and Discontent*, ed. David E. Apter, 206–61. New York: Free Press.

———. 1970. "Attitudes and Non-attitudes: Continuation of a Dialogue." In *The Quantitative Analysis of Social Problems*, ed. Edward R. Tufte, 168–89. Reading, Mass.: Addison-Wesley.

———. 1975. "Public Opinion and Voting Behavior." In *Handbook of Political Science*, ed. Fred I. Greenstein and Nelson Polsby, 4:75–168. Reading, Mass.: Addison-Wesley.

———. 1976. *The Dynamics of Party Support: Cohort-Analyzing Party Identification*. Beverly Hills, Calif.: Sage Publications.

———. 1990. "Popular Representation and the Distribution of Information." In *Information and Democratic Process*, ed. James Kuklinski and John Ferejohn, 369–88. Urbana: University of Illinois Press.

Converse, Philip E., and Gregory B. Markus. 1979. "Plus ça change . . . : The New CPS Election Study Panel." *American Political Science Review* 73:32–49.

Converse, Philip E., Warren E. Miller, Jerrold G. Rusk, and Arthur C. Wolfe. 1969. "Continuity and Change in American Politics: Parties and Issues in the 1968 Election." *American Political Science Review* 63:1083–1105.

Converse, Philip E., and Roy Pierce. 1986. *Political Representation in France*. Cambridge, Mass.: Harvard University Press.

Dewey, John. [1927] 1952. *The Public and Its Problems*. Columbus: Ohio State University Press.

Edelman, Murray. 1988. *Constructing the Political Spectacle*. Chicago: University of Chicago Press.

Erikson, Robert S. 1979. "The SRC Panel Data and Mass Political Attitudes." *British Journal of Political Science* 9:89–114.

Feld, Scott L., and Bernard Grofman. 1988. "Ideological Consistency as a Collective Phenomenon." *American Political Science Review* 82:773–88.

Feldman, Stanley. 1982. "Economic Self-Interest and Political Behavior." *American Journal of Political Science* 26:446–66.

Fiorina, Morris P. 1977. "An Outline for a Model of Party Choice." *American Journal of Political Science* 21:601–26.

———. 1981. *Retrospective Voting in American National Elections*. New Haven: Yale University Press.

Franklin, Charles H., and John E. Jackson. 1983. "The Dynamics of Party Identification." *American Political Science Review* 77:957–73.

Gamson, William A., and K. E. Lasch. 1983. "The Political Culture of Social Welfare Policy." In *Evaluating the Welfare State*, ed. S. E. Spiro and E. Yuchtman-Yaar, 397–415. New York: Academic Press.

Gamson, William A., and Andre Modigliani. 1987. "The Changing Culture of Affirmative Action." In *Research in Political Sociology*, ed. Richard D. Braungart, 3:137–77. Greenwich, Conn.: JAI Press.

Gold, Howard J. 1992. *Hollow Mandates: American Public Opinion and the Conservative Shift*. New Haven: Yale University Press.

Grofman, Bernard, Amihai Glazer, and Lisa Handley. 1988. "Three Variations on a

Theme by V. O. Key." Paper delivered at the annual meeting of the American Political Science Association, Washington, D.C.

Hibbs, Donald A., Jr., R. Douglas Rivers, and Nicholas Vasilatos. 1982a. "The Dynamics of Political Support for American Presidents Among Occupational and Partisan Groups." *American Journal of Political Science* 26:312–32.

———. 1982b. "On the Demand for Economic Outcomes: Macroeconomic Performance and Mass Political Support in the United States, Great Britain, and Europe." *Journal of Political Science* 44:426–62.

Hurwitz, John, and Mark Peffley. 1987. "How Are Foreign Policy Attitudes Structured?" *American Political Science Review* 81:1099–1120.

Jacobson, Gary C. 1987. *The Politics of Congressional Elections*. 2d ed. Boston: Little, Brown.

Jackson, John E. 1975. "Issues, Party Choices, and Presidential Votes." *American Journal of Political Science* 19:161–85.

Jennings, M. Kent, and Gregory B. Markus. 1984. "Partisan Orientation over the Long Haul." *American Political Science Review* 78:1000–1018.

Kernell, Samuel. 1978. "Explaining Presidential Popularity." *American Political Science Review* 72:506–22.

Key, V. O., Jr. 1966. *The Responsible Electorate*. Cambridge, Mass.: Harvard University Press.

Kinder, Donald R. 1983. "Diversity and Complexity in American Public Opinion." In *The State of the Discipline*, ed. Ada Finifter, 389–425. Washington, D.C.: American Political Science Association.

Kinder, Donald R., Gordon S. Adams, and Paul W. Gronke. 1989. "Economics and Politics in the 1984 American Presidential Election." *American Journal of Political Science* 33:491–515.

Kinder, Donald R., and D. Roderick Kiewiet. 1981. "Sociotropic Politics." *British Journal of Political Science* 11:129–61.

Kinder, Donald R., and Walter R. Mebane, Jr. 1983. "Politics and Economics in Everyday Life." In *The Political Process and Economic Change*, ed. Kristi R. Monroe, 141–80. New York: Agathon.

Kinder, Donald R., and Laurie A. Rhodebeck. 1982. "Continuities in Support for Racial Equality, 1972 to 1976." *Public Opinion Quarterly* 46:195–215.

Kinder, Donald R., and Lynn M. Sanders. 1987. "Pluralistic Foundations of American Opinion on Race." Paper delivered at the annual meeting of the American Political Science Association, Chicago.

———. 1990. "Mimicking Political Debate with Survey Questions: The Case of White Opinion on Affirmative Action for Blacks." *Social Cognition* 8:73–103.

Kramer, Gerald H. 1971. "Short-term Fluctuations in U.S. Voting Behavior, 1896–1964." *American Political Science Review* 65:131–43.

Lane, Robert E. 1962. *Political Ideology*. New York: Free Press.

———. 1973. "Patterns of Political Belief." In *Handbook of Political Psychology*, ed. Jeanne Knutson, 83–116. San Francisco: Jossey-Bass.

Lewis-Beck, Michael S. 1988. *Economics and Elections*. Ann Arbor: University of Michigan Press.

Lippmann, Walter. 1922. *Public Opinion*. New York: Macmillan.
———. 1925. *The Phantom Public*. New York: Harcourt, Brace.
Luker, Kristin. 1984. *Abortion and the Politics of Motherhood*. Berkeley and Los Angeles: University of California Press.
Luskin, Robert C. 1987. "Measuring Political Sophistication." *American Journal of Political Science* 25:617–45.
McKelvey, Richard, and Peter Ordeshook. 1990. "Information and Elections: Retrospective Voting and Rational Expectations." In *Information and Democratic Process*, ed. James Kuklinski and John Ferejohn, 281–312. Urbana: University of Illinois Press.
MacKuen, Michael. 1983. "Political Drama, Economic Conditions, and the Dynamics of Presidential Popularity." *American Journal of Political Science* 27:165–92.
Markus, Gregory B. 1988. "The Impact of Personal and National Economic Conditions on the Presidential Vote." *American Journal of Political Science* 32:137–54.
Markus, Gregory B., and Philip E. Converse. 1979. "A Dynamic Simultaneous Equation Model of Electoral Choice." *American Political Science Review* 73:1055–70.
Markus, Gregory B., and Donald R. Kinder. 1988. "Reality and Perception in Economic Assessments." Paper delivered at the annual meeting of the American Political Science Association, Washington, D.C.
Mill, John Stuart. [1861] 1951a. *Considerations on Representative Government*. In *Three Essays*. Oxford: Oxford University Press.
———. [1859] 1951b. *On Liberty*. In *Three Essays*. Oxford: Oxford University Press.
Miller, Warren E., and Donald E. Stokes. 1966. "Party Government and the Saliency of Government." In *Elections and the Political Order*, ed. Angus Campbell, Philip E. Converse, Warren E. Miller, and Donald E. Stokes, 194–211. New York: Wiley.
Mueller, John E. 1973. *War, Presidents, and Public Opinion*. New York: Wiley.
Neustadt, Richard E. 1960. *Presidential Power: The Politics of Leadership*. New York: Wiley.
Nie, Norman H., Sidney Verba, and John R. Petrocik. 1979. *The Changing American Voter*. Enlarged ed. Cambridge, Mass.: Harvard University Press.
Ostrom, Charles W., and Dennis M. Simon. 1985. "Promise and Performance: A Dynamic Model of Presidential Popularity." *American Political Science Review* 79:334–58.
Page, Benjamin I. 1978. *Choices and Echoes in Presidential Elections*. Chicago: University of Chicago Press.
Page, Benjamin I., and Richard A. Brody. 1972. "Policy Voting and the Electoral Process: The Vietnam War Issues." *American Political Science Review* 66:979–95.
Page, Benjamin I., and Robert Y. Shapiro. 1988. "Democracy, Information, and the Rational Public." Paper delivered at the annual meeting of the American Political Science Association, Washington, D.C.

———. 1989. "The Rational Public and Democracy." Paper delivered at the conference "Reconsidering American Democracy," Williams College, August.

Pierce, Roy, and Philip E. Converse. 1981. "Candidate Visibility in France and the United States." *Legislative Studies Quarterly* 3:339–71.

Pomper, Gerald M. 1972. "From Confusion to Clarity: Issues and American Voters, 1956–1968." *American Political Science Review* 66:415–28.

Popkin, Samuel, J. W. Gorman, Charles Phillips, and Jeffrey A. Smith. 1976. "What Have You Done for Me Lately? Toward an Investment Theory of Voting." *American Political Science Review* 70:779–805.

RePass, David E. 1971. "Issue Salience and Party Choice." *American Political Science Review* 65:389–400.

Rivers, Douglas R. 1988. "Heterogeneity in Models of Electoral Choice." *American Journal of Political Science* 32:737–57.

Rivers, Douglas R., and Nancy L. Rose. 1985. "Passing the President's Program: Public Opinion and Presidential Influence in Congress." *American Journal of Political Science* 29:183–96.

Rokeach, Milton. 1960. *The Open and Closed Mind: Investigations into the Nature of Belief Systems and Personality Systems.* New York: Basic Books.

Rosenstone, Stephen J. 1983. *Forecasting Presidential Elections.* New Haven: Yale University Press.

Sanders, Lynn M. N.d. "Against Deliberation." *Political Theory.* Forthcoming.

Schuman, Howard, Charlotte Steeh, and Larry Bobo. 1985. *Racial Attitudes in America.* Cambridge, Mass.: Harvard University Press.

Schumpeter, Joseph A. 1942. *Capitalism, Socialism, and Democracy.* New York: Harper & Row.

Sears, David O., Richard R. Lau, Tom Tyler, and Harris M. Allen, Jr. 1980. "Self-Interest Versus Symbolic Politics in Policy Attitudes and Presidential Voting." *American Political Science Review* 74:670–84.

Smith, Eric R.A.N. 1989. *The Unchanging American Voter.* Berkeley and Los Angeles: University of California Press.

Smith, Tom W. 1984. "Nonattitudes: A Review and Evaluation." In *Surveying Subjective Phenomena,* ed. Charles F. Turner and Elizabeth Martin, 2:215–56. New York: Russell Sage Foundation.

Stimson, James A. 1975. "Belief Systems: Constraint, Complexity, and the 1972 Election." *American Journal of Political Science* 19:393–418.

Stokes, Donald E. 1966a. "Party Loyalty and the Likelihood of Deviating Elections." In *Elections and the Political Order,* ed. Angus Campbell, Philip E. Converse, Warren E. Miller, and Donald E. Stokes, 125–35. New York: Wiley.

———. 1966b. "Some Dynamic Elements of Contests for the Presidency." *American Political Science Review* 60:19–28.

Sullivan, John L., James Piereson, and George E. Marcus. 1982. *Political Tolerance and American Democracy.* Chicago: University of Chicago Press.

Tufte, Edward R. 1978. *Political Control of the Economy.* Princeton: Princeton University Press.

Zaller, John. 1992. *The Nature and Origins of Mass Opinion.* Cambridge: Cambridge University Press.

18

Framing Democratic Discussion

James Farr

"Democracy needs a new way to talk." So urged Harold Lasswell a half century ago in *Democracy Through Public Opinion* (1941, chap. 7). Despite his "maddening methods" (Eulau 1969), Lasswell was sane and sober when discussing the prospects and perils of democracy, even during the dark days of world war. "Democracy depends on talk," he insisted. "The methods of talk need to aid in the discovery of sound public policy. If the practice of discussion does not create a sense of achievement there is contempt for talk. One ominous symptom of our times is the identification of democracy with voluble futility" (Lasswell 1941, 81).

The futility of discussion among the citizenry was soon blamed on the citizenry itself. In survey after survey, study after study, postwar political science showed that ordinary American citizens were blinkered, ignorant, and inconsistent. Mass belief systems were a mess. Democracy was saved—*mirabile dictu*—by political elites in whose company democratic discussion might intelligently continue. Deliberation in the Senate, debate in the House, discussion amid elites—therein lay democracy, or as much of it as political science gave us reason to hope.

It is the "attack on the possibility of democratic discussion implicitly mounted in recent American survey research, especially as set out in the authoritative and influential writings of Philip Converse," that inspires the fast-paced, acid-penned counterattack by Donald R. Kinder and Don Herzog. Unsparingly, they criticize the "antidemocratic" implications of the work of Converse and others on the ideological capacities of ordinary citizens. They argue that, in fact, the American people are more ideological; they may become more ideological still; and most important, they do not even need to be or to become more ideological when it comes to their capacities for democratic discussion. Refusing to be comforted by the nominally democratic argument that all is well that aggregates well, Kinder and Herzog conclude that we should not blame the victim—read "the citizen"—so much as the politicians and news media for our present woes. "Given what passes for democratic debate these days" in *those* circles, "we shouldn't be too surprised by the bleak empirical findings" of mainstream political science. But matters need not remain this way, for "the real hope lies in reforming our politics and practices."

This is altogether in the right spirit. However, save for a few words about the news media, the authors of "Democratic Discussion" do *not* suggest the sort of practical reforms they have in mind. This is extremely unfortunate given the terms of their own argument. Nonetheless, they remove a number of objections raised by influential political scientists to the very possibility of democratic discussion (and, more generally, to the rationality and coherence of popular beliefs and public opinion). Indeed, their discussing democratic discussion at all is a contribution to political science these days, given the curious silence about this constitutive feature of democracy itself. And this is not all. Reaching back to John Stuart Mill, Kinder and Herzog recover crucial arguments for the vision—shared with Mill by Bagehot, Lasswell, Popper, and others, by the way—that democracy is best understood as "government by discussion." They also sketch out, albeit in a purely promissory way, a social psychological theory of "frames" that alleges to supplant Converse's theory of mass belief systems. Frames, they claim, help us to understand the sort of rationality to be found in popular beliefs and public opinion, and to establish the epistemological prerequisites for democratic discussion. Akin to "ideas" (in the very broad sense given to them by John Kingdon, in this volume), frames also reveal the cognitive resources that citizens (or elites) have beyond self-interest in making sense of the real world of democracy around them. Finally—given the premises of this volume and the Democratic Theory Symposium that prefigured it—Kinder and Herzog make evident by their shared labors that an "empiricist" and a "theorist" can readily collaborate and mutually inform the thinking of the other. Indeed, the distinction would be artificial to the point of caricature, in this instance, if one could not see Kinder's hand at work on the empirical literature of public opinion and Herzog's hand at work on the past masters of political theory.

"Democratic Discussion" does not devote equal time to its various tasks. The greater part of the essay, as intimated, criticizes Converse and others who have dominated the literature on public opinion and electoral politics since the 1960s. Some readers of "Democratic Discussion" may feel (as did certain participants at the symposium) that some of the charges against Converse are directed rather more at a straw man than at the erstwhile Dean of the Michigan Model. If true, this would be a shame, of course. No one wants to come off "telling men of straw that they have no brains" (Passmore, n.d., 13, in a different context). In any case, the critique of Converse has been better and more fully undertaken elsewhere (e.g., by Kinder and Sears 1985). Others are in a better position than I am to judge the fairness or adequacy of that critique, and except for a word or two below, I leave such a task to them.

It is the return to Mill (for theoretical justification) and the turn to frames (for empirical guidance) that puzzle me, given the critique of Converse's model of belief systems and the avowed interest in democratic discussion. When all is said and done, Mill and frames are frightfully ambiguous and ambivalent resources for democratic tasks. Even when Kinder and Herzog hint at this, they do not go on to look much beyond elite discourse, to specify the content needed for a frame to be a democratic one, to attend to the actual practices of popular deliberation, or to escape the limiting forum of public opinion and electoral politics. These criticisms are offered in the spirit of "Democratic Discussion"—what with its methodological deck clearing, its diagnosis of our polity in trouble, and its pleas for reform. Thus, it is not inappropriate or impertinent to suggest the limits of its letter or to suggest ways of pressing much further the discussion of democratic discussion.

We may begin, as Kinder and Herzog do, with John Stuart Mill. Mill's vision of democracy, they tell us, accords discussion a central and privileged place. This it surely does. In decided contrast to Rousseau, for example, Mill repeatedly called for "freedom of the press and of discussion as would enable a public opinion to form and express itself on national affairs" (1975, 183). He clearly and steadily advocated "the utmost possible publicity and liberty of discussion, whereby not merely a few individuals in succession, but the whole public, are made, to a certain extent, participants in the government, and sharers in the instruction and mental exercise derivable from it" (230).

However, one readily discovers in these and similar expressions the limits of Mill's advocacy of democratic discussion. These limits are not, by the way, incidental or accidental features of Mill's political theory. They go to the very foundation of it. "Instruction and mental exercise," as Mill puts it in the above quote, suggest the instrumental justification of discussion for liberal and pedagogical ends. Mill wants free speech and discussion to serve the discovery of truth, the cultivation of intelligence, the education of opinion, and the development of individuals. These are laudable ends, to be sure, and they deserve our perseverance in their pursuit. But in Mill's account they may be achieved under widely different forms of government. Although representative government honors them most consistently, we may nonetheless "imagine a despot observing" them (1975, 183). More important, these laudable ends presuppose a devastating critique of the state of the public mind and of the "inferior minds" and "minds of a lower grade" that mainly compose it. "The ignorance, the indifference, the intractableness, the perverse obstinacy of a people, and the corrupt combinations of selfish private interests" require reforms of liberal education, even as they suggest the monumental hurdles that obstruct it (370–71).

It is indeed to his credit that Mill did not seek to circumvent the people, however blasted their brains. He insisted, as noted, on the importance of discussion—or "endless talk" as Kinder and Herzog bluntly put it—to be the very instrument of collective self-enlightenment. However, since the choice of exemplary democrats should matter very much in a discussion between political theorists and political scientists on the issue of democratic discussion itself, what sort of democratic politics did Mill have in mind as he unleashed the tongues of the nation? With equal (and equally frustrating) steadfastness, Mill limits ("to a certain extent") the people's participation referred to above. The "certain extent" turns out to be certainly considerable. "Watch," "control," "superintend," and "check" are the limited and limiting functions that Mill assigns to the people, even as they rap away (1975, 226, 236, 364). These nominally democratic functions are mirrored even by those nominal functions that the people's representatives themselves serve in their assemblies. Although Mill rebuffs the taunts of critics that representative assemblies are "places of mere talk and *bavardage*," he hardly goes on to empower the representatives as they "go on" in their democratic discussions. One longish quote (not mentioned by Kinder and Herzog) captures Mill's views on this score—his giving in one breath, and his taking away in the next.

> I know not how a representative assembly can more usefully employ itself than in talk, when the subject of talk is the great public interests of the country, and every sentence of it represents the opinion either of some important body of persons in the nation, or of an individual in whom some such body have reposed their confidence. A place where every interest and shade of opinion in the country can have its cause even passionately pleaded, in the face of the government and of all other interests and opinions, can compel them to listen, and either comply, or state clearly why they do not, is in itself, if it answered no other purpose, one of the most important political institutions that can exist anywhere, and one of the foremost benefits of free government. Such "talking" would never be looked upon with disparagement if it were not allowed to stop "doing"; which it never would, if assemblies knew and acknowledged that talking and discussion are their proper business, while *doing*, as the result of discussion, is the task not of a miscellaneous body, but of individuals specially trained to it. (1975, 227, quotes and emphasis in the original)

As for professional bureaucrats and legislators—unlike wordy democrats, in and out of assembly—"every hour spent in talk is an hour withdrawn from actual business" (1975, 227).

Mill, in short, is an incredibly ambivalent theorist from whom to draw inspiration for the prospects of democratic discussion. It is not that Kinder and Herzog are completely insensitive to this, for they acknowledge at least a few of Mill's failings, defects, and errors. (For an even less flattering portrait of Mill, warts and all, see Herzog 1985, chap. 3.) It merits the attention I have given it, nonetheless, for at least two reasons.

First, there is the question of balanced treatment (or why the laurels go to whom they go). The praise and recovery of Mill stands in marked and odd contrast to the exceedingly unfavorable treatment that is accorded to Converse and Rousseau. Converse, frankly, should come off not much worse than Mill, considering the overall context of their respective contributions to the prospects and perils of democratic discussion in a representative republic. Indeed the standards that Mill would like to see met for intelligent public discussion as led by those with "superior minds" (1975, 370) make Converse's ideological belief systems pale by comparison and his "indictment" of ordinary citizens much less evidently strident. Converse's failure as a reformer or even as a counterfactual thinker might well be underscored, perhaps; but then Mill's reforms, ambivalent as they are, might be seen as the sort of "utopian fantasy" that Kinder and Herzog reject. Perhaps those reforms are even dystopian insofar as *democratic* deliberation is concerned: let the people talk, it will do their opinions good and the business of government no harm.

Rousseau, as well, might come in for a word or two of democratic appreciation. He certainly deserves criticism for the silent zeal he oddly applauds in the collected citizenry—despite the dramatic gesture that "the voice of the people is in fact the voice of God." However, Rousseau was not simply desirous of "communal affirmation"—with one another or with God—as Kinder and Herzog put it. He was more directly and rightly worried about the "credit or eloquence" of demagogues and assorted modern Cleons. Because of "certain clever persons" like these, he went on, "the general will will be one thing, and the result of the public deliberation another. This is not contradicted by the case of the Athenian Democracy; for Athens was in fact not a Democracy, but a very tyrannical Aristocracy, governed by philosophers and orators" (Rousseau 1973, 122). In his time, Rousseau was rather prophetic, if one looks to the savagery of virtue that revolutionary demagogues unleashed in the 1790s (ironically often invoking his name). In our time, new analysts, opinion leaders, and media pundits manipulate and malform what passes for intelligent public discussion. Indeed, the fear of "freewheeling exercises in pure manipulation" that Kinder and Herzog express, even in the case of their preferred model of frames (to which I turn momentarily) sounds like something that Rousseau shares.

Second, there is the question of what power democratic citizens should have (or which theorist gives what to the people). Rousseau—in striking contrast to Mill—refused to alienate lawmaking to any group of bureaucrats or professional governors. On pain of losing their sovereignty, the people (or their delegates) could not pass off this function. Democracy must entail the active participation of citizens in collective self-governance where actual decisions are made. Rousseau keeps his citizens perversely silent, but at least he requires more of them than an endless series of discussions whose claims to being democratic can be vindicated simply when public opinion finds itself reflected in the legislation of hired pens. If, in short, we want to find in Mill an exemplary democrat who advocates and rationally justifies "government by discussion," let us not forget for a moment how little actual government there is in his view of discussion and how little democratic empowerment it actually entails.

What, then, of those frames that Kinder and Herzog fear even as they forward them? There is not an extended analysis of frames or frame theory in "Democratic Discussion," although the authors refer to recent work by Gamson and colleagues, as well as by Kinder and Sanders. (In this volume, John Kingdon's discussion of "ideas" and the literature he cites are generally relevant here, as well.) Frames, we learn from Kinder and Herzog, "consist of metaphors, exemplars, catchphrases, depictions, and visual images; they often include a rudimentary causal analysis and appeals to honored principles." (Except for the last pair of these, Mill would be utterly horrified that this list is put forward in the name of discussion and deliberation!) Whether as "structures of the mind" or as "interpretive structures embedded in political discourse," frames allegedly provide narrative coherence to a discussion or a series of facts and images by providing an organizing idea or storyline for them. Frames require of their producers and consumers much less by way of rationality, in that those who think or speak in terms of them need not have mastered an ideological system of beliefs as in Converse's account. Thus, frames help lower the threshold, as it were, for what we have reason to expect of the opinions and beliefs of ordinary citizens.

So far, so good. In advocating an alternative theory of social psychology that refuses to blame the citizens for their purported irrationality, Kinder and Herzog lend further credence to the efforts of the late V. O.

Key, Robert Lane, Benjamin Page and Robert Shapiro (in this volume), and many other political scientists (to mention only political scientists, and only in our time). They all help salvage the rationality of ordinary citizens. In so doing, democratic discussion appears to have better prospects. It is important, however, that Kinder and Herzog do not leave the impression that thereby all is fine. Theirs is a darker and more honest appraisal of our present condition. In particular, they do not disguise their concern that frames—"the creation of artful frames"—might nonetheless serve the manipulative interests of political elites.

What is unclear is that frames could be *anything but* manipulative, at least given Kinder and Herzog's emphasis on elites and elite frames. (Lasswell—whose role in the prehistory of frame theory might deserve exploration—spoke of "frames," "frames of reference," and "attention frames" [e.g., Lasswell 1977, 51, 152, 209, 219, 263, 416] in connection with *propaganda*, including what he called democratic propaganda.) Is it enough, in democratic terms, to salvage the rationality of ordinary citizens if, in so doing, that rationality consigns them to being competent listeners, at best, or the objects of elite frames, at worst? "The good news," Kinder and Herzog tell us, "is that frames appear to provide a common vocabulary, one that enables elites to speak clearly to citizens." Why, exactly, is this good news, especially if the so-called common vocabulary can evidently have *any* sort of content whatsoever, democratic or not, and citizens are not discussed in terms of their speaking to one another? Why are only elite frames discussed if we are concerned with democratic discussion? If citizens are always having frames put to them by elites, are they not being framed?

These questions are raised partly in criticism of Kinder and Herzog, but mainly in solicitation of more analysis. What, exactly, puts frames to the service of democratic discussion? Could one not have a frame or be framed without engaging in democratic discussion at all, unless by "democratic discussion" one means any sort of communication whatsoever that goes on in those countries we nominally call democracies? It should be noted in this connection that Kinder and Herzog open their essay with the express "aim . . . to assess the quality of the political conversations that go on between the American public and American leaders." However, by the time the essay concludes, American leaders have done most of the conversing, and "democratic discussion" seems to have figured as an omnibus term that covers free speech, the expression of opinion, the articulation of interests, the campaigning for elections, the casting of votes, and the discourses of politicians and the press. My fear is not only (with Kinder and Herzog) that these things will be manipulated or that they will fail to serve the public good but that we will even think of them as very good examples of "democratic discussion" at all or as the sort of thing upon which a theory of frames will exhaust its energies. In short, as citizens and political scientists, we want more for democratic discussion and more from frames.

What more? First, frame theorists should help us begin to answer some questions about what would be required of an explicitly *democratic frame*. Kinder and Herzog pitch their analysis of frames in terms of their *function*, loosely speaking, in serving democratic discussion. But should we not also wish that democratic discussion proceed in good part in terms of frames that are democratic in their *content*—in their "metaphors, exemplars, catchphrases, . . . and honored principles"? Surely, many frames are more nationalistic, patriotic, heroic, theistic, familistic, or individualistic than they are democratic—even if in some sense elites who use them are trying to serve democracy by creating coherence in public opinion. Doubtless, many problems attendant to frame theory and the concept of democracy are involved here. If "catchphrases" alone suffice as a frame, then the mere catchphrase of "democracy" might seem to make a frame a democratic one. But the catchphrase alone obscures the history of conceptual change that goes into the several and often contested meanings of "democracy" (Hanson 1989). Moreover, the term has surely become "the public cant of the modern world" (Dunn 1979), introduced trivially, incoherently, or manipulatively (never more so than by elites) into all sorts of domestic debates, military interventions, consumer advertisements, and television specials. It is this sort of thing that Kinder and Herzog rightly fear about the use of frames. We might imagine, therefore, discussion being framed democratically if its content is more than a catchphrase. However, if the content is one of, say, "honored principles," how fully articulated, coherent, and consistent must that content be for the discussion to be framed democratically? Would such content start to resemble Converse's ideological belief systems (if not Mill's "minds of higher grade")? And if so, how might that redraw the battle lines between frames and belief systems? Answering these questions means that we need to theorize much more about the democratic content of frames and therefore about the democratic intentions of frame theory.

Second, more might come of our theoretical and empirical research if we look not to public opinion or to elites but to actual discussions held between citizens. That is, we should look at discussion as an actual practice engaged in by citizens who try out different (and one would hope democratic) frames on one another over a range of issues as they deliberate and try to come to some actual decision. One might think of the sort of discussions that are still held in New England town meetings (Mansbridge 1980) or even those that can be experimentally established in focus groups (as discussed by Conover et al., in this volume). A different example of such a practice of deliberation is the jury. Indeed the jury might be the paradigmatic example in this context. A jury proceeds not only in terms of talk but also in terms of deliberation between citizens that issues in an actual decision. But, whatever the example, the general point bears emphasizing. "Democratic discussion" should be conceptualized less in terms of elite frames functionally serving democracy and more in terms of the *actual practices of popular deliberation*. In sum, we should focus less on the ways in which the use of frames makes discussion cognitively possible and more on the ways in which discussion makes the use of frames practically democratic.

There is nothing profound or mysterious in this, Kinder and Herzog have left it to me to point out the obvious. They mention "practices" in passing when discussing Dewey and when they close with their hopes for reform. Yet, in the main, their orientation is driven by the analysis of public opinion, and what they say about democratic discussion is influenced thereby. Here, we may not forget the nondemocratic elements of "public opinion" as revealed in its conceptual history (Gunn 1989) or the fears that it may mismeasure political man and constrict discursive democracy (Dryzek 1988, 1991) or the spiral of silence into which it frequently allows the citizenry to fall (Noelle-Neumann 1984; Habermas 1989).

The only example of democratic discussion (in the sense of an actual practice of popular deliberation, one that empowers citizens by bringing their discussion to a decision) to which Kinder and Herzog devote any sustained attention is the vote. "On election day itself," they tell us, "voters are provided the opportunity to 'talk back.' " But note that the strain in the case is signaled by the very quotation marks used to make it. Even then, one must emphasize how minimal is the discursive element in the silence of the voting booth or the rancorous noise in the campaign that usually precedes it. Then, of course, there are the stretches of time between elections. Here it was Rousseau—not Mill, what with his schemes to give weighted votes to those with better occupations or higher intelligence—who needled the British for their dubious sovereignty: "The people of England regards itself as free; but it is grossly mistaken; it is free only during the election of members of parliament. As soon as they are elected, slavery overtakes it, and it is nothing. The use it makes of the short moments of liberty it enjoys shows indeed that it deserves to lose them" (Rousseau 1973, 240). Rousseau is here characteristically hyperbolic and Anglophobic, but surely he has a point. We want and have the right to expect more from democracy—"government by discussion"—than elections, decisively important as they are.

Empiricists and theorists may yet work together to clarify further what is at stake here, both in theory and practice, by understanding democratic discussion in terms of the actual practices of popular deliberation. The efforts of Habermas (1979, 1981) and Ackerman (1980) represent sustained attempts to analyze discussion *as such* in order to clarify democratic theory and practice (despite the important and, at times, rather humorous criticism of the latter, see Barber 1989 and Herzog 1989). Other democratic theorists (like Manin 1987) have started to elaborate a theory of democratic legitimacy in terms of deliberation itself. This is a decided advance not only over Rousseau (as Manin intends) but also over Mill. (Here, as discussed above, the choice of exemplary democratic theorists matters very much.) Even the jury (as the paradigm of popular deliberation) has hardly exhausted its potential for contemporary political science and political theory. We might follow the lead of certain social psychologists here (Hastie et al. 1983). Empirical work on the juries can surely help us better understand democratic discussion (however much we gain by public opinion, electoral politics, and frames). Indeed, the way in which citizens interpret and construct the law in the course of their deliberations might yet yield methodological insights for political science itself. Here, we might even renew investigations of the sort that helped create the discipline of political science in the first place, as found, for example, in the long-neglected work on interpretation by Francis Lieber, *Legal and Political Hermeneutics* (discussed in Farr 1990). Perhaps the jury can even help to spur the imaginations of democratic reformers in a call for "citizen juries" or similar sorts of deliberative assemblies that might empower ordinary citizens (Barber 1984, chap. 10; Crosby 1990; and, more generally, Burnheim 1985). In the end, we want political theory and political science to help understand, justify, and promote the actual deliberative practices of ordinary citizens as they engage in democratic discussion.

If this looks forward, it also looks back. In *Democracy in America*, Tocqueville (1969, 12) called for "a new political science for a world itself quite new." The new world he found in America was one in which democratic discussion was not only possible but being realized. Richard Krouse—whose voice is missing in democratic theory today and to whom this volume is appropriately dedicated—evidently hoped to bring back what Tocqueville found nearly realized in America (Krouse 1983, 70): "The cares of politics engross a prominent place in the occupations of a citizen in the United States; and almost the only pleasure which an American knows is to take part in the government, and to discuss its measures."

References

Ackerman, Bruce A. 1980. *Social Justice and the Liberal State.* New Haven: Yale University Press.

Barber, Benjamin. 1984. *Strong Democracy.* Berkeley and Los Angeles: University of California Press.

———. 1989. *The Conquest of Politics.* Princeton: Princeton University Press.

Burnheim, John. 1985. *Is Democracy Possible?* Berkeley and Los Angeles: University of California Press.

Crosby, Ned. 1990. "The Peace Movement and New Democratic Processes." *Social Alternatives* 4:33–37.

Dryzek, John S. 1988. "The Mismeasure of Political Man." *Journal of Politics* 50:705–25.

———. 1991. *Discursive Democracy.* Cambridge: Cambridge University Press.

Dunn, John. 1979. *Western Political Theory in the Face of the Future.* Cambridge: Cambridge University Press.

Eulau, Heinz. 1969. "The Maddening Methods of Harold D. Lasswell: Some Philosophical Underpinnings." In *Politics, Personality, and Social Science in the Twentieth Century*, ed. Arnold A. Rogow, 15–40. Chicago: University of Chicago Press.

Farr, James. 1990. "Francis Lieber and the Interpretation of American Political Science." *Journal of Politics* 52:1027–49.

Gunn, J.A.W. 1989. "Public Opinion." In *Political Innovation and Conceptual Change*, ed. Terence Ball, James Farr, and Russell L. Hanson, 247–65. Cambridge: Cambridge University Press.

Habermas, Jürgen. 1979. *Communication and the Evolution of Society.* Boston: Beacon Press.

———. 1981. *The Theory of Communicative Action.* 2 vols. Boston: Beacon Press.

———. 1989. *The Structural Transformation of the Public Sphere.* Cambridge, Mass. MIT Press.

Hanson, Russell L. 1989. "Democracy." In *Political Innovation and Conceptual Change*, ed. Terence Ball, James Farr, and Russell L. Hanson, 68–89. Cambridge: Cambridge University Press.

Hastie, Reid, Steven D. Penrod, and Nancy Pennington. 1983. *Inside the Jury.* Cambridge, Mass.: Harvard University Press.

Herzog, Don. 1985. *Without Foundations: Justification in Political Theory.* Ithaca, N.Y.: Cornell University Press.

———. 1989. *Happy Slaves: A Critique of Consent Theory.* Chicago: University of Chicago Press.

Kinder, Donald R., and David O. Sears. 1985. "Public Opinion and Political Action." In *The Handbook of Social Psychology*, ed. Gardner Lindzey and Elliot Aronson, 2:659–741. New York: Random House.

Krouse, Richard W. 1983. " 'Classical' Images of Democracy in America: Madison and Tocqueville." In *Democratic Theory and Practice*, ed. Graeme Duncan, 58–78. Cambridge: Cambridge University Press.

Lasswell, Harold D. 1941. *Democracy Through Public Opinion.* New York: George Banta.

———. 1977. *On Political Sociology.* Ed. Dwaine Marvick. Chicago: University of Chicago Press.

Manin, Bernard. 1987. "On Legitimacy and Political Deliberation." *Political Theory* 15:338–68.

Mansbridge, Jane. 1980. *Beyond Adversary Democracy.* New York: Basic Books.

Mill, John Stuart. 1975. *Three Essays: On Liberty; Representative Government; The Subjection of Women.* Oxford: Oxford University Press.

Noelle-Neumann, Elisabeth. 1984. *The Spiral of Silence: Public Opinion—Our Social Skin.* Chicago: University of Chicago Press.

Passmore, John N.d. "The Idea of a History of Philosophy." *History and Theory,* Beiheft 5.

Rousseau, Jean-Jacques. 1973. *The Social Contract and Discourses.* New York: Dutton.

Tocqueville, Alexis de. [1835, 1840] 1969. *Democracy in America.* New York: Anchor Doubleday.

19

Political Incorporation and Racial Politics

David H. Tabb

The political incorporation of blacks and Latinos is central to achieving political equality and thereby a more democratic polity. This chapter examines a variety of systematic efforts to achieve incorporation at the local level over the last thirty years.

Mobilization and Incorporation: Fundamentals

Briefly summarized, the concept of political incorporation concerns the extent to which group interests are effectively represented in policy-

This chapter is an expanded and revised version of chapter 12 of *Racial Politics in American Cities* (Browning et al. 1990). In that book, political incorporation is evaluated in twenty-one cities by several urban scholars.

making. The key to control of city government in favor of minority interests is minority inclusion in a dominant coalition, that is, minority participation in a coalition that can dominate city councils and secure repeated reelection. The political incorporation of black and Latino minorities has been measured by assessing the extent to which they were represented in coalitions that dominated city policy-making on minority-related issues (Browning et al. 1984, 20).

This idea of incorporation challenges Gary Jacobsohn's "assimilationist model of incorporation" in which political equality becomes synonymous with co-optation. Political access by blacks and Latinos is gauged by the extent of their inclusion "into a political culture whose essence consists in a commitment to certain regime principles" (Jacobsohn, in this volume). This tradition of democratic theory suggests that efforts to promote political equality of minorities should focus on the procedural rights of individuals rather than on the substantive rights of similarly disadvantaged groups (see Walzer 1983, 152, for a discussion of the norm of equal consideration for individual citizens as applied to blacks), so that, for instance, the implementation of the Civil Rights Act of 1964 was an important step in delegitimatizing "group membership as a criterion in making public decisions about individuals" (Jacobsohn, in this volume). My view is that reducing discrimination by securing procedural guarantees has been at the center of the struggle for political equality of blacks and Latinos, although political incorporation involves a range of possibilities that appropriately go beyond procedural guarantees to include an equal or leading role in a dominant coalition strongly committed to minority interests.

Jacobsohn's concern that affirmative action be based on principles of individualism leads him to argue that my view of incorporation implies certain "claims of entitlement" for blacks and Latinos. Although I certainly disagree with Jacobsohn's neoconservative views on affirmative action, my view of incorporation implies nothing more than what he refers to as "political clout." What I do, I hope, is measure the degree of political incorporation in a more systematic fashion than traditional pluralists.

Assessing the necessary conditions for entering governing coalitions has historically been at the center of the study of political incorporation and political equality, both of which are central to the idea of democratic development (Stinchcombe 1968, 168–81). The question, then, is how minorities become shareholders in dominant coalitions. Withholding for the moment judgment about the value of minority incorporation in city governments, I bring together here findings and their interpretations about resources for incorporation and barriers to it.

Weak and Strong Forms of Minority Incorporation

Representation alone gained little influence for minorities; minority participation in liberal-dominant coalitions led to much stronger minority influence and policy responsiveness; coalitions led by black mayors typically incorporated still stronger minority commitments. As Stokely Carmichael and Charles Hamilton put it in 1967, "When black people lack a majority, Black Power means proper representation and sharing of control. It means the creation of power bases, of strength, from which black people can press to change local or nation-wide patterns of oppression—instead of from weakness" (6). It does not mean merely putting black faces into office. Black visibility is not black power.

Interest-Group and Electoral Strategies

Mobilization that produced sustained incorporation built both on interest-group organization, demand, and protest and on electoral effort, including party or partylike coalition formation. Although electoral mobilization and coalition were the essential foundation of enduring incorporation, it was group organization, demand, and protest that were the foundation for successful electoral effort, in spite of instances where too-intense protest hindered and delayed the formation of coalitions.

Cities in which blacks or Latinos achieved the most powerful participation in electoral coalitions, and subsequently in city governments, were those in which the development of autonomous, solidary minority leadership and organization preceded it, confirming Carmichael and Hamilton's argument: "The concept of Black Power rests on a fundamental premise: Before a group can enter the open society, it must first close ranks. By this we mean that group solidarity is necessary before a group can operate effectively from a bargaining position of strength in a pluralistic society" (1967, 44).

The linkage between the achievement of solidarity within the minority group and the achievement of strong incorporation was very close in the cities my colleagues and I studied. The early strong incorporation of blacks in Berkeley depended on the usually strong organization of black leadership in the Berkeley Black Caucus; the long delay in the election of a black mayor in Oakland was the result in part of the split between the Black Panther party and middle-class black leadership. Failure to achieve solidarity both within and between minority populations in New York explains in part the failure of blacks and Latinos to obtain incorporation corresponding to their population size before the Dinkins election (Mollenkopf 1992). Breaking away from the Democratic machine, organizing a grass-roots process to pull black community organizations together, and including Latinos in a coalition were prerequisites for Harold Washington's victory in Chicago (Starks and Preston 1990).

Jennifer Hochschild provides strong anecdotal evidence suggesting that the solidarity of black leaders is likely to be challenged by other sources as well. She finds among middle-class blacks a "disjunction" between their views on economic and on social justice—sometimes they are more conservative and middle-class than poorer blacks on questions of social welfare policy and more liberal on issues dealing with race and civil rights (Hochschild, in this volume). If correct, the increasing divergence between well-off and poor blacks may have political consequences for both. Although I do not have data to test Hochschild's thesis, it is clear that black leaders often feel pressured from various directions both within the black community and by potential white allies. Neighborhood activists often criticize black mayors, alleging a lack of concern for the black poor at the expense of downtown interests. Their opposition sometimes results in efforts to build competing coalitions within the black community.

The difficulty in maintaining solidarity is reflected in the experience of Andrew Young, the former mayor of Atlanta:

> During the first generation of black elected leaders and appointed leadership in a city, black leaders tend to stick together and to refrain from criticizing one another. It is, of course, wrong to assume that merely changing a leader's color will solve fundamental problems, though new leaders often brought new priorities and understanding. However, all of us must be willing to openly debate our strategies for serving poor as well as middle class constituencies to learn from each other. (Orfield 1991, xi)

The Importance of Coalitions

Regardless of election system (partisan or nonpartisan), in the studies conducted by my colleagues and me the political incorporation of minorities depended on their ability to form and maintain cohesive electoral coalitions. In particular, where blacks and Latinos constituted a minority of the effective electorate, their incorporation depended on the formation of bi- or multiracial coalitions that selected candidates, controlled the number of minority candidates, organized the slate, coordinated campaigns, and controlled city councils and departments.

The fundamental resources of the minority population plus supportive whites formed the basis of these coalitions. Depending on historical patterns of competition and conflict, on leadership, and on the sizes of black and Latino groups and of the supportive white population, coalitions were variously composed of blacks and whites, Latinos and whites, or all three groups.

The Importance of Leadership

Because competition and conflict between groups is typical, the structure, size, and timing of new coalitions depended on the ability of leaders to overcome divisions and to shape issues to minimize antagonism and sustain joint effort. The flow of issues, partly under the control of coalition leaders, and the willingness and ability of the available leadership to reach out across racial boundaries—a difficult task—shaped the structure of the coalitions that actually formed, won control of city government, and maintained their commitment and position. The structure of local leadership, as well as that of group conflict, is shaped by historical experience, as happened in Philadelphia when innovative co-operation took hold and became accepted practice (Keiser 1990).

Barriers to Incorporation

Urban Machines

Boston, New York before the Dinkins regime, and Chicago, except during the tenure of Harold Washington, present characteristics that constitute barriers to minority mobilization and incorporation. In these three cities, strongly organized urban parties have co-opted minorities into their organizations.

The machines are well-institutionalized coalitions that predate minority mobilization of the 1960s. Not oriented toward reform, and determined to protect the power of the organization and the economic interests of its ultimately white leadership and business support, the machine attempts to prevent the formation of multiracial challenging coalitions through co-optation, building on and generating divisions among minority leaders and groups and establishing minority office-holders against whom other minority people find it difficult to run. The machine creates some minority incorporation and produces some minority-oriented policies but prevents the mobilization of a liberal, unified minority-based coalition.

Thus, the machine stands as a barrier to the formation and success of reform-oriented coalitions, in which more autonomous minority leadership would play central and dominant roles. Some benefits flow to minority populations from such machines, as they do from co-optive regimes generally—city government employment, for example, and contracts from the city—but the machines will not undertake efforts to reorient city government across a broad range of policy areas.

In Chicago, unlike New York, a weakened machine was defeated by a multiracial coalition led by black insurgents. Harold Washington's election as mayor and then his success in gaining a council majority show that even a long-entrenched machine and its co-optation pattern can be overthrown, given appropriate leadership, fundamental resources of the minority population, and some support outside the minority community.

The Chicago case also demonstrates the difficulty of accomplishing an overthrow. As Robert Starks and Michael Preston show, Washington's coalition and leadership were unusual (Starks and Preston 1990). The coalition conducted an extraordinary grass-roots mobilization for involvement in the decision to select Washington as the coalition's candidate for mayor in the first place. Washington himself was reaching out across racial lines to Chicago's Latino population, including them as respected partners in his ultimately victorious coalition. Not every leader with the ability to win majority support in his or her own group also has the will and the credibility to create a liberal biracial or multiracial coalition (see Starks and Preston 1990 for a discussion of the importance of black leadership). The fragile dependence of such coalitions on leadership was sadly illustrated when Washington died in office and black candidates competing to succeed him split his coalition, leading to the election of the white machine candidate, Richard M. Daley, in 1989.

Fragmentation of Minority Groups

New York, in addition to being home to a party machine as a barrier to minority mobilization, also illustrates the possibility and consequences of extreme fragmentation of minority groups. The 1980 census counted more than 45 percent of New York's population as black or "of Spanish origin," and these groups probably made up more than half of New York's population by the late 1980s. By the standards of the other cities reported on here, resources of such size should have been more than ample to found a liberal multiracial coalition that could control city government over a long period of time. A major reason why this did not happen is the extent to which both blacks and Latinos in New York have been divided.

Whereas most blacks and Latinos have arrived in California cities since World War II, New York's black and Latino populations have a long history of competition, conflict, established leadership, and political division. This is not new clay that a skillful leader can readily mold into a unified force but a congeries of minority populations between which divisions are deep and solid. Not only are blacks and Latinos in New York split each from the other, they are further split within each group by ancestry and nativity—blacks of West Indian birth or ancestry from Dominicans and other Latino immigrant groups—and by place of residence in the boroughs of the city.

Fragmentation of minority populations in New York also stems from a long history of conflict and competition and the habituation of organizations and leaders to that history, as Mollenkopf notes (Mollenkopf 1990). This is utterly unlike the experience of black communities in the California cites where blacks coming predominantly from the American South are not divided by different ancestry. When organizational structure and leadership were still emerging, they were mobilized by the civil rights and black power movements and were presented with an opportunity to overthrow conservative regimes if they could coalesce among themselves and with others. For California blacks, the civil rights movement was the formative influence for political mobilization.

In contrast, the political fragmentation of New York's black population was well established long before the civil rights movement. Their ability to overcome fragmentation was tested in the 1989 New York mayoral election pitting David N. Dinkins, the black Manhattan borough president, first against the incumbent, Mayor Koch, in the Democratic primary, and then the Republican, Rudolph Giuliani, who ran on the Republican and Liberal lines in the general election. Mollenkopf's analysis of New York shows how several factors came together to unite the previously fragmented minority coalition. The reduction in Mayor Koch's approval rating among whites combined with the successful 1988 Jesse Jackson presidential primary to unite "a coalition of blacks, Latinos and white liberals, with an organizational base in public sector unions and reform political clubs" (Mollenkopf 1990, 86). With Dinkins having won 27 percent of the white vote, biracial politics may indeed have come to New York City. Recent conflicts between blacks and Orthodox Jews in Brooklyn seem destined to test Mayor Dinkins's coalitional skills.

Issues, Interests, and the Loss of White Support

The formation and survival of bi- and multiracial coalitions depend in part on the ideological commitment of liberal whites to the minority cause. Sonenshein's comparative study of New York, Chicago, and Los Angeles delineates the limits of that commitment; the New York case, especially, illustrates the potential for drastic loss of earlier support and the long-term eclipse of progressive multiracial coalitions (Sonenshein 1990).

In some cities, certainly in New York and Los Angeles, Jews have accounted for a large share of total white support for blacks, reflecting the experience of Jews with discrimination and their special moral determination to oppose it. Unfortunately for the cause of coalition, blacks and whites generally, but Jews in particular, have a special potential for conflict of interests around anti-Semitism, city government fiscal problems, residential and labor-market succession, and control over city government functions and employment.

Anti-Semitism. A few black leaders express openly anti-Semitic attitudes; the expression of anti-Semitism and the failure of some black leaders to denounce it must reduce support among Jews for biracial coalitions.

Fiscal problems. In New York, the fiscal crisis of the 1970s turned white supporters away from the problems of minority groups and dominated the agenda of city government for years.

Residential and labor-market succession. In New York in particular, many Jews have been affected in recent years by the transition of Jewish lower-middle- and working-class neighborhoods into black or Latino neighborhoods. Such transitions are likely to kindle racial, class, and cultural antagonisms and thus reduce support for coalitions.

Control over city government functions and employment. In the 1968 school strikes in New York, black activists were pitted as "outs" against a school bureaucracy led and staffed disproportionately by liberal and moderate whites (including many Jews). Liberals were cast as "ins" in traditionally liberal New York City; it was a strike against (white) institutional liberalism. The high degree of black-Jewish conflict produced by the strikes pushed much of the city's liberal base into a moderate-conservative alliance with white Catholics; this link became the base for the Koch regime. The result left blacks without political incorporation (Sonenshein 1990).

It is apparent that conflicts arising from these and other issues can destroy or prevent the formation of bi- and multiracial coalitions. Although the issues described above involved conflict between whites and blacks, it is easy to think of tensions and issues that divide blacks and Latinos or whites and Latinos. Thus, the general problem is the management of issues in order to form and maintain an effective coalition, even in the presence of actual or potential conflict with respect to interests.

Rollbacks of minority incorporation can and do occur, not only in Chicago but also in Philadelphia in the late 1960s and 1970s. As the Philadelphia case shows, it is possible to reform a biracial coalition with an enhanced role for blacks if the conservative regime in office is distasteful to liberal whites as well as to blacks and if an attractive black candidate is available (Wilson Goode).

Latino Mobilization and Incorporation

Latinos are different. They are, first of all, not black, except in small numbers; thus, they do not suffer the stigma of blackness in American society, and many consider themselves to be whites of Hispanic origin. Second, they are much more diverse than blacks, and the diversities count: Cuban Americans are not Puerto Ricans, who are not Dominicans; and Mexican Americans are not Central Americans, either culturally or in socioeconomic status.[1] Third, they are more likely to be Roman Catholics and less likely to see political action as a preferred means of improvement than blacks are. Finally, although poverty continues to be a major problem in many Latino communities, Latinos on average appear to assimilate economically more rapidly than blacks and are less concentrated geographically than blacks.

They are different in other political respects as well. Warren et al. report that of the Latinos in Dade County, Florida, who are registered to vote, about 75 percent are Republicans. Anti-Communism is a central tenet of their political program, even at the local level, and they are strongly growth oriented and increasingly successful in business (Warren et al. 1990).

Regarding San Antonio, with Mexican Americans in the majority but with a weak mayor–city manager system, Munoz and Henry (1990) question whether Mayor Henry Cisneros promoted either his Mexican American identity or the specific interests of that community, although he did promote major economic development in San Antonio, with considerable success.

Federico Pena, mayor of Denver, with a strong mayor form of city government, was not the product of minority electoral mobilization or demand-protest and was not endorsed by established Mexican American politicians. In a city with only 18 percent Latino population (31 percent black or Latino in 1980, but a smaller percentage of the electorate), he did not emphasize his Mexican American identity in his campaign, but he had a "proven track record" with Mexican Americans and liberal whites as a state legislator and was strongly supported by Mexican American voters and the liberal wing of the statewide Democratic party.

When Denver experienced a severe recession, Pena lost the support of important Democratic party leaders, barely won reelection, and never regained control of a majority of the city council. This is clearly not a case of strong minority incorporation, in spite of the election of a Latino to the mayor's office. According to Munoz and Henry, Pena has made some effort to integrate African Americans and Mexican Americans into city government, but his "coalition continues to be dominated by white political and business elites" (Munoz and Henry 1990, 186).

1. With respect to socioeconomic differences among Latinos in the eastern United States, see Fitzpatrick and Parker 1981.

Denver city government has been opened to a modicum of minority participation, but in the absence of organization, solidarity, and mobilization around a minority-oriented program, it is unlikely that much policy change will come of it. However, given the relatively small size and weak mobilization of Denver's minority population, perhaps it is surprising that a Latino mayor was elected at all. A somewhat larger Latino population in San Jose has not elected a Latino mayor; of course, San Jose's black population, which would support a liberal coalition, is very small, unlike Denver's.

Latinos can be mobilized to vote for multiracial coalitions led by whites (Sacramento) or blacks (Chicago and New York), but they are not very likely to generate strongly minority-oriented programs and coalitions themselves. This is not to say that they have not done this to some degree in some cities, such as Miami and perhaps San Antonio, or that they will not do so in the future; but if Latino economic assimilation proceeds with reasonable speed, it is unlikely that Latinos as a group will mobilize strongly around demands of the sort articulated by the black power movement.[2]

In the meantime, Latino incorporation is different. It draws more narrowly from the comprehensive socioeconomic goals of the black power movement, and it has a much more limited view of the proper role of government. Latino political leadership has responded to an electoral base that has been more diverse and, typically, more conservative.

The conservatism of Latino mobilization and incorporation has, of course, implications for the responsiveness of city governments in which Latinos are incorporated. We should expect Latino-run city governments to end discrimination in hiring, certainly, in the routine administration of city affairs and in the award of government contracts to minority-owned businesses. But should we expect such governments to equalize the delivery of city services and improvements generally? Perhaps somewhat, alleviating the most glaring inequities, but not much, if it means significantly reallocating municipal resources toward low-income neighborhoods, their residents, and their businesses.

2. William Julius Wilson (1985, 148) raises the possibility that rapidly growing urban Latino populations, with both continued immigration and high birth rates, might experience a worsening of their social and economic conditions, including an increase in joblessness, crime, teenage pregnancy, female-headed families, welfare dependency, and ethnic antagonism directed toward them.

The studies reported here confirm the difficulty of forming multiracial coalitions including blacks and Latinos. The tensions between these groups are often high because they compete both in labor markets and for political position and governmental benefits. The obstacles seem greatest in New York and Miami, where the two groups are in direct conflict, but political relations are problematic in Los Angeles as well. The most successful black-Latino coalition seems to have been Harold Washington's in Chicago. The process of coalition formation in that city should be a model for similar efforts elsewhere.

Have Blacks Achieved Political Incorporation?

To summarize, all of the twenty-one cities my colleagues and I studied are listed in a rough ranking of the extent of black incorporation:

Strong (bi- or multiracial coalition; black mayors)

Berkeley	1971–85	Warren Widener, Jr., Gus Newport
Atlanta	1973	Maynard Jackson, Andrew Young
Los Angeles	1973	Tom Bradley
New Orleans	1977	Ernest Morial, Sidney Barthelemy
Oakland	1977	Lionel Wilson
Birmingham	1979	Richard Arrington
Chicago	1983–87	Harold Washington
Philadelphia	1983	Wilson Goode

Fairly strong (bi- or multiracial coalition, white leadership or weak-mayor system)

- Sacramento
- Richmond, Calif.

Weak (black representation, not in dominant coalition)

- New York (before Dinkins's election)
- San Francisco
- Denver (coalition controls mayor's office but not council)
- San Jose (very small black population)
- Boston
- Stockton, Calif.
- Miami

Very weak (little or no black representation)

- San Antonio
- Hayward, Calif.
- Vallejo, Calif.
- Daly City, Calif.

New York is especially difficult to classify. Although blacks were not well incorporated in Mayor Koch's administration, they are incorporated in the party organizations of the boroughs; and the organizations, with great influence at the state as well as the local level, are surprisingly supportive on key issues. Blacks in New York might well be termed fairly strongly (but unevenly) incorporated once the complexities of political organization are taken into account, in spite of former Mayor Koch's rhetorical tendencies. They were in fact represented in the party organizations, which are multiracial coalitions with white leadership but commitments to at least some black interests. Blacks have become more strongly incorporated under Mayor Dinkins than under Mayor Koch, although the stability of the regime is still questionable.

What should we conclude from this listing? Of course such a classification is changeable—conservative coalitions may arise and win control of city governments where blacks are now strongly incorporated, and vice versa. Black incorporation is weaker than we might expect on grounds of black population alone in New York, Miami, and Boston. If I had to point to a single limiting factor in those cities, I might note that black and Latino populations in Miami, and until recently in New York, have been especially divided and that Boston's minority population is relatively small compared to cities in which blacks have achieved that especially strong form of incorporation, the bi- or multiracial dominant coalition led by a black mayor.

With the important exceptions of Miami and Boston, blacks appear to be well placed in dominant coalitions in the eight cities of the set in which they constituted at least 20 percent of city population in 1980. They have not achieved stronger incorporation in two large cities, and they have not carved out stronger roles in numerous cities where they constitute a smaller proportion of the population. These are significant limitations. Nevertheless, there is no denying the enormous change from the virtual exclusion of blacks thirty years ago to their assumption of positions of governmental authority and leadership in 1990.

Is Incorporation Enough?

No one who favors political equality objects in principle to the formation of multiracial coalitions or to minority officeholding. The question is, What do minority officeholders and coalitions do with their positions? Do they make city governments responsive to the demands and interests of minority communities? Especially, do they use the powers of city governments to pursue the broader aims of the black power movement, including expansion of assistance and provision of employment to economically marginal populations, largely black, and redistributive allocation of the city resources?

There is "an inherent value in officeholding. . . . A race of people who are excluded from public office will always be second class" (Tom McCain, quoted in the *American Civil Liberties Union News*, 1981). Officeholding does confer legitimacy on a hitherto excluded group, as Perry argues (Perry 1990). These are symbolic but nonetheless terribly important considerations.

Still, some authors set forth criticisms of some largely black regimes and some black leaders, criticisms that lean toward a conclusion that they are not as active as they should be in redistributive efforts, that they are less powerful than their political positions imply, because of the pervasive systemic power of white business interests and a progrowth ideology that may simply ignore the needs of ordinary citizens, and that they are too narrowly self-interested, too focused on their own interests, the interests of the black (and white) middle and upper class.

Clarence Stone, writing on Atlanta, concludes that the city's black middle-class political leadership is in a "tight alliance with the white business elite"; he reports one activist's remark that a meeting of black and white leaders in Atlanta "is nothing but a roomful of people trying to cut a deal" (Stone 1990, 136–37). The city's biracial coalition leaves out a range of lower-class interests, represented, for example, by neighborhood organizations and affordable-housing groups. The dominance of the governing biracial coalition replicates the extreme inequalities in the socioeconomic sphere. Atlanta is second only to Newark in poverty rate among U.S. cities, and the mass of black constituents remains effectively excluded. The moral prestige of former civil rights leader Andrew Young renders the regime all the more invulnerable.

To use Jennifer Hochschild's term, urban black leaders often resolve whatever "disjunction" that exists between their values and the claims of others in favor of middle-class interests. The reasons are not difficult to fathom. In the face of federal cutbacks, taxpayer resistance, and hostile rulings from the Supreme Court, black leaders ally themselves with middle- and upper-middle-class interests in an effort to solve fiscal crises.

One might hope eagerly for black political incorporation but when it arrives find that it is an obstacle to achievement of a broader set of goals. Even if one does not conclude that incorporation is *only* a sham, *only* the illusion of empowerment, it still seems reasonable to suffer a profound ambivalence toward it.

Those who write about incorporation do *not* conclude that black incorporation is only a sham. They agree by and large that biracial regimes have accomplished some good. What has been accomplished varies from city to city.

Have Minority Regimes Been Responsive?

By "minority regimes," I mean city governments dominated by bi- or multiracial coalitions in which blacks or Latinos play significant, usually leading, roles. Primarily these are black regimes.

City Government Employment

All of the minority regimes referred to in this chapter have effectively reduced discrimination in city government employment. Often they have created strong affirmative recruitment and hiring practices that have resulted in minority work forces close to or above parity with the size of minority populations. All of the minority regimes have greatly increased minority representation in professional, managerial, and executive positions, including department heads.

Some commentators deride city government employment as the weakest of weak rewards, "a few government jobs" with which elites buy off minority protest. I do not agree. One analysis concludes that "about 55 percent of the increase in black professional, managerial, and technical employment between 1960 and 1976 occurred in the public sector, and employment in social welfare programs accounted for approximately half of that increase" (Murray 1984, citing Brown and Erie 1981, 308).

This suggests that city government employment gains probably contributed significantly to middle-class black employment gains generally during this period. My own analysis of city work forces in ten California cities showed that minority employees of city governments ranged from 2 percent to 6 percent of total minority residents in the work force, more in the older, larger cities with the highest proportions of black residents—not an insignificant contribution to total minority (especially black) employment.

The argument is also sometimes made that the advantages of city government accrue almost entirely to middle-class blacks and Latinos, but the pattern varies a great deal from city to city. Older cities with broader governmental functions also hire large numbers of blue-collar workers. Bolstering the employment opportunities of middle-class or potentially middle-class minority persons is obviously not the same, from an antipoverty perspective, as enhancing employment opportunities for low-income persons; on the other hand, support for a nascent minority middle-class is not to be scoffed at, either.

Police-Community Relations

Establishment of civilian police review boards was one of the developments in which minority incorporation, in the 1984 California study, did make a difference; progress has been reported in the larger set of cities along these lines (Browning et al. 1984). Police review boards are, of course, only one of several strategies for reducing the use by police of often lethal force against minority people. Minority hiring onto police forces and changing top leadership are common and probably more-effective steps taken by minority regimes. Reviewing the literature on black regimes, Adolph Reed concludes, "Black regimes generally have been successful in curbing police brutality, which often has been prominent among black constituents' concerns. . . . Not surprisingly, black regimes have made substantial gains in black police employment, which contributes to the reduction in police brutality" (Reed 1988, 156).

Development of Minority Businesses

"Development" is typically supposed to be accomplished by set-asides or other special efforts to channel city spending for supplies and services to minority-owned businesses, thus encouraging the growth of the minority-owned and -operated private sector. The record of minority regimes in this area is murky. Perry reports little or no progress in New Orleans and Birmingham (Perry in Browning et al. 1990), and the record in other cities is mixed. Minority contracting is sometimes distorted by favoritism for a few firms with special ties to the regime, as governmental contracting frequently is. In some cities, some minority contractors have been found to be paper corporations, fronts for white-owned businesses. There may actually be success stories of city government support for minority businesses, but the evidence for them is hard to come by. Recent Supreme Court decisions are likely to make set-asides more difficult to implement even when city governments are willing to develop strong programs.

Appointments to Boards and Commissions

Minority regimes, generally, have made substantial numbers and proportions of minority appointments to city boards and commissions. No doubt the significance of these appointments varies enormously. In some cities, they may be entirely symbolic; in others, they are key steps in the extension of control over city government and associated agencies. In Oakland, for example, minority control of commissions with real governmental authority was essential to the establishment of minority control over city departments and over public authorities associated with the city, such as the Port Authority. This in turn allowed the dominant coalition to change the policies of those organizations to emphasize direct minority hiring, employment-related development, increased provision of facilities and services to minority residents and neighborhoods, and coordination with other minority-oriented programs of city government. The same pattern seems to be taking place in New York since Mayor Dinkins took office.

In these respects, the minority regimes studied here have typically been responsive. We simply do not have sufficient evidence about other areas of need in which they may or may not have made substantial progress. Adolph Reed, reviewing the available evidence, concludes that "the presence of a black mayor or regime has some, but less than dramatic, racially redistributive effect on allocation of public resources" (1988, 139). Several authors in our study noted that the regimes they studied had done little to meet the needs or even heed the objections of lower-income minority populations. Yet worsening poverty and other signs of social breakdown in inner-city populations would seem to be critical conditions that a city government must deal with, certainly a government that purports to be responsive to its minority population.

Unfortunately, it is difficult for city governments to have much impact on poverty. Due to cutbacks in programs instituted in the sixties and seventies, the federal government can no longer be depended upon to lead the effort to reduce poverty, and city governments lack both the fiscal resources and the structural capability to reduce poverty on their own, even if they were willing to take up where the federal government left off.

The Structural Limits of Minority Regimes

The painful truth is that many of the forces shaping the conditions under which the mass of low-income minority people live are not under the control of city governments, even governments run by minority regimes (Peterson 1981; Logan and Swanstrom 1990). Big cities with large minority populations are undergoing two radical transformations that have been under way for several decades and are continuing (Kasarda 1985; Wilson 1985; Downs 1985). One of these transformations is economic: the shift from manufacturing and distribution activities to administration, information, and other services, many highly technical. The number of low-skill jobs in such cities is dropping.

Big-city populations are being transformed as well: as blacks and Latinos, mainly poor and unskilled, increase in number, whites are leaving, partly for racial reasons but also as the continuation of long-term trends.

> This transformation is occurring in part because of the white majority's deliberate policy of segregating itself from both poor and nonpoor minority group members. Such segregation . . . operates by excluding nearly all poor households and most minority households from new suburban areas. Segregation is less evident in workplaces, although residential segregation also produces massive racial separation of jobs. . . .
>
> Confronted by a triple handicap of shrinking job opportunities, poor education, and low-quality neighborhoods [and in-

> creasing competition for low-skill jobs from new in-migration and from high birth rates in the inner city], these minority citizens are caught in a situation from which there appears to be no escape. (Downs 1985, 285)

Not only the white population but also its taxable wealth is being suburbanized; at the same time the minority populations of big cities are facing increasingly severe and intractable problems, their cities are losing resources to cope with them.

The roots of this knot of problems and constraints are many; again, they are not easily controlled by city governments. National policies that fight inflation by keeping interest rates high increase demand for the dollar, thereby raising the exchange value of the dollar, raising the prices of U.S. goods, and leading eventually to the closure of older manufacturing plants—deindustrialization—often in big cities. Construction of new regional freeways leads to more development in the suburbs than in the central city. The income tax deduction for mortgage loan interest increases the demand for new homes, which must be built in the suburbs.

The forces operating against big cities and their minority populations are so powerful and manifold that it is difficult to see any direct way out of their dilemmas.

What Can Be Done?

City governments are not, however, entirely without resources. The legal control of city governments over private development within the city, where blacks or Latinos have control of city government, "greatly increases the bargaining power of minorities in relation to major property owners who pay taxes, and increases their political power in Congress and the state legislatures" (Downs 1985, 291).

Minorities need allies, not only to win elections but to mobilize to the fullest extent possible the resources of the community to improve education and job training. Whereas in earlier decades supporters of minority demands for improved education and job training were powerful at the federal level, that is no longer true. Today, as Anthony Downs puts it, "the best natural allies are those who stand to lose most if the minority community cannot produce competent workers. That means businesses locked into the city itself, such as downtown property owners, nonbranching banks, or newspapers. They might support more ghetto enrichment as a quid pro quo for further integrated core development benefiting them" (1985, 292).

Adolph Reed emphasizes the advantageous location of black regimes in cities that are national or regional economic and administrative centers: "Those regimes should be capable of generating and enforcing measures aimed at channeling some of the proceeds of growth to address the needs of their electoral constituency. So far, however, none of the black regimes seems to have made genuine strides in that direction" (1988, 165).

This means "neither a reflexive opposition to economic growth nor an adversarial relationship with concrete business interests." Rather, the goal is to use "public authority to articulate policy agendas that accommodate economic growth as much as possible to the needs of the municipality and its citizenry rather than vice versa" (Reed 1988, 167). A major technique is the use of planning mechanisms to shape desirable private development and link it to an appropriate vision of the urgent problems and future of the city and its people. Downs and Reed both emphasize the leadership role of the minority community, and minority mayors in particular. Reed suggests that regimes use the "cultural authority of office to draw attention to unpalatable conditions that affect constituents but are beyond the scope of municipal control." They can also engage in forms of official protest, such as "passing unconstitutional tax ordinances, to dramatize existing inequities, thereby opening them to public awareness and debate and providing opportunities for political mobilization. Along each of these dimensions of advocacy for justice and equity, the record of black regimes is poor" (Reed 1988, 168).

Downs, too, stresses possibilities for effective advocacy that go beyond the current political efforts of minority regimes. One tactic that might be effective "is constantly emphasizing that spending more on educating minority group children is investing in the city's future, not just aiding the poor." Another tactic "would be launching a series of nonviolent demonstrations in white areas and schools about the poor quality of minority schools," resembling civil rights protests of the 1960s (1985, 292). Such advocacy might lead eventually to metropolitan tax sharing or other measures to channel state or local funds to inner-city schools, investment, and employment programs. Minority regimes could do more to organize and publicize demands on suburban governments in metropolitan regions and on state and national governments for resources and programs to alleviate their problems.

Downs emphasizes self-help efforts in minority communities, including "more internal discipline and leadership than most of them have shown up to now, both politically and socially. . . . Elements of any solution must come from within minority communities themselves, just as happened with other ethnic groups in the past. . . . Self-help efforts can make a huge difference in the welfare of both groups and individuals in a relatively open society" (1985, 292).

Minority regimes can play an important leadership role in this area and, with relatively modest governmental resources or private support, also can organize community self-help activities that involve recyclable financial resources. Leadership in self-help efforts would be an effective tactic politically as well as economically, because it would assure non-minority people that minority communities are doing what they can to help themselves.

This is not a comprehensive list of tactics; I have scarcely scratched the surface of Reed's complex and eloquent analysis. The fundamental point is that many minority regimes, even with the constraints they operate under, could undertake significant new efforts. These efforts could make a difference in revenue and program development. For this to happen, however, may require "greatly increased and informed pressure from the black electoral constituency" (Reed 1988, 196) and from liberal whites; this in turn implies broad public debate on the issues. Although this debate was not heard during the 1992 presidential election, at this point it is too early to assess whether the Clinton administration will target minority concerns in his efforts to develop "universal" and "investment" programs.

Thus, minority regimes should also undertake new efforts in the realm of political mobilization. Incorporation cannot be the limit of minority governmental effectiveness. Minority regimes—and prospective challengers to the leadership of those regimes—possess unique resources with which to pursue renewed mobilization and advocacy, so that issues of poverty, employment, housing, isolation, and inadequate education, for disadvantaged whites as well as for people of color, again find their way onto local, state, and national agendas. Understanding the histories of leadership, mobilization, and coalition formation and incorporation can help people of color and their white allies, both present and future, fashion the vision and the coalitions that will carry to a new plane the historical struggle to build democracy out of the centuries-long practice of racial domination.

References

Brown, Michael K., and Stephen P. Erie. 1981. "Blacks and the Legacy of the Great Society: The Economic and Political Impact of Federal Social Policy." *Public Policy* 12 (Summer): 299–330.

Browning, Rufus P., Dale Rogers Marshall, and David H. Tabb. 1979. "Minorities and Urban Electoral Change: A Longitudinal Study." *Urban Affairs Quarterly* 15 (2): 206–28.

———. 1984. *Protest Is Not Enough: The Struggle of Blacks and Hispanics for Equality in Urban Politics.* Berkeley and Los Angeles: University of California Press.

———, eds. 1990. *Racial Politics in American Cities.* New York: Longman.

Carmichael, Stokely, and Charles V. Hamilton. 1967. *Black Power.* New York: Random House.

Downs, Anthony. 1985. "The Future of Industrial Cities." In *The New Urban Reality,* ed. Paul E. Peterson, 281–94. Washington, D.C.: Brookings Institution.

Fitzpatrick, Joseph P., and Lourdes Traviesco Parker. 1981. "Hispanic Americans in the Eastern United States." *Annals of the American Academy of Political and Social Science* 454:98–124.

Kasarda, John D. 1985. "Urban Change and Minority Opportunities." In *The New Urban Reality,* ed. Paul E. Peterson, 33–67. Washington, D.C.: Brookings Institution.

Keiser, Richard A. 1990. "The Rise of Biracial Coalition in Philadelphia." In *Racial Politics in American Cities,* ed. Rufus P. Browning, Dale Rogers Marshall, and David H. Tabb. New York: Longman.

Logan, John R., and Todd Swanstrom, eds. 1990. *Beyond the City Limits: Urban Policy and Economic Restructuring in Comparative Perspective.* Philadelphia: Temple University Press.

Mollenkopf, John. 1990. "New York: The Great Anomaly." In *Racial Politics in American Cities,* ed. Rufus P. Browning, Dale Rogers Marshall, and David H. Tabb. New York: Longman.

———. 1992. *A Phoenix in the Ashes: The Rise and Fall of the Koch Coalition in New York City Politics.* Princeton: Princeton University Press.

Munoz, Carlos, Jr., and Charles P. Henry. 1990. "Coalition Politics in San Antonio and Denver: The Cisneros and Pena Mayoral Campaigns." In *Racial Politics in American Cities,* ed. Rufus P. Browning, Dale Rogers Marshall, and David H. Tabb. New York: Longman.

Murray, Charles. 1984. *Losing Ground: American Social Policy, 1950–1980.* New York: Basic Books.
Orfield, Gary. 1991. *The Closing Door: Conservative Policy and Black Opportunity.* Chicago: University of Chicago Press.
Perry, Huey L. 1990. "The Evolution and Impact of Biracial Coalitions and Black Mayors in Birmingham and New Orleans." In *Racial Politics in American Cities,* ed. Rufus P. Browning, Dale Rogers Marshall, and David H. Tabb. New York: Longman.
Peterson, Paul L. 1981. *City Limits.* Chicago: University of Chicago Press.
Preston, Michael B., Lenneal J. Henderson, Jr., and Paul Puryear, eds. 1987. *The New Black Politics.* 2d ed. New York: Longman.
Reed, Adolph. 1988. "The Black Urban Regime: Structural Origins and Constraints." In *Power, Community, and the City,* ed. Michael Peter Smith, 138–89. Comparative Urban and Community Research, vol. 1. New Brunswick, N.J.: Transaction Books.
Sonenshein, Raphael J. 1990. "Biracial Coalitions in Big Cities: Why They Succeed, Why They Fail." In *Racial Politics in American Cities,* ed. Rufus P. Browning, Dale Rogers Marshall, and David H. Tabb. New York: Longman.
Starks, Robert T., and Michael B. Preston. 1990. "Harold Washington and the Politics of Reform in Chicago: 1983–1987." In *Racial Politics in American Cities,* ed. Rufus P. Browning, Dale Rogers Marshall, and David H. Tabb. New York: Longman.
Stinchcomb, Arthur. 1968. *Constructing Social Theories.* New York: Wiley.
Stone, Clarence N. 1990. "Race and Regime in Atlanta." In *Racial Politics in American Cities,* ed. Rufus P. Browning, Dale Rogers Marshall, and David H. Tabb. New York: Longman.
Walzer, Michael. 1983. *Spheres of Justice.* New York: Basic Books.
Warren, Christopher L., John G. Corbett, and John F. Stack, Jr. 1990. "Hispanic Ascendancy and Tripartite Politics in Miami." In *Racial Politics in American Cities,* ed. Rufus P. Browning, Dale Rogers Marshall, and David H. Tabb. New York: Longman.
Wilson, William Julius. 1985. "The Urban Underclass in Advanced Industrial Society." In *The New Urban Reality,* ed. Paul E. Peterson, 129–60. Washington, D.C.: Brookings Institution.

20

Political Incorporation and Democratic Theory

Gary J. Jacobsohn

Democratic theory, at least as practiced in the United States, is fundamentally ambivalent about groups. Thus we have Madison's definition of a faction: "a number of citizens, whether amounting to a majority or minority of the whole, who are united and actuated by some common impulse of passion, or of interest, adverse to the rights of other citizens, or to the permanent and aggregate interests of the community" ([1787] 1961, 78). We must, then, be on our guard against the destructive and destabilizing potential of groups, but of course Madison's political solution to the problem that factionalism poses for popular government ultimately relies upon groups. That solution seeks to prevent group domination of the political process by exploiting the rich diversity of an extended republic. The "spirit of party and faction [must be involved] in the necessary and ordinary operations of the government" in order to accomplish "the principal task of modern legislation"—the checking of those very same factions (Madison [1787] 1961, 79).

This ambivalence is manifested in the Constitution itself. Groups are nowhere mentioned in the document, yet many of the individual rights that are guaranteed—for example, free speech and free exercise of religion—ensure that groups will have the right to defend their interests. One may subscribe to a group theory of politics (for many years the dominant school in American political science), while acknowledging, as many constitutional scholars have pointed out, that the Constitution provides very little (if any) support for the concept of group rights (see, e.g., Fiss 1976; Garet 1983; Glazar 1989). The Constitution facilitates the political activities of groups without providing them special recognition. Where constitutional protection is extended to groups, as in the case of the corporation (which is a group organized to operate a business), legal fictions are created that enable us to view the group as possessing the legal rights of an individual. American pluralism acknowledges groups as collections of individuals, not as units whose corporate identity carries with it any claim upon the state for special entitlement.

This is what makes an issue like affirmative action so controversial. Indeed, to the extent that programs designed to advance the interests of racial or ethnic groups are accepted as legitimate, they must be framed in the language of individual rights. Thus, a recent defense of affirmative action by an eloquent spokesman for a more communally oriented American society stipulates that "affirmative action can be seen as a means to promote not separation but integration—and, indeed, as an instrument in the long-term service of individualism" (Karst 1989, 168). The significance of the defense is best seen in the context of the distinction between "liberal pluralism" and "corporate pluralism," the latter entailing a concept of group entitlement and the formal recognition of ethnic and racial characteristics by the state (the distinction is elaborated in Gordon 1981). It is precisely because American constitutionalism is so wedded to the model of liberal pluralism that affirmative action, which in some other setting might be unapologetically related to the enhancement of cultural autonomy, must be defended as a stepping stone to assimilation.

The individualist ethos at the core of liberal pluralism requires assimilation in order to enforce its concept of citizenship. The term "Americanization," for example, does not, from this perspective, project the insidious connotations associated with cultural hegemony but rather connotes the incorporation of the outsider into a political culture whose essence consists in a commitment to certain regime principles. Thus, being an American has nothing to do with *who* one is and everything to do with *what* one believes. The nation is an inclusive concept entailing, in theory, the acceptance of anyone who is prepared to accept the reciprocal obligations that are the only conditions for membership in the political community. The law governing acquisition of membership in the American political community requires that an individual be "attached to the principles of the Constitution of the United States." This oath also serves to remind those who are already a part of the political community that their national identity is manifest in a particular creedal affirmation and that the arrival of new members will not, despite the diversity of backgrounds that will necessarily be incorporated into the polity, undermine the existing sense of what it means to be an American.

Ethnicity, race, and gender have of course been an important component of the American political culture, but they have always coexisted in some tension with the universalist ideal of American citizenship. The evolving antidiscrimination principle in constitutional law and jurisprudence is an expression of this ideal, which holds, at its core, that decisions in the public arena must not be cognizant of group differences. Thus, the underlying aspiration of the orthodox constitutional approach to protecting the rights of minorities is the replacement of ascriptive recognition with a universal standard of transcendent equality, the formal acknowledgment of the primacy of the individual over the group. While particular public policies—for example, the Civil Rights Act of 1964—are appropriately seen as advancing the interests of this or that group of people, the essence of the legislation was the delegitimation of group membership as a criterion in making public decisions about individuals.

The elevation and enhancement of the public profile of groups represents a potential threat to a citizenship based upon principles of inclusiveness. This potential is understood by certain radical theorists whose critique of liberal pluralism is premised upon a rejection of a "citizenship [that] transcends particularity and difference" (Young 1989, 250). Thus, the feminist theorist Iris Marion Young argues for an alternative vision in which "differences are publicly recognized and acknowledged as irreducible" (1989, 258). She stipulates that there are group-based perspectives and histories that can by their very nature never be completely understood by those whose identities are the product of a different group experience. The liberal policy of official blindness to race, gender, and cultural distinctions does violence, she maintains, to the various identities associated with such ascriptive designations. She proposes instead a concept of "*differential* citizenship" as the best way to secure justice in a heterogeneous society. The antidiscrimination principle of mainstream constitutional discourse needs, in this view, to be replaced by a radical acceptance of social diversity.

David Tabb does not subscribe to this sort of radical critique; instead, his work in urban politics reflects the reformist's impulse to push the system to its limits without seeking a fundamental revision in its basic structural commitments. However, a lack of precision in the articulation of his key conceptual variable—political incorporation—opens up the possibility that these limits will be passed, even if this is not the intention.

According to Tabb, "political incorporation concerns the extent to which group interests are effectively represented in policy-making." This definition is not particularly illuminating until we learn what effective representation entails. Tabb goes on, "The key to control of city government in favor of minority interests is minority inclusion in a dominant coalition, that is, minority participation in a coalition that can dominate city councils and secure repeated reelection. The political incorporation of black and Latino minorities has been measured by assessing the extent to which they were represented in coalitions that dominated city policy-making on minority-related issues." It is fair to say that political incorporation has something to do with domination.

It is also an interesting use of the term *incorporation*. Ordinarily when one says that one thing is incorporated into another, the meaning one wishes to convey is that the two things have become so blended together as to render them indistinguishable. The incorporation of one into the other thoroughly unites them to form, in essence, one consistent whole. To incorporate something into something else implies, in this customary understanding, much more than to add something to something already in existence; it means that the something that has been incorporated has become an integral part of the newly enlarged something else. Clearly, however, this is not Tabb's understanding, since his use of the term seems to suggest quite the opposite of blending or fusion. Instead, his notion of incorporation leaves the newly incorporated agent or group in its previously unamalgamated state but in a fundamentally altered power relation with other groups in the society.

Tabb presents us with a comparative picture in which blacks and Latinos display different degrees of incorporation and in which cities vary markedly in the extent to which they have achieved incorporationist goals. The resulting ranking reserves places at the top for cities such as Berkeley, where blacks or Latinos play an equal or leading role in a dominant coalition that is strongly committed to minority interests. Incorporation varies directly with the strength of a particular group's position within a dominant governmental coalition. Latinos for the most part are only weakly incorporated within the political system, for they have generally abjured the "comprehensive goals of the black power movement," instead relying upon a much more limited understanding of the appropriate role of government. Their politics is characterized as conservative incorporation, which, in the Tabb model, comes very close to being a contradiction in terms.

There is of course no contradiction if the more assimilationist model of incorporation is employed; the Latino experience (as described by Tabb), in which an outsider group maneuvers for mainstream inclusion within a framework shaped by the liberal, individualist premises of the existing political arrangements, would then qualify as strongly incorporationist. It may not be a dominant force within the local political environment, but then it is always worth bearing in mind that in a complex federal system there is no guarantee that domination of the local arena will have a meaningful impact on social change. Perhaps there is a need here for less-confusing nomenclature, since what Tabb is really attempting to measure is potential political clout within an urban locale. This would eliminate such awkward descriptions as "rollbacks of minority incorporation," which Tabb uses to portray what has in the recent past occurred in such places as Chicago and Philadelphia. If there is incorporation in the sense of merger, or bringing together into a single whole, then a rollback should logically not occur—which perhaps explains why the word *excorporation* does not exist. But in fact if what we are talking about is political clout, that is, the capacity of a particular group to exert influence over other political actors, then the withdrawal from an alliance, voluntarily or involuntarily, is a perfectly natural and familiar event. Have other groups—Jews, Italians, Irish—experienced the process of incorporation followed by a rollback? These are examples of ethnic groups that have, politically and socially, become more or less assimilated into the larger culture, thus making it extremely difficult to imagine their disengagement and return to outsider status.

If this were simply a matter of semantics, extended commentary would be unwarranted. But the alternative uses of "incorporation" bear directly upon the role of the group in democratic and constitutional theory. The common point of departure for both uses is the simple recognition that in this multicultural society religious, ethnic, and racial groups will seek to improve their condition through the political process. This is a given; nothing in fact could be more "American." And it is also true that group solidarity has been an important variable in measuring the ultimate success of the group in attaining its goals. Whatever one's evaluation of group theory in political science, no one any longer can reasonably contest its basic premise, that understanding the processes of government is impossible without taking seriously the politics of group dynamics. However, the character of those dynamics will either allay or intensify the concerns about groups that were mentioned earlier, namely, that particularistic interests will come to dominate the public agenda and that the universalistic assumptions of the liberal conception of citizenship will be negated. In regard to these concerns, Tabb's notion of political incorporation warrants special notice.

It is particularly noteworthy, for example, that integral to his operational definition of incorporation, Tabb recommends a focus on "the substantive rights of similarly disadvantaged groups" rather than on "the procedural rights of individuals." What does it mean to "go beyond procedural guarantees"? It means "includ[ing] an equal or leading role in a dominant coalition strongly committed to minority interests." The distinction in the alternative versions of political incorporation is effectively captured by the emphasis upon group rights. Unlike group interests, group rights assert a claim of entitlement rather than of consideration, which is to say that they demand satisfaction. Their recognition, in other words, is not simply a political question, it is a matter of basic justice. In a judicial context such claims of entitlement (as applied to individuals) are frequently interpreted to mean that they carry a certain trumping power, so that ordinarily they will prevail over competing claims of interest. By recognizing the rights-based claim, a court is essentially affirming a dominant position for the right vis-à-vis the non-rights-based competitive claim. Within an urban *political* context, the satisfaction of a substantive group right will require an analogous affirmation to legitimate *its* dominant position among the various contenders for public consideration. Thus, it is perfectly understandable that the theme of dominance appears as a constant and ubiquitous motif in Tabb's chapter.

A claim of entitlement is more than an assertion of dominance; it is also a countermajoritarian claim. Courts, therefore, are the appropriate place for such claims to be addressed. When, however, they assert themselves within the political environment, they pose vexing problems for democratic theory. Orthodox pluralist theory, of course, presents its own set of problems as far as majoritarianism is concerned, but these are different in kind from the sort that are implicitly raised by Tabb. The pluralists, after all, insisted that their ideas were supportive of majority rule, and they spent much of their time defending themselves against their detractors' charges that pluralism in operation was countermajoritarian. This contrasts with Tabb's incorporationist framework in which the normative ideal is represented by a reform-oriented coalition in which an autonomous minority leadership plays the central and dominant role in the vigorous pursuit of minority-oriented policies. This means more than that the city government in a fully incorporated urban community will, as the result of its inclusion of a minority presence, display a heightened sensitivity to the problems of minorities and thus seek to address these problems within the context of the total political environment. Rather, it means that in a maximally incorporated city like Berkeley, with a black population of 29 percent, the substantive *rights* of that minority demand that public policy be responsive to its particular claim.

It is not surprising in this regard that the views of Carmichael and Hamilton figure so prominently in Tabb's article, although it is revealing that the more radical implications of their analysis are omitted. The references to *Black Power* speak to the relatively noncontroversial strategic considerations that should inform the political activities of groups seeking to enhance their bargaining position within a pluralistic society. Thus, a bargaining position from strength will be more effective than one from weakness. But this advice speaks to a more fundamental (and theoretically interesting) point made in the context of Carmichael and Hamilton's discussion of what they refer to as the myths of coalition. One of the myths to which they give special attention is that "the interests of black people are identical with the interests of certain liberal, labor, and other reform groups." "Those groups," they go on, "accept the legitimacy of the basic values and institutions of the society, and fundamentally are not interested in a major reorientation of the society" (Carmichael and Hamilton 1967, 60).

By rejecting this myth Carmichael and Hamilton may be understood as questioning precisely those tenets of liberal pluralism that are embodied in Madisonian majoritarianism. When Tabb uses as a measure of incorporation the extent to which a ruling coalition exercises the powers of city government to pursue the broader aims of the black power movement (especially an agenda of redistributive allocation), he is, it would seem, seeking to achieve what Madison's solution intended to prevent, group domination of the political process. Far from being an integrative force, political incorporation assumes an inevitably divisive presence, exacerbating community tensions along the fault lines of race, class, and ethnicity. This divisiveness entails more than the familiar sorts of political conflict endemic to group politics; because it is directed toward the fulfillment of an agenda of minority *rights*—rights that may, as Carmichael and Hamilton maintain, be fundamentally opposed to the interests of other minorities—incorporation actually involves a politics of exclusion.

Even if we assume, as we might be able to in the case of Berkeley, that with the electoral assistance of a minority of the majority, a rule-making majority supports the minority-oriented agenda, meaningful social change is unlikely if (1) the coming to power of this new coalition accelerates the process of middle-class flight from the urban center and (2) the pursuit of a radical redistributive agenda makes it increasingly difficult to attract support, both financial and political, from the white business sector and from state and federal governments. Tabb quite properly focuses on the structural limits of minority regimes. He observes that "at the same time the minority populations of big cities are facing increasingly severe and intractable problems, their cities are losing resources to cope with them." If the policies (real, perceived, or expected) of a strongly incorporated coalition are themselves partly responsible for this depressing predicament, then one might question the desirability of moving in the direction of the black power model. This is not a new issue; one need only recall Madison's penultimate paragraph in *The Federalist* No. 10, where it is pointed out that the triumph of a local political faction will be checked and effectively nullified unless it succeeds in engaging the trust and cooperation of the broader political community. In this connection, Tabb's depiction of the urban machine as an obstacle to incorporation is significant. Thus, "the machine stands as a barrier to the formation and success of reform-oriented coalitions, in which more autonomous minority leadership would play central and dominant roles." Perhaps so, but did not the old and now largely discredited machine play a not inconsiderable role in horizontally integrating many minorities, including blacks, into the local political community and, with respect to the Madisonian argument, vertically integrating them within the federal power structure? It would be worth studying, for example, the role of the machine in the passage of important national legislation in the fields of housing, employment, and civil rights.

The foregoing should in no way be construed as a denial of the proposition that the heightened profile of minorities in positions of political leadership is a desirable development. There seems little question that governing entities operate differently (i.e., they are more sensitive to the concerns of minorities) when they are racially and ethnically integrated. Moreover, to the extent that effective governing is directly related to the level of confidence that the governed have in the governors, the public interest is no doubt advanced when minorities can more closely and tangibly identify with their elected officials. But to the degree that group expectations are elevated to the point where members of the group are conditioned to assume that a particular electoral presence implies a governmental obligation to en*force* their rights, the long-term prospects for legitimacy cannot be so confidently asserted. It is one thing to be frustrated in the outcome of an ongoing political struggle; it is quite another to be repeatedly denied what is one's due.

Finally, there is the likelihood that, intentions to the contrary notwithstanding, Tabb's political incorporation will evolve into some sort of differential citizenship permutation. Thus, the emphasis on group entitlement suggests that one's rights (to a particular result) as a citizen are in fact related very strongly to *who* one is rather than what shared commitments one is prepared to acknowledge. This ascriptive recognition is indeed contrary to "the basic values and institutions of the society." Although it is surely easy to sympathize with and embrace a solution that advances a politics of domination for a historically dominated minority, it may be prudent to question its ultimate worth. Does it make political sense to commend for a minority a solution that links incorporation with domination? And as a strictly normative matter, should we entertain a democratic vision that *incorporates* the concept of domination?

References

Carmichael, Stokely, and Charles V. Hamilton. 1967. *Black Power.* New York: Vintage Books.

Fiss, Owen M. 1976. "Groups and the Equal Protection Clause." *Philosophy and Public Affairs* 5:107–77.

Garet, Ronald. 1983. "Communality and Existence: The Rights of Groups." *Southern California Law Review* 56:1001–75.

Glazar, Nathan. 1989. "The Constitution and American Diversity." In *Forging Unity out of Diversity: The Approaches of Eight Nations,* ed. Robert A. Goldwin, Art Kaufmann, and William A. Schambra, 60–84. Washington, D.C.: American Enterprise Institute for Public Policy Research.

Gordon, Milton M. 1981. "Models of Pluralism: The New American Dilemma." *Annals* 454:178–88.

Karst, Kenneth L. 1989. *Belonging to America: Equal Citizenship and the Constitution.* New Haven: Yale University Press.

Madison, James. [1787] 1961. *The Federalist* No. 10. In *The Federalist Papers,* ed. Clinton Rossiter, 77–84. New York: Mentor.

Young, Iris Marion. 1989. "Polity and Group Difference: A Critique of the Ideal of Universal Citizenship." *Ethics* 99 (January): 250–74.

21

"Private" Coercion and Democratic Theory: The Case of Gender-Based Violence

Virginia Sapiro

The divine right *of husbands, like the divine right of kings, may, it is to be hoped, in this enlightened age, be contested without danger.*

—*Mary Wollstonecraft,* A Vindication of the Rights of Woman, *1792*

All men of any conscience [now] believe that their duty to their wives is one of the most binding of their obligations. Nor is it supposed to consist solely in protection, which, in the present state of civilization, women have almost ceased to need: it involves care for their happiness and consideration of their wishes, with a not unfrequent sacrifice of their own to them. The power of husbands has reached the stage which the power of kings had arrived at, when opinion did not yet question the rightfulness of arbitrary power, but in theory, and to a certain extent in practice, condemned the selfish use of it.

—*Harriet Taylor, "The Enfranchisement of Women," 1851*

Some will object, that a comparison cannot be fairly made between the government of the male sex and the forms of unjust power which I have adduced in illustration of it, since these are arbitrary, and the effect of mere usurpation, while it on the contrary is natural. But was there ever any domination which did not appear natural to those who possessed it?

—*John Stuart Mill,* The Subjection of Women, *1869*

Feminist theory is most often called upon to aid the study of women and their situation. When critics draw feminist and more-canonical political theory together, it is most often to use the feminist theory to criticize the treatment of women in canonical theory. But feminist theory has more to offer political theory than this. Because of its specific

An earlier version of this paper was delivered at the Democratic Theory Symposium, sponsored by the National Endowment for the Humanities, in Williamstown, Mass., July 1989, the purpose of which was to work toward better integration of "empirical" and "theoretical" approaches to the study of democratic theory and practice. I would like to thank George Marcus et al. for a great seminar and very good comments and suggestions.

focus on gender relations and power, it provides a medium to consider some of the problems and limits of politics in neglected but potentially very fruitful ways.[1] This essay considers one such problem: the role of coercion within democratic theory, as it looks from a perspective of feminist theory and research on violence.

Likewise, despite the common practice of political theorists and students of political psychology and behavior to sit at separate tables, there is a strong current of research that integrates the two by investigating what we might call the cognitive practices of specific political cultures, probing the nature and potential of political thinking and behavior with regard to democratic norms. Here I take this approach to the study of violence, coercion, and democratic norms, beginning with general theoretical and conceptual remarks on these relations, then turning to empirical work, drawn largely from psychology and sociology, on gender-based violence against women.

Democratic Theory and Feminist Theory

"Democratic theory" covers a wide range of people and texts. It is therefore prudent to keep working definitions generous, such as Robert Dahl's solution: "At a minimum . . . democratic theory is concerned with processes by which ordinary citizens exert a relatively high degree of control over leaders" (Dahl 1956, 3). Accepting this relatively open definition, many would argue that it follows that a *more* minimal condition of democratic theory is that it be concerned with processes by which ordinary citizens exert a relatively high degree of control over themselves.

This, of course, is by no means the dominant view. "Control over leaders" flags for most of us a clearly political phenomenon. "Control over self" is a more extensive concept, clearly extending beyond what is usually defined as political and into the private and interpersonal. But can we be sure a democratic political theory can truly fulfill its brief, even within the realm of politics conventionally understood, if it focuses only on politics as conventionally understood? At least some influential

1. For further discussion, see Sapiro 1992.

political writers have thought not; Alexis de Tocqueville, for example, clearly defined gender relations, among other "social" phenomena, as an integral part of an understanding of democracy in America (Tocqueville [1835, 1840] 1945, vol. 2, chaps. 8–12).

It makes simple sense that in gender-stratified societies one cannot understand political power without taking gender into account any more than one can understand power in class societies without focusing on class or understand power in nations with apartheid without considering race. To understand the political aspects and implications of sex/gender systems we must, as in all cases, look at governmental organization and processes to evaluate political systems in their full depth and significance for the publics affected by them.[2] This is especially true if we happen to have the barbarians' point of view on Athenian democracy: the view of those left out of the picture.

Feminist theorists have been especially aware of the limits of focusing only on "public" life, primarily because of their concern with conditions of women's lives traditionally defined out of the interest of the mainstream of democratic theory.[3] These concerns revolve mainly around power and coercion in private life and social relations between women and men especially, but not solely, in the family.

The rise of liberal democratic theory has conventionally been described as antipatriarchal in motive and direction. Mary Wollstonecraft, Harriet Taylor, and John Stuart Mill, quoted above, were among the earlier theorists who recognized some of the more ironic limitations to the antipatriarchalism of democrats. The canonical history of democratic theory has been notably silent on its ignorance or, worse, preservation of patriarchal and fundamentally illiberal (in its catholic sense) tendencies with regard to state-recognized and governed relations between women and men within private life (Pateman 1988).

This is not the place to rehearse the wide range of legal and conventional abridgments of women's ability to assert control over their lives, not to mention their political leaders. These were largely based on the notion that while men are governed by varying governmental regimes,

2. For definition and discussion of *sex/gender system,* see Rubin 1974 and Sapiro 1990.

3. Here I enclose "public" in quotation marks because this chapter raises questions about how we define the distinction between what is private and what is public and political. With this understanding the marks will be eliminated from the remainder of the chapter.

women are governed by the marriage contract, the "head of household," and the needs of societies for women's reproductive and household labor.[4] Feminist theorists, for example, cannot help noticing that while theoretical and political debates about the relation between property and political rights and obligations raged in the eighteenth and nineteenth centuries, married women were legally barred even from owning the property on which these hypothetical other rights might be based.[5]

Feminist theorists, then, rarely attempt to understand political relations without reference to private relations and private (especially familial) life. In the historical reality of women's lives, any notion of having a "relatively high degree of control over political leaders" is clearly intertwined with the difficulties of having some control over their own lives. At minimum—the level at which I focus here—feminist theory resists the notion that public and private life are so conceptually distinct that we can seek to characterize the political "system," or "culture," without reference to how private and social life work.

Coercion, Violence, and Democratic Norms

Posing a connection between political structures and relations and those in private life and the family is not, of course, unique to feminist theory. The stunning fourteenth-century allegorical frescoes by Ambrogio Lorenzetti in Siena that depict the effects of good and bad government are graphic testaments to a persistent belief that the goodness and badness of life and government are inextricably intertwined: under conditions of good government people live in domestic harmony, probably in both senses of the word *domestic.*

One of the things that makes bad government bad is the ubiquitous threat of coercive violence; one of the things that makes good government good is security from coercion and violence. For democrats especially, good government does not depend on regular use of force or even the apparent threat of force, and it does not sanction the use of

4. This is not to say that women's lives are the same regardless of the type of political regime.

5. Married women were given the legal right to own property in the United States in the 1840s and in Britain in the 1880s. Without the right to own property, women lacked even the right of management of their own children.

force except under special and carefully considered circumstances. If a government does not rule by terror and violence, neither can any specific social group be governed by terror and violence.

Defining a political culture as democratic depends on the existence of some minimal level of support for democratic norms. Regardless of the nature of public law on civil liberties, for example, we would expect the quality of democracy to be substantially affected not just by the degree of public attachment to generally stated global norms of tolerance and due process but also by how tolerant the public is of different groups within society and how willing they are to allow different groups equal civil rights. Many scholars have investigated public tolerance in order to understand democratic political culture (e.g., McClosky and Brill 1983; Sniderman et al. 1989).

It is a small step to make a similar argument about support for democratic norms with regard to group-based violence. For a society to have a democratic political culture, it cannot encompass substantial public opinion that tolerates or rationalizes social group-based violence any more than it can incorporate substantial intolerance of the rights of social, economic, or political participation of different social groups. It is important to note that *toleration* or *rationalization* of violence does not refer simply to whether people express favorable attitudes toward violence by members of one social group against another. In fact I am more interested in sets of beliefs and orientations that tend to excuse those who have committed such violence, often by displacing responsibility for the violence from the perpetrator to the victim.

We may surmise, for example, that in the earlier part of this century it was not necessary for many whites to accept the statement "It is good for white men to kill black men" in order for them to "understand" and have sympathy for those white men who lynched black men. The actual incidents could be explained away on an *apparent* case by case basis without creating dissonance with the general principle of opposition to murder or genocide. "I'm not in favor of it, but they only brought it upon themselves" is a sentiment often used to excuse the use of force in many settings, especially by members of dominant groups against the less powerful.

A fruitful turn in the integration of normative and empirical theorizing and research on democracy has been to move from straightforward notions of public opinion on key elements of a democratic society to wider investigation of the various cognitive practices underlying interaction in a democratic society. Thus, for example, although it is useful and interesting to know public attitudes toward specific issues and policies, it is also important to know what kinds of schemas tend to bind specific events or people into coherent meaning in the minds of the public within a given culture. It is important to know the relation between reactions to specific incidents and broader ideological principles. This cannot be done simply by studying the documents of a political culture but must include psychological and social psychological research on actual participants in that culture.

Gender-Based Violence

Scholars drawing on feminist theory incorporate in their understanding of political culture the specific relations of power and coercion between women and men. Most early democratic theorists, and even those who criticized patriarchalism, at least assumed (and sometimes have justified) inegalitarian gender relations within the family and even some degree of force. It is interesting how possible it is even in late twentieth-century writing on democratic theory and the family for nonfeminist writers barely to mention women at all, and certainly not to raise questions regarding men's power over women or men's use of force.[6] In contrast, these matters have been central to feminist political argument at least since the time of Mary Wollstonecraft. For feminist theorists and activists, gender-based violence against women is, among other things, a problem of democracy. It is, in part, a public problem rationalized in terms of private motives.[7]

Gender-based violence against women refers to types of violence perpetrated against women by men. More important, they are types of violence generally schematized, explained, or justified specifically with reference to gender relations, gender roles, and gender-based ascriptions about personality. These types of violence include rape, sexual harassment, and spouse abuse, including marital rape. Some writers go further and include incest with children.[8]

6. A list of examples would be too long to provide. Two particularly interesting ones are Schochet 1975 and Fishkin 1983.

7. The echo of Harold Lasswell (1960) is intended.

8. Most cases of incest perpetrated against children by adults involve a male adult and female child. Other forms of child abuse within the family involve a more even balance of females and males as victims and perpetrators.

A review of relevant research and theory indicates that whereas these different forms of violence against women were once analyzed only as distinct problems, they are now understood as linked together through their gender basis (Edwards 1987). The integration of theory on different forms of gender-based violence has considerably aided the specific research done on each of these problems, in large part by providing a useful conceptual framework. Both feminist observers of violence and women themselves generally experience a continuum of violence to which they are subject specifically because they are women (Hanmer 1984; Kelly 1987; Radford 1987). Accounts of the subjective experience of victims, the cultural and legal constructions of these forms of coercion, and the reactions of criminal and civil justice systems are very similar.[9]

The fact that these different forms of violence are often drawn together as an analytical category does not imply that "gender-based violence" is an undifferentiated category. Women experience a continuum of gender-based violence with different impact and implications for them. Liz Kelly (1987), for example, found that women perceive a continuum of sexual violence directed against them that ranges from typical to aberrant, from unharmful to harmful. Where an incident lies on this continuum helps determine the victim's likely response. Thus, for example, verbal sexual violence from strangers is likely to be regarded by most women as both typical and relatively unharmful.

A majority of women are directly or indirectly affected by this violence, either through direct experience or threat or by their fear of it.[10] It is difficult to be precise about incidence because, as the FBI estimates, only a small minority of cases of rape or domestic violence are even reported to the police. Surveys consistently reveal large numbers of women who have experienced rape, battery, or sexual harassment but

9. Rape and spouse abuse fall under criminal law, whereas sexual harassment in the workplace and educational institutions is covered by civil law.

10. For purposes of shorthand, when I say "violence" against women, I am referring to *gender-based* violence of the types listed above. If I were to include all types of violence, men's lives are, of course, more violent than women's (and in the United States, black men are especially likely to be victims of violence). Men are more likely than women to be the victims of all types of crimes other than those that are gender or sexually based; they are the majority of perpetrators except among prostitutes and juvenile runaways. The strength of my argument is not based in incidence rates per se; the social and, especially, political significance of incidence is much more complex and depends on many factors.

who have not reported the attacks either because they believed nothing would be done or, worse, because they believed that the result would be that the perpetrator or the justice system would punish them for speaking out.

The fear of violence plays a special role in women's lives. As Riger and Gordon (1988) show, women, more than men, see themselves as potential victims, and this fear affects their day-to-day lives in many ways, including where and how they travel and how comfortable they feel in different settings. Men are less likely than women to see violence against women as either a widespread or serious problem. They are especially less likely to believe that women are subject to sexual harassment (Jenkins and Dambrot 1987; Jensen and Gutek 1982; U.S. Merit Systems Protection Board 1981; Collins and Blodgett 1981). They are less likely to define "unwanted sexual intercourse between a husband and wife" as rape and less likely to define "a relative having sexual intercourse with a teenager under age eighteen" or "a relative having sexual intercourse with a child" as rape.

There are a number of reasons for this difference in perception. One, of course, is that men are considerably less likely to have suffered any of the forms of gender-based violence, and certainly the fear of it plays very little role in their lives. Also, women do not tend to speak about their experiences very widely among other women; they are even less likely to tell men. Thus, men are probably less aware than women of how many of their acquaintances have been victims.

It is common for men who have been perpetrators not to be fully aware that they have participated in coercion of women. Even convicted rapists tend to deny the violence of their own actions and to transform the event either into one in which the victim consented (actively or tacitly) or in which the victim was otherwise deserving of the treatment she received (Scully 1990; Wolfe and Baker 1980). Wife batterers do the same. Evidence shows that men often have difficulty distinguishing women's friendly behavior from their seductive behavior, in part because they have been socialized to think of women as defined by sexuality (Abbey 1982; see also Shotland and Craig 1988).

Neil M. Malamuth's work on rape proclivity provides a startling picture of orientations toward violence against women. In his surveys 35 percent of young men said there was at least some likelihood they would rape if they thought they could get away with it. In order to investigate the behavioral significance of self-reports of rape proclivity, Malamuth conducted an experiment in which men could choose punishments for error on the part of another person in a problem-solving exercise. The partners in each session were female confederates who, as part of the experimental manipulation, mildly insulted or rejected the subject before the experiment. During the experiments men who had reported higher rape proclivity displayed more anger and aggression toward their partners and reported a greater desire to hurt them (Malamuth 1981). His research is consistent with the bulk of research on rape, showing that rape is not simply a matter of men with overactive libidos (or women with underdressed bodies).

Research such as that cited above and to follow has been widely used by political and policy researchers to consider questions relating to criminal and civil justice systems as well as the delivery of intervention services designed to prevent violence or mitigate its negative effects once violence has occurred. But this work has other implications for political science as well; these concern our understanding of what democratic theory and practice is and how we might define and assess democratic political cultures. Focusing on the gender basis of power and coercion offers a handle on questions of democratic theory and practice that take us beyond consideration of the gender basis of political society, although that is important enough.[11] It also tells us about the degree to which a society has moved away from ascriptive bases of power and those that depend on strength as the basis of legitimacy. In *The Subjection of Women* John Stuart Mill argued that modern political life is marked by rejection of the idea that "might makes right." He further wrote that as the era of slavery drew to a close, the relations between women and men, and especially the justifications generally offered for the power discrepancy, were the single exceptions to the new understanding of politics and political relations. Mill was one of the few male writers to

11. The argument that gender questions and violence against women are important per se is, unfortunately, controversial. In delivering an early version of this chapter, I have noted (and a majority of the other women present have remarked to me on) a common tendency for men's discussion to focus on the relative unimportance of the *gender* basis of violence in the types of violence I am discussing, or the relative unimportance of violence in women's lives as compared with men, or the relative unimportance of studying violence against *women.* The suggestion that women or gender is not a particularly important topic is often made to women's studies scholars.

make note of the role played by violence against women in women's lives and to regard it as a subject of political analysis and a test of women's incorporation into a liberal society.[12]

The remainder of this chapter, then, will explore thinking about gender-based violence against women, and the belief systems of which these thoughts are a part. I look at the public understanding of violence against women to see its relation to the ideological construction of women's roles and status and the gender basis of power and control. Through these studies we can see the circumstances under which violence against women is "understood" in the sense used earlier: rationalized at an individual level but in terms that are group based. I argue that much of the significance of gender-based violence against women lies in the fact that what is demonstrably partly a group-based, political phenomenon is consciously formulated by most people as an individual private and personal problem.

It is important to note that I make no claims here about the causes of this violence and no argument regarding the relation between democratic political processes and structures, conventionally conceived, and the incidence or treatment of gender-based violence against women. One might investigate such connections, but I am not doing so here. My goal is to understand what links there may be between the politics of and thinking about gender and violence against women and the politics of and thinking about democracy.

Victim Precipitation and Rape

One of the central issues in research on violence against women is the assumption of *victim precipitation* that has been found in the general public and, indeed, among agents of the criminal justice system. This term incorporates two things: first, that the apparent victim did something to provoke the act of violence and, second, that in so doing, the victim has assumed responsibility for the violence, or the victim's provocation has at least negated the perpetrator's responsibility. Both

12. Both Mill and Taylor wrote a series of newspaper articles in the early 1850s on the shocking prevalence of wife battery. The early 1850s marked the first public activism against wife battery and family abuse in Great Britain and, especially, in the United States. See Pleck 1987 and Shanley 1989.

conditions are important. There are many cases of crime, for example, in which we can argue that the victim did something that might have provoked a crime or made it easier, but that is rarely held to "excuse" the criminal. There are also no other types of violence in which it is the category of violence itself that leads to a common, even normal assumption that the victim must be at least partly responsible for the crime and that it was somehow beyond the perpetrator's power to avoid engaging in a violent act.

The notion of victim precipitation plays an important role in each type of gender-based violence against women. Susan Estrich, a law professor motivated to study the problem after her own rape, was not the first to note that, in effect, there is a widespread belief that "real rape" rarely takes place, because the women involved have brought the use of force upon themselves or have not actually experienced force in any real sense (Estrich 1987). Women who have experienced rape, battery, or harassment often find if they report what has happened to them, *they* are treated as though they are the guilty parties in need of defense. The experience of women in the justice system has often been labeled the "second assault."

Many researchers have investigated the belief systems surrounding violence against women. This literature suggests the existence of an ideological framework that allows justification of or explanation for individual acts of violence but that does so in large part by drawing on group-based attributions and by reinforcing differential power of women and men as groups.

Martha Burt (1980) did one of the first and most important studies of the ideological construction of rape. She was interested in particular in "rape myth acceptance," a set of beliefs and attitudes that deny the existence of rape, in large part by blaming the victim and removing responsibility from the man or men who rape or simply by assuming women are irrational, lying, or both. Among these myths are the beliefs that "any healthy woman can successfully resist a rapist if she wants to" or that "in most rapes the victim is promiscuous or has a bad reputation" or that "women who get raped while hitchhiking get what they deserve." The logical conclusion of some of these statements is that there really is no such thing as rape.

Burt also investigated two other orientations toward gender and sexuality to see how they were related to rape myth acceptance. One, *sexual conservatism*, consists primarily of statements supporting the notions that women are and should be less sexually interested and active than men and that the purpose of sexuality is procreation. These statements tend to emphasize difference between the sexual natures of male and female and especially the division between male activity and female passivity. The other orientation Burt labeled *adversarial sexual beliefs*. These statements pose the relations between women and men as competitive, adversarial, and manipulative. Among these statements, for example, are "A woman will only respect a man who will lay down the law to her," "A woman is usually sweet until she's caught a man; then she lets her true self show," and "Men only want one thing." Burt found both sexual conservatism and adversarial sexual beliefs related to rape myth acceptance. Rape myths are tied to a syndrome of traditional beliefs about and attitudes toward sexuality and gender.

A study of the United States, Great Britain, Israel, and West Germany also found a significant relation between acceptance of rape myths and restrictive beliefs about women's roles (Costin and Schwarz 1987). In their study of perceptions of date rape, Megan Jenkins and Faye Dambrot (1987) found that men's tendency to define as rape a situation in which a man explicitly forces a woman to have sex was related to their rejection of rape myths.[13] Investigation of the role of rape myths and traditional gender and sexual ideology have become increasingly important as the evidence mounts that men who have been convicted of violence against women do not differ very much from other men in their psychological profiles or sexual history. One study offers an especially instructive comparison of the differences. Ronald L. Scott and Laurie A. Tetrault (1987) studied twenty California prison inmates convicted of rape, twenty inmates convicted of a nonsexual violent crime, and twenty noncriminal participants in a vocational training program. The groups were matched to the rapist group in age, marital status, socioeconomic status, ethnicity, and geographic origin. The participants in the study were asked series of questions tapping attitudes toward and beliefs about gender and sexuality.

Rapists and other violent criminals were similar to each other and more conservative than the normal group in their general attitudes toward women's freedom and independence. Rapists were more conservative than both other groups on four scales: (1) vocational, educa-

13. They also found that women and men were both less likely to perceive a situation as rape if the man paid for the date than if the woman and man shared the cost.

tional, and intellectual roles; (2) dating, courtship, and etiquette; (3) drinking, swearing, and dirty jokes; and (4) sexual behavior. In other words, rapists were found more opposed to the equality of women, more supportive of restricted opportunities, and more supportive of subservient, passive, and stereotypical roles. As Scott and Tetrault point out, their findings are "consistent with the notion that rapists have a need to control women, especially sexually," as many other studies had suggested.

In his study of rape proclivity, Malamuth (1981) also found that men who reported themselves more likely to rape had more callous attitudes toward rape than other men and greater acceptance of rape myths. In a study in which student subjects kept diaries of their activities, researchers found that there was a greater likelihood of sexual aggression against women when the men paid for the date, when they drove, or if they had the complex of attitudes Burt described as supportive of violence against women (Muehlenhard and Linton 1987).

Traditional gender ideology and rape myth acceptance not only frame the orientations of perpetrators, they also shape the experience of victimization. A study of twelve hundred people found that the more strongly women believe in traditional gender divisions of labor and power, the more likely they are to believe it is a woman's own fault if she is a victim of sexual harassment. Indeed, women with traditional gender ideology are more likely to engage in self-blame. They thus also tend to suffer greater psychological damage as a result of the experience of violence.

The prevalence of rape and attitudes toward it vary historically and cross-culturally. Peggy Sanday's (1981) research shows that although in some societies rape is very rare, in others it is a normal and even ritualized common occurrence. The prevalence of rape appears to be related to the status of women and, among other things, the degree to which men participate in child-care.

These studies lead to the conclusion that violence against women in the form of rape can be rationalized and tolerated through a gender ideology that places women in a restricted and subordinate status. They suggest that restrictive views of women's roles and traditional views of sexuality (which also tend to involve statements about the relative roles and natures of women and men) are not mere tangential errors of the unenlightened, but are part of a system of social group differentiation that can be—and has been—supportive of the use of force.

Gender-Based Family Violence

The last decade has witnessed a resurgence of scholarly and policy interest in family violence that far outstrips that of any previous period.[14] Within this area there is a large and growing amount of work on wife battery (for recent reviews, see Finkelhor and Yllö 1985; Margolin et al. 1988; Micklow 1988; Pagelow 1988; Sedlak 1988; Stark and Flitcraft 1988; Yllö and Bograd 1988).

It is notable that, as one review of the literature stated, "theorists and researchers in the field of family violence do not consider family violence as equivalent to criminal violence" (Bersani and Chen 1988, 58). One reason is that "criminal violence" is generally conceived as the illegitimate use of force, whereas the use of similar force against family members is understood as potentially legitimate. Research on treatment of wife battery within the legal system certainly bears this out. Until recently, the mandated role of police in cases of "domestic disturbance," as battery was called, was merely to calm the situation down. As in the case of rape, victims of wife battery face the suspicion or charge of victim precipitation, the view that the victim caused the use of force and that therefore the perpetrator is relieved of responsibility for it.

In her history of social policy on family violence, Elizabeth Pleck concludes that the "single most consistent barrier to reform against domestic violence" has been the ideological construction of the family as a private place, distinct from the public world and public intrusion and, particularly, one that is structured on the basis of certain conjugal and parental rights (1987, 7). Among the conjugal rights was traditionally the right of a husband to discipline his wife. As Pleck observes, "Although abuse has always been separate from correction, the right of discipline has served as a justification for virtually all forms of assault by parents and husbands short of those that cause permanent injury" (Pleck 1987, 8). Due to the marital exclusion in the rape laws of most jurisdictions, another conjugal right is that of a husband to have sex with his wife on demand.

Many family violence scholars agree that an important element in family violence is power seeking. It is often argued that wife batterers accept or take advantage of the social, cultural, and even legal authority

14. On the history of thinking on family violence in the United States, see Gordon 1988 and Pleck 1987. For general reviews of research, see Van Hasselt et al. 1988.

of husbands over wives, but do so as part of a search for unsatisfied power needs.[15] The "choice" of one's female partner is not random and is also not simply due to the fact that she might be close at hand. Reviews of research on abusers show that they tend to be relatively approving of violence, low in self-esteem, and traditional in their acceptance of gender stereotypes. As one review of the literature concluded:

> Although the abuser tends to value traditional characteristics of masculinity (e.g. dominance, success), he actually feels quite inadequate in these respects. This leads to feelings of low self-esteem. His need to maintain an over adequate facade, coupled with the inability to express feelings of vulnerability, leaves the man susceptible to overreaction when he perceives a threat, particularly at home, the one domain where he believes he dominates and is in control. (Margolin et al. 1988, 95)

Many researchers in this area argue that wife abuse depends in part on cultural acceptance of male abuse of women, at least under certain circumstances.

Gender norms as well as notions of the essential privacy of the family provide a rationale for violence against women. They make people "understand" the perpetrator of violence in a way people tend not to "understand" perpetrators of other sorts of violence: it is an understanding that shifts moral responsibility away from the man to some degree and demands that the woman share it.

Public orientations and beliefs legitimize violence by husbands against wives. Studies show that many people approve of spousal violence or believe that it is appropriate under certain circumstances. Evan Stark and J. McEvoy (1970), for example, found that one-quarter of their sample said they approve of husbands or wives hitting each other under some circumstances. Murray Straus describes an experiment in which he and a colleague asked subjects about appropriate punishments for a man who had knocked a female victim unconscious. If the respondents were led to believe the assailant was a husband, they prescribed less severe punishment (Straus 1980).

15. This discussion draws on material that is often cited as an explanation of the cause of wife abuse. Once again, I am trying to demonstrate some of the processes of legitimation or rationalization, not causation.

Violence against women at the hands of their husbands and lovers is more widespread and serious a problem than most people realize. Men have complete legal immunity in many states and most countries if they rape their wives, and most women know it would be pointless to try to charge with rape someone who has been a lover. Battery at the hands of a husband or lover is not considered comparable to the experience of assault and battery by those who are not related to their assailants by love, intimacy, or family ties. This intimate relation does not protect the victim. In 1985 the FBI reported that 30 percent of all female homicide victims were killed by their husbands or boyfriends (Rix 1988). The repercussions can be less direct and obvious. A study of 172 women visiting an outpatient clinic for bulimia found that 66 percent had been physically victimized in the past, including 23 percent who had been raped, 29 percent who had been sexually molested, 29 percent who had been physically abused, and 23 percent who had been battered (Root and Fallon 1988). Violence, of course, is not healthy, even when it is private.

Democracy and Violence Against Women

The literature on gender-based violence against women, including wife battery, rape, and sexual harassment, reveals an underlying system of beliefs and attitudes about the nature of women and men and their relations that allows people to rationalize violence in individual cases. I conclude by suggesting a number of connections between this observation and the pursuit of democratic theory and practice.

Our traditional cultural construction of gender and sexuality, part of a sex/gender system based on male dominance, provides a schema that can be evoked in observation of any given individual case of gender-based violence.

We may hypothesize that like other systems of stereotype this schema can be suppressed by conscious or unconscious motivation. I emphasize conscious as well as unconscious motivation because of recent research on stereotype and prejudice that suggests the importance of *choosing* not to be prejudiced despite the existence of powerful cultural stereotypes, in other words, the decision to think rather than take the cognitive path of least resistance (Devine 1988).

The gender differences in perception of violence against women take on important significance given the degree of institutional gender differences in power. In the United States, men constitute about 89 percent of police officers and detectives, about 95 percent of police and detective supervisors, and 80 percent of lawyers and judges. Most employers, who are legally held responsible for sexual harassment policy enforcement in the workplace, are also men. This difference has a crucial effect both on the likelihood of adequate policy responses to the problems and also on women's expectations regarding the efficacy of policy mechanisms. This is one case in which virtual social group representation among elites and decision makers may make a great difference. It should not be surprising that those from subordinate social groups that are largely unrepresented among justice decision makers are relatively unlikely to "seek justice," because they do not trust the processes (Bumiller 1987). We need to worry about the systemic, institutional forces that lead a large proportion of women to be reluctant to seek justice.

The importance of ideology, and especially gender-based ideology, in the construction of the problem of this violence and its solution is further reinforced by the history of policy change. When Deborah Kalmuss and Murray Strauss (1983) investigated the level of services for abused wives in different states, they found that the level of feminist organization in a state was a more important predictor of programs for battered women than was per capita income, political culture, individual feminist sentiment, or even domestic violence legislation that allocated funds for services. Indeed, many of the programs and services provided for battered women and rape victims have been provided by women who have experienced assault themselves.

We could make a number of arguments about democratic theory and practice and the need for greater balance of power and representation between women and men, but these are relatively well known, and little new is added by extending the consideration of violence. What is worth considering, however, is the significance of these studies of gender-based violence and coercion for the practice of democratic theory and political research.

Why have contemporary political scientists who do not identify themselves explicitly as feminist—empirical, theoretical, and normative alike—so rarely asked questions of gender power and coercion? The history of political theory reveals among our theory "forefathers" of the two centuries past considerably more awareness that understanding political organization, power, coercion, and force requires an understanding of gender relations; this awareness was particularly strong when these theorists were otherwise attempting to argue against coercion, violence, and concentration of power. Numerous feminist theorists have pointed out that women were not ignored in early liberal democratic thought; their role was consciously and carefully defined as subordinate, and that subordination was seen as an important element in the construction of the new liberal state (e.g., Kerber 1986; Landes 1988; Pateman 1988).

Another aspect of the triumph of liberal democratic conceptions of the polity is the historical evolution of not only theories but a widespread ideology that perceives and depends upon a clear and distinct split between what we consider public and private domains. Although we cannot bring our ancestors back for survey research, use of written documents offers strong evidence, even at the individual level, of a schema shift in the late eighteenth and early nineteenth centuries that made this distinction much clearer and more important (Davidoff and Hall 1987).

Feminist theorists, among others, have been preoccupied with the implications of the public-private split for a long time, because the political subordination of women in self-consciously democratic or at least republican and antipatriarchal polities rests on the public-private split (e.g., Elshtain 1981).

One of the difficulties for women's studies scholars in political science is that this conceptual dichotomy also shapes what we take as within the legitimate view of political analysis. Thus, gender-based coercion and violence, which takes place primarily in "private" relations and institutions, has not been subject to "political" analysis by political scientists.

We need rethinking yet again about the relation between family and polity. There was a time when observers posed a relation between the degree of democracy in the polity and the family. Twentieth-century social science witnessed an attempt to explain German fascism by reference to the authoritarian German family, and democracy by pointing to the more democratic (American) family. Looking back to the 1950s, when this work gained influence, contemporary feminists can only sigh. It is certainly true that family structures have varied in their internal authority and power structures, but to label modal families in any of the cultures under investigation as "democratic" from the gender point of view is nothing short of a perversion of the term "democratic."

But, then, what is the relation between the family's structure and authority and those of the polity?

I have underscored my will to avoid drawing causal connections between the ideological construction of violence in what we call private life, on the one hand, and democratic thinking, structures, and processes in what is conventionally called politics, on the other. In doing so, I do not mean to argue that it does not exist. We have made conscious choices at different times to regulate or tolerate coercion in private life through policy processes (Gordon 1988; Pleck 1987). Feminists have not been the only voices to argue that private violence affects the community as a public body. Elizabeth Pleck argues, for example, that the American Puritans thought that family violence threatened social and political stability (1987, 17).[16]

I tried, instead, simply to probe mere connection, asking whether we took the right path when we began to draw a wall between public and private life in political theory. Many theorists, including feminists, have argued that we cannot draw a veil of ignorance over social relations within the community, including those based on gender and sexuality, while we hold conversations about democratic politics.

If we only look at "public" life to measure the degree of democracy, we are left with the absurd conclusion that we can fill our private lives with violence, coercion, and perhaps terrorism without affecting the problem of political democracy. How far can we go in rationalizing coercion of individuals in group-based terms before we consider it incompatible with democracy? What is a democratic understanding of legitimate—or at least excused—uses of force?

References

Abbey, Antonia. 1982. "Sex Differences in Attributions for Friendly Behavior: Do Males Misperceive Females' Friendliness?" *Journal of Personality and Social Psychology* 42:830–38.

Benhabib, Seyla, and Drucilla Cornell, eds. 1987. *Feminism as Critique*. Minneapolis: University of Minnesota Press.

16. I bracket the contradiction between this worry and accusations of witchcraft, which Pleck also discusses.

Berg, Barbara. 1978. *The Remembered Gate: Origins of American Feminism: The Woman and the City, 1800–60.* New York: Oxford University Press.
Bersani, Carl A., and Huey-Tsyh Chen. 1988. "Sociological Perspectives in Family Violence." In *Handbook of Family Violence,* ed. Vincent B. Van Hasselt, Randall L. Morrison, Alan S. Bellack, and Michel Hersen, 57–88. New York: Plenum.
Bumiller, Kristin. 1987. "Victims in the Shadow of the Law: A Critique of the Model of Legal Protection." *Signs* 12:421–39.
Burt, Martha R. 1980. "Cultural Myths and Supports for Rape." *Journal of Personality and Social Psychology* 38:217–30.
Clark, Lorenne, and Lynda Lange, eds. 1979. *The Sexism of Social and Political Theory.* Toronto: University of Toronto Press.
Collins, Eliza G. C., and Timothy Blodgett. 1981. "Sexual Harassment. . . . Some See It. . . . Some Won't." *Business Review* 59:76–94.
Costin, Frank, and Norbert Schwarz. 1987. "Beliefs About Rape and Women's Social Roles: A Four-Nation Study." *Journal of Interpersonal Violence* 2:46–56.
Cott, Nancy F. 1987. *The Grounding of Modern Feminism.* New Haven: Yale University Press.
Dahl, Robert A. 1956. *A Preface to Democratic Theory.* Chicago: University of Chicago Press.
Davidoff, Leonore, and Catherine Hall. 1987. *Family Fortunes: Men and Women of the English Middle Class, 1780–1850.* Chicago: University of Chicago Press.
Devine, Patricia. 1988. "Stereotypes and Prejudice: Their Automatic and Controlled Components." *Journal of Personality and Social Psychology* 56:5–18.
Edwards, Anne. 1987. "Male Violence in Feminist Theory: An Analysis of the Changing Conceptions of Sex/Gender Violence and Male Dominance." In *Women, Violence, and Social Control,* ed. Jalna Hanmer and Mary Maynard, 13–29. Atlantic Highlands, N.J.: Humanities Press International.
Eisenstein, Zillah R. 1981. *The Radical Future of Liberal Feminism.* Boston: Northeastern University Press.
Elshtain, Jeane Bethke. 1981. *Public Man, Private Woman: Women in Social and Political Thought.* Princeton: Princeton University Press.
———. 1986. *Meditations on Modern Political Thought: Masculine/Feminine Themes from Luther to Arendt.* New York: Praeger.
Estrich, Susan. 1987. *Real Rape: How the Legal System Victimizes Women Who Say No.* Cambridge, Mass.: Harvard University Press.
Finkelhor, David, and Kersti Yllö. 1985. *License to Rape.* New York: Holt, Rinehart & Winston.
Fishkin, James. 1983. *Justice, Equal Opportunity, and the Family.* New Haven: Yale University Press.
Fraser, Nancy. 1987. "What's Critical About Critical Theory? The Case of Habermas and Gender." In *Feminism as Critique,* ed. Seyla Benhabib and Drucilla Cornell, 31–55. Minneapolis: University of Minnesota Press.
Gordon, Linda. 1988. *Heroes of Their Own Lives: The Politics and History of Family Violence.* New York: Viking.

Hanmer, Jalna. 1984. *Well Founded Fear: A Community Study of Violence to Women.* London: Hutchinson.

Hooks, Bell. 1984. *Feminist Theory from Margin to Center.* Boston: South End Press.

Hornung, Carlton A., Claire McCullough, and Taichi Sugimoto. 1981. "Status Relationships in Marriage: Risk Factors in Spouse Abuse." *Journal of Marriage and the Family* 42:71–82.

Jaggar, Alison. 1983. *Feminist Politics and Human Nature.* Totowa, N.J.: Rowman & Allanheld.

Jenkins, Megan J., and Faye H. Dambrot. 1987. "The Attribution of Date Rape: Observer's Attitudes and Sexual Experiences and the Dating Situation." *Journal of Applied Social Psychology* 17:875–95.

Jensen, Inger W., and Barbara A. Gutek. 1982. "Attributions and Assignment of Responsibility in Sexual Harassment." *Journal of Social Issues* 38:121–36.

Kalmuss, Deborah S., and Murray A. Strauss. 1983. "Feminist, Political, and Economic Determinants of Wife Abuse Services." In *The Dark Side of Families,* ed. David Finkelhor, R. J. Gelles, G. T. Hotaling, and M. A. Straus, 363–96. Beverly Hills, Calif.: Sage Publications.

Kelly, Liz. 1987. "The Continuum of Sexual Violence." In *Women, Violence, and Social Control,* ed. Jalna Hanmer and Mary Maynard, 46–60. Atlantic Highlands, N.J.: Humanities Press International.

Kennedy, Ellen, and Susan Mendus, eds. 1987. *Women in Western Political Philosophy: Kant to Nietzsche.* New York: St. Martin's Press.

Kerber, Linda K. 1986. *Women of the Republic: Intellect and Ideology in Revolutionary America.* New York: W. W. Norton.

Landes, Joan. 1988. *Women and the Public Sphere in the Age of the French Revolution.* Ithaca, N. Y.: Cornell University Press.

Lasswell, Harold D. 1960. *Psychopathology and Politics.* New York: Viking.

McClosky, Herbert, and Alida Brill. 1983. *Dimensions of Tolerance: What Americans Believe About Civil Liberties.* New York: Russell Sage Foundation.

Malamuth, Neil M. 1981. "Rape Proclivity Among Males." *Journal of Social Issues* 4:138–57.

Mansbridge, Jane. 1980. *Beyond Adversary Democracy.* New York: Basic Books.

Margolin, Gayla, Linda Gorin Sibner, and Lisa Gleberman. 1988. "Wife Battering." In *Handbook of Family Violence,* ed. Vincent B. Van Hasselt, Randall L. Morrison, Alan S. Bellack, and Michel Hersen, 89–118. New York: Plenum.

Mason, Karen Oppenheim, and Yu-Hsia Lu. 1988. "Attitudes Toward Women's Familial Roles: Changes in the United States, 1977–85." *Gender and Society* 2:39–57.

Micklow, Patricia L. 1988. "Domestic Abuse: The Pariah of the Legal System." In *Handbook of Family Violence,* ed. Vincent B. Van Hasselt, Randall L. Morrison, Alan S. Bellack, and Michel Hersen, 407–34. New York: Plenum.

Muehlenhard, Charlene L., and Melaney A. Linton. 1987. "Date Rape and Sexual Aggression in Dating Situations: Incidence and Risk Factors." *Journal of Counseling Psychology* 34:186–96.

Nicholson, Linda. 1986. *Gender and History: The Limits of Social Theory in the Age of the Family.* New York: Columbia University Press.
Offen, Karen. 1988. "Defining Feminism: A Comparative Historical Approach." *Signs* 14:119–57.
Okin, Susan Moller. 1979. *Women in Western Political Thought.* Princeton: Princeton University Press.
Pagelow, Mildred Daley. 1988. "Marital Rape." In *Handbook of Family Violence,* ed. Vincent B. Van Hasselt, Randall L. Morrison, Alan S. Bellack, and Michel Hersen, 207–32. New York: Plenum.
Pateman, Carole. 1988. *The Sexual Contract.* Stanford: Stanford University Press.
Pleck, Elizabeth. 1987. *Domestic Tyranny: The Making of American Social Policy Against Family Violence from Colonial Times to the Present.* New York: Oxford University Press.
Radford, Jill. 1987. "Policing Male Violence—Policing Women." In *Women, Violence, and Social Control,* ed. Jalna Hanmer and Mary Maynard, 30–45. Atlantic Highlands, N.J.: Humanities Press International.
Riger, Stephanie, and Margaret T. Gordon. 1981. "The Fears of Rape: A Study in Social Control." *Journal of Social Issues* 37:71–92.
Rix, Sara E. 1988. *The American Woman, 1988–89: A Status Report.* New York: W. W. Norton.
Root, Maria P., and Patricia Fallon. 1988. "The Incidence of Victimization Experiences in a Bulimic Sample." *Journal of Interpersonal Violence* 3:161–73.
Rossi, Alice, ed. 1973. *Essays in Sex Equality.* Chicago: University of Chicago Press.
———, ed. 1988. *The Feminist Papers: From Adams to de Beauvoir.* New York: Columbia University Press.
Rubin, Gayle. 1974. "The Traffic in Women: Notes on the 'Political Economy' of Sex." In *Toward an Anthropology of Women,* ed. Rayna Reiter, 157–210. New York: Monthly Review Press.
Sanday, Peggy Reeves. 1981. "The Socio-cultural Context of Rape: A Cross-cultural Study." *Journal of Social Issues* 37:5–27.
Sapiro, Virginia. 1983. *The Political Integration of Women: Roles, Socialization, and Politics.* Urbana: University of Illinois Press.
———. 1986. "The Gender Basis of Social Policy." *Political Science Quarterly* 101:221–38.
———. 1990. *Women in American Society.* Mountain View, Calif.: Mayfield.
———. 1991. "Gender Politics, Gendered Politics: The State of the Field." In *Political Science: Looking to the Future,* ed. William Crotty, 165–88. Evanston, Ill.: Northwestern University Press.
Schochet, Gordon J. 1975. *Patriarchalism in Political Thought: The Authoritarian Family and Political Speculation and Attitudes Especially in Seventeenth-Century England.* New York: Basic Books.
Scott, Ronald, and Laurie A. Tetrault. 1987. "Attitudes of Rapists and Other Violent Offenders Toward Women." *Journal of Social Psychology,* August, 375–80.
Scully, Diana. 1990. *Understanding Sexual Violence: A Study of Convicted Rapists.* Boston: Unwin Hyman.
Sedlak, Andrea J. 1988. "Prevention of Wife Abuse." In *Handbook of Family Violence,* ed. Vincent B. Van Hasselt, Randall L. Morrison, Alan S. Bellack, and Michel Hersen, 319–58. New York: Plenum.

Shanley, Mary Lyndon. 1989. *Feminism, Marriage, and the Law in Victorian England, 1850–1895*. Princeton: Princeton University Press.

Shotland, R. Lance, and Jane M. Craig. 1988. "Can Men and Women Differentiate Between Friendly and Sexually Interested Behavior?" *Social Psychology Quarterly* 51:66–73.

Sniderman, Paul M., Philip Tetlock, James Gloser, Donald Philip Green, and Michael Hout. 1989. "Principled Tolerance and the American Mass Public." *British Journal of Political Science* 19:25–46.

Stark, Evan, and Anne Flitcraft. 1988. "Violence Among Intimates: An Epidemiological Review." In *Handbook of Family Violence,* ed. Vincent B. Van Hasselt, Randall L. Morrison, Alan S. Bellack, and Michel Hersen, 293–318. New York: Plenum.

Stark, Evan, and J. McEvoy. 1970. "Middle-class Violence." *Psychology Today,* November, 52–65.

Straus, Murray A. 1980. "The Marriage License as a Hitting License: Evidence from Popular Culture, Law, and Social Science." In *The Social Causes of Husband-Wife Violence,* ed. M. A. Straus and G. T. Hotaling, 39–50. Minneapolis: University of Minnesota Press.

Straus, Murray A., Richard J. Gelles, and Susan Steinmetz. 1980. *Behind Closed Doors: Violence in the American Family.* New York: Doubleday.

Tocqueville, Alexis de. [1835, 1840] 1945. *Democracy in America.* Ed. Phillips Bradley. New York: Knopf.

Tong, Rosemarie. 1988. *Introduction to Feminist Thought.* New York: Basil Blackwell.

U.S. Merit Systems Protection Board. 1981. *Sexual Harassment in the Federal Workplace: Is It a Problem?* Washington, D.C.: Government Printing Office.

Van Hasselt, Vincent B., Randall L. Morrison, Alan S. Bellack, and Michel Hersen, eds. 1988. *Handbook of Family Violence.* New York: Plenum.

Wolfe, J., and V. Baker. 1980. "Characteristics of Imprisoned Rapists and Circumstances of Rape." In *Rape and Sexual Assault,* ed. Carmen G. Warner. Germantown, Md.: Aspen Systems.

Yllö, Kersti, and Michele Bograd, eds. 1988. *Feminist Perspectives on Wife Abuse.* Newbury Park: Sage Publications.

22

Sexual Violence, the Public-Private Distinction, and the Liberal State

Mary Lyndon Shanley

As Virginia Sapiro notes in this volume, sexual violence against women is an important component of the political subordination of women by men. For women, "any notion of having a 'relatively high degree of control over political leaders' "—an essential condition for democratic politics—is "clearly intertwined with the difficulties of having some control over their own lives." The actual sexual violence against women, the fear all women harbor of such violence, and the knowledge that sexual violence is extremely difficult to prosecute remove that sense of control and self-direction from women's grasp. Gender-based violence thus has a profound effect not only on women's private lives but on their political participation and efficacy as well. Commenting upon the relation between societal attitudes toward sexual violence and democratic theory, Carole Pateman has argued that "if 'no,' when uttered by a woman, is to be reinterpreted as 'yes,' then all the comfortable assumptions about her 'consent' are . . . thrown into disarray." If the state, in its reluctance to prosecute rape, is indifferent to whether a woman has in fact consented to sexual activity, there is a need for "radical changes" not only in rape law but in "the heart of the theory and practice of the liberal democratic state" (Pateman 1989, 82). Violence against women is not simply a "domestic" matter but undermines the foundation of democratic politics by helping to silence women.

The failure of advocates of democracy to consider the relevance of sexual violence for their concerns is due in large part to the traditional distinction between what belongs to the "private" sphere, including sexuality, intimacy, and family life, and what pertains to the "public," including economic and political participation. Sapiro's essay is both an analysis of the link between attitudes toward gender-based violence and democratic citizenship and participation, and a critique of academic studies of democratic theory that fail to challenge traditional notions of public and private. Her concerns are clearly relevant to those raised by other authors in this volume, such as the primacy (or not) of "rights" in a liberal polity (Dietz; Tabb; Jacobsohn); the adequacy (or not) of treating all citizens similarly, regardless of race, sex, or other immutable characteristics (Hochschild; Jacobsohn); and citizens' self-understandings of their political roles and activities (Conover et al.; Moon).

The particular form of the public-private distinction that Sapiro argues has affected our understanding of what is "politically" relevant is the one established from the seventeenth century onward by thinkers working within the liberal tradition. For John Locke, whose work laid the groundwork for much of that tradition, the family preceded the formation of civil society and existed independently of state authority. Locke assumed, without discussion, that it was male heads of households, not women, who were parties to the social contract. The virtue of states brought into being by the social contract was justice. The virtue of families brought into existence by human sexual attraction was love. Thus, liberal political thought from its inception embraced and reinforced the notion of the family as the locus of virtues and values distinguishing it from the political world. The principles of equality and consent were important in and applicable to the public realm, but not to the private realm populated by women. This distinction, along with assumptions about the proper authority of husbands over their wives and children, meant that it was possible to think that assault committed in the home was not the same as assault committed in public and that marital rape was not rape at all. Indeed, marital rape was not cognizable in most English-speaking jurisdictions until well into the twentieth century, and still is not in all of them.[1]

Many advocates of battered women invoke the classical liberal value of noninterference or of freedom from assault to strike a blow at the public-private distinction. They insist that protecting women's freedom from interference requires opening certain aspects of domestic life to public view. Police officers, judges, and the laws they enforce must treat domestic violence not as simply a "private" matter that the state may properly ignore in all but the most extreme cases, but as a crime. Assault by a man against a woman does not cease being an assault simply because it is committed within the home or because the two are married. Noting that "between 1.8 and 5.7 million women in the United States are beaten each year in their homes," Susan Okin argues that "the privacy of the home can be a dangerous place, especially for women and children." The notion that state intervention in the family should be minimized, an idea that stems from the public-private distinction, "has often served to reinforce the power of its economically or physically more powerful members." Failure to prosecute sexual and domestic violence thus perpetuates the subordination of women both in the family and in public life. The state sets " 'the background rules that affect people's domestic behaviors' " through marriage and divorce laws, employment policies, welfare regulations, and so forth. The truth is that "the domestic sphere itself is created by political decisions, and the very notion that the state

1. As Sapiro points out, earlier feminists noted the harmful effects for women of the assumption that violence in the family should be treated differently than other forms of violence. (The fact that these feminist voices have been marginalized is itself interesting for thinking about women and political efficacy.) I have studied in some detail a group of feminist activists and thinkers from nineteenth-century Britain who were deeply convinced that the distinction between public and private was used both to keep the state, in the form of police officers and magistrates, from adequately prosecuting sexual and domestic violence and to keep women from taking an active role in political life (Shanley 1989). Similarly, in her historical study of family violence in America, Linda Gordon concludes that "the basis of wife-beating is male dominance—not physical strength or violent temperament . . . but social, economic, political, and psychological power," which makes wife-beating "a social rather than a personal problem" (Gordon 1988, 251).

can choose whether or not to intervene in family life makes no sense" (Okin 1989, 128–29, 130 [quoting Olsen 1985, 837], 111).

The issue of domestic violence reveals the deep ambiguity or tension within liberal democratic theory between treating all citizens as individuals with identical rights and recognizing that biological and cultural differences may generate inequality that identical treatment will do nothing to counteract. In *The Sexual Contract,* Carole Pateman argues that our notions of what constitutes an "individual" and a "citizen" have been so tied to the (false) understanding of "public" life that we must start anew to redefine what citizenship means in a democratic polity. Social contract theories depict human beings existing in a "natural" state of freedom and equality, which they agree to leave in order to put their lives and property under the protection of government. But behind every story of the social contract, says Pateman, is another contract, the "sexual contract" by which men take possession of women and exclude women from the social contract (i.e., political life). Another way of putting this would be to say that while liberal theory seemed to substitute an individualistic and contractarian model of civic life for one based on ascriptive hierarchies, it left gender hierarchies in private life intact. As a result, "citizen," a term that sounds as if it were equally applicable to members of both sexes, in fact refers only to men.

To incorporate women into liberal political theory and, presumably, into democratic politics, Pateman believes, would thus require taking the differences between men and women seriously, attending to the fact that there are no universal or abstract citizens but only "embodied" ones. In her view, political theorists must abandon "the masculine, unitary individual to open up space for two figures: one masculine, one feminine" (Pateman 1988, 224). Making a similar point, Iris Young has argued that the "individual" of traditional liberal theory has been ineluctably male and that such an individual must perforce be thought of either as male or as, literally, nobody—that is, as an abstract, universal, rational agent. Thus she insists that "attending to difference is necessary in order to make participation and inclusion possible. . . . The goal is not to give special compensation to the deviant until they achieve normality, but rather to denormalize the way institutions formulate their rules by revealing the plural circumstances and needs that exist, or ought to exist, within them" (Young 1989, 273). Notions of "universal citizenship" do not open the benefits of democratic societies to everyone equally but, rather, privilege dominant groups and marginalize others.

Other theorists like Gary Jacobsohn and Susan Okin disagree. Jacobsohn views such ideas as a threat to constitutional principles of inclusiveness, a return to the acceptance of ascriptive privileges and obligations rather than those of universal citizenship, and a potentially dangerous invitation to a politics of group domination rather than individual rights (Jacobsohn, in this volume). Paying particular attention to women, Okin believes that basing public policies on perceived sexual differences has been and will continue to be oppressive to women; the only relevant sexual differences for purposes of law and public policy should be the facts that women bear, give birth to, and can breast-feed children. Beyond these, "public policies and laws should generally assume no social differentiation of the sexes." In formulating rules of justice to apply to men and women alike, Okin insists that it should be possible for human beings to "think from the perspective of *everybody,* in the sense of *each in turn,*" and in doing so formulate principles of justice applicable to all human beings (1989, 175, 101).

These arguments about the nature of "the citizen" have a direct bearing on democratic theory and on how our law and social policy will deal with issues that arise out of sexual differentiation. Cases involving sexual activity or gender-based violence (along with cases involving pregnancy [see Finley 1986; Krieger and Cooney 1983]) illuminate the fact that treating differently embodied citizens equally will necessitate radical rethinking of legal practice and theory and of the social preconditions for full democratic citizenship for women and men alike.

The fact that sexual violence is far more frequently directed against women than against men might seem to suggest that the state should reflect that difference in law and public policy, defining sexual offenses against women as more serious than those against men and punishing them more severely. The Supreme Court adopted such a view in its 1981 decision upholding the constitutionality of California's statutory rape law, which made statutory rape (sexual intercourse with a minor regardless of consent) a crime only for men (*Michael M.* v. *Superior Court,* 450 U.S. 464 [1981]). The Court accepted California's argument that the sexes were not "similarly situated" with respect to statutory rape, because intercourse for females, but not for males, can result in pregnancy. Despite the fact that in statutory rape (unlike rape), questions of coercion and consent are irrelevant to the question of the guilt of the person who has had intercourse with a minor, Justice Rehnquist's majority decision was permeated by the notion that men as a group are "offenders" and women are "victims." The Court agreed with California that adult women could be exempted from prosecution for statutory rape; in doing so it perpetuated the cultural stereotypes of men as "naturally" sexually aggressive and women as "naturally" sexually passive. Rather than reinforce such notions, it would have been better, as Wendy Williams argues, if the Court had revised "our understanding of sexual crime, that unwanted sexual intrusion other than male-female sexual intercourse can similarly violate and humiliate the victim, and that legislation which defines sexual offenses in gender-neutral terms . . . is therefore what feminists should support" (1982, 187).

The invoking of sexual stereotypes to sustain rather than challenge traditional sex roles and power relations also arose in *Dothard* v. *Rawlinson* (433 U.S. 321 [1977]), where the Court showed itself unprepared to use women's vulnerability to rape in order to challenge the dangerous conditions under which women live. At issue was whether Alabama could refuse to hire women as guards at maximum security prisons because of the risk that female guards might be raped. Alabama argued, and the Supreme Court agreed, that the risk to women was significantly greater than that to men and that a female prison guard's "very womanhood" could invite sexual assault and undermine her ability to maintain control over male prisoners. But Alabama's chosen form of "protection" amounted to excluding women from relatively well-paying jobs. As Christine Littleton has noted with respect to the decision, the question the case *should* have posed for the Court was not "Why do women attract rapists?" but rather "If women in this context are vulnerable to rape, what is it that creates that vulnerability?" She observes that women's vulnerability to rape does not stem from "something inherent in women; women are not the ones who rape. Therefore one should look at the structure of the workplace itself," that is, at conditions that foster violent outbreaks among prisoners and that put guards with insufficient training on duty. In *Dothard* v. *Rawlinson,* by seeing women as different from men, the Court used conditions in the prison to exclude women when it was those conditions themselves that were unjustifiable (Littleton 1987, 1050).

Female victims of male battering have also confronted legal theories and practices that are deeply resistant to the reconceptualization of issues that must occur when women's experiences and practices are brought to the fore. Many lawyers interested in women's rights have struggled to get the courts to recognize the "battered-woman syndrome" as a part of legal notions of what constitutes legitimate self-defense. Expert testimony on the battered-woman syndrome has established that " 'typically victims of battered woman syndrome believe that their husbands are capable of killing them, that there is no escape, and that if they leave they will be found and hurt even more.' "[2] Hence, many women do not leave their abusers until, subjected to renewed battering, they retaliate with sometimes lethal force. Working for legal acceptance of expert testimony on the battered-woman syndrome, however, has not been without perils for feminists. Invoked as a legal defense, the battered-woman syndrome sets women apart from men and focuses on what appears to be a peculiar female psychological response to violence, rather than on the repetitious nature of a male's behavior that prompts a woman's retaliation. Emphasizing gender-linked differences defends specific women but does not address the social context that gives rise to, and to a large extent tolerates, male violence.

Laws dealing with rape, statutory rape, and other forms of sexual violence and battering (along with policies concerned with pregnancy and childbirth) pose the "hard cases" in debates over whether, and how, the law can treat women and men as "equals." On the one hand, as Pateman and Young demonstrate, regarding women and men as "equals" and then treating them as "the same" under current law has led liberal theory and law to define citizen rights and obligations according to a male pattern. On the other hand, the preceding analyses of cases involving statutory rape and sexual violence reveal how acceptance of sexual difference as a justification for differential treatment can perpetuate unwarranted and harmful stereotypes. Reformers must move beyond the debate over whether the law should treat men and women as "the same" or "different" under current conditions, and must insist that the contexts in which men and women work, live as family members, and engage in public life be restructured to provide genuine equality of experience and opportunity. Such changes are essential to give women the voice to resist violence at home and in the larger society and to participate fully as democratic citizens.

The issue of treatment for incidents of domestic violence also exposes the tension inherent in recognizing both the autonomy and the interdependence of persons who live in a liberal state. As Christine Littleton

2. Littleton (1989, 35) citing *Ibn-Tamas* v. *United States,* 407 A2d 626 (D.C. App. Ct. 1979).

has pointed out, the repertory of state responses to domestic violence is quite limited. Not only has it been difficult to prosecute assault within a family, but very frequently there is little help the state can offer either victim or perpetrator except orders of protection, separation, and divorce. In many cases severing the family tie is desirable, but sometimes what is needed is not physical separation and divorce but help in learning how to live together without violence. In addition to laws that reflect the liberal principle that everyone has a right to live free from violence, victims and perpetrators of battering need social policies that facilitate the human desire and need to live in mutually sustaining relations with others. Here is both a practical and a theoretical problem for a liberal polity that takes as its central task protecting the rights of individuals, but individuals who identify themselves *both* as distinct, or discrete, persons and as persons in relationship: as sons and daughters; wives, husbands, and life-partners; members of local communities; coreligionists; and so forth. It is a problem of "disjuncture" not unlike the one Hochschild documents with respect to political equality and economic equality; people properly wish both to be individuals vested with rights that will protect them from the violence of family members and to have their relations with others given legal recognition and sustained by public policy.

The consideration of sexual violence takes us, then, to crucial questions how sexual difference (and by extension other differences such as those of race and class) may affect our ability not simply to enforce existing laws fairly and vigorously but to formulate, promulgate, and administer laws affecting the traditionally less powerful. It is undeniable that one conclusion we must draw from Sapiro's essay is that it is imperative that crimes of rape, assault, and sexual harassment be prosecuted swiftly and effectively. Only by such means will women receive justice from the legal system. But in a larger sense, diminishing violence against women will require profound changes in the way our society portrays women in popular culture as well as law, punishes perpetrators of violence, and supports women who seek some greater measure of autonomy in both domestic and public life. Indeed, sexual violence will diminish only when we acknowledge that it is not only assault but also a form of personal and public intimidation.

Here, it seems to me, we could learn a great deal from listening to women who have themselves experienced domestic violence and joined the battered women's movement. Their actions have challenged the traditional understanding of the distinction between what is to be kept private and what is public, and they have also taken on the roles of activist and lobbyist. Focus groups of the kind conducted by Conover et al. (in this volume) could explore what led some and not others to become activists and how they perceive their citizen obligations. Are they concerned with rescuing particular women, or do they regard themselves as engaged in a broader social transformation? Did their involvement with the battered women's movement lead them to become activists in other political efforts as well? How does each perceive the relation between her role as family member and as an engaged citizen? We might learn a great deal about the meaning and perception of the public-private distinction and the impact of gender differences on democratic citizenship from such an investigation.

Whether or not such new research leads to a new understanding of how women (and men) understand the public-private distinction and its relevance for their lives as citizens, it is clear that by ignoring or failing to address the issue of sexual difference and by accepting the distinction between public and private, democratic theorists have contributed to the silencing of women and the exclusion of their concerns from political discourse. Sapiro's argument that democratic theory cannot proceed unless and until it seriously engages questions about sexual difference and citizenship is grounded in both philosophical and empirical considerations. The examination of sexual violence is, therefore, a call both for legal and political reform and for the reconstruction of democratic theory itself. To stimulate and aid in that reconstruction is one of the goals of this volume and, as Sapiro demonstrates, a compelling obligation for all advocates of democracy.

References

Finley, Lucinda M. 1986. "Transcending Equality Theory: A Way out of the Maternity and the Workplace Debate." *Columbia Law Review* 83:1118–82.

Gordon, Linda. 1988. *Heroes of Their Own Lives*. New York: Viking.

Krieger, Linda J., and M. Cooney. 1983. "The Miller-Wohl Controversy: Equal Treatment, Positive Action, and the Meaning of Women's Equality." *Golden Gate University Law Review* 13:513–72.

Littleton, Christine. 1987. "Equality and Feminist Legal Theory." *University of Pittsburgh Law Review* 48:1043–59.

———. 1989. "Women's Experience and the Problem of Transition: Perspectives on Male Battering of Women." *The University of Chicago Legal Forum* 23:23–57.

Okin, Susan M. 1989. *Justice, Gender, and the Family.* New York: Basic Books.

Olsen, Frances E. 1985. "The Myth of State Intervention in the Family." *University of Michigan Journal of Law Reform* 18 (4):835–64.

Pateman, Carole. 1980. "The Disorder of Women: Women, Love, and the Sense of Justice." *Ethics* 91 (October): 20–34.

———. 1988. *The Sexual Contract.* Stanford: Stanford University Press.

———. 1989. "Women and Consent." In *The Disorder of Women,* 71–89. Stanford: Stanford University Press.

Shanley, Mary Lyndon. 1989. *Feminism, Marriage, and the Law in Victorian England, 1850–1895.* Princeton: Princeton University Press; London: I. B. Taurus.

Williams, Wendy. 1982. "The Equality Crisis: Some Reflections on Culture, Courts, and Feminism." *Women's Rights Law Reporter* 7 (Spring): 175–200.

Young, Iris Marion. 1989. "Polity and Group Difference: A Critique of the Ideal of Universal Citizenship." *Ethics* 99 (January): 250–74.

List of Contributors

Hadley Arkes is the Edward Ney Professor of Jurisprudence and American Institutions at Amherst College. He has been a fellow of the Brookings Institution, the National Endowment for the Humanities, and the Woodrow Wilson Center of the Smithsonian Institution. He is the author of *Bureaucracy: The Marshall Plan and the National Interest* (1973), *The Philosopher and the City* (1981), *First Things: An Inquiry into the First Principles of Morals and Justice* (1986), and *Beyond the Constitution* (1990).

Benjamin R. Barber is the Walt Whitman Professor of Political Science at Rutgers University. He edited the journal *Political Theory* for ten years and has held Guggenheim and ACLS fellowships. He is the author of ten books, including *Strong Democracy* (1984), *The Conquest of Politics* (1988), the volume accompanying the television series *The Struggle for Democracy* (with Patrick Watson, 1989), and most recently *An Aristocracy of Everyone: The Politics of Education and the Future of America* (1992).

John P. Burke is chair and associate professor of political science at the University of Vermont. He has published numerous articles and chapters on the presidency, public administration, and ethics in government. He is the author of *Bureaucratic Responsibility* (1986), *How Presidents Test Reality: Decisions on Vietnam, 1954 and 1965* (with F. Greenstein et al., 1989), *The Institutional Presidency* (1992), and *Advising Ike: The Memoirs of Attorney General Herbert Brownell* (with Herbert Brownell, 1993).

Pamela Johnston Conover is professor of political science at the University of North Carolina at Chapel Hill. She has written widely on political thinking and women and politics, including *Feminism and the New Right* (with Virginia Gray, 1983). Currently, with Ivor Crewe and

Donald Searing, she is completing a book on citizenship in the age of liberalism.

Mary G. Dietz is associate professor of political science at the University of Minnesota. She is the author of *Between the Human and the Divine: The Political Thought of Simone Weil* (1988) and is the editor of *Thomas Hobbes and Political Theory* (1990), and she has written articles on Machiavelli, Hannah Arendt, and the concept of patriotism.

James Farr is professor of political science and citizen education project director of the Center for Democracy and Citizenship at the University of Minnesota. He is the author of a number of essays in political theory and coeditor of *Political Innovation and Conceptual Change* (1989) and *Discipline and History: Political Science in the United States* (1993).

James L. Gibson is Distinguished University Professor of Political Science at the University of Houston. His research on tolerance and parties has appeared in leading political science journals. He is coauthor of *Party Organizations and American Politics* (1984) and *Civil Liberties and Nazis: The Skokie Free-Speech Controversy* (1985).

Russell L. Hanson is associate professor of political science at Indiana University. He has been a fellow at the Center for Advanced Study in the Behavioral Sciences and is the author of *The Democratic Imagination in America: Conversations with Our Past* (1985). He is also coeditor, with Terence Ball and James Farr, of *Political Innovation and Conceptual Change* (1989).

Don Herzog is associate professor of political science at the University of Michigan. He has been a fellow at the Center for Advanced Study in Behavioral Sciences and is the author of *Without Foundations: Justification in Political Theory* (1985) and *Happy Slaves: A Critique of Consent Theory* (1989).

Jennifer L. Hochschild is professor of politics and public affairs at Princeton University. She has been a fellow at the Center for Advanced Study in Behavioral Sciences, a visitor at the Institute for Advanced Study, and has held a fellowship from the Spencer Foundation and the Andrew W. Mellon Preceptorship at Princeton. She is the author of *What's Fair? American Beliefs About Distributive Justice* (1981), *The New American Dilemma: Liberal Democracy and School Desegregation* (1984), and *Equalities* (coauthored with Douglas Rae et al., 1981).

Gary J. Jacobsohn is the Woodrow Wilson Professor of Government at Williams College. A specialist in constitutional law and theory, he is the author of three books, *Pragmatism, Statesmanship, and the Supreme Court* (1977), *The Supreme Court and the Decline of Constitutional Aspiration* (1986), and *Apple of Gold: Constitutionalism in Israel and the United States* (1993), as well as many articles in professional journals.

Donald R. Kinder is professor of political science and psychology and a research scientist at the Center for Political Studies, University of Michigan. He has written widely on matters of voting and public opinion, including *News that Matters* (with Shanto Iyengar, 1987). He has been a fellow at the Center for Advanced Study in the Behavioral Sciences and is currently completing a book on the politics of race in the United States.

John W. Kingdon is professor of political science at the University of Michigan. He has written widely on American governmental institutions and is the author of *Congressmen's Voting Decisions* (3d ed., 1989) and *Agendas, Alternatives, and Public Policies* (1984). He is a fellow of the American Academy of Arts and Sciences and has been a John Simon Guggenheim fellow and a fellow at the Center for Advanced Study in the Behavioral Sciences.

James H. Kuklinski is professor of political science and research professor in the Institute of Government and Public Affairs at the University of Illinois. He currently is coeditor, with Robert S. Wyer, Jr., of the Cambridge University Press Series in Political Psychology.

Stephen T. Leonard is associate professor of political science at the University of North Carolina at Chapel Hill. He is the author of *Critical Theory in Political Practice* (1990) and coeditor of *Intellectuals and Political Life* (with J. Farquhar, L. Fink, and D. Reid, 1992). He has also written about the development of political science as a discipline.

Jane Mansbridge is Jane W. Long Professor of the Arts and Sciences in the Department of Political Science and a faculty fellow at the Center for Urban Affairs and Policy Research at Northwestern University. She has held fellowships from the Woodrow Wilson Foundation, the National Science Foundation, the Rockefeller Foundation, the Institute for Advanced Study in Princeton, and the Russell Sage Foundation. She is the author of *Beyond Adversary Democracy* ([1980] 1983) and *Why We Lost the ERA* (1986) and is the editor of *Beyond Self-Interest* (1990).

George E. Marcus is professor of political science, Williams College, and executive director of the International Society of Political Psychology. He has published widely on the American voter, political behavior, and public opinion. He is cofounder, and was for ten years coeditor, of *Political Methodology*. He is coauthor of *Political Tolerance and American Democracy* (with John L. Sullivan and James Piereson, 1982).

Roger D. Masters is Nelson A. Rockefeller Professor of Government at Dartmouth College. His publications include *The Political Philosophy of Rousseau* (1968), *The Nature of Politics* (1989), and *Beyond Relativism* (forthcoming). He is also general editor of the *Gruter Institute Reader in Biology, Law, and Social Behavior* and coeditor of *Ostracism: A Social and Biological Phenomenon* (1986), *Primate Politics* (1991), *The Sense of Justice* (1992), *The Neurotransmitter Revolution* (1993), and *The Collected Writings of Rousseau* (1991–93).

J. Donald Moon is professor of government at Wesleyan University. He is the author of a chapter in the *Handbook of Political Science*, "Logic of Political Inquiry," as well as articles on the philosophy of social science and the welfare state. He coedited *Dissent and Affirmation: Essays in Honor of Mulford Q. Sibley* (with Arthur Kalleberg and Daniel R. Sabia, Jr., 1983), and is the editor of *Responsibility, Rights, and Welfare* (1988).

Victor Ottati is assistant professor of political science at the State University of New York at Stony Brook. He received his Ph.D. from the University of Illinois at Champaign-Urbana in 1988. He is interested in political psychology and socialization, public opinion, and political participation.

Benjamin I. Page is the Gordon Scott Fulcher Professor of Decision Making at Northwestern University. He is author or coauthor of several books and articles on public opinion, elections, and policy-making in the United States, including *Choices and Echoes in Presidential Elections* (1978), *Who Gets What from Government* (1983), and, with Robert Y. Shapiro, *The Rational Public: Fifty Years of Trends in Americans' Policy Preferences* (1992).

Larry M. Preston is professor of political science at Northern Arizona University. His research on the meaning of freedom and its relative support by the logic of alternative systems of social exchange has appeared in major political science journals. He is the author of *Freedom and the Organizational Republic* (1992).

Ellen Riggle is assistant professor of political science at the University of Kentucky. She received her Ph.D. from the University of Illinois at Champaign-Urbana in 1990. She is interested in political psychology and socialization, public opinion, and electoral behavior.

Virginia Sapiro is professor of political science and women's studies at the University of Wisconsin—Madison. In 1986 the International Society of Political Psychology awarded her the Erik Erikson Award for Early Career Contribution to Political Psychology. Her works on gender, political psychology, and feminist theory include *The Political Integration of Women: Roles, Socialization, and Politics* (1983), *Women in American Society: An Introduction to Women's Studies* (1990), and *A Vindication of Political Virtue: The Political Theory of Mary Wollstonecraft* (1992).

Norbert Schwarz is at the Zentrum für Umfragen, Methoden, und Analysen (ZUMA) in Mannheim, Germany. He is the coeditor of *Social Information Processing and Survey Methodology* (with Hans J. Hippler and Seymour Sudman, 1987), *Subjective Well-being: An Interdisciplinary Perspective* (with Fritz Strack and Michael Argyle, 1991), and *Context Effects in Social and Psychological Research* (with Seymour Sudman, 1992).

Donald D. Searing is professor of political science at the University of North Carolina at Chapel Hill. He has written widely on British politics, including *Political Roles: Understanding Westminster's World* (1993). He has been the recipient of grants from NSF and NIH and has been a Guggenheim fellow. His current research focuses on the nature and practice of citizenship in the United States and Great Britain.

Mary Lyndon Shanley is professor of political science on the Margaret Stiles Halleck Chair at Vassar College and has been a fellow at the Princeton University Center for Human Values. She is the author of *Feminism, Marriage, and the Law in Victorian England* (1989) and coeditor, with Carole Pateman, of *Feminist Interpretations and Political Theory* (1990). She is currently working on a book on ethical issues in contemporary family law.

Robert Y. Shapiro is associate professor of political science at Columbia University. He is author or coauthor of numerous articles on political behavior and public opinion, including "Effects of Public Opinion on

Policy," "What Moves Public Opinion?" and "Poll Trends" in *Public Opinion Quarterly.* He is also coauthor, with Benjamin I. Page, of *The Rational Public: Fifty Years of Trends in Americans' Policy Preferences* (1992).

Denis G. Sullivan is Remsen Professor of Government at Dartmouth College, is the coauthor of *The Politics of Representation* (1974), and is the author of *Explorations in Conventional Decision Making* (1976), as well as articles on party-nominating conventions. More recently, he has written on the role of political leaders' facial displays in eliciting emotions and cognitions.

John L. Sullivan is professor of political science at the University of Minnesota. He has contributed articles to many social science journals and is cofounder, and for nine years coeditor, of *Political Methodology.* He is coeditor of the Sage Series, *Quantitative Applications in the Social Sciences.* He is the coauthor of *Political Tolerance and American Democracy* (with George E. Marcus and James Piereson, 1982) and *Political Tolerance in Context: Support for Unpopular Minorities in Israel, New Zealand, and the United States* (with Michal Shamir, Patrick Walsh, and Nigel Roberts, 1985).

David H. Tabb is professor of political science at San Francisco State University. He is coauthor, with Rufus Browning and Dale Marshall, of *Protest Is Not Enough* (1984) and coeditor of *Racial Politics in American Cities* (with Browning and Marshall, 1990).

Elizabeth Theiss-Morse is assistant professor of political science at the University of Nebraska, Lincoln. She received her Ph.D. from the University of Minnesota in 1989. Her research interests involve the study of political values, including good citizenship, political tolerance, representation, and democratic leadership.

Robert S. Wyer, Jr., is professor of psychology at the University of Illinois. A recent editor of the *Journal of Personality and Social Psychology,* he also coedited a three-volume work, *Handbook of Social Cognition* (1984). Most recently, he wrote *Memory and Cognition in Its Social Context* (1989).

Index